# A BEHAVIORAL THEORY
# OF LABOR NEGOTIATIONS

# ECONOMICS HANDBOOK SERIES

**SEYMOUR E. HARRIS, EDITOR**

## The Board of Advisors

NEIL W. CHAMBERLAIN
*Yale University—Labor*

JOHN M. CULBERTSON
*University of Wisconsin—Monetary Theory*

SEYMOUR E. HARRIS
*Harvard University—International Economics,*
*Social Security; all other areas*

FRANCO MODIGLIANI
*Massachusetts Institute of Technology—Economic Theory*

RICHARD A. MUSGRAVE
*Princeton University—Public Policy*

MARC NERLOVE
*Stanford University—Econometrics and*
*Mathematical Economics*

# A Behavioral Theory of Labor Negotiations

# A BEHAVIORAL THEORY OF LABOR NEGOTIATIONS

## AN ANALYSIS OF A SOCIAL INTERACTION SYSTEM

### RICHARD E. WALTON

*Associate Professor*
*Krannert Graduate School of Industrial Administration*
*Purdue University*

### ROBERT B. McKERSIE

*Associate Professor*
*Graduate School of Business*
*University of Chicago*

**McGraw-Hill Book Company**

*New York*
*St. Louis*
*San Francisco*
*Toronto*
*London*
*Sydney*

This book is dedicated
to the memory of
*Professor Benjamin Morris Selekman*

# PREFACE

This book is about labor negotiations in particular and social negotiations in general. The entire theory is developed and illustrated in the first ten chapters in terms of labor-management negotiations. In the eleventh, final chapter the theory is applied to two other instances of social negotiations: the interchanges that occur in international relations and the demands of, and responses to, civil rights groups.

This treatment of the negotiation process is intended to be comprehensive. We abstract and analyze four sets of activities which together we believe account for almost all the behavior in negotiations.

The first system of activities comprises competitive behaviors that are intended to influence the division of limited resources. This pure-conflict subprocess is called "distributive bargaining."

The second system comprises activities that increase the joint gain available to the negotiating parties. They are problem-solving behaviors and other activities which identify, enlarge, and act upon the common interests of the parties. This is "integrative bargaining."

The third system comprises activities that influence the attitudes of the parties toward each other and affect the basic relationship bonds between the social units involved. The subprocess is referred to as "attitudinal structuring."

The fourth system of activities, which occurs as an integral aspect of the interparty negotiations, comprises the behaviors of a negotiator that are meant to achieve consensus within his own organization. The fourth subprocess is "intraorganizational bargaining."

The total theory is developed by devoting two chapters to each of these subprocesses. Each subprocess has its own internal logics, which can be represented by a separate model. Accordingly, the first chapter devoted to each subprocess sets forth a theoretical model which draws upon the literature of the underlying disciplines of economics, psychology, and sociology.

Each subprocess has its own identifiable set of instrumental acts or tactics. Therefore, each of the four model chapters is followed by a chapter on the tactics which implement the subprocess. These chapters translate the model into tactical assignments and include an abundance of supporting illustrations from actual negotiations.

Because the four subprocesses are interrelated, they create many dilemmas for the negotiator. For example, a power ploy which is tactical to distributive bargaining may be detrimental to attitudinal structuring, or a gesture designed to achieve an improvement in intergroup attitudes (attitudinal structuring) may violate the expectations of the constituents and make it more difficult for the negotiator to achieve internal consensus (intraorganizational bargaining). The tactical requirements of each subprocess are developed systematically and then compared with those of each of the other three processes in a way that reveals the many tactical and strategic dilemmas which confront the negotiator. These interrelationships are explored at the end of each tactical chapter, and a synthesis is developed in the tenth chapter.

This study should be of interest to several audiences. We believe that the coordinated treatment of the theoretical model of a subprocess and the institutional-tactical material related to that process should be of interest to both students of industrial relations and researchers in the social sciences.

For students and teachers of industrial relations, we have attempted to close the gap between, on the one hand, empirical case studies and the discrete insights they yield and, on the other hand, the literature on bilateral monopoly, decision theory, experimental games, small-group problem solving, attitude change, and role conflict.

For social scientists interested in the general field of conflict resolution, we have attempted to show the fruitfulness of a more or less exhaustive treatment of a specific type of conflict-resolution process in one setting, i.e., negotiations in labor-management. The study develops a great number of propositions which deserve to be researched more systematically in many different settings.

For practitioners of collective bargaining and other persons who are directly involved in international negotiations, civil rights negotiations, etc., we have attempted a comprehensive enumeration of tactical behaviors. Among other things, this has involved making explicit many of the acts of effective negotiators that are intuitive and therefore usually not mentioned by them in describing their own behavior. The book is intended to be a synthesis of theory and practice.

The theoretical framework has been derived by a mixture of inductive and deductive reasoning. Extensive field work and several dozen printed case studies have provided the bulk of our empirical data. The source of the empirical data will be cited for field work of other people. We have found the empirical material reported by Ann Douglas and B. M. Selekman, S. K. Selekman, and S. H. Fuller particularly pertinent.[1] When no citation is used, the empirical data have been collected by the authors from interviews, conversations with officials, and reports from other researchers. To provide continuity, we have used the same company name for illustrations taken from a particular union-management relationship—in some cases a disguised name like Jimson or Utility and in other cases an identifiable name like International Harvester.

These materials were analyzed for the uniformities that they contain. However, in formulating the theory, many existing concepts and frameworks have been useful, especially those of Jan Pen, Ward Edwards, Thomas C. Schelling, Herbert A. Simon, B. F. Skinner, and Fritz Heider.[2]

We want to acknowledge the intellectual stimulus for this study which we have received from many people. Our deepest debt is to the late Professor Benjamin M. Selekman, who transmitted to us his passion for understanding the negotiating process, and it is for this reason that we have dedicated the book to his memory.

We should also like to register our appreciation to the many practitioners of the "art" of negotiations who have provided empirical data on which the framework has been constructed. Some of these people preferred to remain anonymous. Fortunately, however, we are able to express our appreciation to William J. Reilly of the International Harvester Company and Arthur Shy and Seymour Kahan of the UAW for the coooperation and assistance which they have extended. Although we cannot identify the other laboratories, we wish to register our special thanks to Frank M. Sterner, who has helped us collect field material that has provided the basis for many of our examples and insights.

[1] See Ann Douglas, *Industrial Peacemaking* (New York: Columbia University Press, 1962); B. M. Selekman, S. K. Selekman, and S. H. Fuller, *Problems in Labor Relations*, 1st and 2nd eds. (New York: McGraw-Hill Book Company, 1950 and 1958); B. M. Selekman, S. H. Fuller, T. Kennedy, and J. M. Baitsell, *Problems in Labor Relations*, 3d ed. (New York: McGraw-Hill Book Company, 1964).

[2] Jan Pen, *The Wage Rate under Collective Bargaining*, translated by T. S. Preston (Cambridge, Mass.: Harvard University Press, 1959); Ward Edwards, "Behavioral Decision Theory," *Annual Review of Psychology*, vol. 12 (1961), pp. 473–498; T. C. Schelling, *The Strategy of Conflict* (Cambridge, Mass.: Harvard University Press, 1960); H. A. Simon, "A Behavioral Model of Rational Choice," *The Quarterly Journal of Economics*, vol. 69 (February, 1955), pp. 99–118; B. F. Skinner, *Science and Human Behavior* (New York: The Macmillan Company, 1953); Fritz Heider, *The Psychology of Interpersonal Relations* (New York: John Wiley & Sons, Inc., 1958).

Many colleagues have provided valuable help to us during the course of writing this book. We should like to express our appreciation to William H. Starbuck, John J. Sherwood, Karl E. Weick, John M. Dutton, Paul Leitch, John S. Day, Emanuel T. Weiler, Philip Marcus, Donald M. Wolfe, J. David Singer, E. R. Livernash, George P. Shultz, Joel Seidman, Arnold R. Weber, Selwyn W. Becker, Thomas L. Whisler, and Jack Sawyer. These people and others have provided either helpful comments on the manuscript or the approving and supporting climate for interdisciplinary work at the institutions where we worked during the course of this project.

A number of other people have read and commented helpfully on all or portions of the manuscript: Neil W. Chamberlain, Carl M. Stevens, Chris Argyris, Daniel Katz, William F. Whyte, James J. Healy, and Warren G. Bennis. The suggestions of Neil Chamberlain provided the stimulus for an extensive revision of the first draft.

For their excellent research and secretarial assistance we should like to thank Charles R. Perry, Marcel Coté, William Jewell, Ossadell Lambert, and Deanna Parker. Finally, a special note of gratitude is due our wives, Sharon and Nancy, for the grand manner in which they have incorporated this project into the lives of our respective families.

Despite the extensive intellectual contributions from many people, we accept responsibility for the results.

*Richard E. Walton*
*Robert B. McKersie*

# CONTENTS

# CHAPTER I

# INTRODUCTION AND THEORETICAL FRAMEWORK

The purposes of this chapter are to comment upon the orientation of the study, to define the key analytical concepts which will be used throughout the remainder of the book, to compare our theoretical framework with the approaches of others interested in labor negotiations, and to indicate the types of propositions that we shall develop.

## Orientation to the Study

In terms of its meaning to the authors, the study has three touchstones: the field of study of collective bargaining; the emerging field of conflict resolution; and the underlying disciplines of economics, psychology, and sociology.

**Collective Bargaining.** Our first touchstone, the institution of collective bargaining, has long been the subject of research and commentary. Typically, research has focused on particular problem areas, and the commentary has tended to be limited to discrete insights. Too little effort has been made along the lines of developing theory to encompass some major area within collective bargaining. Notable exceptions to this general observation have appeared in the literature in recent years. We should like to comment on the relation of our study to one of these treatments in particular: Professor John T. Dunlop's theory of industrial relations systems.[1] This work has provided a much-needed framework for integrating many diverse aspects of the field. The essential distinction between the Dunlop framework and the one presented here is between a theory of structure and one of ongoing process. Professor Dunlop conceptualizes an

[1] J. T. Dunlop, *Industrial Relations Systems* (New York: Holt, Rinehart and Winston, Inc., 1958).

*1*

emergent internal structure, the "web-of-rules" by which the actors live, and explains this by referring to larger structures in the environment.[2] Both the dependent and independent variables in his theory are structural concepts. In contrast, we shall focus on the rule-making mechanism which is a part of the linkage between these structures. We take as given the goals and structures of the two organizations. We also accept as not requiring explanation the *existing* set of rules which governs their continuous interchange but then ask what the process is by which these rules are changed periodically. Rather than dealing with the rule-making process as an essentially deterministic mechanism, which seems to be implicit in Dunlop's theory, we treat it as a goal-directed activity—a set of instrumental acts which can be more or less intelligently conceived and more or less expertly executed.

**Conflict Resolution.** The second touchstone is the academic field of conflict resolution which has developed in recent years and which has provided a focal point of activity for many psychologists, economists, sociologists, and political scientists. The *Journal of Conflict Resolution* is a major vehicle for the contributions to this field of the behavioral sciences. Two themes run through these contributions which help characterize the field.

The first theme reflected in the *Journal of Conflict Resolution* is in reality a set of assumptions generally accepted by this group:

> Many of the patterns and processes which characterize conflict in one area also characterize it in others. Negotiation and mediation go on in labor disputes as well as in international relations. Price wars and domestic quarrels have much the pattern of an arms race. Frustration breeds aggression both in the individual and in the state. The jurisdictional problems of labor unions and the territorial disputes of states are not dissimilar. It is not too much to claim that out of the contributions of many fields a general theory of conflict is emerging.[3]

The second theme also expressed in the same journal is one of social purposefulness.

> It is clear as we look over the human experience that there are some conflicts which are fruitful and some which are not—some conflict processes which lead to resolution and integration, some which lead to distintegration and disaster. We have a practical as well as a theoretical end in view. Although we believe that the pursuit of knowledge for its own sake is essential for the orderly and secure growth of knowledge, we are also not indifferent to its practical uses. . . . We

[2] The technological, market or budgetary, and power or status contexts in which the parties interact.

[3] Editorial, *Journal of Conflict Resolution*, vol. 1 (March, 1957), p. 2.

welcome insights, theoretical models, and confirmatory tests from all spheres of conflict resolution; for we believe that only as all such areas are drawn on, can we devise an intellectual engine of sufficient power to move the greatest problem of our time—the prevention of war.[4]

The spirit of the current study is consistent with these themes. It is an attempt to build on the work of other social scientists interested in conflict resolution and to contribute to that field. Hence, we conceive of labor negotiations as an example of *social negotiations,* by which we mean the deliberate interaction of two or more complex social units which are attempting to define or redefine the terms of their interdependence. We choose the phrase "social negotiations" because we wish to stress attitudinal and organizational aspects of this process not present in many other instances of commercial negotiations and not treated in many theories of bargaining or games.

The belief that labor negotiations represent a fruitful setting for the study of the larger field of social negotiations is based on several considerations. Most of these relate to the extent to which labor negotiations involve the same type of complexity inherent in other forms of social interaction.

First, the agenda in labor negotiations usually contains a mixture of conflictful and collaborative items. The need to defend one's self-interest and at the same time engage in joint problem solving vastly complicates the selection of bargaining strategies and tactics.

Second, labor negotiations involve more than a transaction of substantive items. Attitudes, feelings, and indeed the tone of the relationship represent an extremely important dimension of labor negotiations. Several characteristics of labor negotiations heighten the attitudinal dimension: the issues themselves often involve human values, and how they are handled affects the overall relationship; the weapons chosen involve sanctions which can exert a strong influence on the tone of the relationship; negotiation of the agreement represents only the beginning of the transaction; and whether the terms of the agreement are fulfilled depends upon the character of the relationship. Moreover, the relationship between the parties to labor negotiations is usually unique, continuing, and long term —the attitudinal dimension providing one mechanism by which the successive negotiations are linked together.

Third, the negotiations of interest to us involve complex social units in which the constituent members are very interested in what goes on at the bargaining table and have some influence over the negotiators. This dimension to negotiations, like the others, makes its own demands upon the negotiator and complicates his bargaining job. Our reasons for emphasiz-

---

[4] *Ibid.,* p. 2.

ing the above dimensions to negotiations will be more apparent after we have elaborated the main features of the theory later in this chapter. These particular characteristics of labor negotiations have important implications for an adequate theory of labor negotiations. But they are characteristics also found in some measure in other interaction systems, such as international relations and civil rights deliberations. In the concluding chapter of the study, more will be said about the translations and revisions necessary to apply the theoretical framework and propositions to other social situations.

**Underlying Disciplines.** Our third touchstone comprises the underlying disciplines of economics, psychology, and sociology. Each of these disciplines became relevant in a significant way, given our commitment to work with the total phenomena and to account for as much as possible of all of the behavior which occurs in the negotiation process. We have tried to incorporate the existing principles and theories of discrete behavioral phenomena from these disciplines whenever the fit was good. In turn the study emphasizes aspects of the negotiation process which may be especially fruitful objects of investigation for these disciplines.

## The Analytical Framework

Labor negotiations, as an instance of social negotiations, is comprised of four systems of activity, each with its own function for the interacting parties, its own internal logics, and its own identifiable set of instrumental acts or tactics.

We shall refer to each of the distinguishable systems of activities as a *subprocess.* The first subprocess is *distributive bargaining;* its function is to resolve pure conflicts of interest. The second, *integrative bargaining,* functions to find common or complementary interests and solve problems confronting both parties. The third subprocess is *attitudinal structuring,* and its functions are to influence the attitudes of the participants toward each other and to affect the basic bonds which relate the two parties they represent. A fourth subprocess, *intraorganizational bargaining,* has the function of achieving consensus within each of the interacting groups.

**Distributive Bargaining.** Distributive bargaining is a hypothetical construct referring to the complex system of activities instrumental to the attainment of one party's goals when they are in basic conflict with those of the other party. It is the type of activity most familiar to students of negotiations; in fact, it is "bargaining" in the strictest sense of the word. In social negotiations, the goal conflict can relate to several values; it can involve allocation of any resources, e.g., economic, power, or status symbols. What game theorists refer to as fixed-sum games are the situations we have in mind: one person's gain is a loss to the other. The specific points at which the negotiating objectives of the two parties come in contact define the issues. Formally, an *issue* will refer to an area of common concern in which the objectives of the two parties are assumed to be in conflict. As such, it is the subject of distributive bargaining.

**Integrative Bargaining.** Integrative bargaining refers to the system of activities which is instrumental to the attainment of objectives which are *not* in fundamental conflict with those of the other party and which therefore can be integrated to some degree. Such objectives are said to define an area of common concern, a *problem*. Integrative bargaining and distributive bargaining are both joint decision-making processes. However, these processes are quite dissimilar and yet are rational responses to different situations. Integrative potential exists when the nature of a problem permits solutions which benefit both parties, or at least when the gains of one party do not represent equal sacrifices by the other. This is closely related to what game theorists call the varying-sum game.

**Attitudinal Structuring.** Distributive and integrative bargaining pertain to economic issues and the rights and obligations of the parties, which are the generally recognized content of labor negotiations. However, we postulate that an additional major function of negotiations is influencing the relationships between parties, in particular such attitudes as friendliness-hostility, trust, respect, and the motivational orientation of competitiveness-cooperativeness. Although the existing relationship pattern is acknowledged to be influenced by many more enduring forces (such as the technical and economic context, the basic personality dispositions of key participants, and the social belief systems which pervade the two parties), the negotiators can and do take advantage of the interaction system of negotiations to produce attitudinal change.

Attitudinal structuring is our term for the system of activities instrumental to the attainment of desired relationship patterns between the parties. Desired relationship patterns usually give content to this process in a way comparable to that of issues and problems in distributive and integrative processes. The distinction among the processes is that whereas the first two are joint decision-making processes, attitudinal structuring is a socioemotional interpersonal process designed to change attitudes and relationships.

**Intraorganizational Bargaining.** The three processes discussed thus far relate to the reconciliation process that takes place between the union and the company. During the course of negotiations another system of activities, designed to achieve consensus within the union and within the company, takes place. Intraorganizational bargaining refers to the system of activities which brings the expectations of principals into alignment with those of the chief negotiator.

The chief negotiators often play important but limited roles in formulating bargaining objectives. On the union side, the local membership exerts considerable influence in determining the nature and strength of aspirations, and the international union may dictate the inclusion of certain goals in the bargaining agenda. On the company side, top management and various staff groups exert their influence on bargaining objectives. In a sense the chief negotiator is the recipient of two sets of demands—one from across the table and one from his own organization. His dilemma stems from conflict at two levels: differing aspirations about issues and differing expectations about behavior.

Intraorganizational bargaining within the union is particularly interesting. While it is true that for both parties to labor negotiations many individuals not present in negotiations are vitally concerned about what transpires at the bargaining table, the union negotiator is probably subject to more organizational constraints than his company counterpart. The union is a political organization whose representatives are elected to office and in which contract terms must be ratified by an electorate.

## Toward a Synthesis

Our framework or theory does not include any major subprocess of negotiations which heretofore has not been discussed by other authors. That is, although we did not originate distributive bargaining, integrative bargaining, attitudinal structuring, or intraorganizational bargaining, we feel that these phenomena have seldom been purposefully or completely abstracted as such.

Regarding the distributive bargaining process, Schelling,[5] for example, has given excellent treatment to commitment tactics. Stevens[6] and others[7] have explored the dynamics of this process. Pen[8] and others[9] have improved our understanding by formulating explanatory models of the outcome of distributive bargaining. Peters[10] has also made important contributions to our insights into this subprocess.

The content and process of integrative bargaining have also been the

[5] T. C. Schelling, *The Strategy of Conflict* (Cambridge, Mass.: Harvard University Press, 1960).

[6] C. M. Stevens, *Strategy and Collective Bargaining Negotiation* (New York: McGraw-Hill Book Company, 1963).

[7] G. L. Shackle, "The Nature of the Bargaining Process," in J. T. Dunlop (ed.), *The Theory of Wage Determination* (London: International Economic Association, Macmillan & Co., Ltd., 1957), pp. 292–314.

[8] Jan Pen, *The Wage Rate under Collective Bargaining*, trans. T. S. Preston (Cambridge, Mass.: Harvard University Press, 1959).

[9] N. W. Chamberlain, *Collective Bargaining* (New York: McGraw-Hill Book Company, 1951); John Nash, "Two-person Cooperative Games," *Econometrica*, vol. 21 (January, 1953), pp. 128–140; J. C. Harsanyi, "Approaches to the Bargaining Problem before and after the Theory of Games: A Critical Discussion of Zeuthen's, Hicks', and Nash's Theories," *Econometrica*, vol. 24 (April, 1956), pp. 144–157.

[10] Edward Peters, *Strategy and Tactics in Labor Negotiations* (New London, Conn.: National Foremen's Institute, 1955).

target of considerable analyses and insights. In a pioneering and impressionistic statement about administration, Mary Parker Follett [11] discusses the concept of integrative bargaining. A study by Slichter, Healy, and Livernash,[12] for example, includes comprehensive empirical treatment of the results of integrative attempts in each of several areas of collective bargaining. The National Planning Association study, *Causes of Industrial Peace*,[13] represents a pioneering effort in improving our understanding of how some firms were successful in integrating the interests of the parties to collective bargaining. Sherif, and Blake and Mouton [14] have made some interesting observations about the conditions conducive to problem solving in intergroup situations.

Furthermore, attitudinal structuring, our third process. has not been neglected by students or observers of collective bargaining. In fact, the NPA study just mentioned, Garfield and Whyte,[15] Whyte,[16] Bakke,[17] Lester,[18] Harbison and Coleman,[19] and Selekman [20] underscore the importance of structuring certain types of relationships and in some instances suggest tactics that work toward this end. Selekman, Selekman, and Fuller [21] have contributed a highly useful scheme for classifying relationships, and the case studies contributed by them reflect a rich

[11] Mary Parker Follett, *Dynamic Administration: The Collected Papers of Mary Parker Follett*, H. C. Metcalf and L. Urwick (eds.) (New York: Harper & Row, Publishers, Incorporated, 1942).

[12] S. H. Slichter, J. J. Healy, and E. R. Livernash, *The Impact of Collective Bargaining on Management* (Washington, D.C.: The Brookings Institution, 1960).

[13] C. S. Golden and V. D. Parker (eds.), *Causes of Industrial Peace under Collective Bargaining* (New York: National Planning Association, Harper & Row, Publishers, Incorporated, 1955).

[14] Muzafer Sherif (ed.), *Intergroup Relations and Leadership* (New York: John Wiley & Sons, Inc., 1962); R. R. Blake and J. S. Mouton, *Group Dynamics: Key to Decision-making* (Houston: Gulf Publishing Co., 1961).

[15] Sidney Garfield and W. F. Whyte, "The Collective Bargaining Process: A Human Relations Analysis," *Human Organization*, part I, vol. 9 (Summer, 1950), pp. 5–10; part II (Fall, 1950), pp. 10–16; part III, (Winter, 1950), pp. 25–29; part IV, vol. 10 (Spring, 1951), pp. 28–32.

[16] W. F. Whyte, *Pattern for Industrial Peace* (New York: Harper & Row, Publishers, Incorporated, 1951).

[17] E. W. Bakke, *Mutual Survival: The Goal of Unions and Management* (New Haven, Conn.: Labor and Management Center, Yale University, 1946).

[18] R. A. Lester, *As Unions Mature: An Analysis of the Evolution of American Unionism* (Princeton, N.J.: Princeton University Press, 1958).

[19] F. H. Harbison and J. R. Coleman, *Goals and Strategy in Collective Bargaining* (New York: Harper & Row, Publishers, Incorporated, 1951).

[20] B. M. Selekman, *Labor Relations and Human Relations* (New York: McGraw-Hill Book Company, 1947).

[21] B. M. Selekman, S. K. Selekman, and S. H. Fuller, *Problems in Labor Relations*, 1st and 2d eds. (New York: McGraw-Hill Book Company, 1950 and 1958); B. M. Selekman, S. H. Fuller, T. Kennedy, and J. M. Baitsell, *Problems in Labor Relations*, 3d ed. (New York: McGraw-Hill Book Company, 1964).

understanding of the process by which attitudes are influenced and relationship patterns are altered.

Similarly, many authors have dealt either directly or indirectly with the intraorganizational bargaining which occurs with the interaction of the parties. In an overlooked piece of work, Weber [22] has studied the process of union decision making during the course of labor negotiations. While centering on other aspects of unions, several investigators have provided considerable illustrative material for an analysis of intraorganizational bargaining. [23]

While it is important to acknowledge previous contributions to our understanding of these aspects of negotiation, it is equally important for our purposes here to state what we regard as the limitations of these contributions. They have tended to deal with the dynamics or results of only one of these processes, or in a few cases, two of these processes. This sometimes has led to an unbalanced view of labor negotiations. For example, some practical treatments and some theoretical efforts focusing on distributive bargaining tactics lead to an unduly cynical concept of negotiations. Similarly, the important contributions of authors focusing largely on attitudinal structuring processes, such as Garfield and Whyte, [24] taken by themselves produce a somewhat naive view of labor negotiations. What claim do we make for our own efforts? We see our present treatment as going beyond these contributions in several ways. We have tried to improve upon the conceptualization of these phenomena. We have endeavored to give as systematic and comprehensive a treatment as possible to the internal dynamics of each of the subprocesses of negotiations. Finally, we have explored the interaction and interrelationship of these simultaneous ongoing processes.

Thus, an important objective of the present work has been to treat concurrently as well as separately the important dimensions of labor negotiations. Similar attempts at synthesis have been made in a number of pioneering books which have been authored in the last several years by Chamberlain, [25] Schelling, [26] Boulding, [27] and Rapoport. [28] Whereas these

[22] A. R. Weber, *Union Decision-making in Collective Bargaining* (Urbana, Ill.: Institute of Labor and Industrial Relations, University of Illinois, 1951).

[23] L. R. Sayles and George Strauss, *The Local Union: Its Place in the Industrial Plant* (New York: Harper & Row, Publishers, Incorporated, 1953); H. S. Parnes, *Union Strike Votes: Current Practice and Proposed Controls* (Princeton, N.J.: Industrial Relations Section, Department of Economics and Sociology, Princeton University, 1956); Lloyd Ulman, *The Government of the Steel Workers' Union* (New York: John Wiley & Sons, Inc., 1962).

[24] Garfield and Whyte, *op. cit.*

[25] N. W. Chamberlain, *A General Theory of Economic Process* (New York: Harper & Row, Publishers, Incorporated, 1955).

[26] T. C. Schelling, *op. cit.*

[27] K. E. Boulding, *Conflict and Defense: A General Theory* (New York: Harper & Row, Publishers, Incorporated, 1962).

books deal with a broader field of conflict resolution, we have focused on the negotiation process in general and labor negotiations in particular.

## The Propositions Generated

What kinds of propositions does our theoretical framework generate?

First, the most fundamental propositions of the study are those that link goals and tactical behavior. We assert that the behaviors which we call distributive bargaining are indices for inferring goal conflict or perceived goal conflict. Conversely, the knowledge that goal structures are in conflict becomes the basis for predicting that class of behaviors we identify as distributive bargaining tactics.

Consider one other process, attitudinal structuring. The observable behaviors we designate as tactics for that process are proposed as an index of the degree of concern about the maintenance or changing of the basic relationship pattern between the parties and as an indicator of the direction of change desired. Of course, the association works in reverse: If you know the party's objectives in this area, you can predict that he will tend to engage in the class of behaviors we have identified as attitudinal structuring tactics. Inasmuch as we may actually identify as many as a hundred behaviors as tactical in a single subprocess, we would have a long list of propositions if we chose to formalize them. We shall not.

The second type of proposition represents a refinement of the first. Because there are often many specific behaviors that can perform any given tactical assignment, it is rather difficult to make precise predictions about behavior from a knowledge of goals or motivations alone. Thus, occasionally our framework and analysis lead to propositions indicating which specific strategies or tactics tend to be used to pursue given goals under given circumstances. This goes a step beyond starting with goal structures and predicting the class of behaviors and represents a step that must eventually be taken if we are to understand the negotiation process in general and tactical choice in particular. We assume that persons act purposefully, even in what they perceive as a fast-moving and fluid situation. Thus, for example, after analyzing the logic of the situation, we offer the hypothesis that the more prior knowledge a management has about the minimum acceptable package to the union, the more likely it is to use a final-offer-first strategy. The final-offer-first strategy is just one of several alternatives within distributive bargaining.

A third type of proposition deals with action-response relations rather than with complex-choice situations. These are explicit or implicit hypotheses that specify the several consequences (noting especially the unin-

---

[28] Anatol Rapoport, *Fights, Games, and Debates* (Ann Arbor, Mich.: The University of Michigan Press, 1960).

tended consequences) of a given type of action: a given tactic has $X$ consequences for the distributive bargaining process, $Y$ consequences for the integrative bargaining process, and $Z$ consequences for the process of attitudinal structuring. For example, our analysis of the several processes suggests that the more management's commitments approximate the final-offer-first strategy, the less problem-solving activity will occur during negotiations, and the more negative will be the sentiments relating the parties. These are both descriptive statements and predictive hypotheses.

The multiple consequences of a single act—due to the simultaneous occurrence of the processes—is the fact which interrelates these processes. And it is this phenomenon that we want to examine closely. We shall be particularly interested in discovering and enlightening the most important dilemmas produced by the conflicting demands of the several subprocesses. How the subprocesses interact and how the dilemmas are resolved must be understood in theorizing about negotiations.

In short, the few propositions which we have made explicit and the other propositions which are implicit in the statement of the theory are about how people actually tend to behave and how elements of the process actually interact. They should lead, therefore, to predictive hypotheses about how people will tend to behave in various circumstances and under varying conditions.

# CHAPTER II

# THE DISTRIBUTIVE BARGAINING MODEL

Distributive bargaining is central to labor negotiations and is usually regarded as the dominant activity in the union-management relationship. Unions represent employees in the determination of wages, hours, and working conditions. Since these matters involve the allocation of scarce resources, there is assumed to be some conflict of interest between management and unions. The joint-decision process for resolving conflicts of interest is distributive bargaining. The term itself refers to the activity of dividing limited resources. It occurs in situations in which one party wins what the other party loses.

This chapter introduces the concepts necessary for understanding the nature of distributive bargaining, outlines a model explaining how the parties reach a settlement, and focuses on the key variables that affect the outcome of distributive bargaining. In the next chapter the vantage point of the negotiator, who wishes to manipulate the key variables to his advantage, is emphasized. There we discuss the strategies and tactics which constitute the process.

Section one in Part 1 of this chapter identifies the essential characteristics of the *issues* over which distributive bargaining occurs and in a preliminary way compares them with the agenda items involved in integrative bargaining. This discussion underscores the opposition of objectives which underlies and gives rise to distributive bargaining.

Section two discusses the range of mutual dependence. In effect, the conflict over issues takes place within an area in which the parties stand to benefit from continuing their relationship. This bargaining range is bounded by *outer limits*. Outside the lower and upper limits the employment relationship itself is no longer profitable. At some lower limit of wages, the company would lose its ability to retain the work force. At some upper limit of wages, the company would be forced to consider other business alternatives. The discussion highlights the institutional factors which influence the location of these limits.

The third and fourth sections help explain where actual bargaining will take place within the larger spectrum. For any point on the spectrum which a negotiator may choose as the settlement point there are two possible outcomes: first, the other party may agree; and second, the other party may disagree and a strike may result. What a negotiator demands and what he actually expects to achieve are influenced by his preferences for various possible settlements. The concept of *utilities* for the possible outcomes is used to characterize this aspect of the negotiator's thinking. The types of factors which determine the shape of the negotiator's utility function are indicated. The negotiator's demands and expectations are also governed by his preferences for avoiding a strike. *Strike costs,* a variation of the concept of utilities, is employed in exploring the influence of the various costs associated with the strike action itself. Strike action usually involves losses or disutilities. Occasionally a strike involves some by-product gains or utilities, in which case the term "strike gains" would be appropriate.

The fifth section attempts to push the above analysis further by discussing *subjective probabilities* and *subjectively expected utilities.* A negotiator's evaluation of various possible settlements becomes more meaningful when he also assigns some probability to the attainment of each of the conceivable settlements.

The sixth section introduces the concepts of *resistance point* and *target.* These points of prominence reflect the negotiator's assessment of utilities, probability, and the resultant subjectively expected utilities. A complicated analysis is required to even roughly explain the negotiator's decisions about what he will attempt to achieve (his target) and what he will insist upon (his resistance point).

Having introduced the key concepts in Part 1, the discussion then turns in Part 2 to the settlement process. The analysis will be inconclusive insofar as specifying the settlement point. The model is indeterminate in the sense that the outcome cannot be predicted from static parameters. The outcome is explainable in terms of several key variables, but these variables are constantly interacting and changing in importance so that it is not possible to predict the outcome prior to the negotiations. It will nevertheless represent a systematic way of thinking about the ways various factors affect the outcome. It provides the framework for our elaboration of tactics in Chapter III.

Before proceeding, a few clarifying remarks should be made. For the purposes of this chapter we are assuming that each negotiator behaves in the self-interest of his organization. He brings neither a generally competi-

tive nor a generally cooperative orientation. Many negotiators do not behave "rationally." Some acts of behavior can be understood only in terms
of the relationship objectives of the institution or the personal needs of
the negotiator. This type of behavior will be considered in the chapter on
attitudinal structuring.

For the present we are also assuming that a negotiator represents the
consensus of his organization. For the most part, we shall not distinguish
here among the wishes of the international union, the rank and file, etc., or
among the desires of top management, staff groups, etc. This matter will
be considered later when we take up the subject of intraorganizational
bargaining. However, from time to time we shall need to relax this assumption in our discussion of distributive bargaining in order to examine
certain behavior critically relevant to this process.


# PART 1 | SETTLEMENT RANGE

### Agenda Items: Issues and Problems

The agenda item appropriate for distributive bargaining is an issue.
Items appropriately handled by integrative bargaining are problems.
When items contain important possibilities for both processes, they are
said to be "mixed situations" or "mixed issues."

The agenda items and processes can be differentiated in terms of two
dimensions of the underlying structure of payoffs: the *total* value available
to both parties and the *shares* of the total available to each party. Distributive bargaining is the process by which each party attempts to maximize
his own share in the context of fixed-sum payoffs. Integrative bargaining
is the process by which the parties attempt to increase the size of the joint
gain without respect to the division of the payoffs. Mixed bargaining is the
process that combines both an attempt to increase the size of the joint
gain and a decision on how to allocate shares between the parties.

**Issues and Distributive Bargaining.** The fixed-sum, variable-share payoff structure is our point of departure for defining an issue. It describes a
situation in which there is some fixed value available to the parties but
in which they may influence shares which go to each. As such there is
fundamental and complete conflict of interests. In labor negotiations there
is an attendant feature to the competitive payoff structure—the possibility
of default. This modifies the extent of the conflict between the parties. If
either party should insist upon a sum greater than the fixed amount

available, or if their combined demands exceed this fixed amount, they suffer mutual losses.[1]

An issue can be represented as in Figure 2-1.

### Figure 2-1

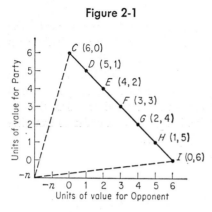

C, D, etc., refer to outcomes.

If one conceives of some spectrum of outcomes C through I, C allows Party [2] maximum satisfaction of 6 units and provides Opponent no satisfaction. Outcomes C through I represent the distribution of values to Party and Opponent 6,0; 5,1; 4,2; 3,3; 2,4; 1,5; and 0,6. Outcomes B and J, which fall outside this series, are accompanied by zero units or losses for both parties. What we have in mind is a demand of 7 by either party or some combination of demands which totals 7 or more. This refers to the mutual losses associated with excessive demands which violate the bargaining range and result in a work stoppage.

Because we intend to make further use of both utility functions and game matrices, we shall illustrate an issue in matrix form (see Figures 2-2 and 2-3).[3]

Figure 2-2 follows the conventional representation of payoff matrices. Party chooses among rows 0 to 7 (here rows represent alternate demands), and Opponent chooses among columns 0 to 7 (his own demands). The units of measurement can be regarded as some objective value, such as money.[4] Coordinating the matrix to labor negotiations, we assume some no-trade point as having less than zero utility and assume some positive range of mutually advantageous trades. (Thus the range might involve 6 cents, from $2.50 to $2.56, the limits to a mutually advantageous trade.)

If the two parties choose demands that add up to 6, they receive the amount of the demands. If their demands add up to less than 6, they

---

[1] For the distributive bargaining issue treated here, we assume that the major bone of contention between the parties, and consequently a strike issue, is the size of the economic package. This is the justification for the assumption that a failure to make compatible demands regarding the issue results in losses and not merely no gain.

[2] We shall use Party and Opponent to differentiate the parties. The labels are intended to apply equally well to the union and company situations in negotiations. If a statement is not applicable to both, we shall use the terms "company" and "union."

[3] Following the convention of game theory, the first entry in each cell specifies the payoff to Party and the second entry the payoff to Opponent.

[4] It will be necessary to modify this later as we introduce and substitute subjective evaluations for objective value units.

receive their respective demands adjusted upward to bring their combined total to 6. If their demands total more than 6, they default and suffer mutual losses, arbitrarily set here at −6,−6.

### Figure 2-2
### Issue Payoffs in Matrix Form

*Opponent strategies*
*(demands)*

| | | 0 | 1 | 2 | 3 | 4 | 5 | 6 | 7 |
|---|---|---|---|---|---|---|---|---|---|
| | 0 | 3,3 | 2½,3½ | 2,4 | 1½,4½ | 1,5 | ½,5½ | 0,6 | |
| | 1 | 3½,2½ | 3,3 | 2½,3½ | 2,4 | 1½,4½ | 1,5 | | |
| Party | 2 | 4,2 | 3½,2½ | 3,3 | 2½,3½ | 2,4 | | | |
| strategies | 3 | 4½,1½ | 4,2 | 3½,2½ | 3,3 | | Mutual losses of | | |
| (demands) | 4 | 5,1 | 4½,1½ | 4,2 | | | −6,−6 associated | | |
| | 5 | 5½,½ | 5,1 | | | | with failure to | | |
| | 6 | 6,0 | | | | | agree | | |
| | 7 | | | | | | | | |

### Figure 2-3
### A Two-choice Issue

*Opponent strategies*
*Soft (1)   Hard (5)*

| | | Soft (1) | Hard (5) |
|---|---|---|---|
| Party | Soft (1) | 3,3 | 1,5 |
| strategies | Hard (5) | 5,1 | −6,−6 |

The possibility of a default is an important aspect of distributive bargaining. In one sense it changes the game to a varying-sum game, in that both parties will be better off if they can avoid the default region of the payoff matrix. For the moment we shall not specify whether the default represents temporary costs incurred by a strike or a permanent breakdown of the relationship.

Figure 2-3 is a truncated version of the matrix in Figure 2-2, in that it allows for only two of the row and column choices. It is sufficient to illustrate the essence of the choice problem but represents a drastic oversimplification of the alternatives usually available in labor negotiations. However, the 2 × 2 or 3 × 3 matrices are most frequently used in illustrations of game theory or in experimental studies of game behavior, and we shall have occasion to employ them ourselves in discussing the relevance of this literature to labor negotiations.

**Problems and Integrative Bargaining.** This process applies to a variable-sum situation in which a wide range of possible total values is available to the pair of parties (depending, for example, on the quality and creativity of their joint decision making) and in which the parties need not be preoccupied at the same time with the question of allocation of the values between them.

They may be relieved from this preoccupation with "who gets how much" by any of several circumstances. For example, in its most fundamental form a problem is one which affects both parties in exactly the same way; each solution considered offers the same inherent benefit to both. Or the parties may have agreed in advance to share equally (or in some other specific proportion) whatever total value is realized by their efforts. This would require prior agreement to make side payments if the alternative outcome (selected because it has the highest joint gain) has disproportionately high inherent benefits for one side. Still another possibility is that, rather than agree in advance to their respective shares of the total value, the parties agree to make this allocation of the joint gain after the outcome. Under each of these arrangements the parties have maximum incentive to choose an outcome with the highest total value. Interests are identical or parallel throughout an array of potential outcomes, as depicted in Figure 2-4.

**Figure 2-4**

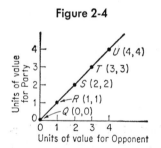

Q, R, etc., refer to outcomes.

Figure 2-4 shows the parties as benefiting equally (although this particular basis for sharing is not essential) in outcomes Q to U, and total values are 0 to 8, respectively. Outcome Q is assumed to be the *status quo,* and only outcomes which improve the joint gain are considered. The possibilities of mutually beneficial outcomes R, S, T, and U are known to the parties only through the process of integrative bargaining.

The payoff possibilities of problem solving can be represented in matrix form (Figure 2-5). The payoff matrix resembles that of coordination games in which the players need to coordinate their game choices without benefit of communication in order to receive preferred outcomes. However, there is an important distinction which prevents us from applying the experimental results of these studies to the integrative process. As we shall develop later in our discussion of integrative bargaining, the task of the negotiators is to *discover* the high payoff possibilities. That is, the various alternatives and their potential benefits are not known to the parties before they engage in integrative bargaining. Given our assumption about coincidence of interests and allowing communication, the parties en-

counter no difficulty in coordinating their choices. And as represented in
Figure 2-5, their choices are nothing more than an intensifying or a relax-
ing of their respective problem-solving efforts. Either party can increase
the payoffs by individual problem solving, but maximum results are
available through joint problem solving. If the parties correctly assume
that there are such potential benefits, they will proceed deliberately to
discover the alternatives that increase the joint gain available to them.
In terms of economic theory each negotiator brings a welfare orientation
to the process. He is not concerned about the payoff available for him, his
primary concern is to increase the total sum.

### Figure 2-5
### Solution Payoffs in Matrix Form

*Opponent choices*
*(degrees of problem-solving activity)*

|                     |   | a | b | c | d | e |
|---------------------|---|---|---|---|---|---|
|                     | a | 0 | 1 | 2 | 3 | 4 |
|                     | b | 1 | 2 | 3 | 4 | 5 |
| Party choices (degrees of problem-solving activity) | c | 2 | 3 | 4 | 5 | 6 |
|                     | d | 3 | 4 | 5 | 6 | 7 |
|                     | e | 4 | 5 | 6 | 7 | 8 |

Total payoffs as a result of problem-solving activity.

**The Content of Issues.** For an issue to arise there must be some dis-
similarity between the value systems of the two parties, and the item in
question must appear to require some choice between the value systems.
Whether or not a party's position is in its own best interest, the fact that
the party's current preferences are opposed to those of the other party is
sufficient to create an issue.

Even though many situational factors strongly influence how agenda
items are perceived and hence how they are resolved, we believe that there
are some items which tend to involve more inherent conflict of interest
than others do. We can distinguish three types of objectives: economic,
rights and obligations, and relationship patterns. When economic objec-

tives are involved, there is often basic conflict. Decisions about wage levels involve a choice between giving more of the "good life" to employees or to stockholders and managers. This is also true of the other direct economic items such as vacations, holidays, and benefit programs. These issues typically involve directly competing claims upon limited economic resources.

Basic conflict can also exist around rights and obligations. One class of issues, which in part reduces to a choice among basic values, is that concerned with union security. For example, privileges and freedom accorded union officials may enhance the status and effectiveness of the union at the expense of management status. A similar type of issue is that which pits employee job rights against management prerogatives and flexibility. Values of this type are often involved in the nature of provisions covering discipline and discharge (which might set job security and justice against plant orderliness and efficiency). Other conflicts between job rights and management flexibility occur in questions of layoff and transfer, work schedules, etc. While these issues usually involve some inherent conflict, they almost invariably also contain some integrative potential. They best illustrate what we refer to as "mixed items."

Let us elaborate briefly here on the question of mixed items in order to explain what we mean by that term. An improvement in the layoff protection for employees usually entails some loss in management flexibility, but inasmuch as there may be several ways of increasing layoff protection, it should be apparent that the amount by which management's flexibility is compromised to provide a given amount of protection can vary considerably. To the extent that the matter is perceived as involving inherent conflict, it will be the subject of distributive bargaining. To the extent that the matter is seen as having some mutual interests or potential for integration, it will also be the subject of integrative bargaining and hence mixed bargaining.

Attitudes and relationship patterns also can be the focus of differing objectives. For example, one party may desire to foster a cooperative relationship, while the other party may desire to preserve an arm's-length relationship. Alternatively, both may desire the same pattern of relationship. Since attempts to influence attitudes and relationship patterns represent a different order of activity from that of bargaining over concrete issues, the subject will be treated separately in the chapters dealing with attitudinal structuring.

Technological, economic, organizational, and other social forces shape the outlook which each side brings to the bargaining table. To explore the connections between these environmental forces and the objectives of the parties would take us beyond the scope of this study. We are less interested in why a particular objective is chosen by a company than in the fact that it conflicts with an objective of the union. We are interested in how these issues are handled and settled.

The point is not that, whenever the items mentioned above are the subject of negotiations, there is necessarily basic underlying conflict of interest. On the contrary, the existence or the extent of inherent conflict is an empirical question, in each case to be examined on its own merits. The first type of issue—that related to direct allocation of economic resources—contains the most inherent conflict, but even this can be overstated. For example, a few companies prefer to be leaders in the wage area and find little conflict with the wage policies advanced by the union. The extent of conflict involved in objectives dealing with union institutional values will depend on the particular issue and on the particular ideological perspective with which management views the union. The objectives centering on job rights and obligations usually involve some inherent conflict and some potential for the integration of interests. The fact that certain items often become the subject of distributive bargaining is explained as much by a party's perception as by the inherent nature of the agenda items.

### Area of Interdependency

Certain long-term limits define the basic area of interdependency and consequently describe the most fundamental limit to the two-party conflict. Beyond each of these outer limits one or the other party would terminate the potentially advantageous relationship.

It is the purpose of this section to discuss the nature of this joint dependency and indicate the factors which limit or prescribe this range.

As we have indicated, the distributive process occurs around many specific issues, both economic and noneconomic. For ease of exposition we shall confine ourselves to the wage issue. In this and the following sections "wage rate" should be taken to represent the overall remuneration from employment.

The area of dependency stems from two sources: market rigidities and jointly created gain. These two sources will be discussed in turn.

**Market Rigidities.** The two organizations engaged in social negotiations stand to benefit by dealing with each other. In the union-management relationship, the lower limit to this area of interdependency would be the point at which the employees would seek a new employer or bargaining agent. At some upper limit, where management would be forced to seek a new relationship, it would invoke its next-best alternative to remaining in the current relationship. Management might move, it might seek another union, or it might hire nonunion labor. If a bargain is to be made between the parties as currently constituted, it must occur within the limits.

We have referred to the limits as if each were the problem of one party or the other. In reality, because the very existence of the business and employment opportunities are at stake at either limit, the two prices are experienced as limits by both parties.[5] That is, neither party has an interest in knowingly going above the higher or below the lower of these prices. Within this range, exchange benefits both parties, but the higher the price, the more the gain goes to labor, and the lower the price, the more this gain goes to management.

Within this range both sides stand to benefit from a bargain, which presumably specifies both price and quantity. Siegel and Fouraker, who review how the price and quantity variables have been handled in the literature, note that quantity (employment) is set so as to maximize the joint gain; i.e., quantity can be considered fixed, and bargaining centers on the question of price.[6]

Thus, at either edge of the range a sharp discontinuity would occur in quantity as the relationship is terminated and employment falls to zero. In actual fact it is unlikely that employment remains constant throughout the range, rather it is likely to diminish steadily as the wage rate is pushed toward the upper limit. This is an important factor in defining utility curves; a negotiator may be hesitant to approach the outer limits of the opponent because of the effects on employment.

At this point we are interested in exploring the sources of the interdependency. In effect, we are talking about a range bounded by two indifference points; at the upper limit the employer is indifferent between other alternatives and remaining in the relationship, and at the lower limit the union is indifferent between other alternatives and remaining in the relationship. These indifference points diverge in part because there are substantial short-run costs to either party for disengaging from the relationship and pursuing an alternative relationship.

*The lower limits.* The employees' lower limit is below their best alternative wage rate to the extent that employees incur costs in transferring to other firms. At this lower price, the expected improvement which would result from other employment would offset the cost of making the move. These costs of disengagement reflect certain institutional and labor market rigidities: the disintegrated nature of the market, the lack of mobility of the workers, the limited knowledge of the market, and the friction caused

---

[5] For a good discussion of these limits and a review of the literature see N. W. Chamberlain, *Collective Bargaining* (New York: McGraw-Hill Book Company, 1951), pp. 213–215.

[6] Sidney Siegel and L. E. Fouraker, *Bargaining and Group Decision Making* (New York: McGraw-Hill Book Company, 1960), p. 9.

by the fact that a certain worker is conversant only with his duties in a certain plant.[7] Finally, any factor such as fringe benefits or seniority rights which tends to lock workers into the employment relationship would depress the lower limit.

These factors influence the extent to which the workers' lower limit is set below alternatives that might be available to them. Obviously the employees' lower limit is also depressed by the extent to which the employer is the only employer in the local labor market. Moreover, the skill level of particular employee groups would affect the location of the employees' lower limits. Highly skilled employees who could readily find alternate employment would not be as dependent on a particular employer, and hence their quit point would be close to their best alternative wage. The degree of unemployment present in the local labor market would have an important bearing on the positioning of the lower limit—the higher the unemployment rate, the lower the outer limit.[8]

Thus far in our discussion of labor's lower limits we have focused on the employees' decision to terminate the employment relationships. However, there may be a different point at which the officials representing the employees would offer maximum and indefinite resistance. To understand this, we can return to another kind of option the employees might exercise at some levels of depressed wages. They might seek to be represented by another union. If the employees would exercise this option earlier, then the union officials might be expected to offer maximum resistance at that point. Presumably they would not agree to terms which would result in their being defeated as bargaining agent.

*The upper limits.* The company's upper limit is somewhat above its best alternative (the wages which would secure other employees) because of the cost of hiring replacements. The costs entailed in severing its connection with large segments of the existing work force are substantial. Extensive termination benefits may be involved, bad public relations may result, and the new work force may require considerable training and orientation. There may also be moving expenses.[9] But there comes a point at which it would be better for the employer to incur these costs than to sign a contract at the demanded wage rate. This point can be thought of as the upper limit of the area of interdependency.

Certain structural arrangements may operate to influence the location of this limit. The union, for example, may control all available labor, and meaningful alternatives for the company disappear. Some unions do

[7] Jan Pen, *The Wage Rate under Collective Bargaining,* trans. T. S. Preston (Cambridge, Mass.: Harvard University Press, 1959), p. 37.

[8] K. E. Boulding, *Conflict and Defense: A General Theory* (New York: Harper & Row, Publishers, Incorporated, 1962), p. 186.

[9] Pen, *op. cit.,* p. 44.

operate within these favorable circumstances in which the labor demand curve is fairly inelastic: labor is a small percentage of the cost structure, the technology requires fixed manning, the company possesses some product-market power and can pass wage increases on to the customer, and so forth.

The following statement summarizes the various circumstances that would create relatively high upper limits for a firm:

> . . . national as contrasted with local product markets, large-scale as contrasted with small-scale operating units, large multiunit companies as contrasted with small companies, locational stability as contrasted with locational fluidity, . . . diverse products as contrasted with . . . fairly simple product structures, (limited degree) of price competition in product markets, . . . industry bargaining contrasted with local bargaining.[10]

The empirical studies which have been made of pattern following support these propositions. Levinson and Seltzer [11] note that size of firm, geographical distance, and product similarity are important variables in explaining deviation from the pattern. In the auto and steel industries, in which the unions enjoy considerable bargaining power, the wage rate has advanced to almost the employers' upper limit. In smaller companies located away from Detroit or Pittsburgh and producing auto parts or fabricated steel, the upper limit is lower and the wage rate is usually commensurately lower.

Many believe that there is no effective upper limit in certain industries, such as construction and trucking. However, there are restraining influences. If the rate moves too high, construction companies will mechanize more rapidly or start using preassembled modules, and trucking companies will lose business as they have in the car-haul field.

On the other hand, it should be noted that many negotiators, particularly on the union side, have a short time horizon and are apt to exploit whatever dependency exists. They are well aware that over the long run a higher wage rate may not be desirable. But they are also aware that in the short run the wage rate can be forced considerably above the other's best alternatives without severe repercussions. They realize that it takes time for alternative arrangements to be adopted. It also takes money. During the short run the company might rather pay higher wages than incur the costs of disengagement.

[10] S. H. Slichter, J. J. Healy, and E. R. Livernash, *The Impact of Collective Bargaining on Management* (Washington, D.C.: The Brookings Institution, 1960), p. 607.

[11] H. M. Levinson, "Pattern Bargaining: A Case Study of the Automobile Workers," *Quarterly Journal of Economics*, vol. 74 (May, 1960), pp. 296–317; and George Seltzer, "Pattern Bargaining and the United Steelworkers," *Journal of Political Economy*, vol. 59 (August, 1951), pp. 319–331.

The decision-making manager may, however, have a more conservative upper limit than that which results strictly from cost-price considerations, since his reputation as a manager is also at stake. Beyond a given maximum wage level the manager can no longer maintain his own status. Managers are unquestionably as sensitive about their reputation among their stockholders and their fellow managers in this type of decision as they are in others. They may be subject to pressure from other employers in the area or industry. For example, canneries put pressure on can manufacturers who supply them with products by urging them to exercise wage restraint. A parent company may be intolerant of high wages paid by one of its subsidiaries if the subsidiary's wages are likely to have company-wide implications. Any of a number of similar factors can influence the point at which the company negotiator offers maximum and indefinite resistance to higher wage levels. See Figure 2-6 for a hypothetical wage spectrum.

### Figure 2-6
### Wage Spectrum

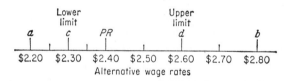

$PR$ = present rate and coincidentally best alternative rate for both employer and employee, $a$ = point at which employees would quit company. $b$ = point at which the company would be forced to move. $c$ = point at which employees would change bargaining agent, $d$ = point at which management would be changed because of its failure to deal effectively with union. $c$-$d$ = outer limits to area of interdependency insofar as union and management negotiators are concerned.

**Mutually Created Gain.** Thus far we have considered only the area of interdependency that stems from market rigidities. Another source of interdependency has been heretofore overlooked. It stems from the fact that collective bargaining is not just a process of dividing existing resources but is also a process sometimes used for creating additional values or mutual benefits.

The creation of additional benefits can take place over both the long and the short run. Over the long run, considerable joint gain can be produced by the attitudes of trust and confidence which exist among employees, union officials, and management. For example, through the mechanism of a union-management cooperation scheme such as the Scanlon Plan, unit labor costs might be reduced to the point at which management would be willing to pay a particular labor force represented by a particular union considerably more than otherwise might be available. The joint gain grows out of the relationship and is something not available to either side elsewhere. The employees could leave the establishment and go elsewhere, but their contributions would be less and their compensation less accordingly. In the given establishment their contributions are higher because of the unique collaboration which produces joint gain.

Another instance of the willingness of employees to accept less than the market rate because of compensations gained from a given plant might exist if the plant were close to their residence or if it provided many social satisfactions of an intangible sort. Again, these factors are not reflected in the market rate since they represent unique attributes of the given company. Thus, it is possible for joint gain to exist because of a unique matching of employee and employer attributes.

Another important source of enlargement of the area of interdependency is the negotiation process itself. As we shall see in the chapter on integrative bargaining, considerable joint gain can be created through the use of problem-solving and utility-matching techniques.

In our discussion we have identified several sources of interdependency. Some of the mutual advantage stems from long-run rigidities in the structure of the labor and product markets. But even when management and labor operate within a configuration that more closely approaches the competitive model, considerable interdependency can be present. For example, the parties may create special gain through a unique sharing of attributes and ideas, or they may have something in common in seeking to avoid the costs of disengagement.

Our interest at this point is to suggest that joint gain exists and focus attention on the activity of distributing this joint gain. Over the long run or even during the short run, the parties enjoy or endure a range of dependency. The point of departure for the next section is that in the given negotiation considerable difference of opinion about how this joint gain should be divided may exist. As long as the range exists, then, there is room for differing desires about how that range should be split.

## Subjective Utilities Associated with Various Settlements

The bargaining spectrum as defined above would consist of all the possible proportions into which the scarce resources could be distributed, each represented by a point or a price. However, bargaining is normally confined to a narrower range than that delimited by the outer limits of interdependency. This occurs for several reasons relating to the utility functions and probability functions of the negotiators. The matter of subjective utilities will be explored in this section.

It is important to distinguish between objective values and subjective preferences or utilities. (In our earlier discussion of issues and their underlying fixed-sum payoff structures we referred only to objective units of value such as monetary units.) Here we do not assume that a party's satisfaction, i.e., utility, is linear with money. Each unit of money added does not add the same amount of subjective utility.

The general question which we shall be working on in this and later sections is: How do certain points or areas on the total conceivable spectrum of outcomes attain unique distinction and prominence in the thinking of the negotiator and provide a guide to his decisions? Consider a spectrum of outcomes regarding a specific issue, say a wage adjustment with an upper limit of an increase of 40 cents per hour and a lower limit of a reduction of 20 cents per hour. At first glance one might imagine that a party simply wants an improvement over the *status quo* and will try to get all that he can. The necessary accompaniment to this is that the person will, in the final analysis, take as little as he must and accept what is necessary. It turns out this is not an adequate conception of the way the negotiator behaves.

What we hope to show by our analysis of utility and probability functions is that parties enter negotiations with more limited expectations about where on the spectrum serious bargaining will take place.

**The Union's Utility Function.** Let us consider the utility function that a union negotiator might have for possible wage levels within the bargaining spectrum. Certainly the union negotiator's preferences would be influenced by his appreciation of the membership's preferences. However, we can now point to an important distinction between the utility functions of the membership and those of the union official. The value which underlies the former is primarily purchasing power of the wages received. The value reflected by the official's preference curve is the security of the institution he represents and the security he enjoys as an official in that institution at the various possible wage levels which he might gain and maintain.[12] It stands to reason that this security is affected by a series of evaluations of the official's specific performances. A union official is sensitive to how well he does in negotiations relative to the settlements negotiated elsewhere. Figure 2-7 presents a curve which reflects these ideas.

The following assumptions underlie Figure 2-7:

1. Present wage rate is $2.40. The settlements reached elsewhere, which are the standards against which the union negotiator believes he will be evaluated, range from increases of 5 to 10 cents per hour. Any change from 5 to 10 cents would be of maximal value to him, since it would greatly influence his relative standing as a negotiator. The 5-cent increase to $2.45 would represent the threshold to this range.

[12] We assume that negotiating an adequate wage level is a necessary, but certainly not a sufficient, criterion for security as a bargaining agent.

2. We assume that no wage increase represents another threshold—
we have designated this point as the point of zero utility on the
diagram. Any increment in the settlement up to 5 cents would be
valued positively but at a lower rate. Hence the added utility between 0 and 5 cents ($2.40 and $2.45) is shown as 2 utiles, contrasted with an addition of 3 utiles for the next 5-cent increment
of 5 to 10 cents.

### Figure 2-7

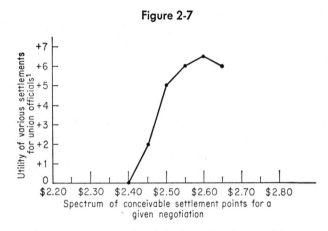

The zero point and units of the interval scale are arbitrary.

3. We assume that increments above 10 cents will be valued less but
still positively. The chart shows the 5-cent increment from $2.50
to $2.55 as adding one utile and the 5-cent increment from $2.55
to $2.60 as adding one-half utile.

4. At some point, represented here as $2.60, the value of higher set-
tlements to the union official actually becomes negative. This is
based on the assumption that settlements can be so high as to
make his life difficult in certain ways. Higher figures might raise
the expectations of the membership to have similar settlements in
the future or to influence the expectations of other groups he also
represents.

What sorts of factors enter into the union negotiator's thinking to influence his preferences? It is not necessary to explain here why certain economic demands or provisions are valued positively, for example, why the
union negotiator's utility curve for employees' wages is generally a rising
one. The question is: What factors explain the discontinuities in the utility
curve? The discussion focuses on three points: zero utility, maximum marginal utility, and maximum total utility.

The *status quo* often represents the point at which a union negotiator
begins to attach positive value to a settlement. A union official often feels

that he must succeed in accomplishing some improvement through negotiations. The point at which the rate of increase in utility is at a maximum is usually associated with "coercive comparisons." [13] Coercive comparisons may stem from the precedent value of prior wage settlements in the given relationship or from the settlements in allied situations. Both precedent and patterns play an extremely important role in creating discontinuities in the utility curves.

The point at which utility starts to decrease absolutely is influenced by many factors. As suggested earlier, the utility of higher wage settlements may be decreased by the problems which the negotiator would encounter in subsequent negotiations with the same company or in concurrent negotiations with other companies.

However, another consideration serves to constrain the utility curve. This involves the subject of outer limits. Each negotiator places less utility on increments in position near the outer limit of the opponent. For example, union officials become progressively less interested in increasing the wage rate as wages reach the upper limit. Depending upon the slope of the company's demand curve, higher wage rates may provoke important employment effects for the union. Thus, to the extent that the company's demand for labor is elastic, there will be some restraining influences on the union's utility curve.

Of course, the outer limit represents the ultimate restraint. As the wage rate approaches the company's outer limit, the company will start to seek other arrangements. The union negotiator who is not sensitive to incremental employment effects may be very sensitive to the possibility of the company being forced to shut down, to move, or to hire nonunion labor. In any event, the outer limits are not precise points, and their very vagueness makes it necessary for each side to be extremely cautious in pressing for a large change in the wage rate.

As with any generalization, there are exceptions. Examples can be found of union leaders who consciously seek wage rates outside the range of dependency. It is not that they purposely want to destroy the relationship, rather they are guided by other concerns. For many years the United Steelworkers demanded that the steel pattern be applied to the paper-cup plants of Continental Can, even though the pattern for the paper industry was lower, and more importantly, even though the union knew that the company was losing business and the workers their jobs. The union adhered to the wage policy since it wanted to maintain parity among its union members and wanted to avoid any break in the national steel pattern.

The Packinghouse Workers Union has been just as adamant in seeking

<hr />

[13] A. M. Ross, *Trade Union Wage Policy* (Berkeley, Calif.: University of California Press, 1948). See also Leon Festinger, "A Theory of Social Comparison Process," *Human Relations*, vol. 7, no. 2 (1954), pp. 117–140.

to preserve the national pattern, even though such a policy has cost it membership through plant shutdowns and relocations.

Another chapter could be written on the complex subject of a union negotiator's preferences for revenue versus employment. Some writers maintain that union leaders are sensitive to employment effects and that their utility curve for higher wage settlements will reflect this fact.[14] They assume that a union negotiator optimizes some combination of revenue and jobs.[15] Other writers maintain that union leaders do not worry about employment effects, either because they feel that employment effects are not involved or because the relationship between wage and employment changes is too subtle and complex. In effect, the utility curve for higher wage settlements reflects primarily political and social consideration.[16]

If we return to the question of how the outlook of the rank and file is different from that of the leadership, additional complexities emerge. Generally speaking, the rank and file is more concerned about the employment effects of higher wages than the leadership is. For example, in meatpacking, some of the locals preferred to make wage and benefit concessions, while the top leadership tried to protect the national pattern.

However, when times are good and there is little concern about employment effects, the wage desires of the rank and file may be considerably more ambitious than the leadership. Here the rank and file will place more emphasis on immediate improvement in the employment relationship, while the leadership will emphasize more the long-run considerations of obtaining similar settlements elsewhere, maintaining membership strength, etc. Just such a situation will provide the setting for the process of intraorganizational bargaining, which we shall consider later in the study.

One writer has attempted to draw these many considerations together.

> Perhaps the most realistic assumption we can make is that unions are interested both in raising wages and in having a large membership, but that the precise weights to be attached to these two objectives will differ from union to union and from time to time. . . . The union will generally be more willing to fight to prevent cuts in present wages than to win increases, and it will be more concerned about preserving the employment of present members than about enlarging the membership. . . . This formulation suggests that many union wage policies can be viewed within a reasonably simple framework of rational behavior.[17]

[14] G. P. Shultz, *Pressures on Wage Decisions* (Cambridge, Mass.: The Technology Press of the Massachusetts Institute of Technology, 1951).

[15] J. T. Dunlop, *Wage Determination under Trade Unions* (New York: A. M. Kelley, 1950).

[16] Ross, *op. cit.*

[17] Albert Rees, *The Economics of Trade Unions* (Chicago: The University of Chicago Press, 1962), p. 54.

**The Company's Utility Function.** Let us now consider the utility curve that a company negotiator might have under the same circumstances. In many respects the curve would be influenced (in a reciprocal way) by the same factors just enumerated (see Figure 2-8).

**Figure 2-8**

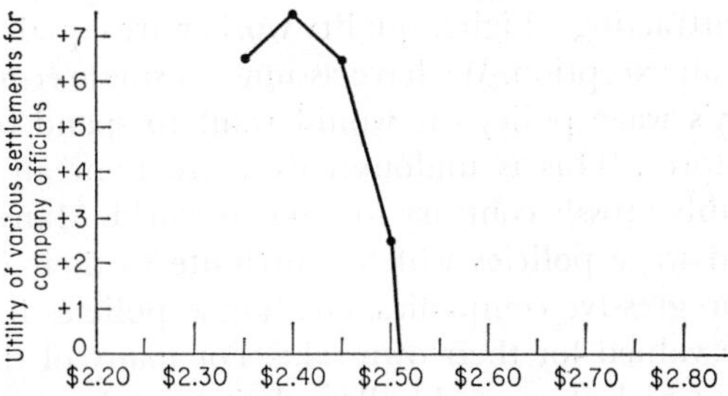

Spectrum of conceivable settlement points for a given negotiation

The following assumptions underlie Figure 2-8:

1. The company has no desire to put through a wage reduction. The point of maximum utility is $2.40, the present wage.

2. Settlements slightly above $2.40 bring some drop in utility but not a great deal. Between $2.45 and $2.50 there is a rapid drop in utility as the wage approaches the limit set by pattern settlements.

3. The point of minimum effective utility represents the "maximum offer" which the negotiator can give without being replaced by top management.

Let us analyze the factors that shape the company's utility curve in terms of maximum total utility, maximum marginal utility, and zero utility.

Like the union, the company is not interested in pushing the wage rate to the opponent's outer limit. Certainly the company would not have any interest in pushing wages below the point at which it would have difficulty in retaining the desired work force, although it might not be deterred from pressing for a wage rate which would induce the employees to abandon the union. Note our assumption that management shares an interest in preventing wages from going below "the level necessary to attract and maintain the desired work force." This has buried within it many complications and prior assumptions. Moreover, there are some important exceptions to the statement itself.

First, look at the complications. The level required to "attract" a work force might be considerably higher than that required to "maintain" a work force. The level which would constitute the point of maximum utility would depend on whether the company needed to attract a new force or merely needed to maintain the present one. "Desired work force" is also a concept needing explanation. Presumably the higher the wage level, the more desirable the quality of the work force recruited. We assume an optimum point at which the marginal wage cost and the marginal productivity resulting from attracting a higher quality worker are equal.

Now, look at an exception. We have assumed a single economic criterion to the company's wage policy—it would want to spend only enough to keep its work force. This is undoubtedly more than an oversimplification; it is probably grossly contrary to the real world. Many business firms have established wage policies which contribute to their images as good employers, as progressive companies, etc. These policies have been internalized and are valued for their own sake. For many of these companies the point below which they would allow their wage level to fall is considerably above the point at which they would begin to lose their work force.

The point of maximum change in utility would be fixed by settlements in other situations. As the wage rate approached the high side of the pattern, the company negotiator would experience sharply reduced satisfaction.

The company negotiator might tolerate a settlement slightly above competition. The company negotiator would experience zero utility in some sense at the point at which he would be in danger of being replaced.

How high a company negotiator would be willing to go depends upon a number of complex factors. If competitors could be required to sign the same contract (as is usual in industry or association bargaining), if the wage increase could be passed on in the form of a price increase, if labor costs represented a small percentage of total costs, or if profits were ample, then the point of zero utility for the company might be considerably higher.[18]

### Subjective Disutilities of a Failure to Agree: Strike Costs

As previously stated, the purpose of this analysis is to determine where, within the long-term area of dependency, actual bargaining will take place in any particular negotiation. Just as the negotiator's preferences for various possible settlements are important, so too is his evaluation of the costs associated with a failure to agree. The negotiator understands that if a particular position he adopts turns out to be unacceptable to the other

[18] All these conditions might also work to raise the company's outer limit. Whether they affect the utility curve directly or indirectly does not really matter for the purposes of this discussion.

party and the parties fail to reach agreement, certain costs are incurred. In collective bargaining the "certain costs" are typically strike costs.[19]

The possibility of a strike and the costs of such a strike for the negotiator is always the other side of the coin to the advantages demanded. The prospect of incurring strike costs encourages caution in a negotiator's thinking. The more costly the failure to agree, the more conservative his expectations will be. In the next section we shall learn more about why this is true when we combine strike costs and utilities with probabilities.

**Types of Strike Costs.** *Labor's costs.* The following are various aspects of labor's costs or potential costs involved in striking:

1. Loss of wages by employees. Drain on financial resources of union.

2. Loss of institutional security. A strike may result in a loss of membership and even threaten the status of the union as bargaining agent. Many employees may find other jobs during the strike and not return after the strike ends. The employee replacements may not be as likely to join the union or may at least delay joining. Other employees who went through the strike may drop their membership. Rival unions or rival factions within the union may exploit a strike situation and acquire employee support for themselves.

3. Loss of goodwill with management. This leads to antagonisms which may not disappear with termination of strike. Management may be more adamant in the future, retaliating in ways of its own. The deterioration in plant relationships can result in a disadvantage to both parties, since the informal accommodations worked out to the mutual satisfaction of both parties may be contingent upon continuing trust and the elimination of trust threatens these working arrangements.

4. Loss of public image. A strike may give the appearance that the union is acting irresponsibly and ignoring the public's interest in maintaining the flow of goods and services.

*Management's costs.* The following are the various aspects of management's costs or potential costs involved in striking:

1. Loss of operating profits (short run) and market position (longer run). Possible damage to plant and equipment through idleness.

2. Loss of management status with higher management or stockholders. If the strike does not seem necessary or if it appears to have

[19] The strike, which is a mutual decision, represents the major alternative to agreement. Failure to agree may provoke other forms of economic pressure such as slowdowns or social pressure such as criticism, but our analysis will center on costs associated with strike action.

been mishandled, the managers responsible for negotiations may suffer a loss of prestige. Their careers may be adversely affected.

3. Loss of goodwill with labor. Both the union-management relationship and employee relations can suffer, resulting in low morale, low productivity, and resistance to changes initiated by management, etc.

4. Loss of public image. The strike can have an adverse effect on attitudes of customers, governmental agencies, or legislative bodies.[20]

*Positive by-products.* Sometimes by striking a party also receives some positive by-products apart from any immediate concessions it may achieve. What are these by-products?

First, the strike which fails to obtain any concessions in the immediate negotiations may nevertheless have some value as a long-term investment. The credibility of a strike threat will be enhanced in the future, whether it is used with the same adversary or with another who only knows of the strike. For example, a union can strike, not to achieve anything in the given negotiation, but to warn others who might try to drive a similar bargain. Such was the approach of the Packinghouse Workers Union against Swift in the 1959 negotiations. By striking at the Wilson, North Carolina, plant the union gained nothing except to communicate the message to other packinghouse companies that if they wanted any opening of the geographical pattern, they were going to have to spend as much money as Swift did (in strike action).

Second, the internal organization of the party may more likely be strengthened than weakened by a strike (of short duration). Identifying an external enemy usually increases the internal solidarity of a group. In addition, winning a strike may gain new members.

Third, sometimes the strike has a positive psychological impact rather than an adverse one. It may serve as an outlet for pent-up emotions of workers. It may even serve to clear the air between the parties and provide a foundation for building constructive relationships.

**The Pattern of Strike Costs.** Strike-cost patterns have two important dimensions. First, there is the question of the *rate* of costs to each party should a strike occur. Typically, this rate will change as the strike progresses. Second, there is the question of the *total time* duration within which a strike can be endured. For each side, some point exists at which it would be forced to capitulate since its resources would have been depleted.

Very often employees will not mind a short strike but will be hurt by a long strike. As the strike progresses and their reserves diminish, greater

[20] For a more extensive review of strike costs see *Preparing for Collective Bargaining: II*, Personnel Policy Study no. 182 (New York: National Industrial Conference Board, 1961), p. 10.

marginal disability will be felt for each week of the continuing strike. Thus, while the weekly cost of the strike in actual dollars may not vary (being the difference between normal wages and strike benefits), the perceived or subjective cost will increase as the bankruptcy point is approached. Apart from the financial drain of a strike, the worker finds the enforced leisure more and more costly psychologically, usually to himself

**Figure 2-9**

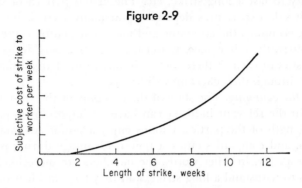

and his family. These factors combine to produce a pattern of increasing marginal costs (see Figure 2-9).

A company may experience a similar pattern of strike costs, particularly if an excess inventory of finished goods is on hand at the beginning of the strike and shipments to customers can continue. In this instance, the curve rises when the inventory is depleted and the customers begin to rely on

**Figure 2-10**

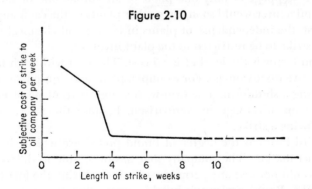

other suppliers; the curve becomes even steeper as financial resources are depleted.

But one can envision the reverse of this situation. In an oil refinery (see Figure 2-10) the cost of a shutdown is greatest at the outset because of the costs of shutting down the equipment and the risks and inconveniences in transfering customers to other refineries. The above diagram suggests that after four weeks the costs of the strike are the fixed costs of idle equipment and management. Of course, if supervisory personnel continue to operate the refinery, then even fewer economic costs would be experienced by the company.

Innumerable patterns exist: unions with low weekly strike costs but little ability to last a long strike, companies with high weekly costs but great ability to last a long strike, etc. The actual pattern of strike costs which each side experiences depends upon many factors, including the state of the economy, the economic and market structure of the company, the technology, the labor market, and the collective bargaining structure. Characteristics of each of these factors influence the bargaining power of the parties through their effect on strike costs.

*State of the economy.* The state of the economy or the economic conditions within the relevant industry can have an important impact on the relative strength of the parties. Unions enjoy a power advantage during good times, and companies enjoy a power advantage during poor times. During prosperity, in other words, the members are more likely to have the savings to withstand a long strike, and they have less fear of being replaced by strikebreakers. Moreover, during an economic boom, the strike would impose a higher rate of costs on the company.

*Economic and market structure of the company.* The extent of the losses imposed by a strike depends upon many economic characteristics of the company. The first is degree of plant specialization. A strike at only one plant of a highly integrated company can be rather devastating. For example, a stoppage at only one plant of an automobile or farm equipment manufacturer would soon force other plants of the company to close. In contrast, the independence of plants in the oil and chemical industries enables a strike to be restricted to the plant involved.

A second factor is the level of fixed cost. The firm with high fixed costs is at a relative disadvantage. For example, plant and equipment costs continue during a shutdown. The firm with a high percentage of labor costs may be at an advantage in comparison, because these costs would be avoided during a strike.

The third factor is the degree of brand preference which characterizes the product market. The company that has been able to differentiate its product would not lose any permanent business during the first few weeks of the strike. Brand preference would suggest that the customers might delay their purchases until the company went back into production. Thus, an automobile manufacturer on strike might not suffer as much damage during the first few weeks of a strike as a steel company would. However, the brand preference is effective only up to a point; eventually the customers will buy an alternate product.

Hence, the postponability of demand plays an important part in the effect of brand preference. Even though a customer may possess strong brand preference to patronize a particular airline or to buy a particular brand of milk, a strike would soon force him to do business with other companies. Having bought the alternate product, he may be persuaded to remain with that new supplier.

Another factor involves the size of individual accounts. The company which supplies only several customers may hesitate to allow a strike for fear of losing a big chunk of its business. This concern is increased if the customer is dependent upon the company for continuous supply. For example, after a long strike at Pittsburgh Plate Glass, which had been an important supplier to Chrysler, the latter announced plans to build its own glass plant. Leland Hazard, who has analyzed the predicament faced by such companies, emphasizes their willingness to take a drop in profits or to raise prices before incurring a strike.[21]

*The character of the technology.* In some industries (utilities, chemicals, and oils) it is possible for supervisors to continue operations. In other industries it is possible to stockpile a finished product and ship it to customers after a strike has started. Clearly, in these situations the impact of a strike on the company is rather small in comparison with that on a railroad, where there is rarely any attempt to operate during a strike and where the product is an instantaneous service.

*The labor market structure.* The structure of the labor market affects the power position of the union. In effect, all the forces that influence the degree of attachment of an individual to a given employer also affect his ability to minimize strike costs. If the employee possesses skills which are generally used and there is a demand for these skills, then he may be able to secure temporary employment during the period of a strike. On the contrary, if he possesses skills unique to his employer or if conditions in the local labor market are "loose," then he may be unable to engage in any alternate activity.

*The collective bargaining structure.* Naturally each negotiator seeks to gain the advantage of relative size.[22] A union negotiator is in a favorable power position when he brings the resources of a large international union to bear on a small company, e.g., the Teamsters' bargaining with a small trucking company.

One large teamster negotiation was described as follows. The union sent telegrams to a large number of companies informing them that a

[21] Leland Hazard, "Wage Theory: A Management View," in G. W. Taylor and F. C. Pierson (eds.), *New Concepts in Wage Determination* (New York: McGraw-Hill Book Company, 1957), pp. 32–50.

[22] A. R. Weber (ed.), *The Structure of Collective Bargaining* (New York: The Free Press of Glencoe, 1961), p. 18.

master contract would be negotiated. At the appointed time and place the union presented the prepared contract. The union leader made a short speech to the effect that the sooner everyone signed up, the easier it would be for them . . . there appeared to have been little cohesion among employers and substantially no negotiation in the process of settlement.[23]

Similarly, a company negotiator enjoys a power advantage when he represents a large company bargaining with a small independent union, as is the case in the chemical and oil industries.

> In one division of a large company bargaining was on a plant basis. The division had about a dozen plants, practically identical in character and widely separated geographically, and dealt with various unions in these plants. The labor relations director explained that they had no "bad" contract clauses in these plants. They simply refused to agree to a clause that was not satisfactory to them. . . . It was perfectly clear that any plant union that struck would have been in a hopeless situation.[24]

To complete the enumeration of possible size combinations, we should note that many instances can be found of large unions facing large companies (steel, auto, rubber, etc.) and small unions facing small companies (craft unions bargaining with small companies). Many bargaining structures fall between the extremes. The industry may be only partly organized or organized by rival unions. The employers may be weakly organized or not organized at all. Such circumstances limit the bargaining power of the union and management, respectively.

Discerning the relative size of the two opposing groups is not easy. Much more is involved than just the size of the bargaining unit formally certified by the National Labor Relations Board. Size is determined by the effective bargaining configuration. The representation unit may cover only the plant group, but bargaining may be conducted on a company-wide basis or even on an industry-wide basis. Even where bargaining is conducted on a plant-by-plant basis, a high degree of coordination may exist between locals of the same union or between different unions through the operation of bargaining councils.

On the employer's side, a high degree of coordination may exist between companies, even in the absence of a formal employers' association (as in the

---

[23] Slichter, Healy, and Livernash, *op. cit.*, p. 942. For a good discussion of bargaining in trucking see Ralph and Estelle James, "Hoffa's Acquisition of Industrial Power," *Industrial Relations*, vol. 2 (May, 1963), pp. 67–95 and "Hoffa's Leverage Techniques in Bargaining," *Industrial Relations*, vol. 3 (October, 1963), pp. 73–93.

[24] Slichter, Healy, and Livernash, *op. cit.*, p. 942.

case of the automobile manufacturers). Even where there is no explicit coordination, the pattern-setting–pattern-following syndrome may operate, thereby linking developments in one negotiation to developments in other negotiations. The subject of the bargaining structure is complex and involves employer associations, mutual-aid pacts, multiunion bargaining councils, etc.[25]

## Probability Functions and Subjectively Expected Utilities

We have discussed only utility functions for issues and cost functions associated with a strike. These functions alone do not determine the locus of bargaining. We must turn to the question of the likelihood of attainment for each of the various possible outcomes. One school of decision theory makes a definitive point of combining utilities and probabilities into a composite concept: The subjectively expected utility (SEU) of an alternative is the product of the subjective utility and the subjective probability of success associated with that alternative.[26] The theory holds that a person will choose the alternative which maximizes subjectively expected utility. Let us trace out the implications of this formulation without becoming committed to the precise significance of the figure it produces.

Inasmuch as there are both potential positive and potential negative consequences associated with a given demand, the SEU of an alternate demand $(x)$ is its utility $(U)$ times the probability $(P)$ that it will be acceptable *plus* the strike costs $(S)$ associated with a failure to agree times the probability $(1 - P)$ that the demand will not be acceptable.

$$SEU = P(x) \cdot U(x) + [1 - P(x)] \cdot S(x)$$

But what are the probabilities associated with the bargaining spectrum? What is the probability that an insistent demand at any particular level would be successful? We return to our illustration of the union official's thinking. Thus far we have analyzed and illustrated four types of considerations associated with a given level of union demand: the utility of such a settlement for the union, the (negative) utility of that settlement for the company, the cost of a strike for the union, and the cost of a strike for the company. These utilities and costs are the basis for probability estimates.

The union official's subjective probability function is constructed out of his assumptions about the responses of management under various circumstances. He might ask himself, "Suppose I absolutely refused to go below 20 cents ($2.60)? Would management be likely to agree without a strike?"

[25] For a good treatment of these issues see Weber, *op. cit.*
[26] Ward Edwards, "Behavioral Decision Theory," *Annual Review of Psychology*, vol. 12 (1961), pp. 473–498. See also Pen, *op. cit.*

First, the union official would need to make some assumption about the (negative) utility of the various settlements for management. The union would be especially interested in knowing the general shape of management's utility function for the possible wage settlements. Where is management's maximum marginal utility? To know this would be to improve the union's ideas about where along the spectrum management might offer the most resistance. Within this sensitive area of the spectrum (as viewed by management), the union might expect more rapid changes in the probabilities of success of alternate demands. *The more disutility involved for management, the lower would be the union's estimate of its probability of success.* Simply stated, management is more likely to fight for issues it thinks are important.

Second, the union official would be concerned about the strike costs the company would face. *The lower the company's strike costs, the lower the union's estimate of the probability of success.* Essentially, management would be more willing to take a position which risked incurring a strike that would be less costly.

Third, the union official also would be concerned about his own strike costs. *The higher the union's strike costs, the lower the union's estimate of the probability of success.* In effect, the less a strike would cost the company and the more a strike would cost the union, then the more the union can expect the company to use coercion in furthering its objectives in the distributive bargain.

Let us assume that the union official's assessment of these factors led to a probability function like that in Figure 2-11.

### Figure 2-11

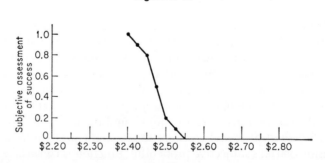

Spectrum of conceivable settlement points for a given negotiation

The probability figures shown in Figure 2-11 can then be combined with the utility curve shown earlier. The results are the positive expectations associated with alternate demands (see Figure 2-12a).

Let us assume that the strike will have a disutility of 2 (coordinated with the positive utility scale of 0 to 7).[27] Using $1 - P(x)$ for the probability of a strike and $- 2$ for the utility of a strike, we can calculate the expected

### Figure 2-12a
### Table of Calculations

| Increase of x | U(x) | × | P(x) | = | Total |
|---|---|---|---|---|---|
| 0¢ | 0 | | 1.0 | = | 0 |
| 2½¢ | 1 | | .9 | = | .9 |
| 5¢ | 2 | | .8 | = | 1.6 |
| 7½¢ | 3½ | | .5 | = | 1.75 |
| 10¢ | 5 | | .2 | = | 1.0 |
| 12½¢ | 5½ | | .1 | = | .55 |
| 15¢ | 6 | | 0 | = | 0 |

### Figure 2-12b
### Table of Calculations

| Increase of x | S(x) | × | [1 − P(x)] | = | Total |
|---|---|---|---|---|---|
| 0¢ | −2 | | .0 | = | 0 |
| 2½¢ | −2 | | .1 | = | −.2 |
| 5¢ | −2 | | .2 | = | −.4 |
| 7½¢ | −2 | | .5 | = | −1.0 |
| 10¢ | −2 | | .8 | = | −1.6 |
| 12¼¢ | −2 | | .9 | = | −1.8 |
| 15¢ | −2 | | 1.0 | = | −2.0 |

costs associated with each demand (see Figure 2-12b). Figure 2-13 shows the net subjectively expected utilities which result when one subtracts the subjective strike costs associated with each possible level of increase from the positive expectations.

[27] The calculation of this figure can be done as follows: The lump-sum costs represented by a strike can be converted into a stream of costs comparable to wages by a discount calculation. For the company the discount period would closely parallel the payout period used for any analysis of capital appropriations. For the union the payout period might be approximated by the length of the collective bargaining agreement. While this conversion from a lump sum to a stream of costs may not be operationally easy, it does not contain any conceptual problems. In his calculations, Cartter chooses a 20 per cent discount rate for the union and a 10 per cent discount rate for the company. See A. M. Cartter, *Theory of Wages and Employment* (Homewood, Ill.: Richard D. Irwin, Inc., 1959), p. 119. Reder also discusses how this calculation can be made. See M. W. Reder, "The Theory of Union Wage Policy," *The Review of Economics and Statistics*, vol. 34 (February, 1952), p. 38.

The maximum *SEU* (1.2) is at 5 cents. What is the meaning of this figure? If the contest were one in which the union entered a single sealed bid without further haggling, this figure would be its optimum bid. But

Figure 2-13

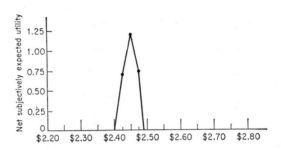

Spectrum of conceivable settlement points for a given negotiation

other points on the spectrum are important to the union negotiator. Between 2½ and 7½ cents subjectively expected utility is reasonably high (.7 and .75 respectively). Outside of these points expected utility drops sharply. The union negotiator would hope to approach 7½ cents, but he also recognizes that he may not do as well and the settlement may be closer to 2½ cents. This is suggestive of the idea of target and resistance points, concepts which will be introduced in the next section.

**Response Patterns in Decision-making Situations.** Before discussing the significance of the points of prominence which emerge on the curve of subjectively expected utility, let us comment on two ways in which individuals differ in their response to decision situations.

First, a person's probability estimates for an event may be more or less influenced by his desire for the event. Some persons tend to overestimate the likelihood of desirable events and underestimate the likelihood of undesirable ones. One negotiator may tend to set his objectives more on the basis of what he feels he needs, with less independent assessment of his chances for success. He brings demands to the bargaining table that are held with strong fervor, with little regard for the objective chances of success.

Second, for those negotiators who are sensitive to probabilities another distinction can be made, between persons who like and those who dislike risky situations.[28] Atkinson distinguishes between the motive to achieve success and the motive to avoid failure. He proposes that there are two kinds of people, those in whom the motivation to achieve success is greater

[28] J. J. Stone, "An Experiment in Bargaining Games," *Econometrica*, vol. 26 (April, 1958), pp. 286–296.

than that to avoid failure and those in whom the reverse is true.[29] Persons of the first kind—those with a high need for achievement and a low fear of failure—will tend to prefer bets of intermediate probability of success, i.e., near .5. Persons with low need for achievement and high fear of failure will prefer bets with a probability of success near 1 or 0.

## Target and Resistance Points

While our discussion of *SEU* was not developed in order to identify a single objective or decision choice for a negotiator, it did serve to focus attention on a portion of the bargaining spectrum where the alternatives involved relatively high expected utilities. We have termed the boundaries of that range as target and resistance points.

The need for distinguishing multiple points rather than a single objective results from the particular type of decision situation facing the negotiator. Inasmuch as a fixed deadline will terminate negotiations, a party is forced to a decision rule about settling or striking. Hence his need for a resistance point or a level of achievement below which he would choose to sustain a strike over the issues still unresolved. We assume that the negotiator anticipates the need for such a decision rule well in advance of the zero hour, formulating a tentative resistance point as one guide to his behavior at the bargaining table.

Another feature of labor negotiations explains why negotiators need an additional decision rule, a target. We have already said that negotiations are not one-shot decision-making situations, even though the ultimate exchange before a strike deadline might be so represented. Negotiations involve a series of decisions interspersed with performance activities—in short, they are situations involving complex goal strivings. The negotiator can do more than enter an "optimum bid"; he can influence the area in which final bids will be exchanged. If this is an achievement situation, the negotiator needs something to aim at, so to speak.

There is additional anecdotal support for the idea that a negotiator identifies more than one intermediate position (in addition to his conception of the outer limits or the area of long-term dependency). Support for this assertion comes from the language used by negotiators. Consider the following statements: "I hope to get 7 cents, and must have at least 5 cents"; "I'd be happy with an 11-cent package, but we couldn't go below the pattern of 8 cents under any circumstances." The words or phrases such as "hope," "happy with," on the one hand, and "must have at least" and "couldn't go below," on the other hand, certainly refer to different

[29] J. W. Atkinson, "Motivational Determinants of Risk-taking Behavior," *Psychological Review*, vol. 64 (November, 1957), pp. 359–372.

points of prominence on the bargaining spectrum as conceived by a negotiator.

Figure 2-14 contains a graphic representation of these distinctions. The resistance and target points are aspirations. Aspiration level theory explains the process of goal formation by reference to the same variables of utility and probability. Although the theory usually prescribes a point, one can think of the range bounded by the target and resistance points as an aspiration zone.[30]

### Figure 2-14

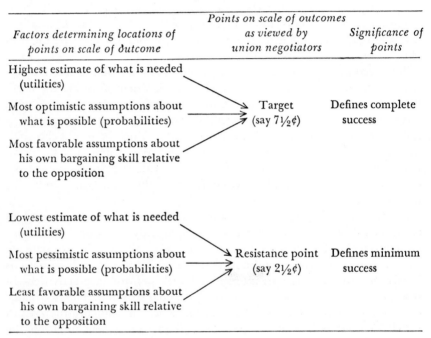

| Factors determining locations of points on scale of outcome | Points on scale of outcomes as viewed by union negotiators | Significance of points |
|---|---|---|
| Highest estimate of what is needed (utilities) | | |
| Most optimistic assumptions about what is possible (probabilities) | Target (say 7½¢) | Defines complete success |
| Most favorable assumptions about his own bargaining skill relative to the opposition | | |
| Lowest estimate of what is needed (utilities) | | |
| Most pessimistic assumptions about what is possible (probabilities) | Resistance point (say 2½¢) | Defines minimum success |
| Least favorable assumptions about his own bargaining skill relative to the opposition | | |

For the reasons mentioned earlier we believe that the latter view is more appropriate to bargaining activity. True, as negotiations unfold, this range narrows and approaches a point, but it is just this process by which a negotiator establishes a particular referent for his ultimate decision that we want to understand in all of its complexity. For convenience we shall use the term "aspiration" when we want to refer to both target and resistance point. Whether the term describes a range or a point will depend upon the stage of negotiations.

**Settlement Range.** The area between the parties' respective resistance points is referred to as the "settlement range." The range, however, can be

[30] W. H. Starbuck, "Level of Aspiration Theory and Economic Behavior," *Behavioral Science*, vol. 8 (April, 1963), pp. 128–136.

positive or negative. In the positive range the resistance points are compatible. In the range bounded by these two points both parties would settle in preference to sustaining a work stoppage (see Figure 2-15). The negative settlement range depicts the situation in which the resistance

### Figure 2-15
### Positive Settlement Range

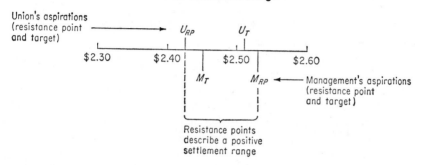

points are incompatible (see Figure 2-16). There is no settlement which would be minimally acceptable to both parties.

In practice, the target of one is usually selected in a way that represents the best estimate about the other's resistance point. Thus, for all intents and purposes a party usually behaves as if his own resistance point and target describe *the* settlement range. However, the settlement range as defined here is only determined objectively by combining the private aspirations of the two parties.

### Figure 2-16
### Negative Settlement Range

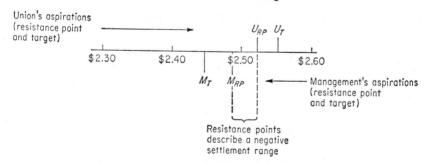

Perhaps the most common configuration is one in which both parties (1) prefer and entertain hopes for positions which are incompatible but (2) are resigned to accept other less ambitious positions which are compatible. The targets are not compatible, but the resistance points are.

The resistance points of parties will tend to be compatible if each party has a relatively accurate picture of the other's utilities. Whether these resistance points are compatible at the outset of negotiations depends in part upon the existence of stereotype utility functions.[31] Of course, these stereotype functions need to be appropriate for the particular negotiator, i.e., to approximate his true utility function. When there are well-established traditions and role requirements for each of the negotiators and when the specific pressures bearing on them are generally known, the negotiators tend to enter bargaining with more or less consistent expectations about each other's utility function.

*Influence of patterns.* Whether the resistance points describe a positive or a negative settlement range depends in more specific terms upon all the factors previously enumerated in this chapter. A few words need to be said about the influence of patterns, since their impact is usually to define a fairly narrow range, whether positive or negative. In some instances, the union views the pattern settlement as a floor from which to bargain upward, and the company views it as a ceiling from which to bargain downward (that is, both interpret the pattern in a way most favorable to themselves and then regard it as their resistance point). In this situation a small negative range will exist; but it may be hard to close, nevertheless.

When the parties are free to set their own pattern, the settlement range is likely to be large, although it cannot be said whether it will tend toward the negative or the positive direction. The willingness of a company to become a pattern setter in wages or benefits may create a positive range. By making a breakthrough, the company gives the union an important advantage over and above the substantive gain of the settlement. The new pattern strengthens the union's bargaining position in subsequent negotiations. In return for this advantage, the union may adopt a restrained position in other areas, even to the extent of giving the company concessions. But it is just as likely that the pattern-setting situation could produce a negative range. When uncertainty exists, the union and the company may well be overambitious in formulating their aspirations.

Some empirical work on strike activity is pertinent here. The frequency of strike activity can be one indicator of the prevalence of the negative range. In a study of strike activity, Albert Rees relates the business cycle and the tendency to develop incompatible expectations. The negative range is most likely to occur just prior to the peak of business activity.

> Why does the strike peak consistently precede the reference peak (high point of the business cycle)? The strike peak is probably a maximum in the divergence of expectations between employers and

[31] J. C. Harsanyi, "Bargaining in Ignorance of the Opponent's Utility Function," *Journal of Conflict Resolution*, vol. 6 (March, 1962), pp. 28–38.

unions. Unions pay close attention to employment, which generally does not lead at the peak. They are also influenced by previous wage increases received by other unions and by increases in the cost of living. The attention of employers is likely to be focused on some of the activities which do not lead at the peak, and they will thus resist demands for which the unions are still willing to fight.[32]

*Prevalence of positive or negative settlement range.* From a practical point of view we should like to know whether the many structural factors involved generally tend to produce a positive or a negative range. There is no systematic evidence on this question. Our own research has yielded a mixed pattern. Ann Douglas's conclusion regarding the four cases she studied is of interest here.

> One can now make a prediction about the content of final settlement which was not possible before—namely, that the final settlement figure (or arrangement) will fail to incorporate everything that is literally obtainable. In other words, there will be something left over after settlement from the total resources which the parties bring to the table prepared to spend if necessary. It should be feasible to test this prediction in concrete cases. What the present study has to offer is a finding which at first seemed incredible: that in the Marathon, the Irving Mining, and the Crescent City cases (the reader will be left free to make his own judgment about the Atlas case) there was one party in each instance which did not have to yield to the ultimate limits for which it was in readiness at some point. In these cases it can be declared with the greatest confidence that a party's failure to tap with its minimal demands the maximum available to it from the other did not prohibit it from accepting the settlement with satisfaction.[33]

Edward Peters, an experienced negotiator, concludes:

> The large majority of bargaining relationships are characterized by consecutive periods of negotiations where the parties confine their differences to areas which do not exceed the minimum bargaining expectations of either group. These periods are interrupted in off years by tight negotiations where attempts are made to affect basic changes in the relationship—even through an economic contest.[34]

[32] Albert Rees, "Industrial Conflict and Business Fluctuations," *The Journal of Political Economy*, vol. 60 (October, 1952), p. 381.

[33] Ann Douglas, *Industrial Peacemaking* (New York: Columbia University Press, 1962), p. 199.

[34] Edward Peters, *Strategy and Tactics in Labor Negotiations* (New London: National Foremen's Institute, 1955), pp. 40–41.

# PART 2 | MODEL OF THE SETTLEMENT PROCESS

Part 1 set forth the factors which delimit the area for bargaining activity. These factors are assumed to influence the negotiator's thinking as he enters into the bargaining process. He is aware of limits to the basic interdependency of the parties in their present relationship. Within this broad area, each alternate settlement point has a certain utility for him. He also takes into account the costs of a failure to agree. And for each point he estimates the probability that the other would agree. Thus, the potential settlement points have different subjectively expected utilities for him. A limited range of these points which have relatively high expected utilities establishes his expectations. Specifically, we suggest that he identifies a target and a resistance point and that he coordinates his bargaining behavior to realize achievement between these points. He may assume, but he cannot be certain, that his opponent's target and resistance points define the same general area for bargaining so that there exists an actual positive settlement range.

Subjectively expected utility theory was essential, and it was also adequate for explaining the general location of bargaining activity. We may note that others have extended the underlying logic of this *SEU* analysis to a determinate solution, i.e., to specifying the single outcome of bargaining.[35] We do not carry through with this analysis here because it does not, in our opinion, contribute to an understanding of purposive behavior in the bargaining process in the same way that game theory and commitment do.

We might note that theories which predict outcome strictly from the utility parameters without further enlightening the behavioral process, such as the arbitration formulas of Nash and Raiffa, are even less relevant for our purposes in developing a theory of convergence activities.[36]

As our point of departure for a discussion of the settlement process, we return to a $2 \times 2$ payoff matrix in which the underlying objective payoffs are "fixed-sum, with default possibilities," such as that presented earlier in

[35] F. Zeuthen, *Problems of Monopoly and Economic Welfare* (London: Routledge and Kegan Paul, Ltd., 1930); Jan Pen, "A General Theory of Bargaining," *American Economic Review*, vol. 62 (March, 1952), pp. 24–42; and J. C. Harsanyi, "Approaches to the Bargaining Problem before and after the Theory of Games: A Critical Discussion of Zeuthen's, Hicks', and Nash's Theories," *Econometrica*, vol. 24 (April, 1956), pp. 144–157.

[36] John Nash, "Two-person Cooperative Games," *Econometrica*, vol. 21 (January, 1953), pp. 128–140; and Howard Raiffa, "Arbitration Schemes for Generalized Two-person Games," *Contributions to the Theory of Games: II*, Annals of Mathematics Study no. 28 (Princeton, N.J.: Princeton University Press, 1953), pp. 361–387.

Figure 2-3. But now we assume that the cell entries represent "utilities," the parties' subjective evaluations of the four possible outcomes.

We assume that negotiations have just begun and that Party now perceives the basic alternatives essentially as represented in the matrix in Figure 2-17. If Party's perceptions of the alternatives and associated payoffs did not change, he would eventually be forced by the deadline to choose between a cautious strategy that would net some modest payoff and a bold strategy that would lead to either a high payoff or a high cost. Which choice would Party make? What would Party assume Opponent would do?

## Figure 2-17

| | | Opponent | |
|---|---|---|---|
| | | *Soft* | *Hard* |
| Party | Soft (to achieve RP of 2) | Outcome 1 6,6 | Outcome 2 2,10 |
| | Hard (to achieve T of 10) | Outcome 4 10,2 | Outcome 3 −6,−6 |

How does game theory contribute to our understanding of which choice Party and Opponent would make and of their prechoice influence activities?

**Game Solutions.** Game theory is a branch of mathematics that analyzes various problems of conflict and decision by abstracting common strategic features for study in theoretical models. Mathematicians have advanced many theoretical solutions for both two-person fixed-sum and variable-sum games. The solutions, however, fall short of persuasiveness when applied to real-choice situations.[37] Moreover, the experimental evidence available which supports proposed solutions generally is for games with payoff structures not relevant to those studied here.[38]

The most persuasive mathematically derived solutions are offered for fixed-sum games. In such games, a truly equilibrium position is available through minimax choice rules referred to as "saddle point" or "mixed strategies." [39] However, where the games deviate from strictly fixed-sum because they include a default cell, the normative theory is less powerful and convincing and the experimental findings more variable.

[37] H. W. Kuhn, "Game Theory and Models of Negotiation," *Journal of Conflict Resolution*, vol. 6 (March, 1962), pp. 1–4.

[38] Anatol Rapoport and Carol Orwant, "Experimental Games: A Review," *Behavioral Science*, vol. 7 (January, 1962), pp. 1–37.

[39] R. D. Luce and Howard Raiffa, *Games and Decisions: Introduction and Critical Survey* (New York: John Wiley & Sons, Inc., 1957).

Another criticism of the game theory approach is its oversimplification of alternative courses of action open to each of the parties in order to make the analysis manageable. A more serious deficiency of game theory is the assumption that participants act as if they attached constant numerical values to the possible outcomes.[40] The fact is that evaluations of the outcomes are not constant during the course of negotiations. *Indeed, apart from the final single moves of the two negotiators by which they make a choice and conclude negotiations, the negotiators' bargaining activity serves primarily to estimate these utilities and to alter them.*

Despite its limitations, which we must be frank to admit, the game format is extremely useful to an understanding of certain convergence activities. First, it provides a vivid way of specifying the prechoice influence activities. Second, it adequately characterizes the final-choice situation in a way which underscores the importance of certain game rules, such as whether final choices are made in sequence or simultaneously.

**Prechoice Change of Perceived Utilities.** The entries in Figure 2-17 represent Party's utilities and his assumptions about Opponent's utilities for the four possible outcomes. The reader will recall that by utilities of alternatives, we mean a party's subjective evaluation of the consequences associated with each alternative outcome. Because of the complex nature of the issues in labor negotiations the specific consequences which one associates with the demand, as well as his evaluation of these consequences, are subject to considerable change during the course of negotiations.

Game theory does not prescribe a choice for Party confronted with this payoff matrix. Party's choice between $S$ and $H$ would depend upon his expectation about Opponent's choice. But theory is no more help to him in predicting Opponent's choice than it is in advising him on whether to choose $S$ or $H$. However, if Party can modify Opponent's perceptions of the utilities of the outcomes, he can change the likelihood that Opponent will make a particular choice. We shall assume that Party's views of his own payoffs remain constant in order to focus on his influence activities. Figure 2-18 presents the payoff matrix as Party would have it perceived by Opponent. Each of the entries has been modified slightly by Party's influence efforts.

First, regarding Opponent's perceptions of his own utilities and disutilities, outcomes 1 and 4 which result from Opponent strategy $S$ become more attractive to Opponent. Outcome 2, which Opponent still favors, becomes somewhat less attractive, and the default cell 3, which is a risk associated with strategy $H$, becomes more costly. These perceptions in themselves increase the likelihood that Opponent will choose $S$ rather than $H$.

Second, note the change in Opponent's perceptions of Party's utilities

[40] Kuhn, *op. cit.,* pp. 1–4.

and disutilities. He now sees outcomes 1 and 2 as less attractive to Party, whereas the positive outcome 4 associated with Party strategy $H$ is more attractive to Party and the default outcome less costly to him. Inasmuch as this information would increase Opponent's expectation that Party would choose strategy $H$, these perceptions also make him (Opponent) less inclined to choose strategy $H$ and more likely to choose strategy $S$.

### Figure 2-18

|  | | Opponent | |
|---|---|---|---|
|  | | S .67 p .83 p | H .33 p .17 p |
| Party | S | Outcome 1 6,6 5,7 | Outcome 2 2,10 1,9 |
|  | H | Outcome 4 10,2 11,3 | Outcome 3 −6,−6 −5,−7 |

To the extent that Opponent's perceptions of utilities have been modified in the direction indicated above, Party himself can choose $H$ with increased confidence, even though *he* does not perceive the utilities any differently than before. What he does perceive differently are the probabilities. If Party had assumed that Opponent's disposition to choose $H$ before was about 1 in 3, he might now estimate it at, say, 1 in 6. Thus, the expected value for Party of his strategies $S$ and $H$ have decreased and increased respectively, not because his utilities have changed, but because the probabilities of actually attaining certain preferred outcomes have increased. For example, one would calculate Party's expected utilities for $S$ by combining Party's stable utilities and his newly perceived probabilities for outcomes 1 and 2: $(6 \cdot .83) + (2 \cdot .17) = 5.32$. The expected utilities of $H$ would be now greater: $(10 \cdot .83) + (-6 \cdot .17) = 7.28$.

The amount of bargaining time available, the situational opportunities, and the degree of success Party meets for his efforts will determine how actively and with what persistence Party continues to attempt to modify Opponent's perceptions of the utilities associated with alternate outcomes. In turn, the difficulty with which Party is able to modify Opponent's perceptions, as well as the extent to which Opponent succeeds in modifying Party's own perceptions, brings about a modification of Party's aspiration levels. To represent this change in Party's target and resistance points, we could present successive matrices, each showing less divergence between the payoffs for Party associated with a "hard" and a "soft" strategy.

**Commitments.** It is difficult for Party to ensure that Opponent and he have similar perceptions of the utilities for the four outcomes. At some point it is easier to coordinate expectations about their choices of strategy (even if chosen arbitrarily) than to further coordinate assessments of the underlying utilities and disutilities involved.

The purpose of commitment is to affect the choice of Opponent by influencing his perception of what Party intends to do. "Commitment" refers to the act of pledging oneself to a course of action.[41] It is often implied by the taking of a bargaining position. A commitment may communicate something about the probabilities of Party's choice not necessarily consistent with the payoffs represented in the matrix. It is a statement of intentions; an open selection of a strategy in advance for influencing the other's choice. The statement may be a threat in the sense that the strategy selected will have adverse consequences for Opponent conditional upon Opponent's choice. These statements range from absolutely binding commitments (where no freedom of choice is reserved) to commitments involving various degrees of uncertainty. The statement is a *tactical* commitment if it communicates a higher probability of a choice than appears appropriate given the payoffs in the matrix. If it communicates probabilities consistent with the matrix utilities for Party, it is an *inherent* commitment. We refer here to tactical commitments.

Figure 2-19 shows Party committing himself (with a $.95p$) to strategy $H$ irrespective of Opponent's choice. Thus, to the extent that Opponent is persuaded by this new information about probabilities, he is more likely to choose strategy $S$ to avoid the default outcome.

### Figure 2-19

|  |  | *Opponent* | |
| --- | --- | --- | --- |
|  |  | $S$ | $H$ |
| Party | $S .05\ p$ | 6,6 | 2,10 |
|  | $H .95\ p$ | 10,2 | −6,−6 |

However, Opponent may not be readily persuaded that Party will actually follow through with this choice of $H$, especially if Opponent should manage to move first and choose $H$ himself (or commit himself to choose $H$). Party is in a position of having asserted that he would act in this contingency in a way in which he now would manifestly prefer not to act. Party may make his commitment (i.e., his exaggerated probability statement) credible by actually structuring the situation so that his payoffs shift in a way consistent with his stated intentions. He may do this by invoking a penalty on his own failure to pursue a strategy to which he has indicated commitment. Figure 2-20a shows Party subtracting

[41] Our use of the concept of commitment follows generally that of T. C. Schelling, *The Strategy of Conflict* (Cambridge, Mass.: Harvard University Press, 1960).

a penalty of 3 from his payoffs in all cells which do not correspond to the indicated strategy $H$. This should serve to increase Opponent's estimate of the probability that Party will choose strategy $H$. In order for Party to be maximally persuasive, he could subtract 9 from payoffs associated with strategy $S$. The resulting payoff matrix shown in Figure 2-20$b$ now contains a dominant strategy in the game theoretic sense: regardless of Opponent's choice, Party can do better by strategy $H$. Party's strategy $H$ and Opponent's strategy $S$ now become a stable solution.

Figure 2-20$a$          Figure 2-20$b$

|  |  | Opponent | | Opponent | |
|---|---|---|---|---|---|
|  |  | S | H | S | H |
| Party | S | 0̸,6 / 3 | 2̸,10 / −1 | 0̸,6 / −3 | 2̸,10 / −7 |
|  | H | 10,2 | −6,−6 | 10,2 | −6,−6 |

The importance of an actual shift in payoffs available to Party in commitments is underscored by Schelling in his analysis of game moves and communications: ". . . moves can commit him to actions when speech often cannot. . . ." [42] One may state repeatedly that some options are no longer available to him or are available only at some new enhanced cost, and he will not be believed until he somehow demonstrates this fact. Thus, moves support or substitute for verbal communication, a point of great significance for our tactical discussion in the next section.

**Focal Points.** Most situations provide some clue for coordinating behavior, "some focal point for each person's expectation of what the other expects him to expect to be expected to do." [43] One of the many outcomes minimally acceptable to both may be more prominent than the others. The prominence may inhere in the payoff matrix, based on uniqueness, symmetry, or simplicity. For example, an experimental study by Joseph and Willis found that the availability of a central solution increased the number of agreements reached, fewer offers were required to reach agreement, and the central solution itself was chosen a disproportionately large number of times, especially when the bids and offers were made sequentially.[44] In this experiment structural prominence inhered in the central position where there were five rather than six possible positions of agreement.

Prominence is equally likely to derive from other aspects of the negoti-

[42] Schelling, *op. cit.*

[43] Again we cite Schelling, who has pointed out the importance of this phenomenon in interdependent decision making: Schelling, *op. cit.*, p. 57.

[44] M. L. Joseph and R. H. Willis, "An Experimental Analog to Two-party Bargaining," *Behavioral Science*, vol. 8, no. 2 (1963), pp. 117–127.

ating context, such as tradition or a recent settlement in a pattern industry. Joseph and Willis failed to get statistically significant support for the proposed effect of prior settlements in a laboratory experiment in which some of the subjects were informed that a particular solution in a previous replication of the experiment had been agreed upon most frequently.[45] However, there is an abundance of anecdotal evidence on this point from the real world of labor negotiations. After a key negotiation in an industry, subsequent settlements are arrived at more peacefully with less prolonged negotiation, and they tend to involve remarkably similar terms. With this form of prominence, as with others, the party for whom the choice is relatively unfavorable very often takes it simply because he knows the other will expect him to.

Focal points, like commitments, tend to modify Opponent's choice tendencies apart from his perception of the underlying utilities. However, it is in Party's interests to rely upon a focal point only if it operates to his advantage. The fact is that usually there are several points which have uniqueness, or are potentially more conspicuous than others. However, it would be getting ahead of the story to delve into the tactical opportunities for giving prominence to some particular outcome that would be more favorable to Party.

**Convergence in Positive and Negative Ranges.** What distinction can we make between bargaining in the context of a positive versus a negative range? Referring to the situation portrayed in Figure 2-17, we assume that Party entered negotiations with a resistance point of 2 and a target of 10. In this case we can also assume that Opponent had a target of 10 and a resistance point of 2. These resistance points would define a positive range, and any settlement between 2,10 and 10,2 would be minimally acceptable to both. Their targets are not compatible with each other, and it is precisely when both attempt to achieve their target of 10 that they both lose. Party's strategy $S$ would ensure him of at least 2, perhaps more. Strategy $H$, which held out the promise of reaching his target of 10 but contained risks, was nevertheless also attractive—especially if he could decrease those risks associated with that strategy. The several distortions achieved in Figure 2-18 and the commitments represented by Figures 2-19 and 2-20 all acted to lower Opponent's expected utilities associated with his $H$ strategy and to increase his tendency to choose an $S$ strategy. Consequently, Opponent's target would be modified toward being less ambitious.

Thus, when a positive range exists at the outset of negotiations, the effect of the interaction will be to close the range to a settlement point. That is to say, that one or both of the parties will gain information on which to become more ambitious than indicated by their original re-

[45] Joseph and Willis, *ibid.*

sistance point. At the same time each side will attempt to exploit opportunities to restructure the situation in such a way that the other party not only does not close in on an initial positive range but also may even become less ambitious in his resistance point. Since by definition in the positive situation there exists a range within which both parties would accept a settlement rather than let a strike occur, if either could force such a choice on the other party near the latter's resistance point, he would capture the lion's share of the initial range. It is true that the more optimistic targets of the parties need to be modified if they are not initially compatible, but this is a less wrenching experience and involves no retreat in the decision rule invoking a strike. In an initially positive range the role of strike costs in the modification of bargaining positions is minimal. As we shall see in the next chapter, references to strike costs and other power tactics are nevertheless important in establishing the credibility of tactical threats. However, implicit in the definition of compatible resistance points is some preexisting consensus about the basic power situation. If a strike occurs, it is because of miscalculations which were made and acted on during the negotiation process.

Figure 2-21 presents a game matrix for a situation in which the parties'

**Figure 2-21**

|  |  | Opponent | |
|---|---|:---:|:---:|
|  |  | S | H |
| Party | S | −6,−6 | −6,−6 |
|  | H | −6,−6 | −6,−6 |

*RP*'s are incompatible, i.e., a negative range exists. Actually a game matrix is meaningful only if it is a representation of the intersection of the (two or more) strategies being considered by the parties. According to Figure 2-21, all the strategies considered by the parties themselves would lead to default outcomes. When we use the payoff matrix as perceived by one of the parties in order to predict his choice, we normally assume that he is considering only alternatives which allow him at least his *RP*, and hence the matrix would not include strategies which certainly lead to a loss. The matrix in Figure 2-21 has more meaning as a description of outcomes perceived by a third party.

When the parties sense their predicament, they will usually attempt to avoid the strike. If a settlement is to occur, the basic decision rule of one or both of the parties about at which point to invoke a strike must be modified in the direction of conservatism. The negative range usually exists because there are differences in perceptions about the strength of their respective preferences and about the strike-cost realities.

Thus, in his prechoice influence activities Party may be content to give Opponent more realistic, not distorted, views of his (Party's) utilities and intentions. He attempts to convince Opponent how important the issues *really* are. Similarly, the attempts by Party to influence Opponent's perceptions of Party's intentions or commitments may be limited to the real or inherent limitations and not to the tactical ones.

Clarification of these factors provides the basis on which the parties modify their resistance points to the point of convergence. Thus, in the context of the negative range, strike costs become critical. A negotiator will generally modify his resistance point only when he is convinced that the costs of conflict are greater than the portion of the bargaining spectrum that he will lose by abandoning his resistance point.

By making a distinction about the bargaining which occurs in the positive and negative settlement ranges, we should be clear about what we are saying and what we are not indicating. The essential difference in the two cases is the direction of the modification of resistance points. A different kind of tension is involved for the negotiator, depending upon whether he is, on the one hand, attempting to maneuver in such a way as to allow him to raise his minimum expectations or, on the other hand, scanning the situation to ascertain how much he must lower his minimum expectations. But while there is an important conceptual difference (e.g., that some commitments are inherent rather than tactical), we do not wish to make too much of this difference as it affects tactical bargaining behavior. The overt tactical behavior of the negotiators in the two situations does not differ in appearance, and for obvious reasons: the parties may not in reality know that the range is positive or negative, and even if they believe it is positive, it is to their advantage to behave as if it were negative.

In negotiations, information is never complete. Even though both sides entertain compatible resistance points, this fact may not be known until agreement is actually reached. As will be seen, the tactics of distributive bargaining are designed to obscure, not to clarify, resistance points. If one side reveals his resistance point, this will probably induce the other side to press for at least this amount.

**Final-choice Situations.** The game matrix presents at the "moment of truth" the results of all the ongoing influence efforts. Striving activity of Party becomes telescoped into one highly defined decision situation. We should readily admit that the game presentation does not do justice to all the striving activity that involves successive evaluation, decisions, and adjustments. However, we feel that the format is an accurate representation of the point in time when all the earlier activities are focused into a decision. Usually this moment of truth comes at the deadline.[46] At the

---

[46] In his analysis of labor negotiations Stevens has placed primary emphasis on the role of the deadline. See C. M. Stevens, *Strategy and Collective Bargaining Negotiation* (New York: McGraw-Hill Book Company, 1963).

deadline each side is face to face with the dilemma: "Should I remain pat, or should I concede?" The reason the game format comes into sharp focus at the deadline is that precisely at this point the default possibility has the most meaning. During the early phases of bargaining Party may realize that aspirations are incompatible and that there is a good chance of a strike at the deadline, but this prospect is still in the future. It is only at the deadline, when the alternatives are truly specified, that the decision about which strategy to choose becomes relevant.

The structure of the bargaining situation is critical to the nature of the decision which confronts each party. Do the parties make simultaneous final moves, or do they make their last moves in a sequence. Figures 2-22a and b illustrate the alternative matrices which result.

Figure 2-22a
Simultaneous Choice

|  |  | Opponent | |
|---|---|---|---|
|  |  | Concede | Stand pat |
| Party | Concede | 1,1 | 0,2 |
|  | Stand pat | 2,0 | −5,−5 |

Figure 2-22b
Moves in Sequence

|  |  | Opponent (2d move) | |
|---|---|---|---|
|  |  | Accept | Reject |
| Party (1st move) | Concede | 0,2 | Not applicable |
|  | Stand pat | 2,0 | −5,−5 |

The advantages and disadvantages for Party of each of the two structures are apparent from an analysis of the payoffs. The situation depicted in Figure 2-22 would result when the two parties have narrowed their explicit positions to a range of 2 and when they are both apparently, but not absolutely, committed to a position involving no further concession. Each has a target of 2 and a resistance point of 0.

The simultaneous-choice situation favors a concede strategy. In part, this solution derives from the uncertainty of Opponent's move, and in part, it results from the fact that a concede strategy probably will result in a compromise 1,1 payoff rather than a 0,2 payoff.

In the situation allowing first and second moves, Party (with the first move) is more likely to be bold and select a stand-pat strategy. For one thing, the probability that Opponent will accept the bid is greater in this situation. In addition, the concede strategy has a lower expected value for Party—he certainly receives nothing.

The greater tendency for both players to choose cooperative strategies in games requiring simultaneous moves rather than nonsimultaneous moves has been confirmed in a laboratory experiment by Morton Deutsch.[47] Thus the structure of the bargaining situation plays an important role in

[47] This experiment is reported in Rapoport and Orwant, op. cit., pp. 15–17.

determining whether final convergence takes place as a result of mutual concessions or as a result of a stand-pat commitment by one side.

**Settlement Dynamics during a Strike.** All our analysis thus far has considered the settlement process that takes place prior to the onset of a strike. The assumption has been that the basic parameters and the skill of the two negotiators produce a convergence toward a settlement point. Indeed, if commitment is completely credible, there should be no need to carry through on the threats that accompany the statement of commitment.

However, strikes do occur, precisely because the negotiators are not clear about the real intentions of the other side. Consequently, it is desirable to discuss briefly the settlement process that takes place once a strike has started.

Negotiations take a dramatically different turn once a strike starts. Usually after a strike starts, the stated positions of both sides become more rigid. An analysis by Livernash [48] indicates that their underlying aspirations are also revised in a more ambitious direction. According to his analysis, the union's minimum settlement terms undergo the following changes with the onset and unfolding of a strike (see Figure 2-23). What are some of the reasons for the sequence depicted in this chart?

Figure 2-23

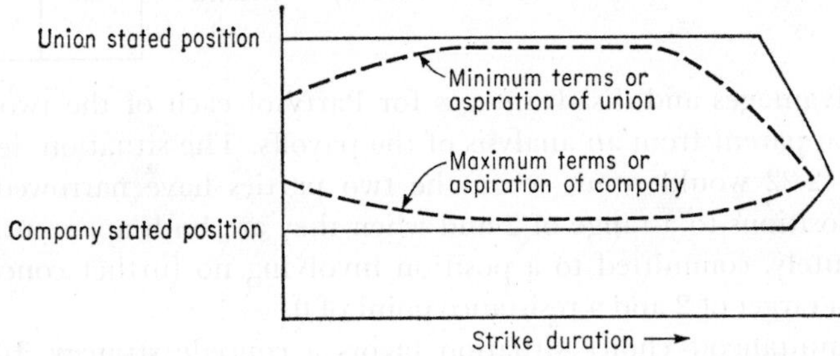

What happens is that the union views the strike costs already incurred as costs to be recouped rather than as "sunk" costs. As the strike continues, the union continues to revise its aspirations upward in an attempt to offset the costs of the strike.

The company's position may become equally adamant. Some companies have been known to revise their offer downward after a long strike, saying that the ability to pay which existed prior to the strike had been depleted by the strike. Clearly things can get worse. What started out as a gap between bargaining positions turns into a deadly test of strength. The outcome is now influenced by basic power to inflict losses on the other and

[48] E. R. Livernash, "The Relation of Power to the Structure and Process of Collective Bargaining," unpublished.

to sustain losses oneself; the encounter also becomes a test of strength for the loyalty of the employee group and becomes less a matter of searching for solutions at the bargaining table.

The company may remain adamant in its position also because it knows that any concessions made by it after the onset of a short strike can be viewed only as the fruits of that strike. The company does not want to establish a pattern of behavior whereby the union will assume that if it goes out on a short strike, it can improve the terms of settlement. Thus, a company may be entering upon a strike prepared to go the full route of forcing capitulation by the union. This would be in line with the Livernash formulation.

Thus, with the onset of a strike the issues typically become first *more difficult* to settle than they were during prestrike negotiations, but then at some point they become *more amenable* to resolution. Whether this is after a lapse of weeks or months depends in part on how much hardship is entailed in strike action. Fatigue and resignation are predictable as eventual responses, but it is difficult to predict when they will set in.

Usually in bringing about a settlement, the negotiators establish an arbitrary deadline. The focal point may be provided by the entrance of a mediator, by a time deadline that one negotiator has to meet in order to get back to other business, etc. Both sides agree on the new time deadline, and they work actively to come to an agreement. Here the dynamics of bargaining are similar to those analyzed throughout this chapter; the main difference is that none of the agreed-upon "deadlines" during a strike has the force of the one which marked the end of prestrike negotiations. If the parties cannot come to an agreement before some self-imposed deadline, then they enter another phase of idle waiting.[49]

[49] Peters, *op. cit.*, pp. 177–178.

# CHAPTER III

# STRATEGIES AND TACTICS
# OF DISTRIBUTIVE BARGAINING

The preceding chapter introduced the variables important in the distributive bargaining process and discussed the manner in which they first delimit the settlement area and then operate to produce a settlement. The discussion of the settlement process made a distinction between the influence of changes in perceived utilities and the influence of changes in probability estimates resulting from commitments and focal points. In this chapter Parts 1 and 2, respectively, analyze the tactical operations associated with these two influence mechanisms.

The distinction between Parts 1 and 2 is fundamentally one of emphasis. In Part 1, Party is purporting to communicate about the basic utility parameters in order to shape Opponent's expectations in a general way. Party is trying to influence Opponent's view of the nature of Party's inherent strength—the strength of his needs and coercive capacity. In Part 2 attention is focused upon communications about bargaining positions. Party's initiatives are less concerned with influencing Opponent's view of the basic utilities than of Party's intentions. For this purpose, it is only necessary to convince Opponent of the strength of Party's tactical position, about which more will be said in Part 2. Part 3 will present some of the dilemmas and problems inherent in distributive bargaining.

# PART 1 | MANIPULATING UTILITY PARAMETERS

A brief review of some propositions implicit in the model of distributive bargaining will suggest the various ways by which the negotiator can influence the outcome by directly influencing the other's perceptions of utilities (including values associated with the issue and strike action). We view these from the point of view of one negotiator, Party, whose general tactical assignment can be thought of as inducing Opponent to adopt a relatively lower (less ambitious) resistance point and to take explicit bargaining positions throughout negotiations consistent with the lower resistance point.

First, *Opponent's resistance point varies directly with the utilities he* [1] *attaches to possible outcomes.* Thus, Opponent's resistance point will be lower if he places a lower value on the conceivable outcomes, that is, if the whole or a major portion of his utility function is shifted appropriately. Party can manipulate Opponent's view of Opponent's utility function so that Opponent does not see as much advantage in maintaining his position. Opponent must be convinced that a proposal of his own is of less value to him than he originally thought or that a demand of Party is less unpleasant to him than he first thought.

According to our analysis of subjectively expected utilities (to which the resistance-point decision rule was coordinated), the resistance point also varies directly with subjective probabilities. Since the later value varies inversely with one's own strike costs, directly with the other's strike costs, and inversely with the other's utilities for the outcomes, we have the following additional derived propositions:

Second, *Opponent's resistance point varies inversely with his subjective strike costs.* Thus, Opponent's resistance point will be lower if he places a higher estimate on his own strike costs. Party can manipulate Opponent's view of his strike costs so that Opponent is somehow convinced that a strike would provoke a higher cost than he had originally assumed (either because of increased rate or increased duration).

Third, *Opponent's resistance point varies directly with Party's subjective costs of a strike.* Thus, Opponent's resistance point will be lower if he places a lower estimate on Party's strike costs. Party can convince Opponent that the former will experience a low rate of costs and perhaps that Party would derive some positive by-products from the strike which would tend to offset these costs.

Fourth, *Opponent's resistance point varies inversely with Party's util-*

---

[1] We are interested here in the magnitude of the utilities whether they be positive (value in obtaining his own demand) or negative (value in resisting Party's demands).

*ities of possible outcomes.* Thus, Opponent's resistance point will be lower if he places a higher estimate on how much Party values the conceivable outcomes. Party can convince Opponent that Party attaches greater importance to issues than Opponent had earlier realized.

The explicit positions that Opponent takes at any time during negotiations, as well as his resistance point, are assumed to be subject to the influence of these basic parameters. Therefore, Party can influence the process and the outcome of bargaining by manipulating Opponent's subjective assessment of any or all of the four utility parameters.

Before discussing the specific tactical assignments implied by these propositions, it is necessary to deal with the matter of controlling information. The role of information or the lack of information is of such tactical importance in distributive bargaining that it needs to be handled at the outset. It affects all the other tactical operations.

The relative values of the four parameters change in response to the information generated and exchanged during bargaining. It is not necessary for the objective conditions to change; it is only necessary for the perceptions of these conditions to change in order for a negotiator to alter his position. In contract negotiations objective knowledge virtually never becomes complete in the sense that the true nature of all factors is accurately understood by both sides. Thus, it is only necessary to change the other's perceptions in order to alter his bargaining position. This is not to say that parties do not influence each other through more basic changes in the conditions underlying utilities and probabilities. The point is that the purpose of changing the actual conditions will be to influence Opponent's perception. If the latter does not occur, then the tactical operation has not been successful. The following statements are suggestive of the attempts at manipulation and efforts of resistance that can take place at the *informational* level:

> I do not think that you really feel that strongly about the issues that you have introduced.
>
> I believe that the strike will cost you considerably more than you are willing to admit.
>
> I believe that a strike will cost me almost nothing in spite of your statements to the contrary.
>
> I feel very strongly about this issue regardless of what you say.

Part 1 will discuss four tactical assignments as follows: The first section treats a preliminary tactical requirement, namely, assessing Opponent's utilities. The second section treats the tactics which influence Opponent's perceptions of Party's utilities. The third section will discuss the tactics used by Party to manipulate Opponent's perceptions of his own utilities. In the second and third sections we shall be interested in both the content of communication and the techniques employed. The emphasis is primarily on attempts to influence perceptions of the utility parameters without changing objective conditions affecting the utilities themselves. Some tactics actually alter the objective costs of disagreement. This will be our subject in the fourth section.

## Assessing Opponent's Utilities for Outcomes and Strike Costs

Party's first tactical assignment is to assess Opponent's utilities and strike costs and if possible ascertain his resistance point. Party may know that the parties hold differing objectives regarding the resolution of an agenda item; that is, he knows that he is dealing with a distributive issue. But what is not so obvious to Party is just how important the objective is to Opponent, particularly in terms of how much gain (loss) on the issue would be minimally acceptable to him. Moreover, while a negotiator usually knows whether a strike would be costly to the other party, he does not know *how* costly!

Knowledge about the relevant parameters is critical in deciding whether to maintain or abandon a position. Such knowledge enables Party to make in turn intelligent probability assessments. These assessments tell him how far he has to go in further manipulating the parameters in order to bring about movement on Opponent's part. They also tell him whether he had better consider altering his own position.

Party has two general ways in which he can gain knowledge about Opponent's resistance point. He can use an indirect route of assessing the factors which underlie each parameter, or he can attempt to obtain more direct clues regarding the resistance point which Opponent has at least tentatively set for himself. Much of the required information for both methods of assessment has to be obtained from Opponent himself. Other information is available through more public channels.

**Indirect Assessment.** Many factors affecting economic power, and in turn the resistance point, can be assessed by both parties: they include inventories, alternate production or warehousing facilities, market conditions, the percentage of the work force unionized, the size of the strike fund, the numbers involved in a strike vote, mutual assistance arrangements, etc. The "grapevines" supply this information to unions and management with varying degrees of accuracy.

More systematic research methods are often used. For instance, managements frequently hold prenegotiation conferences with their first-line supervisors to get their estimates of how strongly employees feel about certain issues and how willing they are to strike.

Some companies have their foremen conduct informal meetings with employee groups. The purpose of this is to understand the needs and problems faced by the employees. Foremen are in a good position to understand the strength of feeling about these matters and the willingness of the employees to strike.

One negotiator claimed that he could walk through the shop and by some kind of intuitive assessment of the atmosphere tell what was on the minds of the workers. As a negotiator he knew the range of issues, but by walking through the shop, he sought the intensity of feeling behind these issues and whether people were furious enough to force a showdown.

Managements sometimes have the industrial relations staff make an analysis of the content and patterns of the grievances processed to various stages of the machinery in order to discover any clues regarding the importance the employees and the union may attach to certain issues.

General Motors reportedly utilizes automatic data-processing equipment for this prenegotiating analysis. By tabulating the incidence of each issue persisting in upward movement through the grievance machinery, management is in a position to estimate the importance of most of the union's demands.

Managements occasionally ask their personnel research staff or some outside agency to administer opinion surveys to their employees to learn how employees feel about issues and striking.

Opinion polls taken before and during the early stages of the 1959 negotiations in the steel industry served this purpose for the steel companies. They indicated that the employees had been influenced by "inflation thinking" and did not feel strongly about a wage increase. The employees' feelings about the work-rule issue, whether tapped by this method or not, proved to be quite another matter.

If, with sufficient effort, some knowledge can be gained about issue utilities and strike costs, making the appropriate translations and then computing Opponent's resistance point is more difficult. Actually the problem is even more complicated—it is one of simulating how Opponent interprets these factors and how *he* computes his resistance point. After all, Party is interested in learning what Opponent's resistance point *is*, not what it should be. This being so, it is often more rewarding for Party to try to induce Opponent to betray his own resistance point than it is to attempt to estimate it indirectly.

The validity of the inferences that Party makes about Opponent's position is enhanced, if the former has ever been in the latter's position. Members of management who have been employees or union officials can "put themselves in the shoes" of the union negotiators. Short of this, management can with a little empathy visualize the kinds of factors that would influence feeling in the union organization. Management can examine pattern settlements or precedent-setting circumstances in past settlements. Of course, the union engages in the same kind of vicarious thinking. It seeks to understand management's true position by examining such indicators as the profit and loss statement.

**Tactics to Elicit Clues.** When we turn to the problem of obtaining more direct clues about Opponent's resistance point, we must consider the ongoing negotiation process. Sometimes the efforts flow along ethically questionable channels and involve cloak-and-dagger operations, e.g., utilizing an informant from Opponent's headquarters or bugging Opponent's caucus room. The following incident is reported to have occurred during the 1959 negotiations between the International Union of Electrical Workers and the Gray Manufacturing Company, producers of electronic equipment:

> The second incident which Mr. Hogan (IUE official) related to the case writer also occurred during the negotiations before the strike. The union committee was offered the use of Mr. Ditmar's (the company president's) office for their caucuses during one of the negotiating sessions. While the union committee was in caucus, one of the members discovered a microphone hidden under the radiator. A quick search revealed another microphone behind the wall clock. Hogan claimed that he "ripped them out of the wall." Mr. Bennett, federal mediator assigned to the negotiations, told the case writer that he went to the office to find Hogan standing with the two microphones in his hand and cursing them. The union moved its caucus to the union office which was near the plant.[2]

Informal conferences with negotiators of the other party are sometimes employed in order to sound them out regarding reactions to various types of proposals. Typically, however, reliance is placed on bargaining-table tactics. Some of these tactics are intended to elicit reactions that become data in estimating the resistance point. The most obvious way is to ask questions designed to clarify both the meaning of the proposal and its underlying rationale. Sometimes Party will direct such questions to some of the "less-coached" members of Opponent's team.

[2] Floyd Brandt, John Glover, and B. M. Selekman, "Gray Manufacturing Company (C)," (Copyright by the President and Fellows of Harvard College, 1959), p. 10.

In reporting upon the practice of one company, a negotiator had this to say:

> Before drafting any counterproposals, meetings are held with the union, and each of the union's proposals is discussed in detail in order to determine the precise intent of the union in each case. Since the atmosphere in these meetings is completely informal, it is possible for management, when necessary, to sow doubt in the union's mind about certain proposals, to recall operating requirements that may have been overlooked, and to test precisely how the union really feels about these issues.

By probing Opponent's team members regarding a specific proposal, Party can determine how well prepared they are, using this information as one basis for inferring how seriously they are advancing their proposal.

Tactics involving personal abuse may be introduced to induce or provoke Opponent into revealing more than he wishes. What we have in mind by "abuse" is well illustrated by an excerpt from a chemical company's negotiations:

> **Heath (U)** And when you say you have discussed it, you are a damn liar. You can take that any way you want to take it, see. If you want to take it with coats off, we will take it with coats off as far as I am concerned; or if you want to select anybody on your side of the table to do it, I'll take my coat off.[3]

Ann Douglas describes how pressure and abuse can break an opponent down and force him to reveal his true position. She quotes a company negotiator who operated on this theory:

> And I think a direct personal attack—a vicious personal attack on U2 would break him. Just—he'd just break under the thing.[4]

Tactics of exaggerated impatience which make it appear as if the negotiations were rushing headlong into their final stages may force the inexperienced negotiator into prematurely revealing the bargaining room he has allowed himself. That appears to have been the case in the Fanco Oil Company negotiations in which in the very first session the first two remarks below apparently induced the third:

> **Hayes (U)** The morale of our men on the boats is very bad. More than 50% of the men are not paying dues, and I have instructed the

[3] B. M. Selekman, S. K. Selekman, and S. H. Fuller, *Problems in Labor Relations*, 2d ed., (New York: McGraw-Hill Book Company, 1958), p. 342.

[4] Ann Douglas, *Industrial Peacemaking* (New York: Columbia University Press, 1962), p. 26.

delegates not to collect from them. We are not getting anywhere, so I think we may as well adjourn and let matters take their own course. . . .

*MacIntosh (U)* No sense for further meetings, if we can't agree now on 7 and 7. . . .

*Downs (M)* If we add $25 monthly income to each man, you would be interested?

*Black (U)* It makes a lot of difference. . . .[5]

In one move Downs offered a monthly increase of $25, virtually everything the negotiating team had to bargain with. What frightened Downs, who was just gaining negotiating experience, was an implicit threat that the independent Fanco union would get discouraged and affiliate with the nearby International Longshoremen's Association. That threat was implicit in the apathy of workers mentioned by Hayes. Still the fact is that this was only the first negotiating session. Furthermore, regardless of how dreaded the consequences of the threat might have been, the threat itself actually was not very credible, because it is unlikely that the officials of the independent union actually had any serious intention of sacrificing an arrangement so beneficial to them.

The tactics discussed above—personal abuse and exaggerated impatience—are not without their risks. In his excitement the other negotiator may take a stronger position than he had originally planned and then become obliged to maintain that position.

Testing techniques are particularly useful for assessing Opponent's resistance point late in negotiations. Sometimes in order to test Opponent's position, Party will suggest calling in a mediator. If Opponent accepts the suggestion, this is taken as an indication that he sees the problem as one of exploring a way by which the positions of the parties can be brought together; he would presumably have some "give" left himself. If he rejects the bid, this may indicate that he has no room to move unless he had reason to believe that Opponent is just looking for an excuse to move all the way himself. Another tactic is for a union to bring the parties up to a strike deadline, arrange a last-minute postponement, and then bargain up to the new deadline in order to test and retest the company's limits.

**Tactics to Record and Analyze Reactions.** Even in the absence of "baiting" tactics, the verbal and nonverbal behaviors of members of Opponent's negotiating team are often rich with clues about the degree of interest they have in the items being discussed or passed over and about their expectations regarding these issues. The following is an excerpt

[5] Selekman, Selekman, and Fuller, 2d ed., *op. cit.*, pp. 568–569.

from a conversation among members of one team as they process the clues available to them:

> ... soon as he finishes I'll give ya a ... full report ... on what took our discussion here and how I think the thing had to go. And it's going all right. *He showed disappointment. Now, a man that shows disappointment, his mind is open on that question.* What's *in* his mind or how far he'll go to buy that we have to find out. ... But you're not gonna find out now, immediately.[6]

In a continuous relationship the negotiators learn in various subtle ways how to assess the position and intentions of the other person.

> When you have been negotiating with the union for as long and as often as I have this one, you get accustomed to the habits and ways of doing things. These may be famous last words, but I think I have Midge figured down to a "T." [7]

Several tactics are used to take full advantage of this source of data regarding Opponent's resistance point.

First, Party may have a man-to-man policy in composing his own negotiating team. Many managements find it useful to have one management committeeman for each union committeeman, so that the latter can be under constant observation during negotiation proceedings.

> One newspaper publisher told of a technique by which he organized his team on a two-platoon basis. By rotating committee members, he was able to keep them fresh and alert and in a position to constantly observe the reactions of the union committee. In addition, he assigned technical people who could understand the real meaning of the union's presentation on detailed subjects such as job evaluation.

Second, Party may be even more sophisticated in this practice by making a continually revised assessment about the influence of each member of Opponent's negotiating team. Since negotiations are not an isolated event but occur as part of a continuing labor-management relationship, most members of the negotiating committee are known to the opposite group. Respective individuals work together during contract administration, on problems and grievance handling. This type of familiarity enables each side to better assess the intentions of the other side. In his analysis of collective bargaining in the steel industry, Ulman notes the practice of analyzing the reactions of local union representatives.

[6] Douglas, *op. cit.*, p. 576.

[7] Edward Peters, *Strategy and Tactics in Labor Negotiations* (New London, Conn.: National Foremen's Institute, 1955), p. 17.

Nor is the sounding off by local union representatives mere sound, for, by carefully listening to the local people, the top negotiators can frequently obtain a truer ranking, in order of their significance to the membership, of the multitude of items included in the wage policy committee's shopping list.[8]

## Modifying Opponent's Perceptions of Party's Utilities

This tactical assignment is to conceal or misrepresent the utilities for Party inherent in the agenda items. In a sense, this becomes the counter-measure to the first tactical assignment. If we assume that all of the verbal and nonverbal behaviors of Party are being scanned by Opponent for clues about Party's utilities, then Party has two responses. He can be in-scrutable, that is, behave in a minimal or irrelevant way, or he can disguise his utilities by deliberately misrepresenting them. Of course, sometimes the best Party can hope to do is to accurately represent the importance of some particular demand, if, for example, Opponent is very likely to underestimate it.

**Minimizing Clues.** The earlier discussion of assessing Opponent's re-sistance point suggests certain tactical countermeasures which Party can take to minimize the number of revealing clues he admits. It is especially important for Party to minimize clues early in negotiations rather than fashion misleading ones, to the extent that he has not already developed clear notions about what his ultimate resistance point is in these negotia-tions. The point is that the negotiation process itself is a mechanism whereby Party gathers much of the information he needs to test the ap-propriateness of his own resistance point.

Perhaps a basic step in this direction is for Party to maintain a low rate of activity and interaction. He makes a deliberate effort to remain quiet, letting members from Opponent's committee do most of the talking. An-other way in which Party sometimes ensures that minimum clues, or rather appropriate clues, will be produced is by using a single spokesman or a chairman who controls the participation of other members of his com-mittee. The importance of such control can be illustrated by an instance in which it was not operating or at least could not cover the more subtle aspects of behavior at the bargaining table.

The union negotiator, Watoski, had let it be known to management that the union placed considerable importance on the waiting-time issue. Employees were losing incentive pay, because in their opinion poor management practices resulted in excessive waiting time. After an initial proposal for a higher guaranteed rate for waiting time,

[8] Lloyd Ulman, *The Government of the Steel Workers' Union* (New York: John Wiley & Sons, Inc., 1962), p. 66.

the negotiators agreed that management should attempt to commit itself to remedial and preventive actions in a letter to the union. In the session in which management finally submitted its offer—the letter it had composed—the following took place:

Scott, the management negotiator, passed out copies of the waiting-time letter to the union committee. At the suggestion of Watoski, Scott read the letter aloud point by point. After he had finished reading it, he waited for comment. One member of the union team, Jernas, asked, "What color is this paper?" Everyone chuckled. Since the letter had been duplicated, the paper used was a special type that was light blue. After Jernas's comment, everyone on the union team except Watoski—who was carefully reading the letter—indulged in light conversation. After a few minutes, the union committee returned to the letter and asked several questions.

The point of the illustration is this: Jernas and then the committee by their lighthearted responses had revealed their general approval of the company's proposal. This was most clear when this particular response was contrasted with the more bitter and sometimes sullen way in which the committee had reacted on other occasions when they had not been happy with the company's position. In fact, in this instance the company had gone far in committing itself to action, but the tactical point is that only Watoski, the chief negotiator, appreciated that there were other items to be resolved and that it was too early to give the union's candid reaction to this aspect of the company's package.

Another tactic is for Party to compose the committee of people who obviously cannot reveal clues, because they themselves do not have significant knowledge of their party's resistance point. In fact, the chief negotiator may be such a person. This tactic of "calculated incompetence," as one union official has termed it, also can have other important tactical assignments which we shall note later. Consider an instance in which this tactic was used:

The union negotiator had been demanding information from the company regarding its cost under the company's current insurance program. The union was urging a new insurance program from a different insurance firm and needed the current cost information to substantiate its arguments. The company had been adamant in its refusal, and the chief negotiator could effectively argue that neither he nor anyone else on the team had the information to give. In a surprise maneuver, the union negotiator brought in a representative from the insurance company whose program he was advocating. Both the union and company negotiators were interested in selling their respective proposals to the union committee. Therefore, the company negotiator's immediate reaction was to think of bringing in someone from the company's insurance firm or from the financial department. Later management decided against this because it would have exposed to the union negotiator a person who had the cost information being sought. The policy of calculated incompetence was observed.

Of course in some instances Party controls information about his own utilities by only appearing uninformed. At the base of the person's behavior is a rational and logical scheme, but on the surface he may appear completely ignorant about the important forces.

Party may make it difficult for Opponent to ascertain Party's true utilities by the tactic of submitting a large number of proposals. "Many demands cover up the hard core which one might accept as a settlement and mask the relative importance which the side making the demands ascribes to the various demands." [9]

The above are efforts to minimize the flow of information. Attempts to modify Opponent's perceptions of Party's utilities often involve some of the positive communication acts which we turn to now.

**Conveying Deliberate Impressions.** Party will attempt to communicate those facts which create the most advantageous impressions of his inherent demands and threats. When it is advantageous, he will provide Opponent with information which gives the latter a better appreciation of the basic importance of an issue. Party advances cogent reasoning and engages in emotional behavior in order to underscore the importance of a particular issue to him. For example, Party can convey the appropriate impression by informing Opponent of the costs that he faces. Several tactics have this as their purpose.

One tactic adopted by management with more frequency in recent years is to take the initiative by introducing positive demands of its own, and the function of these demands is to focus attention on difficulties encountered under the *status quo*. It allows management to focus attention on areas in which they can demonstrate basic costs or difficulties—areas which the union might not anticipate or fully consider. Even though these demands will relate to only a portion of the bargaining agenda, the tactic tends to create the appropriate overall impression.

Another tactic for Party is to ensure himself that he has informed Opponent of all Party's costs associated with a given demand. Thus, it often takes the form of reporting: "Consequences for me of demand $D$ include $C_1$, $C_2$, and $C_3$, whereas I have reason to believe that you were only aware of consequences $C_1$." The reporting can occur in relatively general terms.

Management of Utility Mfg. Co. took pains to inform the union of the prospect of a drop-off in government contract business and of

[9] J. T. Dunlop and J. J. Healy, *Collective Bargaining: Principles and Cases,* rev. ed. (Homewood, Ill.: Richard D. Irwin, Inc., 1953), p. 54.

increasing competition from the entry of other producers into the market. It was equally conscientious about explaining the probable impact that these developments would have on the company's profit picture. Then it reported in frank terms the minimum profit expectations imposed by the parent company on the management of Utility, it being only one of many subsidiaries. Management had reason to believe the union had not fully appreciated that the "gravy train," which the company had enjoyed for the past three years, was about to come to an end, with important implications for management's inherent demands and threats. Management was, of course, selective in the facts that it reported.

The consequences of demands can also be discussed in somewhat more specific terms.

In recent years many unions have asked for a voice in the investment of health and welfare funds. In some instances management has refused on the grounds of principle, e.g., management's rights. In other instances management has attempted to avoid the arrangement by asserting that the involvement of the union would probably result in higher-risk investments, that investments of this type would require the company to lay aside more money, and therefore that the union was asking for the company to contribute more money for the health and welfare funds.

The above statements by Party convince Opponent that Party perceives a real need to avoid the demand. Opponent does not need to accept the importance of costs from his own viewpoint, all that he needs to do is recognize that costs are something that motivate Party's behavior. In effect, Party is saying to Opponent, "if you were in my shoes, this demand would look like the following. A rational person in my shoes would resist such a demand because it has these contingent costs."

The use of specific cost information heretofore unknown or not even considered by Opponent sometimes involves precise disclosures.

During the 1958 negotiations of an agricultural implement company a question developed regarding whether the company should share certain cost information. Line management advised against this action, arguing that issues should be settled on their "merits." Yet, to bring about a settlement, the chief negotiator believed that he needed to do this to convince the union that the company would move no further. Thus, he informed the union that the new administrative procedures covering piecework were costing the company a penny and a half. This apparently came as news to the union negotiators and gave them additional insight into the basis on which the company was opposing its requests.

The tactical use of economic cost information can get rather involved and contains liabilities. All the observer can be certain about is that *prior* to the signing of the settlement, the company is trying to convince the union that a given set of demands will cost too much, while the union is seeking to convince the company that the costs will not be as great.[10]

In 1959 one company showed the union actual cost figures to demonstrate that it was spending 2 cents an hour more on certain health and welfare benefits than its competition was. Significantly, the additional costs did not result from higher benefits but rather from the fact that the company carried a higher share of the burden relative to the employees than, for example, its major competitor did.

In 1961 the union brought into negotiations with the company estimates of what the pattern had cost its competitor. The company knew by comparison that its cost figures would indicate that the pattern would cost it less; not less in fact, in its opinion, but less in comparison with the union's figures, which the company believed were exaggerated for the occasion. Partly for this reason the company chose not to release cost figures.

When the importance of a demand is not merely underscored or slightly overstated but rather is grossly exaggerated, this tactic contains important risks. Peters quotes the observation of one seasoned negotiator:

You've got to be careful how you handle some of these minor issues. You can be so anxious to sew them up, that you sound off too loud and too long about them. Then what happens? A slick management negotiator starts fighting back like they really were big issues. Then, before you know it, he surrenders with a big hullaballoo as if he were giving you the combination to the safe. Now he's jockeyed you into a weaker position when you get down to brass tacks on the major issues. . . .[11]

Clearly there are other risks in communicating misinformation. The point may come in distributive bargaining when Party would like to talk about his true feelings and his true perceptions as a way of closing a negative settlement gap. But it is very difficult to be oblique in one negotiation and accepted as a faithful reporter in the next negotiation. Moreover, unless one is consistent in the types of arguments he advances, his positions lose credibility. In certain situations one can influence perceptions by communicating cost information. Such information may give Opponent a

[10] *After* the signing of the settlement the positions of the parties reverse for reasons that we shall explore later.

[11] Peters, *op. cit.*, pp. 169–170.

better appreciation of the inherent importance of an issue. But if the use of cost information is turned on and off, then when it is not advanced, Opponent will assume that Party's position is weak and his arguments are designed to mislead.

Many other difficulties emerge from the tactical use of information. Opponent will be able to counter with tactics of his own. What then results is a buildup of misinformation on top of misinformation. Instead of negotiations progressing to more common perceptions, they may lead in the opposite direction. Such a spiraling of misinformation can lead to greater uncertainty and miscalculation.

Aside from the question of how communicating misinformation affects the distributive bargaining process, certain value judgments are involved. There is a fine line between misrepresentations which are viewed as "natural" and those which are viewed as "lies" and consequently provoke hostility. Since collective bargaining is a continuing relationship, abuses along these lines will eventually receive their due.

## Modifying Opponent's Perceptions of His Own Utilities

The objective of this tactical assignment is to alter Opponent's subjective utility function either by changing his view of the value of his own demands to himself or by changing his view of the unpleasantness of Party's proposals. We see these efforts to revise Opponent's utilities as primarily consisting of bringing to bear the right information and arguments at the right point within Opponent's organization. We shall first discuss the substantive aspect of these tactics, i.e., the types of information and arguments employed, and then turn to the procedural aspects of these tactics, i.e., the problem of introducing these arguments into Opponent's decision-making apparatus.

**Tactical Arguments.** In the preceding tactical assignment Party attempted to selectively report the consequences of a certain demand for him. In the present tactical assignment Party is enlightening Opponent about the consequences Opponent will face if the latter should succeed in maintaining his position on a certain issue. The distinction can be characterized as follows: In the first instance Party was communicating, "Here is why I definitely can't concede this item to you in a settlement." In the second instance, the one we are concerned with here, Party is saying, "Even though I'm not saying whether you could have it or not, here is why for your own good you should not insist upon this item."

Generally, this maneuver takes the form of a union trying to convince the company that the union's demands are costless and the company trying to convince the union that the union's demands are valueless to the union. Stated in terms of a general example, the union would say something like this to the company, "Your proposal to cut crew size will not save you money; morale will suffer and overall output will drop significantly." Similarly, the company says something like this, "Your proposal for a change in the seniority system is really not going to be that valuable to you because of the repercussions that will take place in your own organization."

Negotiators use colloquial and colorful language in their effort to force the other person to reassess the cost and value of different issues. Such phrases as the following are frequently encountered: "it could backfire"; "it might come back to haunt you"; "you can't have your cake and eat it too"; "the cost of this proposal will eventually be shifted to you"; "increases in cost will hurt our ability to compete, meaning fewer jobs and less security for you"; and "don't kill the goose that lays the golden egg." But whatever the language, the intent is the same, namely, to force the other person to reappraise the utility of a given issue.

The disadvantages to Opponent of his position may be more or less immediate and may be more or less certain in their effect. Some undesirable consequences possibly not considered by Opponent may be shown to be "part and parcel" of his demand.

> During the 1958 negotiations, the union asked for an early retirement arrangement. The company said that it would be willing to grant this demand but that it would retire a number of people unilaterally. When the union realized that in asking for early retirement benefits they might be giving the company the right to weed out certain key people, they retracted the demand.

> During the 1961 negotiations the UAW asked for uniform salary continuation benefits. It desired to bring the lower benefit plants up to the higher plants. The company successfully squelched this demand by saying, "the Harmon plant, which had the highest salary continuation benefits, had to be closed."

One variant of this argument is the idea that "it could backfire" or that "it might come back to haunt you." An example showing how management used such an argument in negotiations is as follows:

> A 7-hour day would mean that we'd be cutting production back . . . it wouldn't mean any more employees. We don't have room for more equipment; we wouldn't wanta buy more equipment. We couldn't have a 1-hour or ½-hour shift to make up the difference; that wouldn't work. In the long run, it would mean that we'd give less service to our customers, we'd be producing less; and that, in turn, would prob'ly build up. We would gradually lose much of the special type of business we get now, which is based on service. On top of that,

it would increase our costs tremendously in an area where . . . our prices are higher than competition in many of our products. This would make the thing even worse. It would—it would hurt everybody.[12]

The content of the above tactics involves the sharing of information with Opponent. The same purpose, namely, influencing Opponent's estimate of the true value to him of a specific issue, may be accomplished by the selective *withholding* of information.

In the Utility negotiations management withheld from the union officials information they had regarding future plans for technological changes which would result in layoffs, in which the effect of that knowledge would have been to cause the union to include in its minimum acceptable package some concrete language on separation pay and layoff procedures.

It should be noted that this tactic—enlightening the Opponent about certain costs he will face should he achieve a particular demand—runs the risk of patronizing. Presumably Opponent believes that he is capable of assessing the advantages and disadvantages of a particular demand; hence, one is usually cautious in telling him what is good for him.

*Gambon* Look, Len, pardon me for sayin' this, but will you, for Christ's sake, let us start to worry how to—to portion this money out? Don't be tellin' us how to use it. . . . Let us try to determine what's needed here.[13]

In distributive bargaining each side is wary of the intentions of the other side. Consequently, it is difficult for Party to convince Opponent that the advice is being given solely for the latter's benefit. In distributive bargaining each correctly suspects the other side of having some ulterior motive or some personal gain at stake. Nevertheless, Party often succeeds in sowing sufficient doubt about the wisdom of the issue that Opponent will take a hard look at his position.

**Procedural Tactics.** The foregoing material dealt with the content of the arguments. How does Party introduce these arguments most effectively into Opponent's organization? There are several possibilities. First, Party may invite a higher official from Opponent's organization to participate in negotiations. Such officials may have wider experience in the industry, may better understand Party's language, may be better aware of the bigger picture; hence, if Party's logics are good, they may have more impact on the

[12] Douglas, *op. cit.*, p. 477.
[13] *Ibid.*, p. 480.

higher official. It is in this vein that the union often asks to speak to the company president or to a higher authority than that represented in the company's bargaining team. Management may seek to involve a representative of the international union for the same reason.

Second, Party may communicate directly with Opponent's principals. Employees, for instance, may be less familiar with the issues and hence more easily convinced by illogical but persuasive arguments, or the principals may be assumed to have some doubt about their bargaining agent or the importance of the union's bargaining positions and hence can be reached by arguments that are couched in terms of what is in the workers' best interest. Letters sent to employees' homes telling them about the "generous company offer" represent this kind of procedural approach.

Third, in situations which have features opposite to those above, it is sometimes tactical for management to try to deal strictly with local union officials. This is used when many of the union's demands are believed to have originated at higher levels of the organization and may contain mixed blessings for the local unit of the organization.

> In a negotiation between a teamster local and a large newspaper, the international representative made a demand that all route salesmen be provided with automobiles. The company negotiator countered this by calling on some individual members in the negotiating committee who were driver salesmen and asked them, "You know what we're doing?" By directing the question to people from the local organization, the company negotiator was able to get the union to admit that the company's compensation practices were not that inadequate.

Generally, the objective is to locate someone in Opponent's organization who will evaluate the issue in a way more favorable to Party. One union studied in a recent negotiation tried this technique rather successfully. They contacted company officials up and down the line until they found someone who was sympathetic to their position. This tactic is particularly effective when top management is strongly oriented toward maintaining principles and local management is strongly oriented toward administrative convenience. The union can obtain relief on issues by searching out the official who is not overly sensitive to the day-to-day costs inherent in the union's position.

### Manipulating Strike Costs of Party and Opponent

In this section we consider two remaining tactical assignments which operate on strike costs: increasing Opponent's potential strike costs and minimizing Party's. They are considered together for reasons of convenience inasmuch as single tactics chosen by negotiators often operate simultaneously on both sides of the power equation. In the discussion of the distributive model we indicated that we would be limiting our treatment of the costs of disagreeing to that of strike costs. However, it should be understood that pressure can be inflicted in ways other than precipitating a strike. Consider the following interesting example:

> Instead of striking a restaurant, as a restaurant owner had expected and prepared for, a union arranged to have hundreds of the sympathizers enter the restaurant just before the noon rush hour, order a cup of coffee, and sit down. When the regular customers of the restaurant entered, they found all of the tables taken. As the coffee drinkers are strictly within their rights, the management could not eject them.[14]

In some negotiations, one side or the other will attempt to impose pressure by going to outsiders—the National Labor Relations Board, the courts, etc. This practice is more prevalent among white collar unions who are unable or unwilling to engage in strike action.

> Since the Association lacked strike power, its most dramatic weapon was the filing of an unfair labor charge with the NLRB, which brought publicity that the company might find distasteful or injurious in recruiting.

> While one cannot conclude that the Association deliberately filed unmeritorious charges for the sake of such publicity, it must be recognized that this was one of the strongest formal weapons at its disposal. Another publicity device used by the Association was the issuance of bulletins during bargaining negotiations. Widely read within the management structure, the bulletin was credited by some Association leaders with winning influential members of management to the support of its position on occasion, with the result that the company's position was changed. Moreover, the bulletins provided a medium for shaping membership opinions on bargaining issues. The combination of membership meetings, informal group discussions, and bulletins permits the Association to use morale as a bargaining weapon in a way that would be impossible for unorganized professional employees.[15]

---

[14] A. T. Jacobs, "Some Significant Factors Influencing the Range of Indeterminateness in Collective Bargaining Negotiations," unpublished Ph.D. thesis, Ann Arbor, Mich., University of Michigan, 1951, p. 296.

[15] Bernard Goldstein, "Unions for Technical Professionals: A Case Study, 1957," unpublished Ph.D. thesis, Dept. of Sociology, University of Chicago, August, 1957, p. 21.

Sometimes the third party is the specter of a rival union. Independent unions may threaten to abandon their independent status, which the company typically values.

> In several negotiations in the oil industry the following sequence has taken place: the independent union drags its feet in bargaining, the membership believes that the delay is due to the company's failure to bargain, soon a militant union like the Teamsters or the Oil, Chemical, and Atomic Workers appears on the scene offering to represent the employees, and a certification election is held. The election is decided in favor of the independent union, but when negotiations resume, it turns out that the contract is quickly signed and the company makes additional concessions.

In most situations the company cannot go out of business, but sometimes there are steps that can be taken short of this.

> In an important negotiation between the musicians union and the Chicago Symphony Association over contract terms for a summer music festival, management announced that it was canceling the season's concerts when the union failed to accept its offer by a certain time. As it later turned out, the cancellation was only "on paper," and the concerts were held once an agreement was reached. However, cancellation of the season's concerts can be a very powerful form of economic pressure.

Since the total effect of a strike involves more than immediate economic losses, a party may try to enhance these collateral costs.

> In a long strike between the OCAW and the Shell Oil Company, the union made much of the hard feelings that were developing between the foremen who were running the plant and the striking workers. The union knew management would be sensitive to the tenor of long-run relations between the foremen and the employees, since once the strike ended, these employees would have to return to the plant and work under the foremen who had been operating the plant. It was clear that the strike was not hurting the company in terms of economic losses, but the union was sure that it was hurting it in terms of foreman morale and management's concern about foreman-employee relations.

A frequently used device is to physically exhaust Opponent to the point at which his fatigue overwhelms his desire to attain his objective. This is often characteristic of the closing phases of negotiations. However, as the following two examples illustrate, it can be used throughout negotiations:

A management person quite successful in the newspaper field told how he scheduled bargaining for the evening hours as a way of placing pressure on the union team. For one thing, they were tired after having worked a full day. In addition, the company was not paying them for the time spent in bargaining. He claimed that if the company could get away with it, it was the best way of putting pressure on the union bargaining team.

In the public employment field, in which the economic strike is not a possibility, other forms of pressure have been developed. In one negotiation the employees just kept meeting, hoping to wear management down. The management officials, who were anxious to return to their desks, finally gave in on some issues, not because they felt that they should, but to end the time-consuming process of negotiations.

Many other examples could be given of the imaginative use of pressure tactics, particularly in situations in which the strike option is not meaningful. These include such devices as picketing in front of the president's home, appearing at stockholder meetings, adhering rigidly to safety rules, shifting tags of destination on luggage, boycotting a briefing session for insurance agents, etc. The techniques of labor protest are manifold. However, our discussion concentrates mainly on economic duress through the strike action.

In deciding how to place an opponent at a strike disadvantage, many structural and strategic questions are involved. In the short run it is difficult for a negotiator to manipulate the rate of cost that his opponent will experience should open conflict develop. However, in the long run many possibilities are available. Some of these are suggested by the factors outlined in the model chapter. For example, changes can be made in the structure of collective bargaining. Each side can attempt to alter the structure in a favorable direction. Companies may move toward industry-wide bargaining or move to strengthen one another's position through the development of mutual-aid arrangements. On the union side action may be taken toward the development of cooperating councils.

Either side also can alter the power equation by altering the location of the appropriate outer limit or reservation price. If the union enjoys great power because management has few other alternatives, management can take steps over the long run to lower its resistance point by constructing new plants, etc. Similarly, the union can do such things as improving the skill level of the workers, vesting pension rights, etc.—efforts designed to raise the lower limit and thereby increase the bargaining power of the workers.

Similarly, the effect of cyclical and seasonal factors can be handled by a skillful manipulation of the date of the contract expiration. The union prefers to have a contract expire when employees have more need for leisure time (for example, during hunting and fishing seasons or during the warm weather). The union would hesitate to have a contract expire near the Christmas season, when financial demands on employees are heavy. On the company's side they would prefer to have the contract expire during a slack period of the year.

Over the long run either party can maneuver the expiration date in its favor. However, it may be necessary to forego certain short-run gains in order to achieve a more favorable expiration. Obviously Party's objective is to have the contract expire when costs of conflict are greatest for Opponent and least for himself.

> This was illustrated in the case of a skyscraper office building under construction in New York City some years ago. In New York City the renting season for office space almost invariably begins on May 1st and occupancy for tenants must then be available or they cannot move from their old locations. The union campaign was so timed, that cessation of work would make the completion of the building by May 1st impossible.[16]

In the absence of a favorable expiration date it is often possible, more for the union than for management, to continue working until the time is favorable for a showdown. The UAW adopted this strategy during the 1958 negotiations, when at the contract expiration date there was an abnormally high inventory of cars available. As Leonard Woodcock expressed it, "We rocked and rolled through the summer." The UAW only became serious as the critical model changeover period approached.

Besides enabling the union to bide its time, the technique of working without a contract has another advantage. It forces management into an uncertain period which can have severe economic costs if as a result the company's customers regard it as a less reliable supplier and begin to divert orders to competitors.

Beyond manipulating the structural factors, many other steps can be taken by each side to gain the favorable side of the power equation. These tactics work on both the rate of strike cost and the amount of total resources available for withstanding a strike. A few of these tactics can be quickly summarized for the union and the company.

**Union Tactics.** First, the union can attempt to increase membership solidarity. The union can strive to bring all the employees within the bargaining unit, to quell factionalism, and to take other steps designed to create solid support for a strike.

Second, the union can increase the availability of other activities and

---

[16] Jacobs, *op. cit.*, p. 296.

benefits. Prior to the strike the union can survey the availability of alternate employment and make arrangements for various kinds of supplementary benefits. Over the long run the union can push for legislation that would provide state unemployment compensation to striking workers.

Third, the union can build strike funds and enter into mutual assistance pacts. Funds are usually collected and paid out by national headquarters. In preparing for the 1955 automobile negotiations, the UAW set the goal for their strike fund at $25 million. That would appear to be a large amount, but it would probably cover less than two weeks' normal earnings for striking General Motors employees.[17]

David Dubinsky reportedly had an imaginative technique for getting the most psychological impact out of the limited funds of the garment workers. He would open an organization campaign in a new area by depositing a substantial sum to the account of the union in a leading local bank. When local garment manufacturers learned of the deposit, they would assume that the union was able to finance a long strike and capitulate. Only later might they learn that the entire sum had been placed locally on the express condition that it be returned intact after serving its psychological purpose.[18]

Fourth, the union can encourage employees to increase their personal savings and place an upper limit on their fixed weekly financial commitments, such as regular payments for durable goods purchased on time. Both efforts limit the employees' dependence on continuous income.

The use of these and other tactics is revealed in a report in a union publication which summarizes the steps that can be taken by unions to prepare themselves for strike action.

> *Health, Welfare and Retirement Benefits.*—Unions have found it possible in many cases to work out arrangements for preserving the workers' stake in these funds and in some cases for continuing these benefits to union members during the strike. *Support of other unions* —Unions on strike have found it to their definite advantage to make certain that other interested unions in industrial areas are kept up to date regarding strike developments. *Support of local community*—In certain cases, unions have been able to win support for the strike (or at least neutralize the opposition) from certain enlightened elements in the business community. *Easing the financial burden of strikers*— Many unions have found it possible to make special arrangements with local merchants, banks, insurance companies, and credit agencies, under which striking union members would be given considerations in meeting with financial obligations. *Special assistance to*

[17] Alfred Kuhn, *Labor Institutions and Economics* (New York: Holt, Rinehart and Winston, Inc., 1958), p. 183.
[18] *Ibid.*

*strikers*—A variety of resources is often available to help individual strikers and their families suffering severe hardship during a strike.[19]

**Company Tactics.** First, the company may take steps to keep the plant open. It may go so far as to hire strikebreakers and proceed to replace the work force. Short of this the company can attempt to operate the plant with supervisors and regular employees who have been encouraged to return to work.

Second, the company can build inventories. The objective is to continue shipments during the course of the strike. Whether this can be done depends on the location of the firm's warehouses and the general questions of how easy and inexpensive it is to store materials. It also involves the question of who normally stores the inventories—customers or suppliers?

Third, the company can transfer production to alternate plants not represented by the union. If a plant is only one of several company plants which have similar production facilities, the company can reduce the cost of a strike by transferring production to other plants. The net cost of supplying customers from alternate production facilities will depend upon added transportation costs, amount of excess capacity available, how much adaptation of other production facilities is required, etc. Still an additional production capability may be achieved by subcontracting operations to another firm or otherwise arranging for them to supply customers.

Fourth, the company can secure financial resources in order to withstand a long strike. Many things can be done to avoid capitulation because of the lack of financial resources. Extra cash can be acquired. Resources from other parts of the company can be shifted into the plant.

Again, let management speak for itself. Consider the following analysis of an aircraft company official regarding the impact of strike action:

There are some points that should be made clear:

Only two major divisions are involved: Lockheed Missiles & Space Company, where the union has only 5,700 members out of a total work force of 31,200, and Lockheed-California Company, where the union has 11,600 members out of a total work force of 24,000.

We currently are in a good schedule position for deliveries of most of our important programs. Many are research, development, and engineering programs, which we can maintain with minimum delays. The effect on production programs would be more immediate and direct, but Lockheed intends to continue operations and will make every effort to minimize this effect.

*Whether any of our programs would be moved away from Lockheed would, of course, be for the government to decide. Such action obvi-*

[19] AFL-CIO Collective Bargaining Report, "Strikes," vol. 3 (November, 1958), p. 71.

*ously would be as harmful to employees and to the community as to the company.* In our opinion, there would be less added expense and schedule delay in leaving a project at Lockheed even during a strike than in moving the program to another plant and organization.

What we have been talking about are the steps that each side can take to influence the actual power equation. Of course it is also necessary to affect the other party's perceptions before these actual changes can be made to influence him.

# PART 2 | COMMITMENT TACTICS

Part 1 discussed the many actions and arguments available to Party to directly influence Opponent's perceptions of the values of the basic utility parameters (and indirectly influence his probability estimates). These efforts affect the bargaining positions taken by Opponent during negotiations. Thus, we are enlightened about a major way in which the parties eliminate the initial area of indeterminateness through information exchange. However, little or nothing was said about one particular form of behavior available to Party which can influence the outcome, namely, Party's manipulation of his own bargaining position. Opponent will draw inferences about Party's target and resistance point from Party's bargaining behavior. This fact creates an important opportunity for Party to behave in a way that develops the appropriate impressions and leads to a settlement favorable to himself.

The concept introduced in the model chapter to handle the manipulation of bargaining positions is *commitment,* by which we mean the taking of a bargaining position with some implicit or explicit pledge regarding a future course of action. The content of the communicative acts referred to as commitments can be either primarily demands or threats but always involve some element of both. Commitments can be minimal, indicating *flexibility,* or maximal, indicating *firmness.*

When compared with the tactics in Part 1, commitment tactics have a less direct and less basic influence on utilities—but they are not necessarily any less potent. At this point we shift *from* an interest in the tactical modification of perceptions of basic forces in the larger negotiation context *to* an interest in the tactics which exploit derived forces set in motion by the interaction process itself. In Part 1 the parties were viewed as relying to a substantial degree upon rational persuasion about inherent demands and threats. Now, as we turn to commitment tactics, the parties are viewed as concerned with more arbitrary persuasion techniques, i.e., demands and threats which are obviously tactical. The possibility of such tactics arises because the convergence process by which parties modify their stated positions during negotiations has its own logics apart from the basic utilities involved. The external standards for the point of settlement decline in importance during negotiations as negotiators have more data about each other, particularly about each other's expectations and intentions. Hence, the importance of commitment tactics.

Commitment tactics will be the central concept employed to discuss the second major way in which the parties eliminate the range of indeterminateness, whether it be a positive or a negative settlement range. Perhaps a brief review of the broad function of distributive bargaining tactics would be helpful here. If there is a positive range, the process consists of successive efforts on the part of each party to narrow the range to a settlement point more favorable to itself. Thus, the lion's share of the range of indeterminateness represents the prize for skillful distributive bargaining. On the other hand, if the parties enter negotiations with a negative range, the efforts of the two parties can also be conceived as designed to eliminate it in a way that is to their respective advantages.

The strategies of commitment are based on a simple proposition well expressed by Schelling [20] along these lines: *If Party can make an irrevocable commitment to a position near Opponent's resistance point* [21] *in a way that is unambiguously visible to Opponent, Party can squeeze the range of indeterminateness down to the point most favorable to himself.*

We can illustrate the idea briefly.

> Assume that at a particular point in time the company has a resistance point of a 15-cent increase. It would prefer to take a strike rather than settle above 15 cents. Assume that the union's *RP* is 9 cents. If the union could somehow irrevocably and conspicuously commit itself to a position of $14\frac{1}{2}$ cents and therefore claim virtually all of the settlement range, the company would be in a position of taking it or leaving it. It would have to take it by definition of its own resistance point.

Making a firm commitment has great potential advantage for Party. It works directly on Opponent's perceptions of his own probabilities of success (i.e., attaining his preferred outcomes without a strike) since it

[20] T. C. Schelling, "An Essay on Bargaining," *American Economic Review*, vol. 46 (June, 1956), p. 283.

[21] The assumption is that there is a positive initial settlement range. If there is a negative gap capable of being closed, the propitious commitment for Party would be one near his own current resistance point. For purposes of simpler exposition in discussing commitment tactics, we shall make the constant assumption that there is a positive gap between the resistance points of the two parties.

conveys information about Party's intentions. In effect, Party is arbitrarily altering probabilities in order to influence the position of Opponent.

As discussed thus far, the idea of commitment strategy raises as many questions as it answers. When one applies the idea to actual labor negotiations, certain difficulties become apparent. What if Opponent's resistance point is not known to Party? What means are afforded by the institutional framework of collective bargaining for making an "irrevocable commitment visible to Opponent"? What if both Party and Opponent make such commitments? Corresponding to each question are one or more tactical assignments for commitment strategy.

What if Opponent's resistance point is not known to Party? Since an irrevocable commitment might fall outside the settlement range and result in an inadvertent strike, Party fashions his commitments with caution. It is a question of balancing firmness and flexibility. Party's first tactical assignment in commitment strategy is to determine the degree of commitment appropriate to the situation. The second tactical assignment we shall consider is to communicate the appropriate commitment.

What means are afforded by the institutional framework of collective bargaining for Party to make an irrevocable commitment visible to Opponent? Although absolutely irreversible commitments may be impossible, there are many techniques available for lending credibility in varying degrees to a commitment. Thus, the third assignment is to make Party's commitments credible.

What if both parties make firm commitments which are incompatible? Again, a strike may result. In an effort to minimize this eventuality, Party periodically must perform one or more of the three following tactical assignments: Prevent Opponent from becoming committed, enable Opponent to revise commitments, or abandon Party's commitments.

In a moment we shall turn our attention to the various types of tactics which are important in each of these tactical components of commitment strategy. However, before we do, let us attempt to state what constitutes the optimal commitment strategy: The practical ideal of a commitment strategy is for Party to develop his position in such a way that Opponent believes Party is firmly committed to an outcome most favorable to himself but at the same time leave himself an avenue of retreat known only to himself which will permit him to demonstrate that he never was in fact committed to this preferred outcome, should it develop that this becomes untenable.

### Determining Appropriate Degree of Commitment

A central issue in distributive bargaining strategy is the question of how rapidly in the sequence of bargaining moves does one approach a particular point which he will pose as his final position. The execution of one's commitment strategy is comprised of the tactical decisions which the negotiator must make about when to actually make a concession, when to indicate flexibility, and when to hold firm. These tactical decisions have several aspects, since at any given point in the bargaining sequence he will indicate his current position, the degree of resoluteness he attaches to that position, and the course of action he intends to follow should his position not be acceded to.

**Communicating Firmness versus Flexibility.** Here we assume that Party does not intend to make a concession at this precise moment but considers that he must communicate something about his current position. The need to communicate may grow out of a preference to take the initiative, or it may be necessary to respond to an initiative by Opponent. What factors does Party consider in deciding how much firmness should be communicated at any particular point in time?

*Limits to firmness.* Certain considerations limit how early in the bargaining sequence one can make an irrevocably firm commitment. Stated more generally, these considerations influence how much firmness one dare communicate at any point in time. To the extent that Party is uncertain about Opponent's perceptions of utilities and strike costs, maximal commitments by Party run the risk of violating Opponent's resistance point. By taking a maximally committed position, a negotiator makes it more difficult for himself to abandon an untenable position—he can do so only by risking internal dissension within his own organization and embarrassment at the main bargaining table. By its very nature firm commitment requires that the initiating party go through with the consequences.

Therefore commitment does more than indicate the utility of an outcome—it also shapes and increases utility associated with that outcome. The negotiator who becomes identified with a particular position has gone on record with respect to the importance that he gives to his position. As a result the act of taking a committed position arbitrarily changes his utilities. This explains why negotiators often hold to positions which incur the costs of protracted strike action. The costs of the strike action are less than the cost of "losing face." What started out as an inconsequential issue to both sides takes on increased importance.

*Reasons for flexibility.* The point of the discussion above is that firmness contains risks. However, Party's reasons for wishing to convey flexibility rather than firmness in his current position may be of a more positive nature. Party may desire to communicate the possibility that he will reduce his demands or concede something to Opponent's demands. Party may, for example, wish to make this change contingent upon some concession by Opponent, or Party may have other reasons for wishing to suggest that he has the latitude to accommodate Opponent's position without actually making that a binding promise.

Party may desire flexibility in his present position for another reason—

in order to increase his demands later should that become feasible or necessary. Some of the factors which might contribute to this are as follows: First, there is the possibility that a strike might ensue, in which case it might be better to increase one's demands. If a strike is going to occur, it is desirable to possess as much trading room as possible. It may also be necessary to win more benefits to justify the strike to the membership. For these reasons the union negotiator will often remain vague about his position in the event that he needs to take a higher position than he initially envisioned. This is facilitated by the ground rule often adopted specifying that "nothing is final until everything is wrapped up." Second, Party may wish to add a new demand or otherwise increase his position during negotiations as a credibility tactic. We shall see in the next section that one sometimes convinces the other that he is serious by this technique—"You will see what will happen if you persist in your position!" Third, the possibility exists that a pattern that would justify higher demands may develop during negotiations. Fourth, Party might concede more in one area than is presently contemplated, making it necessary to tighten up on a position in a related area.

Remaining flexible and not taking a committed position has the advantage of allowing the negotiator to continue to test the feasibility of various positions. Flexibility enables the negotiator to increase his aspiration as well as to reduce his aspiration in the light of the unfolding negotiations. In effect, a flexible position minimizes the risk of a strike.

The negotiator needs to balance two considerations. On the one hand he needs to wait until he has enough information about the intentions of his opponent—until he can decide whether his opponent will take the first step in narrowing the range. On the other hand, by seizing the initiative and taking a committed position, he increases the probability that his opponent will move first.

**Communicating Flexibility versus Actual Concession.** Here we assume that Party does not intend to communicate extreme firmness in his present position. His choice now centers on whether to merely communicate some degree of flexibility or to actually make a concession. What factors does Party consider in deciding this question at any particular time? This is the question of pacing the convergence process and controlling its final point of intersection.

Peters emphasizes the importance of sophisticated treatment of this tactical decision area:

> In skillful hands the bargaining position performs a double function. It conceals, and it reveals. The bargaining position is used to indicate —to unfold gradually, step by step—the maximum expectation of the negotiator, while at the same time concealing, for as long as necessary, his minimum expectation.

By indirect means, such as the manner and timing of the changes in your bargaining position, you, as a negotiator, try to convince the other side that your maximum expectation is really your minimum breaking-off point. . . . Since you have taken an appropriate bargaining position at the start of negotiations, each change in your position should give ever-clearer indications of your maximum expectation. Also, each change should be designed to encourage or pressure the other side to reciprocate with at least as much information as you give them, if not more.[22]

While we cannot set forth the specific decision rules which Party will utilize to decide whether or not to move, it is possible to suggest some of the considerations he will take into account. The factors are framed as questions.

*How far is each side from Party's target?* Whether to communicate some flexibility or to actually move is influenced by the relative distances between the current positions of Party and Opponent and the point Party holds as his target. If Party is the farther from this point, he is more likely to make the next move. An illustration of this sort of reasoning is reported in the Jimson negotiations:

The company's strategy was clear. It did not plan to concede any more until Watoski had made additional concessions. This was prompted by the fact that the company was very close to having given all that it wanted to grant. Not making any more offers was apparently a tactic for convincing Watoski that the company was firmly committed to a package which was somewhat smaller than what he was hoping for.

This reasoning influences the choice of first moves, especially the employer's first move. The timing and size of the employer's first offer can be a troublesome question, as reported by Peters:

If the pattern is 5-10¢ and the union is still at 30¢ plus fringes, and management offers something, how can it ever hope to settle for 6¢? Management's first offer can only come when it is possible for management to alternate moves, inching toward the eventual figure. Moreover a small offer doesn't give the right impression. But to not make any offer looks like management isn't bargaining, and the union can use this to club management, since management can't afford to appear unreasonable.[23]

*Who made the last move?* Certainly, Party will consider who made the last move and whether that move was regarded by the other as an "ade-

22 Peters, *op. cit.*, p. 112.
23 Peters, *op. cit.*, p. 35.

quate" move. Party cannot afford to move out of turn, if he can avoid it. Alternating moves is almost a convention of collective bargaining. The rule carries the aura of equity or fair play.[24] One side may not be happy with the amount of concession made by the other, but he is under considerable pressure to respond with some concession of his own.

The alternation of concessions is not a mechanical process. Each side is alert to the meaning of the other's concession. Consider a union negotiator with an aspiration of 10 cents. A concession from 15 to 11 cents means more than one from 30 to 15 cents. In the example below the company underestimated the extent to which the union had revised its position:

> The contract was due to expire on November 15. The day before the expiration the union submitted a revised proposal. Instead of the earlier listing of 50 separate demands, the union put its position on one piece of paper and phrased its demands in general terms. The company failed to respond with a similar revision, claiming "the union had not really dropped a thing—they were cloaking all their demands in general language." After the strike started, the company pointed to the fact that the union continued to press all its original demands.

The example can be used to make several important points. The company missed the tenor of the union's concession and failed to respond in kind. Clearly the union was protecting itself with the general language, which is the character of most concession probes made during the convergence process. Once the strike started, the union reverted to its earlier position. In effect, the company's statement that the "union really hadn't changed position," turned out to be a self-fulfilling prophecy.

Further evidence regarding the importance of matching the spirit of the opponent's concession comes out of the Douglas study. A mediator is cautioning management against failing to reciprocate a substantial concession by the union.

> Now look. That union has got right into the realistic area. If you come up with a cent or 2¢ you are going to damage these negotiations beyond repair. Now you know you have to settle this and you know that you have a—a limit. The question is—I know what you're tryin' to do. You're tryin' to get to that limit without jeopardizing your bargaining position, and I'm here to help you do that, but don't make it harder on me. The union has made such a *substantial* move, and now you *know* they're in the realistic area. If you come out with

[24] The role of "rules for play" are well analyzed by C. M. Stevens, *Strategy and Collective Bargaining Negotiation* (New York: McGraw-Hill Book Company, 1963).

a penny you're gonna insult them. You're goin' to make them feel that you're not bargaining in good faith. If I were you I would throw out at least *80%* of what you're going to give them—and I didn't know what you were—what the company was going to give them.[25]

***Have the parties exhausted the topic under consideration?*** Ann Douglas suggests that positions are revised, not so much because Party feels it cannot obtain its demands after analyzing the strength of Opponent, but because it becomes exhausted in the process of pressing its demands. This is the crux of timing. Related questions are: How much urgency is provided by the approaching strike deadlines? How adequate is the rate of concessions when considered against the time available for negotiations?

***Would a move by Party be interpreted as a sign of weakness?*** Whether it would be so interpreted will depend both on the context in which the move occurs and the way the concession is handled. Modification of one's bargaining position step by step must avoid giving the impression of weakness. This is best achieved if one can ensure that his opponent will reciprocate with a step for each step that he takes.[26] In other words, Party would be less likely to move unless he had some reason to believe that he could force Opponent to make the next move.

The answers to the above questions will influence whether Party chooses to offer a concession or merely to indicate flexibility in his position. If Party should decide that he must make a move despite the fact that in some respects this might not be wise, Party will often try to communicate his misgivings to Opponent. In the Jimson case, the company negotiator felt that the union had got stuck on a figure which was too high. After he could wait no longer for the union to make the next move, the company negotiator prefaced his offer with, "We have an offer to make to you today. We think we're really too far apart to make an offer, but we're going to anyway."

Bargaining over whose move it is and how much is adequate "to throw the ball to the other side" is precisely the way the parties factor or fractionate the larger distributive bargaining process. Therefore, any bad decision along the line can well affect the outcome. It is hard to offset the implications of a move not really intended. Consider a discussion between a mediator and a union negotiator:

"You have offered the employer no inducement—none whatever—to take another step. The employer has made it clear. He's not tipping his hand any further. Not until you show him where you're going. When you're up at thirty cents, you're telling him nothing. When

[25] Douglas, *op. cit.*, p. 278.
[26] Peters, *op. cit.*, p. 45.

you come down to a point where he can guess roughly where you're going, then he'll reciprocate."

"Nuts!" retorted the business agent. "He beats that drum every year. But what happens when we do come down before we're ready to? We end up two or three cents under what we should've gotten."

"Sure," I said, "it's possible to come out on the short end by dropping down too fast, but you're so far away from the real bargaining area, you haven't even come to grips with the employer yet. The time to get cagey is when the dentist's drill is near the nerve. Then there's some advantage in forcing the other side to move before you do." [27]

Note that the mediator stresses that who moves how much is especially critical in the final stages of negotiations: "The time to get cagey is when the dentist's drill is near the nerve."

Party can take a stance of initiative or one of response regarding the control of the pacing phenomenon. He can adopt one of two contrasting decision rules about concessions: (1) "After Opponent has cut his position, I'll alter mine. How much I alter my position will depend upon how much Opponent has altered his and what expectations he communicates." (2) "I'll cut my position first and signal how much of a cut by Opponent I think would be adequate in order for me to regard it as my move again."

**Commitments in the Final Convergence.** The final phase of bargaining, in which the two negotiators attempt to converge on a settlement point, presents the same tactical questions regarding degree of commitment that have been present throughout bargaining, except that they are now sharpened by the impending deadline and the possibility of a strike. Each negotiator must decide upon the timing and the size of the concessions which bring him to the settlement point.

Information is now more complete. Each side has gained a fairly good picture of the other's resistance point and whether a settlement is possible short of a strike. The problem facing each negotiator is to approach the settlement point in such a way that he does not display weakness or enable his opponent to seize the advantage. Assuming a positive range, Party must approach the settlement without prompting Opponent to revise his aspiration upward.

We shall consider the tactical questions facing Party in two connections: the *timing* and the *amount* of final position changes.

*Timing.* A good example of how Opponent aspirations can change in a direction unfavorable to Party because of a poorly timed concession schedule is provided by a mediator interviewed by Douglas:

Right after the war, there was a manufacturer here in the metropolitan area who was . . . in negotiations with this union. And he

[27] *Ibid.*, p. 114.

felt certain the union would accept 10¢, and I did, too, but under certain conditions and at—*at* a certain time . . . he was a—a very excitable man. . . . And these kind of meetings just aggravated heck out of him and he couldn't control himself. So he said to me in caucus, "Now, let's stop all the bickering. Let's get 'em in here and give 'em a dime." I said, "Mr. Neifach, you may do that, but if you do, don't say I haven't told you." He said, "Do you mean to tell me they'd reject a dime? I *know* . . . they want 8¢." I said, "You put a dime on the table now and you can kiss it goodbye. They'll take it, but they ain't gonna stop there. They've got another week." . . . "Well," he said "they won't get anything." I said, "Then you'll— then you'll push them into a position where they'll strike." "I don't believe it." . . . So we went in, and he told them . . . "Now! I know there's going to be a lotta haggling and I have a good idea where it's gonna end up, and I have an offer to make. And here it is. I wanta end this thing up. I'm gonna get—wrap it up and get out of here tonight. 10¢ an hour." . . . They sat there and *not a word.* And you could see the look of disappointment on his face. . . . Art Smith was the negotiator. He said, "Mr. Neifach, we'd like a caucus to *consider* your offer." He says, "*Consider!*" . . . I thought he was gonna jump out that window. And he started. Oh, he just—he said, "There'll be *no* considering. You'll take it or else!" And he walked out. . . . Don't you know we had a strike? [28]

Timing of a final offer as premature as the one above is an exception. The timing of final concessions usually takes place within the shadow of the deadline. It is the deadline which gives the final phases of bargaining a characteristic quality of urgency. And it is the deadline with the prospect of default that provides the incentive for both sides to make final concessions in order to reach agreement.

Thus, final concessions need to be made rather late in bargaining—the very timing of these concessions gives them a finality.[29] But if the concessions are made too close to the final deadline, they may not be heard in the "din of battle." In other words, Opponent may assume that you are not going to concede further, and he breaks off negotiations in order to prepare his organization for strike action.

In several negotiations between the UAW and a large company, the company's offer came too late to stop a strike. The company was forced to delay making its economic proposal until the pattern had been established.

In 1958 this delay extended for several months. During this period the local union leaders grew impatient and took strike votes,

[28] Douglas, *op. cit.*, pp. 280–281.
[29] Stevens, *op. cit.*, p. 6.

and even though the company made its offer prior to the strike deadline, the momentum toward the picket line was too strong to be stopped.

Consequently, the announcement of the final position has to be late enough to be believed and yet not too late to be heard.

*Amount.* Ideally each negotiator only wants to concede as little as possible to bring about agreement. He wants to state a position that just meets the resistance point of the opponent. But knowledge about this point will never be complete. Party will have to fashion his concession schedule in terms of the movements in position already made by Opponent and his best estimate of the settlement or convergence point.

The final concession needs to be large enough in amount to be dramatic and symbolic of closure. A small "final" concession will create the impression that something is being held back by Party. Contrastingly, the large final concession may prevent Opponent from arguing that Party has not reached his resistance point. The belief that Party has reached his final position will have a sobering effect on Opponent; it will force him to think carefully about strike action, and it may even induce him to modify his resistance point. The importance of the size of the final concession is well illustrated by the following quotation from a mediator who is counseling one of the parties during this phase:

> Let me also prove . . . what I'm trying to say by . . . telling you about something that happened, again in the ABC negotiations. We were at 7¢. The company had offered first 5 and then 2. . . . The company called me into caucus, and they said, "George, we think we oughta make a move. You know where we're going." . . . "We're going to 10." And I know these people. When they tell me that, that *is* it. . . . "Now, we're at 7. We'll give you a counter-proposal. We'll give them 8 and some fringe." I said, "Jim, knowing that you're going to 10 I advise against your throwing them a cent now, because when the chips are down that 2¢ that's left isn't going to be big. I would rather you hold at 7 and then when my *right time comes,* that 3¢ is going to look a *lot* better than 2." So they went along on it.[30]

The most difficult aspect of making a concession at any point during negotiations is to be sure that it is coupled to a concession from Opponent. The greatest danger in revealing a new position is that Opponent will not reciprocate, in fact he will take the move as evidence that Party is capitulating. The need to couple concessions is particularly acute at the deadline. Some negotiators (usually on the company side) have experienced the agony of making a final concession to achieve agreement only

---

[30] Douglas, *op. cit.,* p. 377.

to find that agreement has eluded them. The solution is for a negotiator to reach agreement with Opponent on coupling before releasing the content of the concession. How this is done involves the subtle art of tacit communication, discussed in the next tactical assignment.

### Communicating Party's Commitment

We now asume that Party knows what degree of commitment he wishes to express and with what implicit contingencies, if any, he wants his present position to be regarded by Opponent. The subject of implementing commitment decisions will be discussed in two parts: in this section, verbal and tacit communications of commitments; in the next, confirming or credibility tactics of commitment.

The communications of interest here may have any of four purposes. First, Party may wish to convey firmness in commitment which is complete and which accurately represents Party's present position and future intentions. Second, Party may wish to convey firmness in commitment that is more apparent than real. Third, Party may want to communicate positive flexibility in its current position, such that Opponent can expect Party to make further concessions. This entails a type of "minimal commitment," approaching the form of a promise. Fourth, Party may wish to indicate that his present position might have to be revised to the disadvantage of Opponent. This would require a minimal commitment of a different variety. Throughout the discussions of this section we shall want to keep in mind the above distinctions about purpose.

**Verbal Communications.** *Dimensions of commitment statements.* In general the firmer the commitment which Party intends, the clearer the communication he selects; the weaker the commitment, the more ambiguous the communication. However, degree of commitment has several dimensions—we suggest that it has three. The anatomy of a *complete* statement of commitment is comprised of three tactical parts: first, the *degree of finality* of the commitment to a specific position, second, the *degree of specificity* of the position to which the commitment is made, and third, the *consequence* to be associated with a positional commitment, in other words, the threat.[31]

In order to illustrate the importance of these three dimensions, we can analyze the following hypothetical statement by a union negotiator who

---

[31] Although the communication of commitments often contains reference to the how or the why of the commitment to the particular position, this merely verbalizes a confirming tactic; it does not elaborate the commitment itself. Of course, these confirming tactics are essential, since one need not take the verbalized commitment at face value. The two types of tactics must ultimately be considered together. However, here we are interested in illustrating the tactical elements of a statement of commitment.

has received an offer from management late in negotiations: "We must have the 12½-cent package and the seniority provisions which we proposed. We are prepared to strike, if necessary." The above statement is firm along all three dimensions. (1) "We must have . . ." indicates a high degree of finality. (2) ". . . the 12½-cent package and seniority provision we proposed" is quite specific. (3) The consequences seem reasonably clear from the phrase, "We are prepared to strike, if necessary." Commitment could be weakened by altering any one of the three dimensions of the statement.

First, less finality in the union's position would be implied if the statement began, "The committee expects management to give more consideration to the . . ." rather than, "We must have. . . ."

Second, less specificity would result if the statement were revised to read: "We must have the kind of package and seniority provision we have been discussing here. We are prepared. . . ."

Third, the statement would be weakened by modifying the consequences linked to the failure to comply with the demand: "We must have the 12½-cent package and the seniority provisions which we proposed, or this committee is going to have to work hard to sell this to the membership." All the union is saying here about consequences is that they will experience difficulty "selling" the membership. This does not obviate the possibility that the membership might vote for ratification even if it isn't exactly "sold" on the package. It certainly does not state that there will be a strike.

What purposes are served by statements such as those above? The first basic statement would be used to convey a firm commitment completely and accurately. However, each of the modifications of that statement contains both a degree of commitment and some qualification or reservation. The apparent firmness still remains, but the real commitment is less than binding. That is, each contains a phrase that can be interpreted in such a way that the party could later abandon the commitment without great loss of face.

We can better discuss commitment statements relevant to the other purposes after we have examined several statements made by spokesmen during labor negotiations (Figure 3-1). In examining Figure 3-1, we are interested both in the degrees of commitment represented by each of the statements and in the nature and purpose of the qualifications or reservations inherent in most of these statements. Column 1 lists several statements of commitment. Column 2 contains an analysis of the degree of finality of the position taken; column 3, a comment regarding the degree of specificity of that position; and column 4, a comment on the associated consequences explicit or implicit in the situation.

Thus, to sketch out the extremes suggested by the framework and the analysis presented above, statements of commitment range in degree of firmness from *maximum firmness* via a statement that the current position, spelled out in unambiguous terms, is absolutely final and that this position is taken in full awareness of the worst consequences which can be contemplated under the circumstances (usually a work stoppage) to *maximum flexibility* via a statement that the current position, alluded to in uncertain terms, is the company's current position, based, for example, on an analysis of the circumstances still in process. In the latter statement reference to the consequences associated with that position would have to be stated in the absolute minimum or be scrupulously avoided entirely.

The illustrations in Figure 3-1 also serve to impress us that language offers an almost infinite variety of ways of expressing the finality, the specificity, and the associated consequences of a party's current position. The situation is further confounded by the fact that any given statement comes to carry its own unique meaning in a particular context in a particular relationship.

All the statements in Figure 3-1 seem to be intended to convey an impression of a firmer commitment than they in fact contain. Other statements might deliberately signal flexibility, hinting of possible future concessions. Or they might indicate tentativeness, hinting the possibility of withdrawing present concessions. In each of these later cases the ambiguity in the statement would have a different purpose from that in the statements illustrated above.

*Significance of dimensions.* Perhaps we can suggest some considerations which influence the negotiators' choice of dimensions on which to be firmest and those on which to be most tentative.[32] Suppose Party has the need for, and capacity to achieve, substantial gains, but is relatively indifferent about the specific package. If Party knows that he must make considerable gains but has considerable latitude in the areas in which these gains can come, then he might from the outset be final in his commitment to an acceptable package and tough about the consequences associated with a failure to agree but not be specific about what constitutes an "acceptable package." As negotiations proceed, he would become increasingly specific about that. Unions, in particular, have adopted this technique. In recent negotiations the UAW has taken the posture of indicating the

---

[32] This is a particularly intriguing issue as it arises in international negotiations. For example, along which dimensions should the United States have been most firmly committed on the Berlin issue in 1960–1962? Should the United States have indicated that it was ultimately and irrevocably committed to defend Western rights in Berlin and that violation of Western rights would lead directly to wholesale retaliation, without specifying in meaningful terms what it regarded as those rights? Should the United States have been more specific regarding the rights that it was intent upon defending, and should it have been perhaps equally final in that position but less clear on the consequences to be associated with that position? There were numerous possible combinations, each of which had some logic to defend it.

**Figure 3-1**

*Interpretive comments about the degree of firmness in statements of commitments*

| Statement of commitment (1) | Degree of finality of commitment to a position (2) | Degree of specificity of that position (3) | The consequences or implications associated with a position (the threat) (4) |
|---|---|---|---|
| *From a negotiation involving a middle-sized manufacturing plant in 1953:* "We have looked very seriously and must present this (10-cent package) as our final offer." | The statement "must present this as our final offer" is not as strong as, for example, "this is our final offer." The strength of the word "final" is somewhat hedged by the more tentative phrase "must present this as." | The reference to the "10-cent package" was fairly specific. | No reference to the consequences. What the other party is expected to associate with the company's position would depend on the company's reputation or other confirming tactics. It would seem to imply that company is ready to take a strike. |
| A union replied later, "The membership disagreed" with the company's economic proposal. "The present contract will not extend beyond 12:00 tonight." | Significantly, the membership was reported as only having "disagreed"; it did not "reject." | Reference to "economic proposal" is not specific. Hence the degree of disagreement is unclear. | By stating "the present contract will not extend," they do *not* state that there would be a strike. And in the particular context it was not clear that they would strike. |
| *From the public statements regarding to the 1955 negotiations between the UAW and The Ford Motor Company:* Henry Ford II suggested alternate ways of achieving security "without piecemeal experimenting with dangerous mechanisms or guinea pig industries. . . ." This was a statement of opposition to the union's GAW proposal. | The statement contained no hint about the finality of commitment of opposition. | The phrase "piecemeal experimenting . . ." clearly avoided reference to just what was objected to. | There were no references to the consequences to be associated with ultimate failure to agree. |

| | | | |
|---|---|---|---|
| *From the transcripts of a negotiation in the oil industry:* Management stated, "If you say now or never or else (on a wage increase demanded by the union), I would say go ahead; we are prepared to take the consequences." * | This was an explicit, binding commitment. | The company's position was also clear in this instance—it was not prepared to make any concession on the issue at hand. | Company was indicating its readiness for a work stoppage. |
| Later the union spokesman replied, "My advice to your employees will be not to become a party to any agreement which binds them to present wages." † | Regarding what the union leader's advice will be, that is final. It says nothing about the finality of that position of the party, however. | The advice "not to become a party to any agreement which binds them to present wages" is hardly specific. Any increase would meet the test of this statement. In fact, even a reopening clause would avoid "binding the union to present wages." | Although at first glance this statement seems to commit the union to a wage increase "or else," it leaves them the option of continuing with no contract and with signing a contract which has a way of adjusting wages in the future. The context did nothing to clarify just what consequences were to be associated with the union's position. |
| "I don't believe that they (the rest of the union committee) can recommend acceptance" (of the company's offer).‡ | "I don't believe" is more tentative than "I know they cannot." | "I don't believe that they can recommend acceptance" leaves unanswered whether the union committee would recommend that the membership not accept the offer or merely make no recommendation. Moreover, the reference is only to the company's offer *as it now stands.* | Not specified here, but the union had begun to refer to economic sanctions. |

* B. M. Selekman, S. K. Selekman, and S. H. Fuller, *Problems in Labor Relations*, 2d ed. (New York: McGraw-Hill Book Company, 1958), p. 221.

† *Ibid.*, p. 226.

‡ *Ibid.*, p. 233.

acceptability or lack of acceptability of the company's offer. Rather than stating a firm position of its own, it uses such adjectives as "woefully inadequate" to describe the company's offer. This technique is used when the issue is money or some other matter that lends itself to incremental movement.

Precisely the same combination appears to be appropriate for a slightly different situation. Assume that Party is certain that his principals have the willingness and capacity to sustain a work stoppage but that Opponent may be known to have some doubt about that. Assume further that Party has had little basis on which to determine Opponent's resistance point. Under such conditions it would be wise for Party to represent himself as "resolutely determined" (great finality) to achieve an "appropriate settlement" (little specificity) "or else" (implicit costly associated consequences), provided, of course, that the context itself adds very little to the precise meaning of the words "appropriate settlement" but does convey clearly that "or else" means costly consequences, such as a long and bitter strike.

When there are few issues or when the issues are discontinuous, a party is forced into a different commitment configuration. If only one subject is under discussion and there are only two positions one could take on the subject, each one favoring a different party, the parties would have no choice but to be absolutely specific about their current position. Any tentativeness in their bargaining posture must be reflected in the lack of finality of their current position or in the severity of the consequences they were willing to attach to a failure to agree. An illustration of this is provided by the UAW, which assumes just this type of commitment on matters that involve principles, in contrast to the way that it handles issues of money.

**Tacit Communications.** There is no sharp distinction between the "verbal communications" discussed above and the "tacit communications" we turn to now. It is largely a matter of degree. By tacit communications we refer to those communications which do not rely upon ordinary usages of words but rely more upon the unique configuration of signs and circumstances for their meaning. In this sense, tacit communications may resemble our illustrations of verbal communications which conveyed only the appropriate meaning when viewed in the total context. With that caution, let us turn to what is referred to variously as tacit communication, sign language, or shared meanings.

In this section we have stated the several purposes of communications. Sign language is particularly useful in communicating flexibility without really promising a concession. Consider the following interchange taken from the Jimson negotiations:

*Scott (M)* We plan to give something to the employees. (Pause) What's the thinking behind proposal number 6?

*Watoski (U)* We've proposed this, because some people have been asked to work through their lunch hour.

*Scott (M)* Do you know any other company that gives what you're asking for?

*Watoski (U)* Not for lunch, no. But it's hard on a guy to have ordered a hot lunch and then have to work instead of eating it. When he finally gets to it, it's cold.

*Scott (M)* Has this happened often?

*Watoski (U)* Not real often, no.

*Scott (M)* This is an approach to the thing that I haven't seen before. If there is a lot of this, maybe it should be corrected. Can we hold this for the present?

*Watoski (U)* (Reading another agreement.) This contract pays time and a half for lunch after 10 hours of work.

*Scott (M)* Well, let's hold this for now. This doesn't mean we will give it. By the way, is it OK if we use orange paper for the cover of the agreement this year? We've got some left over from last year.

By closely examining this sequence, we see several tacit communications from Scott to the effect that the company could give on this item if it were important to the union. The first sign was his reference to this specific union proposal immediately after his general statement that the company planned "to give something to the employees." A second sign was the noncommittal "Can we hold this for the present." The third sign that might be interpreted in the same way was his almost irrelevant mention of the color of the cover to the agreement. Perhaps reference to the agreement symbolized Scott's confidence that this sort of issue could be resolved without difficulty. But these communications did not add up to a firm promise. In fact, Scott could always remind Watoski that he had specifically said, "This doesn't mean we will give it." Moreover, Scott also suggested that the solution to the problem might be through preventive action by management, rather than by a new premium for employees.

Silence in response to an issue may be a sign of willingness to concede the point, provided other issues are settled to Party's satisfaction. An even stronger sign is indicated when a union official says about one of the union's demands, "Well, let's pass over this for now. I don't see much here." His counterpart will probably take this to mean that he is dropping the issue, which may have been included to satisfy some group within the union. The comparable signal from a management negotiator who is willing to give on an item, but not quite yet, is, "Well, let's pass over it for now. I don't see much of a problem here."

Tacit communication is a way of protecting one's bargaining position while at the same time indicating the possibility of a concession. "Sign language enables you to offer concessions without having your actions interpreted as weakness. It gives you the flexibility to move in the direction of peace—or to *move back* to a position of strength." [33] Peters illustrates this point by citing several tacit communication tactics which can be used to indicate a willingness to move—but only if the move will be reciprocated.

> The industrial relations director might say, "I'll try to get something, fellows, I don't know how, believe me, it's tough this year, but if you tell me you'll take five cents, I'll break my neck trying to sell it to the front office."

> The industrial relations director has his counterpart in the union spokesman who appears to be stepping out ahead of his committee. "I haven't even talked this over with the committee, and maybe they'll over-rule me, but I personally would be willing to try to sell this. . . ." He then lowers the union's bargaining position. If management shows no immediate response to the feeler, someone on the union committee might shake his head quickly, "Oh, no—I wouldn't go for it if you did try to sell it." [34]

Sometimes the tacit probe does nothing more than test the posture of Opponent. It does not convey a concession, only a willingness to move toward settlement. The probe is phrased in such a way that Opponent can perceive it as a gesture toward convergence, but if Opponent does not reciprocate, then Party can protect himself by reinterpreting his gesture as a posture of firmness. In the following statement we see a good example of a union tentatively accepting the company's wage offer without directly saying so:

> If we cannot come together on these two issues, wages and retroactivity, and you say that is your final and best offer, I will ask for a conciliator to come in. Even if the membership was to accept that [wage] offer, we are still in doubt as to the retroactive date. [35]

The union negotiator indicated the concession on wages in an oblique way in order to preserve his bargaining position on that issue should the

---

[33] Peters, *op. cit.*, pp. 153–154.
[34] *Ibid.*, pp. 156–157.
[35] Selekman, Selekman, and Fuller, 2d ed., *op. cit.*, p. 278.

company not concede on the other issue, namely, retroactivity. If the union were to come out and openly say that the only point of disagreement was the retroactivity question, it might find itself with too little still at issue to call a strike.

In order for the parties to utilize tacit communication, they must not only learn the signs over time and reciprocate them, but they must also use them with at least a minimum of integrity. It is true that an important attribute of the sign is its ambiguity, but Party must be careful how it exploits that ambiguity.

Occasionally a negotiator will commit an act breaching the good faith. Reneging sometimes occurs.

> Yet there are negotiators—and desperation is no excuse for it—who attempt to entice an offer from an opposing negotiator by giving a hint of reciprocity, and yet, when the offer is made, they fail to come through with the indicated counteroffer. Then they want to use the changed position of the other party as a new floor from which to bargain. When accused of reneging, they blandly stand on the literal meaning of the words they had used, and deny any hidden implications to the statements they had made.[36]

Another violation occurs when a party soft-pedals an issue, suggesting that it isn't important, and then "springs" it on the opponent after he has achieved his other objectives.

An incident known to one of the authors provides a dramatic example in which an alleged violation of the sign language virtually ruined the reputation of a union negotiator, to say nothing about its adverse effects on the particular negotiations in which it occurred.

> A difficult issue resulted from a local strike at one of the divisions of a large manufacturing plant. It occurred during the contract year and centered on the layoff status of a group of gals. Finally, Max, the international representative, who had been called into the situation, received word that the company might be ready to settle. He called the divisional manager, Foster, who asked, "What's it going to take to settle this thing?" Max indicated the union's terms. Foster inquired, "Well, if we do that, can you give us some relief on the equalization of overtime during the rush season?" Max replied, "I'll talk to the committee."

> Foster had received the critical sign; he assumed that the matter was settled. He recalled that whenever he had conferred with Max about pending grievances, and Max had said, "I'll talk to the committee," the grievances would disappear.

[36] Peters, *op. cit.*, p. 211.

In the meetings which followed, the committees gradually arrived at the terms for settling the layoff dispute which had been indicated to them by Max and Foster. Every time that the management committee tried to inject the overtime issue, Max would say something to the effect, "One thing at a time." Finally, they signed an agreement on the layoff issue. A management representative asked, "OK, what about the overtime question?" Max replied frankly that he had discussed it with the committee but that they weren't prepared to go along. The reaction of management, especially Foster, was violent. Max was accused of a double cross; the situation almost produced physical blows.

Max stressed that he had only promised to "talk" to the committee and that Foster's interpretation of his "sign" was correct for grievances but not for negotiations. In reporting the incident later, Max accepted some blame for the situation. He was severely shaken, "All a guy like me has is his reputation for keeping his word, for honest dealings. If you ever lose that in this circuit, you're washed up!" Shortly after the incident he suffered a heart attack, which he believed resulted from the trauma of the incident.

Another illustration points out the frustrating experience of both negotiators when they cannot manage to communicate the real situation at the bargaining table. This underscores the need for an adequate vocabulary of signs.

In the Jimson case, in which the chief negotiators had a close working relationship, Scott, the company negotiator, had informed his union counterpart, Watoski, that the union could expect to get an improvement in the Sickness and Accident Benefit, an item that the union had not previously requested. The union had been disappointed on most of its own proposals and this issue offered Watoski an opportunity to gain something for his committee; therefore, at the appropriate moment Watoski asked management for the Sickness and Accident Benefit. Meanwhile, however, Scott and others on the company committee had received instructions that they must not give the Sickness and Accident Benefit unless absolutely necessary. Scott was in a box. How could he abide by his instructions and say "no" to Watoski but at the same time signal to the latter that if the union became insistent enough, he probably could get permission from top management to concede the benefit? There were no opportunities for a private discussion. As it happened, their sign language was not adequate to the job. When Scott declined on the S and A Benefit request, Watoski reacted dismayed, angry, and embarrassed, but he didn't react in the one appropriate way, namely, "insistent."

## Making Party's Commitments Credible

Another tactical assignment is to find a way of making Party's tactical demands and threats credible. Credibility can be viewed as a probability assessment: "The perception by the threatened party of the degree of probability that the power wielder will actually carry out the threat if its terms are not complied with or keep a promise if its conditions are not met." [37]

Party takes steps other than verbal and tacit communication to convey the degree of his commitment to his demands and associated threats. But *how* does he commit himself? We have shown that he can verbalize his commitment, but certain actions may speak louder than words. We recall that earlier analysis suggested that the bargainer should be able to commit himself *irrevocably* to a position and to certain associated consequences. Taken literally, this simply does not appear to be possible in collective bargaining. However, the institutional apparatus of collective bargaining does permit commitments of varying degrees of firmness. For example, a verbal commitment can be reinforced by arousing the principals to support one's position, by taking a stand publicly or by behaving in an assertive manner at the bargaining table. These are just a few of the ways in which Party can demonstrate his resoluteness. They tend to confirm verbalized or otherwise inferred statements of commitment. They may tend to underscore the finality of a position, the specificity of the position, or the consequences to be associated with it.

**Commitment to Whom?** An important and strategical issue is deciding to whom one commits himself. A negotiator can commit himself to his own organization, to some third party not directly involved, or to his counterpart across the bargaining table. In each instance, the technique for commitment is to pledge one's bargaining reputation. It should be noted that so much depends upon the reputation that the party has already gained. He cannot pledge what he does not have; hence, the importance for the present of having fulfilled threats made in the past; hence, also, the importance for the future of not making present commitments one cannot fulfill.

Somewhat different risks and other implications are associated with each of the three targets of commitments. We shall discuss each of the targets, in turn.

*Commitment to own organization.* The tactic of building the expectations of the union membership and then exhibiting its militancy is an important way of demonstrating commitment. In the process the union

---

[37] R. C. Snyder and J. A. Robinson, *National and International Decision-Making* (New York: The Institute for International Order, 1961), p. 164.

negotiator may have effectively limited his own authority to revise his commitments. The membership would not let him. This type of tactic comes as close to effecting an irrevocable commitment as any to be observed in collective bargaining, because it may effectively alter the strength of the membership's aspirations. There is a limit, however, to how far a negotiator can go in appearing "helpless." The negotiator who can convince his opponent that he has no control over his membership or that his "hands are tied" on a particular issue may gain some bargaining advantage at the negotiating table, but he must suffer the consequences should his opponent not accommodate his adamant position.

*Commitment to third parties.* The tactics Reuther utilized during the early 1950s which involved associating himself publicly with a particular issue—the guaranteed annual wage (GAW)—committed him to obtain some significant gains on that issue. The strategy involved more than commitment to the companies with which he negotiated and to the UAW membership; it included commitment to third parties—to the other AFL and CIO unions and to the public at large. Therefore, he was staking his broader reputation, indeed probably his career, in the labor movement.

Bargaining through the newspapers has become an important facet of contract negotiations. In recent years negotiations in the steel, railroad, and airframe industries have given ample evidence of the technique used by each side for taking a committed position before outsiders, the public and their representatives. As the structure of collective bargaining becomes more centalized and as the aggregations of power grow larger on each side of the bargaining table, then the government either willingly or unwillingly becomes a party to each contract negotiation, and the jockeying for a favorable position with respect to the government becomes an important activity for each negotiator.

Note has been taken that commitments can be made to people who are not present at the bargaining table. As indicated in the model chapter, these commitments to third parties constitute a type of side bet. While these side bets do not directly involve the other negotiator, they do increase the credibility of the bargaining position of the first negotiator by increasing the cost that the first person would face in revising his position. In effect, he says, "This matter is so important that I am willing to stake my reputation with outsiders on the question of whether I shall achieve this objective."

*Commitment to the adversary.* Ultimately these commitments to principals or third parties must be visible to Opponent, for it is only in this way that the latter will be induced to modify his position. The majority of credibility tactics do not involve this roundabout process of impressing Opponent. They involve a side bet directly with the Opponent: "I am demonstrating my resoluteness in such a way that if I should back off from the indicated position, I would lose face with you." For example, the tactic of adjourning the meeting without suggesting another tends to demonstrate commitment to one's present position. One's strategy is to commit himself to that position before his adversary. Therefore, if he later has to revise his position, it is his bargaining reputation with the adversary which suffers. Thus, the credibility of not only the revised commitments but of all commitments in future negotiations will be affected adversely. Inasmuch as the parties are in continuous relationship, whether one's "word" is accepted by the other attains considerable importance. For the most part the commitment tactics that will be discussed below involve taking a position before Opponent at the bargaining table.

The credibility tactics are to be considered separately; they may or may not be used in combination. They are grouped by types, according to whether they tend to increase the prominence of the demand, emphasize the intrinsic viability of demands, identify officials with demands, manifest psychological propensity to fulfill threats, involve overt preparations to fulfill threats, or create and fulfill minor threats. The first few types tend more to underscore the finality and specificity of the demand; the later ones underscore the likelihood and severity of consequences.

**Underscoring Demands.** *Increasing prominence of demand.* Tactics may be intended to increase the credibility of a demand by making the demand more prominent. They seek to convince the other of Party's interest in the issue. The following tactics are of this type:

First, Party can present the issue and also his position on the issue before Opponent manages to state his. This idea of presenting proposals first is particularly effective if done by the company, since it runs counter to custom. This was a key tactic for the management of Gardner Board and Carton, whose bargaining strategy paralleled General Electric's "Boulwarism." One particularly revealing interchange occurred at the beginning of the 1952 negotiations.

> When the session opened on July 16, the union wished to present its proposal first. To this the management replied, ". . . [the company desires] to present its proposals first so the union could have something to compare their proposals against. The company determines the right thing in its offer . . . it doesn't hold anything back." The company proceeded to present its complete offer.
>
> The company remained firm on its proposals throughout. . . .[38]

Second, Party can engage in repetition of demand and devote a considerable amount of time to discussing it. This tactic makes the most sense for the party seeking to change the *status quo*. In other words, in most

[38] Selekman, Selekman, and Fuller, 2d ed., *op. cit.*, p. 600.

circumstances one would find the union repeating a demand and devoting considerable time to discussing it as a way of indicating the importance of this demand. Conversely, one would not expect to find a company using this technique as much. If the company desires to preserve the *status quo,* constant reiteration of it might keep the issue alive long after the union has desired to drop it.

Third, Party can reduce demands to writing or use transcripts or minutes to further record his demands and elaborate and clarify his position. This is assumed to increase the likelihood that Party will stick to anything he says.

**Emphasizing intrinsic viability of demand.** Tactics may tend to underscore the intrinsic viability of Party's demands under the circumstances. They are usually intended by Party to convince Opponent that Party sees an inherent fairness in the particular demands. Three tactical operations are suggested.

First, Party can note the face validity of the demand or the obviousness of a particular position based on the idea of a round number (an element of symmetry), a pattern, a precedent, and other referents visible to both. Second, Party can cite principles which require that he adhere to the demand, as such. By attaching policies, principles, or matters of integrity to his position, he ensures that if he should subsequently make concessions, the principles would be discredited. Third, Party can arrive at settlement in intersecting negotiations against the backdrop of a consistent policy of making identical settlements in both negotiations. Thus Party may arrange for simultaneous bargaining with slightly staggered (successive) termination dates.

**Identifying officials with demands.** Tactics may have the effect of increasing the identification of important officials of Party's organization with certain of his demands. These tactics tend to pledge the prestige and bargaining reputation of Party's organization in general, and these officials, in particular. Party can take several steps toward this end. He can promise results to principals and permit these promises to be reported to adversaries. He can take a position in the presence of both principals and adversary, for example, by utilizing committees of larger size and with more varied composition or by allowing observers. Party can also report his position to all elements of Opponent and sometimes to third parties such as the public.

Moreover, Party can involve more prestigeful negotiators. They may enter and lead negotiations. However, higher officials may be involved without actually being present in negotiations, as the following practice illustrates:

> When one of the divisional industrial relations managers in a large company wanted to take a more committed position, he would say,

"Well, I've been to the top and I had a hell of a fight, but we'll take a new position." The vice-president of industrial relations himself would say, "I've been to the board of directors, and this is as far as we can go."

**Underscoring Threats.** As we indicated in our discussion of commitment statements, one way of exhibiting resoluteness is for Party to outline the steps that will be taken if his position is not acceded to. In collective bargaining the ultimate threat is typically a work stoppage. The task of making the ultimate threat itself more credible is the topic of the subsequent discussion.

The strike acts as a deterrent. It is effective only as a threat; in other words, it prevents the other person from doing something by presenting him with contingent costs of such a magnitude that he is prevented from pressing his position. For a deterrent to be effective, there must be some credibility to the threat of carrying out the action. In the words of Schelling, "We have learned that a threat has to be credible to be efficacious, and that its credibility may depend upon the cost and the risk associated with fulfillment for the party making the threat." [39] Thus, for a threat to be credible, the threatener must demonstrate that the cost to him of carrying out the threat would not be excessive. A threat is more plausible if the action does not cause worse damage to the person making the threat than to the threatened party. Boulding maintains that small threats are ignored and large threats are not believed. In between is a threat which is taken seriously enough to have high expected value. [40]

In passing, we might note some of the risks entailed in overt threats.

As it happens, threats are not only the most dangerous, but usually the least effective form of indicating strength. . . . As often as not, people who make threats find it necessary to do so because they are bluffing. An experienced negotiator will tell you that if you have the strength, you don't need to make threats; if you haven't the strength, when the showdown comes you must choose between taking some suicidal action, or eating your words.

When you hurl a threat, you buy some militancy, but often at too high a price. . . . You have served notice on the other party that if he yields to you, he openly acknowledges himself in retreat. You may have scared him a bit, but in all likelihood you have made it much harder for him to accede to you. . . . [41]

[39] T. C. Schelling, *The Strategy of Conflict* (Cambridge, Mass.: Harvard University Press, 1960), p. 6.

[40] K. E. Boulding, *Conflict and Defense: A General Theory* (New York: Harper & Row, Publishers, Incorporated, 1962).

[41] Peters, *op. cit.*, p. 44.

For this reason the less overt, less blatant threats are usually the more effective.

There are certain ways that Party can underscore the importance of the threat without throwing down a challenge which must be returned in kind. One way is to stress the unpleasantness for Party associated with preparing for the strike action.

> Frankly, we don't want to strike. We have been put to a lot of trouble. The other night I drove 400 miles, half of it in a fog, to go up and be sure that we had a vote for a strike at Norton; and we got it. Do you think that I like to do that? [42]

Another way to minimize the risks associated with the threat is to place them in an offhand or humorous communication. Consider the following exchange:

> *Michelsen (M)* Well (laughing), don't ask me to do it, then. I'm going to—I'm saying to you just what I've said before, that this is the company's position. This is it, period! (Pause.) Now—
>
> *Gambon (U)* Well, I'm trying to determine whether it's time for us to go out and buy a shotgun. (Pause.) [43]

*Manifesting willingness to fulfill threat.* Tactics may operate to make Party's threats more credible merely by conveying the idea that Party has a taste for a fight. How can Party create this impression?

He can act irrationally by attaching great emotional importance to what seem to be little things. He can indicate that he has "an itchy trigger finger." While the inner strategy is rational, the posture appears irrational, perhaps even foolish. A similar effect is created by pounding the table, stomping, shouting, and cursing or by alluding to other strikes, pickets, boycotts, whether these were successful or not.

Party can indicate a willingness to fulfill threats by stating that other elements of his organization are in an aggressive mood and then assume for himself a posture of helplessness. Very often a union negotiator will say to management, "I cannot control the membership; they are ready to strike unless you do so and so." The negotiator may even indicate to management that he is working to convince the membership that the package is acceptable, while behind the scenes he actually is working to bring in a negative vote.

A mediator may be used to convey to Opponent the seriousness of Party's intentions. Consider an instance reported by Peters:

[42] Selekman, Selekman, and Fuller, 2d ed., *op. cit.*, p. 337.
[43] Douglas, *op. cit.*, p. 316.

Management said, "Let them strike, perhaps some of these hotheads who are listening to the labor bosses will sing a different tune after they've missed one or two weeks' wages." Then the mediator came back, "I wouldn't count on that, McKeon's an old hand at this—seldom makes mistakes. He wouldn't be pulling the pin if he were not sure he could hold them out for a long, long time." However, in this instance the mediator performed the same activity with the union, advising the union committee, "Oh, just that I don't think he's bluffing. If you ask me, he's going to the end of the line." [44]

*Making overt preparations to fulfill threat.* Tactics which evidence actual preparations for fulfilling a threat can have profound confirmation value. Party intends that these tactics will convince Opponent both about his willingness and capacity to bring about the consequences or to accept them, as the case may be.

The question of Party's ability or capacity to bring about given consequences was considered in the earlier section. Many of the steps that can be taken to affect the rate at which costs will be incurred (should a strike develop) can also indicate intent. For example, stockpiling inventory will minimize the cost of a strike, but it also can be done in such a way that it indicates willingness to engage in conflict. At this point we are interested in the latter aspect of power, and the illustrations will concentrate on this facet.

The union can prepare members for a strike vote. Taking a strike vote is extremely important. In a study of the subject,[45] Parnes found that most strike votes are used as a bargaining tactic rather than as an attempt to ascertain rank-and-file attitudes toward a work stoppage. Many of the strike votes are taken early in the negotiations, and the negotiator is allowed to call the strike if and when he feels it is necessary. While such an early vote of confidence may not be too convincing to the employer, still it is a step in the direction of fulfilling a threat.

Once the union leader sets out to conduct a strike vote, he needs to obtain a resounding plurality. Parnes found that "authorization of strike action by majorities of 9 to 1 or better was the most typical result of the strike votes for which data were obtained." [46] The participation in strike votes is also important. Parnes concludes, "In only one instance out of 26 did less than 50% of the eligible union members participate." [47] While these turnouts and the percentage favoring strike action are impressive,

[44] Peters, *op. cit.*, pp. 6–8.

[45] H. S. Parnes, *Union Strike Votes: Current Practices and Proposed Controls* (Princeton, N.J.: Industrial Relations Section, Department of Economics and Sociology, Princeton University, 1956).

[46] *Ibid.*, p. 51.

[47] *Ibid.*, p. 50.

experts learn to look for small deviations from past displays of solidarity. For example, a 90 per cent strike vote may look impressive to an outsider, but to a company official it may be a sign of a softened membership when compared with the usual 98 per cent mandate.

A formal notice of Party's intentions to terminate the contract can be considered an act preparatory to threat fulfillment. In most negotiations the contract expires at a specified time, and neither party seeks to extend it. However, in some negotiations the contract expires only on specific notice from one side. Moreover, in other situations the contract may be extended pending termination by one party. In these situations, establishment of the contract expiration date activates the strike deadline.

Jacobs lists still other devices used by unions to signal physical and psychological readiness.

> Mass meetings and strike votes are standard union devices. More effective have been the ostensible renting and furnishing of strike headquarters, the printing of picket signs and strike banners, the leakage to the press of the union's strike intention should the employer not better his offer, the more violent emotions displayed at the negotiating conferences, the open solicitation of strike funds from other unions and sympathetic merchants, etc.[48]

*Creating and fulfilling minor threats.* Often the most effective way of convincing Opponent that Party means business about certain tactical demands and threats is to carry out a minor commitment which was explicit or implicit in the negotiations. These tactics offer direct evidence of Party's willingness and capacity to act and tend to build the reputation of Party as one which fulfills its tactical threats.

Party can first threaten to introduce new demands into negotiations and then proceed to do it. Consider the statement of a management negotiator:

> The company's seniority provisions are among the most liberal in industry, and the company will not agree to change that which will add to the cost of operating or contribute to inefficiency of seniority applications. If any changes are to be negotiated, the company will want changes itself.

The threat to alter Party's bargaining position may be effective because negotiations represent a totality, and movement or lack of movement on one issue can be linked to other issues. However, the threat to retaliate with a reversal of bargaining position is sometimes difficult to make credible. The other side can in effect say, "If you weren't interested enough in that change to introduce it early in the bargaining, why are you holding

[48] Jacobs, *op. cit.*, p. 313.

it over my head now?" To overcome this disbelief, the threatening party needs to find a way of justifying the threat. It attempts to do this by linking its course of action to the belligerence or obstinacy of the other party. In effect it counters with this argument, "Initially, I didn't take your demand seriously, but if you really stick by your position, then I am going to have to obtain compensating benefits."

Other prevalent ways of first making a minor threat and then enforcing it are union slowdowns or "quickie" strikes. A company can employ a speedup or certain restrictive actions. The following harassment activities by workers served this purpose:

> At one plant the forge-shop employees walked out for a few hours; at another plant the workers voted not to work overtime until the negotiations were concluded; in another plant some sabotage took place: Several cans of paint were perforated and allowed to drip down over inventory items, several foremen were soaked with fire hoses, and inventory tags were changed to confuse the filling of orders.

Paradoxically, the major threat may be less credible after fulfillment of this type of minor threat. The frustrations dissipated by the excitement of even a two-day quickie strike may reduce the forces operating to support a contract strike.

There are innumerable steps that can be taken which have the effect of creating and fulfilling minor threats. The following is a list of those encountered frequently in labor negotiations:

1. Party first declares there are certain preconditions to further negotiations and then proceeds to abide by that statement.

2. Party persists in his bargaining position, refusing to revise it even when Opponent makes a concession.

3. Party employs delaying tactics, refusing to engage in effective bargaining on issues on which he has communicated his position.

4. Party adjourns the meeting without suggesting another meeting and then waits for Opponent to take the initiative in resuming negotiations.

### Preventing Opponent from Becoming Committed

This tactical assignment for Party is to prevent Opponent from making or communicating a commitment which Opponent is prepared to make. Usually it is in Party's interest to do what he can in order to prevent Opponent from becoming more than minimally committed, if committed at all.

However, under certain circumstances it may be preferable for Party to pin Opponent down. If, as mentioned earlier, Opponent is remaining flexible in order to increase his bargaining position, then it may be completely functional to force him to take a committed position. In this case the purpose is to "put a lid on his position." Several negotiations in which this approach was taken by the company were studied. In the face of a union that occasionally revised its position upward, the dominant orientation of the company negotiator was to force the union to state a specific position. In effect, the company negotiator felt that he gained more by preventing the union from increasing its position later in the negotiations than he lost by enabling the union to develop support for a particular position.

In the more typical case a negotiator enters bargaining with his boldest position and then proceeds to take a more modest position. For these situations it is functional to prevent the other side from becoming committed. Three alternative courses of action are available: Party may take steps to block the action which Opponent might take to confirm his commitments, he may attempt to prevent Opponent from communicating either verbal commitments or reporting on his confirming tactics, and/or he may receive such information but ignore it or pretend not to comprehend it.

**Blocking Action Which Confirms Commitments.** The previous discussion of the ways in which one party can commit himself are suggestive of the methods that a party can use to make it more difficult for the other to commit himself. Thus, theoretically each of the credibility tactics has its defensive counterpart, although as a practical matter some defenses are more effective than others. For example, a few of the more common defensive tactics would be to avoid transcripts, galleries, and publicity; to prevent Opponent from reducing his position to writing; etc.[49]

In one case management tried to minimize any repetition and discussion of Opponent's demands by making the commitment medium, i.e., discussion time, scarce.

> During 1961 negotiations the company made the following statement: "For the company to review every issue of every subject in the negotiations for the sole purpose of merely refuting the union's charges would be a waste of time. We should be working toward agreement and not toward disagreement."

In another instance in the same company, management stalled and delayed in answering the union's original statement of proposals, thereby preventing the latter from further developing its supporting arguments.

[49] There may be a conflict between Party's need to create a medium which *he* can use for a commitment credibility tactic and his need to eliminate this medium in order to prevent Opponent from using it.

The company took considerable time for investigation of the union's demands before it answered them. It hoped to move its answer closer to the strike deadline, when the pressure would be on the union to cut its position before it had acted in a way to strengthen its commitment. However, the tactic was used by both sides. The union skillfully delayed on the testing issue. It knew that the company had a very strong opposition to any change in the testing field. The weight of persuasion and logic was also on the company's side. Consequently the union did not reintroduce the issue for several weeks, thereby preventing the company from stating and restating its opposition to this issue.

Still another variant of this tactic is to keep an item in subcommittee because Party knows that Opponent is likely to make a commitment if it is brought back to the main table.

**Interposing Obstacle to Communication.** Party may attempt to interpose some obstacle to communication—one which prevents Party from receiving either verbal commitments or information about confirming tactics. Ideally the arrangement would be asymmetrical, in the sense that it would still allow Party to communicate to Opponent his own commitment, but this ideal is not always achieved. Presumably Party would use only a symmetrical obstacle when he believes Opponent is more prepared than he to make a tactical demand or threat.

Party may completely sever communication from Opponent in order to avoid receiving any information from him. In the Atlas case reported by Douglas we observe Party calling for a timely adjournment.

The mediator had said to the company that they should put their counterproposal on the table before adjourning for dinner; then, without allowing any time for discussion and possible No's, the meeting would adjourn, which would give the union a chance to go over the proposals at dinner and come back in an amenable frame of mind.[50]

In another case more drastic action was taken—certain officials of the union resigned, while others left town.

The situation at the Seneca Paper Company had reached crisis proportions. The company was intent upon proceeding with its modernization program. The union was equally opposed to letting management take the first step. After the union had established the issues involved as subject to discussion, perhaps negotiation, it attempted to make its own commitment and then break off all communications.

[50] Douglas, *op. cit.*, p. 76.

*Scott (M)* "Could we get together Wednesday, day after tomorrow?"

*Machetti (U)* "Not very well. I am leaving town for two weeks. The grievance committee and shop stewards have plans for the week and will be too busy. We will get in touch with you later. In the meantime we shall consider that our problems are still under negotiation." [51]

Shortly thereafter management received several letters, each sent by registered mail with return receipt request. They contained notification of the resignation of the union vice-president and all shop stewards in the department affected. The company was concerned, for these moves cut off all communication with the officials with whom they could negotiate and effectively "take a position."

Party may convey that as bargaining representative he does not have authority to make concessions and does not communicate all threats or demands to the officials in Party's organization who do make decisions. Thus, Opponent cannot efficiently communicate with Party's decision makers. Sometimes consultants are used as bargaining agents for this purpose. At other times lesser officials who allegedly have little or no authority are used. The union negotiator for a professional union felt especially frustrated when the company used this tactic:

The personnel officers are puppets who are only authorized to receive concessions, not to make any. There is a federation of departments instead of one company, as far as the union is concerned. When we deal at the top level, the supervisor's authority is represented as complete and practically untouchable. When the members and representatives try to obtain concessions at the department level, they find, naturally, that the supervisor has negligible influence.[52]

Party may maneuver around situations in order to avoid enumeration of issues when he is in doubt about whether the other has actually dropped one of his demands, or Party may suggest that the parties move on to another issue or recess when he anticipates a commitment is coming from Opponent. Some diversionary tactics like jokes and casual conversations are intended to head off a commitment. Still a more obvious move is to avoid requesting a commitment. Consider, for instance, a tactical error by a union negotiator:

Toward the end of September the company presented its full economic proposal to the union. This was an important session, in

[51] Selekman, Selekman, and Fuller, 2d ed., *op. cit.*, pp. 119–120.

[52] R. E. Walton, *The Impact of the Professional Engineering Union* (Boston: Division of Research, Graduate School of Business Administration, Harvard University, 1961), p. 34.

which top officers from both sides were on hand. The chief spokesman for the union asked the company after the full presentation whether this was the company's final offer. Immediately the company negotiator responded, "I'm glad you asked me that question. We are not holding anything back. This will be our offer as of the contract expiration." Immediately the union realized that it had made a mistake by giving the company an opportunity to take a committed position in such a clear and unambiguous manner.

**Ignoring Commitments.** A third line of defense is for Party to ignore commitments or simply not to comprehend them. This has more significance, of course, if Opponent's strategy is one of commitment to Party. If Opponent is committing himself to his principals or to a third party, less is gained by Party's ignoring the commitment.

Party is presented a difficult choice when he receives a strike threat from Opponent. If Party must make his own commitment, then he acknowledges the threat and proceeds to cite counterpressures which might be taken or costs which Opponent might incur. If these other tactical assignments are not paramount at the time, Party would probably attempt to ignore or minimize the other's commitment.

Opponent's commitment might be minimized by ridiculing the threat if Party believes it is not backed by real pressure—if he thinks Opponent is using idle threats—or Party might divert attention from Opponent's threat statement by cracking a joke or introducing casual conversation, just as he uses these techniques to head off a commitment before it is made. In some instances Party has no better way of coping with an unwanted commitment statement than by passing it by without flinching or reacting in any other way. Consider the following interchange from the Jimson negotiations, in which each negotiator is determined to get his own commitment on the table and to ignore the other's. They seem to be talking past each other.

> *Scott (M)* So far, we have offered you 5 cents plus the ½ cent. We have also agreed to raise the third shift differential to 12 cents. Our package cost up to this point is 5.6 to 5.7 cents. Is that what you have, Jim?
>
> *Watoski (U)* (Ignoring the question just asked.) Our proposal was 9½ cents.
>
> *Scott (M)* (Ignoring Watoski and checking his figures.) Our offer comes to about 5.6 cents. Our offer on major medical is still open. (Pause.) I think we've reached a point where I should say what I have to offer. (Pause.) Jim, this is all I have to offer. I have another cent to offer on wages. That's 6 cents. That's all I have, and I'm serious about it. The major medical is still open. (Pause.) I guess that's all I

have to say at this point, Jim. We would be willing to make the wage increase retroactive to August 1.

*Watoski (U)* Let's go over the union agenda. On number 1, since we'll have a one-year agreement, that means the dates will be from August 1, 1961, to August 1, 1962.

### Enabling Opponent to Revise Commitments

Just as one attempts to prevent the other from becoming more than minimally committed, he attempts to make it as easy as possible for the other to revise a previous commitment—without apparent loss of bargaining reputation. In the next section we shall discuss the various tactics Party might use to rationalize his own revision. Exactly the same rationalizations and mechanisms are contemplated in these two tactical assignments, except that in this one Party merely collaborates or takes the initiative in finding rationalization tactics for Opponent. Rather than duplicate these rationalizations here, let us clarify why one party has an interest in accommodating the revising party. For instance, when a settlement represents a defeat for Opponent, why do both parties agree to express it in terms other than those used during negotiation and thereby obscure just what relationship the settlement bears to the earlier positions of the parties?

We refer to this as letting the other guy "save face." More precisely, it is letting the other guy save his reputation as an effective bargainer. It is still more accurate to state that the parties are refraining from exposing the fact that Opponent abandoned a position previously labeled "final," or "best," or "minimum." Now Party, with whom he is currently bargaining, will know this—which cannot be helped—unless even Party pretends to be fooled. However, others with whom the actually defeated Opponent deals will not have this information on which they could revise their own strategy in negotiating with him. Thus, by this favor, Party makes it easier for Opponent to settle below his earlier commitments.

There are still other reasons for letting the defeated Opponent save face: Party may otherwise increase Opponent's insecurity with his principals and make him less rational in the future (and hence, perhaps, plunge both parties into a foolish strike); and Party may otherwise set into motion within Opponent a psychology of deliberate revenge.

### Abandoning Party's Commitments

This tactical assignment is to abandon Party's previous commitments, if necessary. Party attempts to revise any commitment which becomes untenable as negotiations develop, by rationalizing the move in such a way that Opponent is not certain that there ever was any real commitment.

Under most bargaining strategies commitments must undergo continual revision. New positions are reached as Party gains better estimation of Opponent's resistance point and as he anticipates the timing and position of Opponent's commitments. These are relatively minimal commitments in the early stages, and abandoning them does not require elaborate rationalization tactics. Nevertheless, whenever possible, a party attempts to relate changes in positions on specific issues to "something"—to changes external to the present negotiations or to appropriate aspects of the bargaining activity itself.

Naturally, when a firm commitment has been made—whether this occurs early or late as the culmination of the progressively firmer commitments—only severe developments can prompt the abandonment of that tactical commitment. Let us assume that a deadlock has occurred in negotiations. Both parties are committed to incompatible positions. Party must either enable Opponent to revise his commitment, abandon his own commitment, or see his own commitment through. Party's preference, of course, would be to have Opponent revise his commitment. Here we assume that attempts to do this have failed, and we focus on whether Party should abandon his commitment and, if so, how? If it is more costly (considering the costs of a strike versus losses through settling at Opponent's terms) to maintain the commitment than to abandon it, the only reason for Party to maintain it is to preserve his posture of strength—to lend credibility to commitments in the future.

A negotiator does not like that choice and will search for a third way out. He will reason there *must* be a way of avoiding the cost of pursuing the commitment (to a work stoppage) and yet avoiding the creation of an image of one who does not carry through on a firm commitment—as one who backs down on a threat. The more skillful negotiator will plan for that eventuality, if it can be done without the other party recognizing that an avenue of escape exists for the first party. This latter qualification should be stressed. As Schelling has emphasized, the availability of any avenue of retreat, if known, is a direct subtraction from the commitment itself.[53] The question becomes one of finding a means for abandoning a previous firm commitment which minimizes the harm done to one's bargaining stature.

In some instances nothing more is required than that Party silently drop the issue. However, in most cases in which a truly firm commitment by Party was understood by both parties, Party needs to rationalize dropping the issue in some way. We can turn to some tactics which accomplish this.

A classic example of the need for rationalization tactics occurred in the Barrington Oil Company negotiations.[54] This is a study of a company in

[53] Schelling, *op. cit.*
[54] Selekman, Selekman, and Fuller, 2d ed., *op. cit.*, pp. 221–239.

"graceful retreat." Early in negotiations management was bargaining with local officials with whom management seemed singularly unimpressed. Management appeared quite opposed to meeting the union's wage demand. In fact, the chief negotiator said at one point, ". . . you are too impatient. However, if you say now or never or else, I would say go ahead; we are prepared to take the consequences." [55] In short, the company negotiator had become firmly committed in his rejection of the union's demand.

Later the international union entered negotiations in behalf of the local union, balancing the sides in terms of both bargaining skill and power. In reviewing the situation in light of these developments, management wisely decided that a substantial wage increase as well as additional concessions would be required. The tactical problem for the negotiator was to find ways of abandoning his earlier firm commitment.

One tactic that the company negotiator used was to cite changes in the Opponent's arguments. That is, changes in the basis upon which the union had presented its proposal. Thus, he picked up the fact that whereas the union previously had been arguing largely on the basis of cost of living, it was now approaching the question on the company's "ability to pay."

> *Malcolm (M)* You are attacking the problem from a different basis than the committee had before. You are giving major emphasis now to different criteria for wage adjustments. But I still have to say at the present time we cannot see eye to eye with you. . . .[56]

He was laying the groundwork for further retreats. Therefore he asked for time to go back to management.

> *Malcolm (M)* I think it seems only logical since we are approaching the subject on a different basis . . . that I have an opportunity to present your idea to the management.[57]

There was now a new dilemma to Malcolm's situation. The aspect of the situation which he had hit upon to rationalize "reopening" the wage question—the union's argument of ability to pay—happened to be one which he couldn't possibly use to justify the next step of the retreat, namely, the making of an offer. Typically companies are unalterably opposed to ability to pay as a wage criterion.

Another tactic for abandoning a commitment is to do it out of concern for the public or in the interest of national security. This happened to be the rationalization tactic employed by management in the Barrington

---

[55] *Ibid.*, p. 221.
[56] *Ibid.*, p. 227.
[57] *Ibid.*, p. 229.

case. The following took place just 24 hours after Malcolm had agreed to "reopen" the question with his top management.

> *Malcolm (M)* We might as well get down to business. We have been considering your request very carefully and we are glad to make an offer *on the basis of national defense.*[58]

The fact that a Federal mediator had entered the case that day facilitated the use of that tactic, especially since the mediator had actually interjected a patriotic note into the proceedings.

The entry of a mediator is often used as a pretext for making adjustments in Party's position previously regarded as "out of the question." This was undoubtedly one service performed by the entry of Vice President Nixon and Secretary of Labor Mitchell into steel negotiations during the 1959–1960 strike.

Changes in the available facts can be used as a reason for abandoning a commitment. An example of this is provided by the Gardner Board and Carton Company, which utilized a final-offer-first approach, a strategy involving maximal commitment.

> The company remained firm on its proposals throughout. It did withdraw, however, a proposal for incorporating of rotating shifts at Lockland *when the foreman reported to the management committee* that it was untenable because of strong opposition by senior employees.[59]

The Gardner management saved face on revisions that it could attribute to its own assessment of the employees' needs based on information gathered by the management organization subsequent to its last previous offer. In order to implement its maximal commitment strategy, it scrupulously avoided revisions in response to union influence during negotiations.

Other examples of the type of facts utilized in this way are national wage patterns or cost-of-living figures which often change during negotiations. The point here is that the party which wishes to use them as a rationalization tactic usually is advancing exaggerated implications of the changes.

Party may cite changes in the basic relationship between the parties and the promise it offers. Late in negotiations Utility management made the following commitment: "We have looked very seriously and must present this as our final offer." However, after the union had indicated that an exceptionally well-attended membership meeting had "disagreed" with

[58] Italics supplied. *Ibid.,* p. 233.
[59] Italics supplied. *Ibid.,* p. 600.

the company's economic offer and that the "present contract will not extend beyond 12:00 tonight," the company revised its position with this statement:

> In light of our negotiations we are going out and beyond what we can afford to give. Because of new relationships we have established here, we feel we can offer another 2 cents.

Party can confuse the evaluation of the settlement in various ways. This is sometimes accomplished by stating the settlement in terms other than those used throughout negotiations in order to obscure precisely what was conceded by whom.

> During the 1961 negotiations in farm equipment the company's methods of costing the package under consideration consistently produced higher figures than the union's methods. Once the agreement was signed, the tactical representation of the cost impact reversed. Thus, the union officials estimated that the union had done better than the auto settlement, and the company officials estimated that the union had done poorer than the auto settlement. Both wished to understate their own concessions. Because of the complexities in computing costs both could cite evidence to support their contention.

Another way by which the evaluation of the final settlement is confused is by incorporating in the settlement issues which were not crucial to final stages of negotiation and which do not make apparent who conceded what. Thus, sometimes Party requests that Opponent add something of no continuing value or little utility to either party to the package.

Party may portray the concession as a favor for which he ultimately expects to receive some value. Management might state, for example, that it is bailing the union and employees out of their mistake and that they are indebted accordingly.

This last point, portraying the revision as a favor, leads to the general observation that Party will often try to get as much mileage as he can out of making an important concession. For this reason he may simultaneously highlight the importance of the issue being abandoned and rationalize the act of abandoning it. In effect, the negotiator says, "I wanted this issue, and I'm only giving it up grudgingly." The point is that by highlighting the importance of the issue, the negotiator hopes to establish some kind of *quid pro quo*. The expectation may be that his opponent will drop something that is equally important. By pointing to the high utility of something being dropped, Party can hope to induce Opponent to drop something which has high disutility for Party. The main difficulty is that if Party had been forced to abandon a firm commitment, this may be indicative of his weakness. Therefore, he might not be in a very favorable position for getting an additional concession which he can call a *quid pro quo*. If that is the case, Party may simply rationalize his revision in position by citing some concession or benefit received from Opponent earlier.

# PART 3 | DILEMMAS OF DISTRIBUTIVE BARGAINING

In this concluding discussion of distributive bargaining we shall address ourselves to several aspects of strategical decision making. If we are to subject distributive bargaining to scientific study, we need to begin to delineate the areas in which explanation and prediction are possible. After we have examined the problem of how negotiators select specific tactics to perform a given tactical assignment, we shall identify several issues of a strategical nature. We are particularly interested in the dilemmas negotiators confront. Wherever possible we shall present predictive hypotheses about how certain conditions affect strategical decision making.

## Selecting among Alternate Tactics

We have reviewed each of about 10 tactical areas, which we contend are embraced by distributive bargaining. These areas are conceived in functional terms—each is comprised of those tactics which are believed to perform a certain function for the bargaining party. According to our analysis there are many different acts that may tend to perform the required function. How then does a negotiator *choose* among these acts which purportedly have the same or similar functions for the distributive bargain? Often the question is not which one of several tactics to utilize, but rather which combinations of the tactics related to an assignment one should utilize. Often the many tactics are not redundant but rather are supplementary.

We have not endeavored to treat in any systematic fashion these questions as they relate to each tactical area. However, it would appear that selecting among tactics listed for accomplishing any particular tactical assignment involves several considerations.

First, the institutional framework and the actual situation make some alternative tactics more appropriate or available to a party. Consider a direct survey of workers' opinions intended to produce information from which a company could make inferences about the union's resistance point. Such a tactic can be used more effectively where the population of the bargaining unit resides in a concentrated geographical area, minimizing the effort required to conduct interviews in the homes of workers. Moreover, such a survey is more appropriate for obtaining a measure of strength of interest about simple issues, such as wage increases or certain well-publicized benefit programs, and less appropriate for complex seniority or wage-classification issues.

Second, some tactics may conflict with other requirements of the distributive bargain. For instance, tactical behaviors designed to confuse the other negotiator in order that he might be induced to reveal more about his resistance point contain the risk that it might also cause him to make a resolute commitment earlier and more ambitiously than he otherwise would.

Third, some distributive tactics may be in conflict with the requirements of integrative bargaining, attitudinal structuring, or intraorganizational bargaining. For instance, for a company to include a union man on the bargaining team who could be helpful in picking up and analyzing clues from the behavior of the union team might also antagonize the union team and undermine the relationship, with perhaps ill effects also for integrative bargaining. This particular act would be especially provocative if the existing union-management relationship were one characterized by a low trust and a high militancy. This type of consideration—how distributive tactics influence other subprocesses—will be treated in a systematic way throughout the study.

## Issues in Bargaining Strategy

**Commitment Strategy.** Let us return to the strategy issue in distributive bargaining mentioned earlier; namely, at what point in the sequence of bargaining moves does one make his maximum commitment—one which is final and precise and which has important associated consequences?

In essence the alternate commitment strategies are as follows in their extreme formulation: (1) On the one hand, Party can state his final position at the outset, even before Opponent can indicate his own initial position. (2) On the other hand, Party can at the outset and then continuously through subsequent moves take only unclear or tentative positions along the bargaining spectrum until bargaining terminates, when Opponent indicates his own final position and leaves Party with the option of either taking it or leaving it. Strategies which approximate the first type we shall designate as strategies of "early firm commitment." Those which approximate the second type will be referred to as strategies of "gradually increasing commitment."

Some companies,[60] General Electric, for example, have adopted a strat-

[60] The issue also arises in international diplomacy—in some instances a country will set forth in relatively unambiguous terms and very early in the development of a crisis

egy of "factual bargaining," in which they make their "final offer first"; while others engage in "blue-sky bargaining," taking an obviously unrealistic position at first and gradually modifying their position in subsequent bargaining moves, at the same time increasing their resolution not to make further concessions.

Why should not the party with the first move commit himself to a position near the other's resistance point and thereby settle on terms most favorable to himself? We hypothesize that the following factors will bear on the choice of commitment strategies and that they will affect the rate at which Party becomes committed to a particular point on the bargaining spectrum: [61]

**Hypothesis 1** *The more knowledge Party has about the resistance point of Opponent, the fewer the bargaining moves before Party commits himself to a final position.* Recall that the "knowledge" is in fact usually derived from one of two sources: (a) clues from the bargaining table and (b) inferences based on information regarding Opponent's utility preferences or strike costs. When he has made these assessments, he is in a position to calculate the probability of obtaining each position within the settlement range. Then, depending upon his risk preference and general psychological orientation, he will commit himself to a particular position. Support for this proposition comes from the experimental work of Siegel and Fouraker. They found that when Party was given information about Opponent's payoffs, he tended to adjust his opening position, or gambit, closer to the final settlement point.[62] As a general matter, few negotiators obtain sufficient information in sufficient time about their own or Opponent's situations to adopt the early-firm-commitment strategy.

**Hypothesis 2** *The more understanding Party has about his own resistance point and the factors which combine to determine this point, the fewer the bargaining moves before Party commits himself to a final position.* The point here is that Party does not always think through in advance of the first bargaining move precisely how far he can go in accommodating Opponent. He depends upon the bargaining process to either (a) stimulate explicit thinking about this problem, or (b) generate more information about exact implications of the various possible outcomes. As we shall see later, Party often needs to (c) obtain more consensus within his own organization than he has at the outset of negotiations.

---

the solution or set of conditions they can tolerate, whereas in other instances the same country will be much more cautious in arriving at such a statement of what is tolerable; for example, one could probably distinguish between the strategies of the United States in the Korean, Berlin, Suez, Congo, and Vietnam crises along these lines.

[61] These propositions are being tested in a series of two-person bargaining experiments being conducted by W. H. Starbuck and R. E. Walton at Purdue University.

[62] Sidney Siegel and L. E. Fouraker, *Bargaining and Group Decision Making* (New York: McGraw-Hill Book Company, 1960), p. 94.

*Hypothesis 3 The more available to Party the tactical operations for convincing Opponent that Party will not under any circumstances revise his current position, the fewer bargaining moves before Party commits himself to a final position.* Devices for communicating and confirming commitments are not always equally available, and the lack of availability limits their use.

*Hypothesis 4 The more prominent the expected settlement position, the fewer bargaining moves before Party (and Opponent) commits himself to a final position.* If a particular position possesses a focal quality because of pattern settlements, etc., it is likely that the parties will converge rapidly, and the side having the more accurate perception will reach the position in fewer moves. This proposition has been supported by experimental work.[63]

*Hypothesis 5 The more available to Party the tactics for rationalizing the abandonment of a "final" commitment to Opponent, if necessary, the fewer bargaining moves before Party will make that apparently final commitment.* Like confirming tactics, the situation largely determines what rationalization tactics are available.

*Hypothesis 6 The greater the expectation on the part of Party that Opponent will become committed in a small number of moves, the fewer bargaining moves before Party commits himself to a final position.* The value of waiting for progressively more information diminishes if the other will become committed shortly.

*Hypothesis 7 The smaller the costs associated with a strike which results from mutually incompatible commitments, the fewer bargaining moves before Party commits himself to a final position.* The choice of strategy depends among other factors upon a negotiator's weighting of "loss of face" versus breakdown. The early-firm-commitment strategy minimizes the descent and hence the loss of face—it establishes bargaining credibility for future negotiations—but it maximizes the possibility of miscalculation and deadlock. On the other hand the gradually increasing-commitment strategy avoids the danger of taking an untenable position, but it involves considerable descent and, in that sense, loss of face.[64]

Later we shall explore other conditions which we believe affect the choice of commitment strategy; for example, we shall show how the requirements of integrative bargaining, the need to preserve a certain relationship between the parties, and the internal consensus process of one or both parties may constrain the use of an early-firm-commitment strategy. However, these hypotheses and the assumptions which underlie their for-

---

[63] M. L. Joseph and R. H. Willis, "An Experimental Analog to Two-party Bargaining," *Behavioral Science*, vol. 8, no. 2 (1963), pp. 117–127.

[64] G. L. Shackle, "The Nature of the Bargaining Process," in J. T. Dunlop (ed.), *The Theory of Wage Determination* (London: International Economic Association, Macmillan & Co., Ltd., 1957), pp. 292–314.

mulation can best be taken up after we have examined the three other subprocesses of labor negotiations.

**Modifying Utilities versus Commitments.** Although we do not intend to discuss all the strategical or important tactical issues raised by our analysis of the component activities and functions of distributive bargaining, one in particular needs further exploration: What conditions influence whether Party's bargaining strategies rely upon clarifying the basic utilities and strike costs impinging on the parties or upon executing commitment tactics?

According to the analysis in Part 2, making tactical commitments and making certain points prominent play a large role in bringing about a convergence in distributive bargaining. We indicated in Part 1 that this convergence also occurs as a result of attempts to influence perceptions of underlying utilities associated with the alternate outcomes. Thus, Party has available to him two types of influence mechanisms. Sometimes they are utilized in a way supplementary to each other, and sometimes they are considered as alternatives. A major resort to the more arbitrary commitment mechanism is often made only when the other influence mechanism shows little promise of success.

The mix of tactical operations between, on the one hand, those involving persuasion to modify the other's perceptions of underlying utilities and strike costs and, on the other hand, those involving commitment mechanisms may influence the nature of the type of negotiating outcome.[65]

*Hypothesis 8 Because the commitment mechanism which involves more arbitrary influence tends to create more tension, it is more likely to precipitate a breakdown in negotiations.* "Breakdown" refers to a nondeliberate bolting from the bargaining situation—to be distinguished from an outcome of "no agreement" at the customary deadline, an outcome which could occur after reliance on either mechanism.

The analysis can be carried a step further. Assuming an agreement is reached, the extent to which the parties have relied upon these two mechanisms (for achieving a convergence of their expectations and explicit bargaining positions) may have important consequences for their feelings of satisfaction about the ultimate decision and their future adherence to it in spirit and letter.

*Hypothesis 9 Satisfaction and compliance are greater under contracts in which reliance was relatively greater on manipulating perceptions of utilities and strike costs and less on commitment tactics.*

---

[65] An extremely significant point made by Carl Stevens in his analysis of negotiating tactics appears also to be applicable to the somewhat different distinction we make here between influence mechanisms. Stevens distinguishes between Class I tactics (those designed to induce Opponent to avoid his own position) and Class II tactics (those designed to reduce Opponent's opposition to Party's position). C. M. Stevens, *op. cit.,* p. 24.

# CHAPTER IV

# INTEGRATIVE BARGAINING MODEL

In Chapter I we suggested that labor negotiations comprised four inter-related processes—distributive bargaining, integrative bargaining, attitudinal structuring, and internal bargaining. The two preceding chapters have explored one of these processes, distributive bargaining. We have treated this particular process first, because, as the wage-setting mechanism, it related to the basic rationale for conducting labor negotiations. By completely abstracting this process from the total phenomenon, we were able to examine its internal logics; and by setting forth the tactical assignments which emerged from this examination, we have provided ourselves with an adequate basis for comparing the distributive process with the other processes involved in contract negotiations.

However, we are misleading if we imply that the distributive bargain is always the most important aspect of negotiations and that the requirements of that process invariably represent the most important criterion for all behavior at the bargaining table. Often, equally important objectives can be attained only through another process, integrative bargaining. Indeed it is rare when the agenda of labor negotiations does not include significant items which can be pursued only through some combination of the two processes.

The purpose of this chapter is to set forth a model of integrative bargaining. First we shall discuss and illustrate some of the agenda items which frequently are the subject of integrative bargaining. Next, we shall attempt to abstract the integrative process, detailing its internal aspects, such as defining the problem, searching for alternate solutions, and applying utility functions to compare solutions and to select a solution. In the next chapter we shall analyze an array of tactics commonly observed in negotiations strictly in terms of their implications for the integrative process. Finally, we shall focus on the many tactical dilemmas raised by the confluence of distributive and integrative bargaining. We shall discuss some of the ways in which the negotiator handles the mixed situation.

# PART 1 | AGENDA ITEMS AND INTEGRATIVE POTENTIAL

**Issues and Problems.** We referred to the subject matter of distributive bargaining as issues. The subject matter of integrative bargaining is problems. The two subprocesses involve dramatically different activities because they deal with quite different potential payoff structures. The distinction between the payoff structures which underlie issues and those which underlie problems was analyzed in detail in Chapter II. The contrasts can be summarized briefly. Issues involve a fixed total objective value which can be allocated between the parties in various shares or proportions. Problems, on the other hand, are agenda items which contain possibilities for greater or lesser amounts of value which can be made available to the two parties.

In its extreme, or pure, form an issue would require that whatever gains are available to one necessarily entails a corresponding and equal sacrifice by the other. Similarly a problem in its purest form would be an agenda item for which the parties would assign the same preference ordering to all possible outcomes and about which the two parties would be equally concerned. For an issue the interests of the two parties are diametrically opposed; for a problem the interests are identical or completely coincidental.

In actual fact, few items correspond to these pure types. Thus, we have tended to employ issues, problems, and mixed items in a somewhat more relaxed fashion. Issues are those items in which gains to one *tend* to involve corresponding sacrifices for the other. Our discussion and illustrations of distributive bargaining have applied to the broader conception of *predominantly* conflict situations. Distributive bargaining tactics were viewed as instrumental to the extent that the payoff structure approached the pure "issue" type.

Similarly, the concept of problem covers more than the situation in which gains available to one necessarily allow corresponding and equal gains by the other. It is applied to situations in which the total payoff is varying sum in a significant way, even though both parties may not share equally in the joint gain, and indeed one may even suffer minor inconveniences in order to provide substantial gains for the other. Presumably, when the direct results of a problem solution are high benefit–low sacrifice, the slightly inconvenienced party can receive some side payment or reciprocal treatment in another problem area. However, this gets ahead of the story—here we are interested in the fact that for certain agenda items some outcomes allow significantly larger joint payoffs than other outcomes do, without concerning ourselves with the allocation of these payoffs between the parties.

We complete the spectrum by defining a mixed agenda item as one in which there are both significant issue aspects and problem aspects and where there is more than token conflict potential and integrative potential. We shall treat the mixed items in detail in the next chapter as a part of the discussion of the dilemmas of distributive and integrative bargaining.

Issues, problems, and mixed items have different types of outcomes. Issues result in compromise solutions. Problems result in integrative solutions in some degree. Mixed items can result in either compromise or integrative outcomes, depending upon the orientation of the negotiators and their tactical approach to the agenda item.

The distinction made here between compromise and integration is similar to that made by other observers of joint decision making.

> The conflict in this case was constructive. And this was because, instead of compromising, they sought a way of integrating. Compromise does not create, it deals with what already exists; integration creates something new. . . .[1]

> The agreement involved in compromise is to be distinguished from that involved in integration. In the former case, each party is able to identify the precise extent of his losses and gains; in the latter, new alternatives are accepted of such a kind as to render it extremely difficult to discern the balance between concessions made and concessions received.[2]

**Integrative Potential.** The range of situations assumed by the integrative bargaining model and tactics includes agenda items of two types. In the first, one (or more) possible resolution(s) of the agenda item by itself offers both parties a gain in absolute terms over their respective positions in the *status quo;* for such a resolution neither party experiences any loss.

---

[1] Mary Parker Follett, *Dynamic Administration: The Collected Papers of Mary Parker Follett,* H. C. Metcalf and L. Urwick (eds.) (New York: Harper & Row, Publishers, Incorporated, 1942), pp. 34–35.

[2] H. D. Lasswell, "Compromise," *Encyclopedia of the Social Sciences,* vol. 4 (New York: The Macmillan Company, 1937), pp. 147–149.

This may mean that the utility functions of the two parties are identical or parallel, but this need not be the case. The necessary condition is that at least one arrangement different from the *status quo* would allow each to move to a more favorable position on his relevant utility curve. These absolutely integrative solutions to an agenda item may not be obvious to the parties, but if in an objective sense they exist, the situation is said to be of this first type.

The second type of integrative situation is less clear cut. None of the possible solutions of a given problem permit improvement upon the *status quo* for both parties. We have in mind a situation in which the many possible solutions represent widely varying sacrifice-benefit ratios, but where one solution involves no more than token sacrifice. Thus, the parties must determine the best of the partially integrative solutions.

We can illustrate situations that have high integrative potential by discussing some common problem areas and alternate solutions in collective bargaining. Agenda items involving strictly economic values are much less likely to contain integrative possibilities than are items referring to rights and obligations of the parties.

It is just a fact of economic life that "money is money." With money, one side's gain is the other side's loss. Money can only be divided into units; it cannot be reformulated into an arrangement that may be an improvement for both sides. Thus, inherent integrative potential is more apt to be found in qualitative issues—in matters that involve the rights and obligations of the parties. To quote a participant in the Humans Relations Committee in steel: ". . . the joint study approach is least effective when applied to wages, very useful on fringes, and has its greatest future promise on 'job security' issues." [3] Consequently most of the following examples fall in the area of rights and obligations, and many pertain to job security. We have organized the examples around such collective bargaining matters.

***Individual job security and management flexibility.*** Often the provisions of the contract achieve some measure of one of these values only at the expense of the other value. For every increment in employee job security provided by seniority rights, management has incurred a corresponding loss in flexibility in managing manpower or operations. In these cases the bargaining outcome is fundamentally and strictly a compromise between the two values. However, parties sometimes achieve considerable integration of these twin interests in job security and management flexibility, in part because the unique circumstances allow for this possibility and in part because of imaginative and diligent problem solving. In the following

[3] Bureau of National Affairs, *Labor Relations Reporter* no. 198 (Washington, D.C., Oct. 10, 1963), p. 2.

discussion we shall analyze several facets of the situation and provide illustrations of solutions both of a relatively compromise and relatively integrative character.

One aspect of providing job security involves arrangements about "competitive" rights, namely, the rules for allocating jobs among competing employees. Consider the solution adopted by the parties to one negotiation in the meat-packing industry:

> Many plants were being closed. New plants were being opened at distant points. The union wanted employees from the old plants to be able to move to the new plants with full seniority. The company, which often established a new plant because of inducements provided by local officials, was anxious to hire employees from the adjoining area. In one situation it was proposed that the old employees carry one-half of their seniority. The arrangement seemed acceptable to both sides since it protected somewhat the vested interest of the older employees and at the same time did not give them an overwhelming edge on newer employees for whom management felt considerable responsibility.

The solution providing for old employees to carry one-half of their accumulated seniority to new plants probably represented a good balancing of the interests of the parties. Nevertheless, it would appear to have been more of a compromise than an integrative answer to the underlying concerns of the parties.

A somewhat different problem arose in the agricultural equipment industry in this general area of competitive job rights and provides another illustrative solution.

> In the closing down of the McCormick Works of International Harvester, the following issue arose: As soon as the company announced the shutdown of the plant, the union wanted employees released so that they could apply for work at other International Harvester plants. For its part, the company desired to keep many of these employees since they were necessary in the phasing-out operation. The solution reached established a "pegged" seniority date at other plants, if at any point after the company announced its plans to shut down the plant a job opened at other plants which the given employee could fill. Thus, the employee continued on in the plant being terminated, all the time acquiring seniority at the plant to which he would be eventually transferred.

By the imaginative arrangement devised in this case both job security for employees and management efficiency were achieved. This solution apparently was more integrative than compromise.

The job-security–management-flexibility question often takes the form of an issue about the relative weight of length of service and ability in layoffs. The solution to this problem in one case took the following form:

> The union had demanded that more weight be given to experience in promoting people in the clerical area. The company had been placing primary reliance upon test results which the union claimed favored the junior employees. A satisfactory solution was reached when the company proposed that a certain number of points, pro-rated according to service, be added to each test score; thereby achieving a blend of ability and seniority.

Although this represented a compromise of the two competing criteria for layoff decisions, it provided an imaginative mechanism for implementing the compromise—a procedure in which the discretion of supervision was limited.

It is useful to examine how the same type of problem has been handled differently in the case of one professional engineering union.

> The layoff formula in the union contract incorporates (a) retention ratings based on the company's evaluation of worth (this rating being subject to the grievance procedure) and (b) points accumulated for months of continuous service. Supervision assigns the retention ratings to employees during March and September of each year, using a range from 60 to 120 points. The supervisors are further required to discuss the rating with each employee. Lists of retention ratings are made up for each job classification, ranking employees on the basis of the average of their last two retention ratings, and are distributed to union representatives after each rating. In the event of a layoff, only ratings established more than 60 days prior to the date of layoff are used, unless there are no prior ratings for an individual.

> When a layoff situation develops, the employees with the lowest retention ratings are those termed "eligible" for layoff. The number on the list of "eligibles" is somewhat greater (usually 20%) than the number actually to be laid off. This is where length of service counts. For each month of seniority of each of the employees on the eligible list one point is added to that employee's average retention rating, producing a "modified" rating. The names on the eligible list are then rearranged in the order of their modified rating, and layoffs are made from the bottom of the list.[4]

In what ways was this somewhat complex procedure an integrative solution for the parties? In order to answer this question, it is absolutely

[4] See R. E. Walton, *The Impact of the Professional Engineering Union* (Boston: Division of Research, Graduate School of Business Administration, Harvard University, 1961), p. 187.

essential to be able to state the underlying concerns. The engineers wanted equity in their present employment, that is, they desired rights based on tenure and other specified job inputs as protection against arbitrary release. In addition, they desired predictability—they wanted to know in advance what their status would be with respect to a future layoff, however secure or vulnerable that status might be. Strict seniority would have been an answer but an unnecessary one. In a sense the engineers were less concerned about the precise criteria used to govern the order of layoff than that these criteria be stated and applied equally and in a way open to appeal; they were less concerned about influencing their status than about knowing it in advance so that they could act on this knowledge. For its part, management was most concerned about being forced to make a decision based on factors other than ability. In an innovative manner characteristic of the engineering participants involved, the parties' solution allowed an individual to know where he stood in advance of a layoff but allowed the most heavy weighting to be placed on ability factors.

In another case in which few senior employees were being promoted because of a lack of the requisite skills, the parties transformed an issue into a problem.

> At first the company and the union were in dispute about why so few senior employees were being promoted. One solution offered by employees was that seniority be given more weight in promotions. After considerable discussion, it was agreed that the company would inaugurate a "self-help" program for employees. It would pay for outside education and do everything possible to help the employees improve their skills in advance of promotion opportunities.

By this solution the union achieved its objectives of improving the promotional opportunities of senior employees and management retained its preferred criteria for making promotion decisions. It is not clear whether the solution enabled both parties to gain over the *status quo* (that would depend on how management valued the improved opportunities for senior employees), but the solution appeared to be at least a high-benefit–low-sacrifice one.

An important matter which has produced a number of innovations is the question about the rights of displaced employees.[5] The Brookings study reports on the area-availability arrangement used in southern Michigan. This plan is used in the Ford Motor Company and enables a pres-

---

[5] Several reviews have been published which summarize the innovations in this area: Derek Bok and Max D. Kossoris, *Methods of Adjusting to Automation and Technological Change* (Washington, D.C.: U.S. Department of Labor, no date); and *Recent Collective Bargaining and Technological Change*, BLS Report 266 (Washington, D.C.: U.S. Department of Labor, 1964).

ently employed worker to have priority over a new worker. Often the company's interest is coincident with that of the union when the skills of the displaced employees are needed in the new plant. "The plan did not provide interplant bumping rights, but it established a preferential hiring policy and therefore it was a part of a system of enhancing seniority rights." [6]

A number of special retraining programs have been developed to help the employee who has been displaced from his former plant. An example is the work done under the Armour Automation Fund. The many efforts that the parties have pursued to meet the needs of displaced employees while keeping the financial liabilities of the employers within limits have been described and analyzed by Thomas Kennedy.[7]

*Preserving jobs and management efficiency.* Often the arrangements which serve the union's interest in preserving jobs entail a corresponding sacrifice to the company in terms of its operational efficiency. Subcontracting is a matter which has important implications for these two interests.

The parties often invoke incompatible principles in the area of subcontracting.[8] The starting point for the union would be to prohibit subcontracting. The starting point for the company would be to claim unilateral and unfettered rights. Stated in this way, the matter is an issue and is subject only to compromise.

However, by exploring the various reasons which underlie the parties' interests in the issue, new possibilities may emerge. The union's reasons can include the following: (1) to protect normal employment opportunities for its members, (2) to preserve the particular union's jurisdiction and strength, (3) to enlarge work opportunities of its members, (4) to combat escaping from unionism, and (5) to protect union standards against competition. The reasons for the company's interest in subcontracting include some of the following: (6) more rapid completion, (7) more adequate skills, equipment, or plant, and (8) lower cost. Unless the company's reasons also include specifically antiunion objectives, such as to reduce employment opportunities for union members, to escape unionism, or to subvert union standards; and unless the union has comparable anti-company intentions, there is probably some integrative potential.

Let us turn to integrative potential. There are different ways in which either absolute prohibition of subcontracting or unfettered freedom can be modified. Management's rights could be qualified by procedures it must

[6] S. H. Slichter, J. J. Healy, and E. R. Livernash, *The Impact of Collective Bargaining on Management* (Washington, D.C.: The Brookings Institution, 1960), p. 166.

[7] Thomas Kennedy, *Automation Funds and Displaced Workers* (Boston: Division of Research, Graduate School of Business Administration, Harvard University, 1962).

[8] Slichter, Healy, and Livernash, *op. cit.*, pp. 280–316.

follow preliminary to a subcontracting decision, such as prior notification to the union, consultation, mutual agreement, etc., or they can be modified by specifying conditions under which subcontracting is permitted, i.e., by indicating decision criteria. Whichever of these two general methods of limiting management's rights represents the most integrative solution will be the one which provides maximum protection to the union (in the terms 1 to 5 listed above) for the minimum sacrifice of flexibility and efficiency on the part of the company (in terms of 6 to 8 listed above).

Now suppose that the parties explore the second method, that is, the conditions under which management is permitted or is not permitted to subcontract. Several criteria are sometimes incorporated into contract clauses governing subcontracting: Are present employees working a short work week, a full work week, or are they working overtime? Do present employees possess or lack the requisite skills? Is work to be performed on or off the premises? Again, in order to achieve the best integration of interests, the parties must subject each criterion to the test of the particular utilities of the parties in the situation. Often a specific criterion carefully worded affords the workers precisely the protection they are most concerned about without any sacrifice of the flexibility wanted by management.

Other solutions to the conflict between jobs and efficiency can be found in a number of the cost-reduction or incentive plans that have been developed over the years. Under the West Coast Mechanization Fund the union agreed to let the shipping companies do away with work rules in return for an annual contribution of $5 million to a fund from which the union would pay for short-work-week, early-retirement, and other benefits that might be needed because of the increased mechanization. This solution gave the union an alternative to a blind and opportunistic opposition to management's attempts to automate, which would indeed have achieved a slowing down of mechanization but at higher cost to the employers. Similarly, the solution contained obligations for management and benefits for displaced employees which were predictable and therefore could be planned for by both the firms and the worker households involved.

Sometimes the solution is much more positive and involves active cooperation on the part of the union to save the jobs and help the finances of the business. Such is the case in the Scanlon installations and in the suggestion systems which were established on the railroads in the early 1920s.[9]

*Expanded benefits and limited costs.* In the union's quest for new programs and benefits there are bound to be many points of conflict. Sometimes these are inherent in the union's and company's objectives. Other times the agenda items are amenable to integrative solutions.

[9] *Ibid.*, pp. 292–293 and 841–878.

During the 1955 automobile negotiations the UAW vigorously pressed for some form of guaranteed annual wage. The demand was important to the union because of the need to take care of unemployed automobile workers. The specific form of the program advanced by the UAW conflicted with several of management's objectives, but eventually an accommodative and quite integrative arrangement was worked out—one that limited the company's cost liability, coordinated the Supplemental Unemployment Benefit plan with state unemployment compensation, and kept the level of benefits at a point where there was still some incentive to work. These had been the critical concerns of management. From the union's point of view, the plan went a long way toward securing the objectives of the originally proposed GAW and was regarded as an important union achievement.

A good example of maximum union gains within cost limitations occurred in one International Harvester negotiation.

> The union entered bargaining with over 100 inequity demands. The company had only a limited amount of money to spend on classification adjustments. The solution which was reached was to emphasize *progress* toward a master book. While the union did not gain a great deal of money, it did gain satisfaction on many small issues which in a qualitative sense moved it along toward a master book. For its part, the company met its objective of not spending too much money on the inequity problem.

In the above example there was no "elegant" solution to the whole problem area under consideration, but elements of the problem could be handled in such a way to allow for mutual gain. The company held an objective of increasing the rationality and stability of the job classification system. For its part, the union desired to minimize inequities and unfavorable comparisons that might be made by local groups. The two parties differed about what specific adjustments would bring different wage rates into proper alignment. The master book was an integrative solution in that it enabled each side to achieve the more important of its objectives. Beyond that, however, the parties continued in conflict. For example, the objectives each held about specific adjustments were not always amenable to an integrative solution. In addition, the parties held different points of view on the question of how adjustments would be made in the future. The company desired to work toward the master book on a systematic or industrial engineering basis. In other words they wanted to consider inequity problems on their merits. On the other hand, the union wanted a means by which it could stay involved in the settlement of classification disputes. In this respect no integrative solution was found, although the adoption of a formal job-evaluation scheme might have satisfied the procedural requirements of both sides.

*Institutional security.* The area of union security provides the substance for many issues that occasionally can be converted into problems. Most unions press adamantly for union shop arrangements. Most companies resist requiring their employees to join the union as a condition of employment. Here is a conflict between the "free-ride" argument and the "right-to-work" argument. In some situations the agency shop, wherein the employee pays a fee to the union for the bargaining services provided, has been adopted and found satisfactory by both sides.

A study of collective bargaining by the National Industrial Conference Board illustrates another way in which a mutually beneficial arrangement was realized.

> The company recognizes that as exclusive bargaining agent in this bargaining unit the union is obligated to represent nonunion as well as union members and that in carrying the burden of contract administration, the union performs some service for all employees in the bargaining unit. Therefore, in recognition of these things, and in consideration for the pledge of the union that its officers or members will not intimidate or coerce employees into joining the union, and in the interest of harmony, the company agrees when new employees have completed their probationary period as provided in this contract, the personnel manager or his representative will place in the hands of such employee a copy of the union contract together with a letter from the company recommending that the new employee join the union.[10]

Occasionally important goals of the two negotiating parties are such that they can be accommodated by the same means. An instance of this is provided by the first postwar negotiations between the UAW and the Ford Motor Company. The years 1941 to 1946 had been marked by an extremely large number of wildcat strikes in Ford, a fact which had been experienced by the company as a considerable handicap to its production efforts. An important objective of the company in the 1946 negotiations was to establish a means for reducing the number of unauthorized work stoppages. The union officials, for their part, had been embarrassed and were less effective on several occasions because they had not been able to maintain internal discipline within their ranks. Although they objected to the company's early proposals for curtailing wildcat strikes and could not show open support for the company's intentions, these union officials were interested in establishing more central control in this area. Consequently, the parties were able to devise a set of procedures and penalties for unauthor-

[10] J. J. Bambrick and M. P. Dorbandt, *Preparing for Collective Bargaining,* Studies in Personnel Policy no. 172 (New York: National Industrial Conference Board, 1959), pp. 14–15.

ized work stoppages which allowed both union and management to largely attain their respective objectives. The eventual means chosen represented for both an improvement over the *status quo*.

Other problem areas occasionally provide an opportunity for mutual improvement over the *status quo* if the parties can just find the right solution. Allocation of overtime, when it has been troublesome for both parties, might provide such potential. Absenteeism is another such area.

# PART 2 | THE INTEGRATIVE PROCESS MODEL

Thus far we have been talking about the types of situations which contain integrative potential and about the characteristics of the outcome of integrative bargaining. At this point we turn to the process itself. Integrative potential can be exploited only if it is first discovered, its nature explored, and it is then acted upon by the parties. Before getting into the techniques and mechanics of how this is done, let us consider an abstract model of the process, essentially a problem-solving model involving three steps: [11]

1. Identifying the problem

2. Searching for alternate solutions and their consequences

3. Preference ordering of solutions and selecting a course of action

**Steps in the Model.** The model is a statement of the steps of problem solving and the necessary conditions for these steps to occur. In a rough and oversimplified way, we might say that the three steps parallel the sequence through which bargaining usually passes. The early phase of negotiation, possibly even the prenegotiation phase, involves the uncovering, identifying, and understanding of problems. As negotiations progress, the attention turns toward the search for possible solutions to these problems. Finally, under the pressure of a deadline, decisions are reached.

A few elaborating words can be said about each step. The process is also diagrammed in Figure 4-1.

*Step 1.* Step 1 involves a maximum exchange of information about the problems perceived by each party in order that these problems be identified and defined in their essentials. The problem is formulated in a clear

[11] H. A. Simon, "A Behavioral Model of Rational Choice," *The Quarterly Journal of Economics*, vol. 69 (February, 1955), pp. 99–118.

### Figure 4-1
### Joint Problem-solving Process

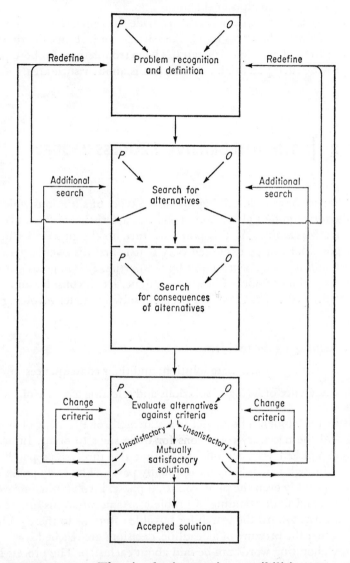

and accurate manner. That is, the integrative possibilities are exploited only if potential is first discovered through the identification of mutual problems. The way the problem is defined will have great influence on how operational the criteria used to evaluate solutions are. The model assumes redefinition of the problem as the problem-solving process continues, either as search fails to generate acceptable solutions or as new information suggests a connection with other problems not originally considered.

*Step 2.* The model assumes that alternative courses of action (potential solutions) are not immediately apparent but rather have to be discovered or invented. It also assumes that the full consequences of a course of action are again not obvious; instead they have to be inferred from an analysis of all the facts available.[12]

Therefore, this step involves thorough and accurate gathering of information about alternatives and their consequences. The parties attempt to be imaginative in perceiving alternatives and persistent in exploring the fullest range of alternative solutions. Invention and creativity are essential in order for appropriate arrangements to be developed for coping with the problems.

*Step 3.* This step entails the identification of the larger sum of net utilities possible in the situation. The parties attempt to be as clear as possible about their basic utility functions, combining these in some way in order to arrive at the final solution. The model assumes that neither of the following procedures and decision rules govern the selection of a solution: (a) the parties have a fixed idea at the outset about how much to search before selecting the "best" solution; or (b) the parties have a fixed idea about what would be a minimally acceptable solution and search until they discover or invent an "acceptable" solution. Instead the parties engage in successive comparisons among alternatives and between a given alternative and a tentative idea of an acceptable solution. Aspiration level dynamics connect one's latest definition of what would be minimally successful with one's current estimate of what is feasible in a way that governs one's future choice between whether to (a) accept the best solution generated thus far or (b) continue to search for a more acceptable solution with or without a redefinition of the problem. It should be obvious that in joint problem solving there may be a lack of coordination between persons in this choice and in other procedural phases of the process.

**Facilitating Conditions for Problem Solving.** Effectiveness of the problem-solving process depends upon the presence of several psychological and informational states: motivation, information and language, and trust and a supportive climate.

*Motivation.* The parties must have the motivation to solve the problem. The participants must regard the problem as significant enough to take time to discuss. When there are differences between the motivational states of the parties, they encounter certain difficulties in the process.

[12] J. G. March and H. A. Simon, *Organizations* (New York: John Wiley & Sons, Inc., 1958), pp. 137–172.

To the extent that the parties are exploring a problem in which it is inherent that some (low) amount of sacrifice by one will be associated with (considerable) gain on the part of the other, there will also be tendencies along the following lines: to disagree about how the problem should be defined, to disagree about what criteria for settlement will be considered and what weight will be given to these criteria, to suppress or disregard certain alternatives which might be considered, and to withhold certain facts relevant to understanding the consequences which will flow from certain alternatives under consideration.

Even when the two parties are motivated in the same direction, differences between Party and Opponent in the strength of motivation lead to some lack of coordination in the following ways: The party with higher motivation will make a relatively greater attempt to make relevant information available at the negotiating table; that party will also tend to prefer to engage in search efforts for a longer period of time; and that party will develop higher standards for an acceptable solution.

*Information and language.* Those participating in the process must have access to the information relevant to each step and be authorized to use it. They must also have language and other means and skills of communication adequate to exchange this relevant information.

When information is low, the result will be a less adequate definition of the problem (e.g., a definition less in terms of basic concerns and more in terms of solution characteristics which are easily communicated); fewer alternatives will be generated; and the potential consequences of these alternatives will be less explored. Finally, when the information is relatively low, the parties will produce relatively low-grade solutions. Under conditions of low motivation *and* low information, the parties will engage in relatively short-duration search processes. When the motivation is high and information is low, the search process will be of relatively longer duration.

In general, the effect of inadequate language, that is, when the meanings of words are not shared fully, is similar to that of low information, described above. However, one additional consequence is that a lack of shared meanings makes implementing the agreed-upon solution more difficult. There are more likely to be problems in compliance or in coordinated implementation.

Because information is crucial to problem solving, there is relatively great emphasis on fact-finding processes. Because the parties may not have confidence in their joint efforts to gather unbiased information, given the more general posture they must take in distributive bargaining, they may choose to delegate aspects of this activity to a third party, to technicians from their own organization, or to a subcommittee of their negotiating team not centrally involved in the distributive bargaining activities.

Communication patterns available to the group can have important influence on the effectiveness of problem-solving efforts. In problem solving, communication tends to be among all members present rather than confined to a single spokesman for each side. One can conceive of the alternative communication networks adopted by the parties in a way diagrammed in Figures 4-2*a* and *b*.

| Figure 4-2*a* | Figure 4-2*b* |
|:---:|:---:|
| 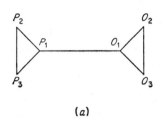 | 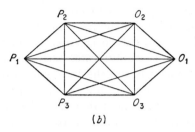 |
| (*a*) | (*b*) |
| Communication is free within Party and Opponent teams; only chief spokesmen $P_1$ and $O_1$ communicate across team boundaries. | All possible communication channels are open among six participants forming one problem-solving group. |

The level of performance is definitely related to the communication channels for small groups. Experiments have shown the superiority of networks allowing for channels between more group members over those between a limited number.[13] In particular, one study found that the opportunity for free feedback (questions and other responses to the communicator) produced greater accuracy in communication, led to better rapport among the communicators, and resulted in greater confidence in the decisions that were made.[14]

***Trust and supportive climate.*** A supportive and trusting climate facilitates joint problem solving. Defensive and low-trust atmospheres inhibit the process. A supportive climate is marked by encouragement and freedom to behave spontaneously without fear of sanctions. A defensive atmosphere is one in which the parties perceive threat and risks associated with provisional behavior. Why is climate important?

First, when support is lacking and a person anticipates threat, he behaves defensively, diverting energy from the problem-solving task.

[13] E.g., G. A. Heise and G. A. Miller, "Problem Solving by Small Groups Using Various Communications Nets," *Journal of Abnormal and Social Psychology*, vol. 46 (July, 1951), pp. 327–335. For a review of studies of the effect of communication network on problem solving, see A. P. Hare, *Handbook of Small Group Research* (New York: The Free Press of Glencoe, 1962).

[14] H. J. Leavitt and R. A. Mueller, "Some Effects of Feedback on Communication," *Human Relations*, vol. 4, no. 4 (1951), pp. 401–410.

> The person who behaves defensively, even though he also gives some attention to the common task, devotes an appreciable portion of his energy to defending himself. Besides talking about the topic, he thinks about . . . how he may win, dominate, impress, or escape punishment, and/or how he may avoid or mitigate a perceived or an anticipated attack.[15]

Defensive behavior on the part of this person tends to create similarly defensive postures in others, and the ensuing circular response becomes increasingly destructive of problem solving.

Second, if trust is lacking, the sender will control information or deliberately miscommunicate. Each participant must have sufficient trust that the other will use the information only for purposes of problem solving and not for some other purpose (such as distributive bargaining). It has been demonstrated that an individual will distort his opinions and the facts available to him in communicating them to a person he distrusts.[16]

Third, trust and support lead to more complete and more accurate reception of problem-relevant communications. The more supportive the climate, "the less the receiver reads into the communication distorted loadings which arise from projections of his own anxieties, motives, and concerns. As defenses are reduced, the receivers become more able to concentrate on the structure, the content, and the cognitive meaning of the message." [17] Experimental evidence of the biasing effect of competitiveness and defensiveness on comprehension of another person's position is provided by Blake and Mouton.[18]

Fourth, support allows for more experimentation with attitudes and ideas and more testing and retesting of perceptions and opinions. Problem solving produces more thorough and innovative solutions if there is a phase "of stimulation and sharing, during which ideas get kicked around, elaborated, and defended—this is the process of finding new meanings that would not occur to one by oneself." [19] As Stock and Thelen point out, "To engage in this process with others requires conditions such that one not only can take the risk of sticking his neck out but will, in fact, be rewarded for so doing. . . ." [20]

[15] J. R. Gibb, "Defensive Communication," *Journal of Communication,* vol. 11 (September, 1961), pp. 141–148.

[16] E.g., see G. D. Mellinger, "Interpersonal Trust as a Factor in Communication," *Journal of Abnormal and Social Psychology,* vol. 52, no. 3 (1956), pp. 304–309.

[17] Gibb, *op. cit.,* p. 142.

[18] R. R. Blake and J. S. Mouton, "Comprehension of Own and Outgroup Positions under Intergroup Competition," *Journal of Conflict Resolution,* vol. 5 (September, 1961), pp. 304–310.

[19] Dorothy Stock and H. A. Thelen, *Emotional Dynamics and Group Culture,* Research Training Series no. 2 (Washington, D.C.: National Training Laboratories, 1958), p. 257.

[20] *Ibid.,* p. 257.

Fifth, participants who are threatened and who experience anxiety suffer a loss in efficiency in processing the information they receive. They may, as individuals, show a loss in their ability to abstract and in other flexibilities of intellectual functioning.[21]

Some caution is required in relating conditions of trust and support to effectiveness in problem solving. We are convinced that some minimum level of trust and support is a precondition to the process—for the reasons enumerated above. However, there is no clear evidence that a completely harmonious context is the one most productive for problem solving. Consider the finding of one experimental study which suggests the positive stimulation value of a degree of competition:

> When the system of emotional control is constant, groups with a primary valency to *fight* differ from the others in their ability to dig into a problem, to raise issues, and to settle them in one way or another. Their products show the widest range of ideas employed in problem solution, a high level of specificity within a flexible organization, much attention to causation, and a high amount of emotional involvement and commitment to act on their proposed solutions.[22]

While moderate amounts of conflict may produce an optimum climate for problem solving, this ingredient is almost automatically provided when this process occurs in the context of negotiations. Hence Party's task is invariably that of reducing conflict and defensiveness.

[21] E. G. Beier, "The Effect of Induced Anxiety on Flexibility of Intellectual Functioning," *Psychological Monographs*, vol. 65, no. 9 (1951), pp. 3–26.

[22] J. C. Glidewell, "Work-Emotionality Characteristics of Total Group and Their Relation to Group Problem Solving," in Stock and Thelen, *op. cit.*, p. 126.

# CHAPTER V

# INTEGRATIVE BARGAINING TACTICS

The implications of the problem-solving model might be succinctly stated: For optimum results in integrative bargaining situations, Party must induce the maximum exchange of information relative to mutual problems, so that the problems are identified and defined in their essentials, the fullest range of alternative solutions are explored, and the solutions reached represent the relatively higher joint gains possible in the situation. Party can facilitate this process by increasing the motivation of Opponent to solve the problem, by ensuring that the relevant information is available to the two negotiators, by facilitating communication between them, and by structuring the situation to allow for trust and emotional support between them.

While the integrative and distributive processes are related and are sometimes difficult to separate in actual contract negotiations, it should be remembered that conceptually they are very distinct. As we shall see later in this chapter, the techniques for fostering the integrative process are generally the reverse of the techniques for implementing the distributive process. Typically, in both processes the parties start with differences in viewpoints, perceptions, and tentatively preferred solutions. In both processes they are seeking to realize the most satisfaction possible. But the means and manner by which they settle these differences and obtain the most satisfaction possible out of the interaction are quite different. The implementing techniques for these two processes generally stand in an antithetical relationship.

In Part 1 of this chapter, we first examine the tactics which implement the three steps of the integrative process and then turn to the tactics and mechanics relative to establishing the necessary conditions for the process to function.

In Part 2, we treat the dilemmas associated with mixed agenda items and analyze the mutually interfering nature of the tactical operations involved in distributive and integrative bargaining.

# PART 1 | TACTICAL ASSIGNMENTS

## Identifying the Problem

In this decision process one party and then both parties recognize that an agenda item or some combination of items has integrative possibilities. This entails an exchange of information about one's own concerns and one's perceptions of the situation. Party endeavors to get at the genuine underlying concerns and to state these concerns as problems as accurately and as meaningfully as possible. In bringing this about, several tactical matters are involved.

*Timing of negotiations.* Problems are most easily understood when the negotiators are close to them. This argues for frequent negotiations or at least for the ability to convene negotiations whenever a problem arises. Several companies have adopted open-ended bargaining, wherein, at the request of either side, negotiations can be inaugurated. Rather than postponing the solution of a problem until the expiration of the agreement, the parties deal with the matter as soon as possible. The Rogers Company of Rogers, Connecticut, has been a strong proponent of this approach to bargaining.[1]

In many respects, the criteria for effective grievance handling also apply to integrative bargaining. The experience of the UAW and International Harvester in modifying grievance procedures, viz., on-the-spot discussions, quick handling, no written records, etc.,[2] is relevant to the process of identifying problems in integrative bargaining.

*Agenda.* The matter of determining the negotiation agenda has important implications for integrative bargaining. The integrative bargaining model would require that the parties attempt to include those items which contain good potential for increasing combined utility. It seems clear that strictly from the viewpoint of increasing the opportunities for exploiting

[1] "The Story of a Pioneer in Crisis-free Bargaining," *Business Management* (March, 1964), p. 43.

[2] See R. B. McKersie and W. W. Shropshire, Jr., "Avoiding Written Grievances: A Successful Program," *The Journal of Business*, vol. 35 (April, 1962), pp. 135–152.

low-sacrifice–high-benefit situations, Party would include a large number of items on the agenda.[3]

However, there are limitations to this general rule. The parties would want to avoid having an overwhelming number—so that the negotiators are not overloaded and do not need to devote too much time sorting through items to the detriment of genuine exploration of particular items. The items presented by Party would reflect the screening out of (1) those items not of genuine concern to himself and (2) those which he knows represent imbalance or little utility to himself and great disutility to Opponent. Party advances items he knows to represent some sacrifice to himself if promising considerable benefit to Opponent. Items which have potential for integration rather than those which have considerably less such potential but are slightly more important to Party are selected.

*How the agenda item is stated.* Does it make any difference how Party presents the item? We think that this matter does have implications for integrative bargaining.

Are subjects raised by Party by stating them in terms of "the problem he experiences" or the "solution he proposes"? The former contemplates and allows for more integrative bargaining.[4] Consider the contrasting approaches which might be taken by a union bothered about the matters of internal stability and control over the membership. The union can enter bargaining and frankly talk about the internal union problems. Or it can enter bargaining with the demand for a union shop. The first approach focuses on a *problem,* the second approach on a *demand;* the first approach talks frankly about the union's needs, and the second approach may even obscure the real needs; and the first approach does not prescribe the solution, while the second approach formulates the answer.

Consider an illustration from one negotiation. A relatively integrative solution was found only when the parties directed their attention to their underlying concerns.

> In the clerical area the parties initially seemed to be in opposition about tests. The company was opposed to their abandonment, and the union was demanding that they be dropped. Toward the end of the negotiation both sides were talking about constructing tests which achieved what the union wanted, namely, tests that were more in line with the practical aspects of the job, and which enabled the company to avoid any drastic compromise of the testing program.

---

[3] L. E. Allen, "Games Bargaining: A Proposed Application of the Theory of Games to Collective Bargaining," *The Yale Law Journal,* vol. 65 (April, 1956), pp. 679–693.

[4] N. R. F. Maier, *Problem-solving Discussions and Conferences* (New York: McGraw-Hill Book Company, 1963), p. 63.

A somewhat related distinction is whether the problem or a recommended solution is stated in terms of abstract principles or in terms of specifics. In integrative bargaining a party can fruitfully explore the agenda item in the specifics of the problem under consideration.

To argue in general about whether brotherhood, equality, job security, management's right to schedule the work, and industrial democracy are practicable and desirable often means that neither knows what the other is talking about. In some cases apparently divergent views are eliminated by converting a discussion of principle into one of amount.

> During recent negotiations the union demanded that certain incentive allowances be abandoned and payment be made at average earnings. This was a demand of principle. The wage and salary people within the company responded immediately and pointed out that such an arrangement would have a disincentive effect on the employees. At some point in the negotiations this issue was changed into one of amount by the following solution: The company and union negotiators isolated the plants that were having difficulty with allowance payments. Rather than abandoning the concept of allowance payment, they merely changed the level of the guarantee. The union received great gain by having this political problem settled, and the company did not give much ground.

In other cases, apparent consensus in principle hides disagreement over remedial action. Progress in effective problem solving depends as much upon revealing divergence in views about means as it does in discovering underlying areas of agreement. Thus, Party accomplishes the necessary clarification of the source of latent disagreement by stating the problem or the solution in terms of specifics rather than principles.

> It has been observed that it is very easy to get a group to accept broad principles, but there are wide variations in the application of the principles to specific situations. Everyone will agree, for example, that a foreman should not play favorites because of the adverse effects on morale and discipline. But discussions of specific actions of foremen that may cause them to be suspected or accused of favoritism frequently produce many differences of opinion.[5]

In brief, matters allow for more integrative bargaining when they are formulated as problems and not as solutions and when they are stated in terms of specifics, not principles. It is dysfunctional to state matters in terms of final-contract-type language rather than the-essence-of-it lan-

[5] G. V. Moser, *Problem Solving Conferences*, Studies in Personnel Policy no. 176 (New York: National Industrial Conference Board, 1960), p. 20.

guage. As Mary Parker Follett observed, "The first step towards integration is to bring the differences into the open." [6] With real insight she criticizes negotiators who deal obliquely with each other and who obscure their real needs, even if these are somewhat in conflict. Integrative solutions cannot emerge if both sides are not candid with each other.

The communication task is twofold. First, it requires that Party faithfully communicate to Opponent his essential needs. To do this he needs to gather information that accurately portrays the situation that he faces. Second, he needs to listen to the situation presented by Opponent. William F. Whyte has stated the essence of this task:

> When a man states a point of view on which you disagree, there are two contrasting ways of meeting the situation. You can immediately bring in counter arguments to show him that he is wrong. Or you can express interest (not approval) in his point of view and ask him to tell you more about it. Why does he feel the way he does? What is behind his thinking?

> These two moves lead in opposite directions. The first move leads to increasingly sharp disagreements, marked by brief and rapid interchanges, interruptions, and rising emotional tension.

> The second move leads to relaxed tension and makes agreement possible. The man does not feel under pressure to get out a statement in a hurry and prepare for counterattack. He is able to talk to the subject and around it, in an informal, exploratory manner. Both parties are then better able to size up possibilities of getting together.[7]

### Searching for Alternate Solutions

Effective joint problem solving requires that more, rather than fewer, alternate solutions be identified and mutually considered, especially when the parties are likely to have access to quite different types of information relevant to the problem at hand. Thus, the implications of the problem-solving model is that many alternative solutions tend to be actively and mutually considered for a problem which arises. It also implies that there will tend to be accurate statements by both parties regarding the consequences of a given alternative. Again several tactical matters are involved for Party as he pursues integrative bargaining.

*Advance notice and negotiating time.* A longer time over which nego-

[6] Mary Parker Follett, "Dynamic Administration," in H. C. Metcalf and L. Urwick (eds.), *The Collected Papers of Mary Parker Follett* (New York: Harper & Row, Publishers, Incorporated, 1942), p. 36.

[7] W. F. Whyte, *Men at Work* (Homewood, Ill.: The Dorsey Press, Inc., and Richard D. Irwin, Inc., 1961), p. 332.

tiations are scheduled allows more time for study and discussion of agenda items with beneficial effects for integrative bargaining. Moreover, the provision for more, rather than less, time spent in negotiating sessions allows for more search activity.

A related question involves alerting Opponent of Party's intentions before negotiations. Advance notice improves the chances that both parties will have done their homework—will have explored alternate solutions and their relative utilities and disutilities, given the data available. Consider the statement of a company negotiator:

> The merit system and layoff procedure proposals required months of study before they could be agreed to by the company. Yet they did not advance these proposals until late in the negotiation procedure. A more mature and competent leadership would not have made these mistakes, which resulted in bitterness and misunderstanding, damaged relationships, and affected morale. It would also have achieved more of its objectives, as company study would have revealed ways in which these could be accommodated.[8]

This preparation permits a negotiating committee to enter negotiations with more specific ideas about the kind of information they need to gain from the actual interchanges.

The UAW has frequently used the technique of advance notice to alert management about an area of concern. Many observers would regard this as a distributive bargaining tactic, but integrative aspects are involved. Starting in 1950, the UAW began building a campaign to "win" the GAW from industry. While publicly the companies resisted the idea, behind the scenes they were fashioning an amazingly innovative approach to alleviating the burdens of unemployment which underlay the desire for the GAW. It was this approach presented by Ford that provided the basis for the SUB program agreed upon during the 1955 negotiations. Again in 1958 the UAW put the companies on notice about the objective in the area of profit sharing, and in 1961 American Motors came forward as a collaborative partner in such a venture.

The best statement of the UAW's approach in areas in which they believe there is integrative potential appeared in a document prepared for the 1961 auto negotiations and was significantly entitled *Workers' Problems Are Democracy's Problems.*

> We shall present management not with rigidly fixed programs, to solve our problems, but with clear statements of the problems them-

[8] R. E. Walton, *Impact of the Professional Engineering Union* (Boston: Division of Research, Graduate School of Business Administration, Harvard University, 1961), p. 37.

selves, and with a full range of the alternative solutions that have emerged from the democratic discussions within our Union. We intend to enlist management in a joint exploration of all those alternatives, and we shall examine with open minds any others that management may propose. We hope to embark with management on a joint search for the best solutions to problems that are as much theirs as ours because they are the problems of the society of which we are both members and upon whose welfare their future as well as ours depends.

We are confident that solutions can be found. We are determined that they shall be found. We unite to assure that they shall be found.[9]

***Preliminary discussions.*** Occasionally Party may request that a particular complex and unfamiliar item be discussed jointly but in an informal and exploratory way. Such discussions may be able to perform an important function for integrative bargaining. Discussions without the time pressure and without a threat of sanctions in areas in which it can be more exploratory may be conducive to problem solving. Again, this relates to the earlier statement about study groups and efforts that give the parties time for deliberate and unhurried search.

There is plenty of evidence that the approach of taking things away from the compressed time period of formal negotiations is a step in the integrative direction. The use of study groups such as the Human Relations Committee in the steel industry or the joint group which grew out of the American Motors–UAW profit-sharing plan are examples of the arrangement in which ample time is given for differences to be discussed. In 1963 the idea was extended to other firms in the auto industry in which management had long resisted this type of involvement. The auto companies accepted Reuther's proposal to form joint committees to meet one year prior to the 1964 auto negotiations. Reuther explained:

> The proposed joint study committee would not be authorized to bargain. It would be confined to assembling relevant data and to exploring and studying objectively and in good faith the problems that we will face when bargaining begins.

Automobile management had rebuffed such overtures in earlier years out of the feeling that Reuther would have used the preliminary talks only for building more militancy in the membership rather than for a joint search for beneficial arrangements. On both sides, a more mature approach to collective bargaining has been adopted. Moreover, with the success of the Human Relations Committee in the steel industry, auto management

[9] United Automobile Workers, *Workers' Problems Are Democracy's Problems* (Detroit: Solidarity House, 1961), p. 18.

was in a position in which it had to match the cooperative posture of steel management.

**Sequence of agenda items considered.** Here we have a host of subquestions. There are many possible ways of considering issues. Issues can be considered in the order in which they appear in the contract or the order in which they appear in the union's or the company's agenda, a decision rule can be made to consider noneconomic issues first and economic issues second, or one may follow the procedure of considering relatively less important issues first, moving on to the more important issues later in the negotiations.

Integrative bargaining proceeds most vigorously when the parties see a high likelihood of success. The appropriate impression is created by a pattern of early success. Therefore the parties often prefer to take up those issues in which the integrative potential is greatest and easiest to discern. The success in the search process on these initial issues prepares the way for search on the tougher issues.

Another consideration involves the inherent nature of the issue and the extent to which it is probably integrative or mixed. Issues that contain even minor elements of conflict are not as appropriate for the early stages of bargaining as those which are purely integrative. Mixed issues present difficult problems, and there is always the danger that the situation will be converted into deadly serious power bargaining. Consequently Party usually considers noneconomic issues or those issues with the most integrative potential early in negotiations.

For purposes of integrative bargaining, too much stress can be placed on sequencing agenda items. It is probably more important to ensure that the parties utilize repeated and varied search techniques. Integrative bargaining is a type of kaleidoscope in which the parties look at matters from all perspectives. Problems are considered, but if a solution is not readily apparent, it is laid aside. Other individuals may be called in to search for solutions. A period of extended recess often brings fresh perspectives and new ideas. Several brief sessions may be held in lieu of one longer one.[10] The negotiators avoid commitment or rigidity and constantly stay flexible in their thinking.

The convention of having everything tentative until everything is agreed upon suits integrative bargaining, because a solution for one problem may affect the solution of another problem. This favors keeping the total bargaining agenda fluid. If discussions uncover new possibilities, then integrative bargaining may be enhanced by allowing new agenda items to be added after negotiations get under way. However, as we have noted elsewhere, this can open the door to tactical threats instrumental to distributive bargaining.

[10] Moser, *op. cit.*, p. 40.

The format of the Human Relations Committee in the steel industry is illustrative of many aspects of integrative bargaining. Before entering into the deliberations, the members agreed on certain ground rules: freedom to advance an idea without committing one's self to accept it in the last analysis, ability to change position frequently, and freedom to make a proposal without consulting the parent organization.[11] All these rules facilitate the search process. They leave a person free to explore an area without fear of having an opponent make the person "live with" a remark.

*General orientation.* By now it must be clear that the secret to the search process is not any one or a combination of tactics but a certain frame of mind or orientation, merely reflected by the tactics discussed above. Innovation or bright ideas do not come from any following of procedures by rote. The creative process is elusive and unpredictable. "Creativity is rarely a matter of gradual, step-by-step progress; more often, it is a pattern of large and largely unpredictable leaps after relatively long periods of no apparent progress." [12]

The search process is most apt to be successful when both sides drop their preconceptions and jointly look at problems in the most flexible way possible. One test of the extent to which the search process is really functioning is the extent to which the union and management abandon their respective offensive and defensive postures. In true problem solving the institutional roles are dropped and the identity of the participants becomes unimportant.

In a very interesting study, Douglas submitted the transcript of an actual negotiation to a panel of judges. She asked them to identify the participants by union and management roles (she had removed all information relating to union and management designations. The distinguishability of the participants was noted early in bargaining and again just before the deadline, but for the major portion of the negotiations the differences of opinion existed as much within a committee as between management and labor. The inability of the judges to identify the institutional connection of the participants for much of the negotiations attested to the presence of problem solving.[13]

The participants suspend evaluations of each alternate solution offered. Rather than having a union proposal presented and countered by an

---

[11] By its very nature the Human Relations Committee has not revealed itself to the outside world. Nevertheless, some information about its mode of operation has leaked out. For the best description of this interesting development see A. H. Raskin, "Nonstop Talks Instead of Non-stop Strikes," *The New York Times Magazine* (July 7, 1963), p. 12.

[12] G. A. Steiner, "The Creative Organization," Selected Paper no. 10 of the Graduate School of Business, University of Chicago, no date.

[13] Ann Douglas, *Industrial Peacemaking* (New York: Columbia University Press, 1962), pp. 140–161.

alternate proposal, the group explores the widest possible spectrum of alternate solutions in a tentative way prior to evaluating them.[14]

It should be noted that it is probably more difficult for management to remain tentative than it is for the union. It is natural for the union to be probing and advancing different ideas and more natural for the company to be on the defensive in attempting to maintain the *status quo*. Integrative bargaining is most effective when both sides are flexible—willing to make tentative advances. Thus, management is probably under a greater burden to alter its normal negotiating style.

In the study *Causes of Industrial Peace* several illustrations are given of managements which did alter their negotiating style (with beneficial results for both sides). For example, the study of Sharon Steel reports:

> The second characteristic is management's open-mindedness and flexibility. The seniority issue, for example, was not prejudged and no dogmatic take-it-or-leave-it proposals were put forward by the company. Instead there was a willingness to give full consideration to the union's suggestions.[15]

## Selecting the Best Alternative

The time pressure that usually prevails in negotiations works to limit the search processes, and this restricts the number of actual alternative solutions which can be considered and evaluated. The time limit also curtails the systematic comparison of alternatives. As a consequence, the parties not only fail to produce an optimum solution, but they also may not even be certain that they are choosing the best alternative raised. A number of other tactical questions are involved in selecting the "best" alternative.

*Reporting of respective utility functions.* An important point about exploring utility functions is that the evaluations that people bring to agenda items are constantly changing during negotiations. "One of the most important reasons for bringing the desires of each side to a place where they can be clearly examined and valued is that evaluation often leads to re-evaluation." [16]

For integrative bargaining to be effective, both sides must accurately report their preferences or utility functions. This is the phase of integrative bargaining that is most susceptible to distortion whether it be delib-

[14] R. R. Blake and J. S. Mouton, "The Intergroup Dynamics of Win-Lose Conflict and Problem-solving Collaboration in Union-Management Relations," in Muzafer Sherif (ed.), *Intergroup Relations and Leadership* (New York: John Wiley & Sons, Inc., 1962), pp. 94–139.

[15] C. S. Golden and V. D. Parker (eds.), *Causes of Industrial Peace under Collective Bargaining* (New York: National Planning Association, Harper & Row, Publishers, Incorporated, 1955), p. 142.

[16] Follett, *op. cit.*, p. 38.

erate or inadvertent. One factor contributing to distortion is selective perception.[17] We assume here that the motivation to distort is minimal because we are dealing with solutions in which a party is called upon to make only slight sacrifices. Deliberate distortion will become a problem of considerable proportions when we turn to mixed situations.

One means for being faithful about utilities is for Party to present actual data about his cost structure. This is easier for the company than it is for the union, since for the company, utility is pretty much described in economic terms, while for the union many political overtones are involved. Thus, the union must often discuss internal politics and other affairs.

The age-old problem of interinstitutional or interpersonal utility comparisons is involved in this section of the integrative process. Except in the case of purely integrative situations, inevitably a comparison has to be made between the sacrifice that a given solution poses for one party and the amount of gain that it gives to the other party. These kinds of comparisons are difficult but essential. To put the issue more sharply: theoretically, interpersonal comparisons *cannot* be made; in practice, such comparisons *are* being made every day by most of us,[18] aided by psychological projection, empathy, analogy, and stereotyping.

Of course, more may be involved than just communicating information. Party may gain information not deliberately communicated by Opponent. Essentially, this treats the question of the usefulness for integrative bargaining of the indirect assessment techniques enumerated in the distributive chapter—grapevine, prenegotiation conferences, content analyses of grievances, and opinion surveys. These methods of indirect assessment permit Party to increase his understanding of the shape of Opponent's utility curve. To this extent Party is in a better position to suggest action in the areas in which there is the minimal sacrifice of Opponent's utility for each unit gained in his own utility and maximum gain for Opponent associated with modest sacrifices for himself. In effect, Party is attempting to locate the most integrative solution by gaining access to the relevant information about Opponent without disclosing too much information about himself.

*Combining or dividing proposals.* As we have noted before, items that are framed in terms of all or nothing do not lend themselves to integrative bargaining. An item which is divisible and which can be looked at in its parts is more susceptible to integrative bargaining. For example, the proposal for a union shop can either be granted or not granted—it is difficult

---

[17] D. C. Dearborn and H. A. Simon, "Selective Perception: A Note on the Departmental Identification of Executives," *Sociometry*, vol. 21 (June, 1958), pp. 140–144.

[18] For an analysis of the debate on the feasibility of interpersonal comparisons, and the approximate methods suggested by social psychology, see C. A. Hickman and M. H. Kuhn, *Individuals, Groups, and Economic Behavior* (New York: Holt, Rinehart and Winston, Inc., 1956), pp. 143–180.

to break it into parts. However, the proposal for union security can be divided into different parts, namely, union shop, maintenance of membership, etc. Hence, before the utility scanning process can take place, the respective utilities and disutilities need to be known for the various parts or subsolutions of a given problem.

On the other hand, it does make sense to take joint action on agenda items that have some functional relationship to each other, just as they are often defined and explored together. It is important to have a viable basis for connecting different items on the bargaining agenda. For example, during the 1958 International Harvester negotiations the union asked for changes in the manner in which grievances were processed prior to arbitration. The company used this as a means for introducing some of its problems in the area of day-to-day contract administration. Together these issues took the form of a problem in which discrete remedial actions could be conceived of as a part of a general solution.

### Conditions Which Facilitate the Steps in Problem Solving

The above discussion of the tactics which implement the integrative process should help us understand the necessity for certain conditions to prevail before the process will function. These facilitating conditions will be discussed in the following terms: motivation, information and language, and trust.

**Motivation.** Both parties must be motivated to solve the problem. The process model made clear the importance for the parties to be similarly motivated to search for alternate solutions, to be equally prepared to maintain agreed-upon criteria for an acceptable solution, to redefine the problem if necessary, and so on.

Motivation to work on an agenda item as a problem assumes a certain type of insight-discovery of the integrative potential in the situation. Often the achievement of comparable motivation between the parties is primarily a problem of gaining similar or complementary perceptions of the problem area. Thus, if the key participants have a relatively long time horizon, they are more likely to perceive integrative potential and be more motivated to engage in problem solving.

One often wonders why under similar circumstances some negotiations produce innovative solutions and others produce deadlock and conflict. For example, many relationships have been caught in economic adversity. In some of these, innovative solutions such as the Kaiser Plan and the West Coast Mechanization Fund have been developed; yet in others, distributive bargaining continues—the union fights a rearguard action and eventually management abandons the plant. Why the difference? Clearly, the security of the firm should be of importance to the union, insofar as the long-run survival of the firm means the long-run preservation of jobs. However, in the short run such an identity of objectives may not be present.[19] Some labor leaders are able to hold a long time horizon, while others are forced into short-term considerations because of the political pressures impinging upon them. Harry Bridges could look ahead and see that the defensive action of the International Longshoremen's and Warehousemen's Union was only leading it down the road to destruction. As a result he took the initiative to sign a pioneering agreement that met both the needs of the companies for changes in the work rules and the needs of the workers to have the shock of technological change cushioned. On the other hand, some labor leaders in the meat-packing industry, who have not been so politically secure, have had to fight the company at every turn: demanding that wages not be reduced, that plants not be abandoned, etc.

We do not mean to imply that nearsightedness only characterizes the union side of bargaining. Many management officials are equally insecure and under great pressure to achieve short-run results. Likewise, they find it difficult to consider arrangements or solutions which would really benefit both sides over the long run.

The negotiator should be able to see interrelationships between certain alternatives and his own goal structure.[20] The negotiator who suffers from myopia will fix on his objective and assume that there is only one alternative for getting there. The more skilled negotiator will be able to discern the connection, complex though it be, between some new alternative and the objective which he seeks. When the UAW demanded a form of GAW, the automobile companies could have seen this as directly in conflict with their objectives of maintaining managerial flexibility. Rather, they saw a chain of connections as follows: the union and workers were concerned about the inadequacy of unemployment compensation; if no changes were made in the unemployment compensation picture, then new laws would be passed; new laws would mean more obligations for the company; consequently it would be an advantage for the company to take the initiative to improve the unemployment compensation picture for its employees. With such a chain of reasoning, a managerial negotiator could view the proposal for GAW somewhat differently. He could then move to find an alternative that met the objectives of preserving managerial flexibility and limiting cost obligations while it met employee needs.

---

[19] George Brooks, a former union official and observer of the collective bargaining scene, puts the point succinctly, "most union members will show a vital interest in economic success in the company in which they work, *if they can perceive it.*" See G. W. Brooks, "Unions and the Structure of Collective Bargaining," in A. R. Weber (ed.), *The Structure of Collective Bargaining: Problems and Perspectives* (New York: The Free Press of Glencoe, 1961), p. 128.

[20] K. E. Boulding, *Conflict and Defense: A General Theory* (New York: Harper and Row, Publishers, Incorporated, 1962), pp. 311–312.

In some instances the integrative potential is overlooked because one or both of the parties lacks the ability to examine local problems. Either side may bring to a specific negotiation certain objectives which are based on considerations external to the given situation. For example, a union can insist on eliminating a geographical wage differential in furtherance of its national policy of wage uniformity. The policy is not related to local considerations and can be explained only in terms of broader economic or institutional factors. Similarly, management may bring to the bargaining table an objective to contain the union—an objective originating in the wider managerial ideology of opposing encroachment from any direction on their decision-making authority. Again, such an objective might not be in the long-run economic interest of the individual firm, but many companies would rather go out of business than cooperate with unions. All these forms of myopia limit the chances for integrative bargaining.[21]

**Information and Language.** The process is completely dependent on the communication of certain kinds of information. Certain decisions regarding negotiating procedure and mechanics greatly determine whether the relevant information will be exchanged.

The composition of the committee is important. If a larger team of actual participating members (either in session or caucus) includes a greater variety of relevant information and points of view, this will tend to facilitate integrative bargaining, although there is an upper limit to group size and variation imposed by the limitation of communication channels. Some companies compose their teams of people with varied backgrounds, representing industrial relations, production, industrial engineering, marketing, accounting, and public relations. Including a team member who has had actual experience on the other side of the bargaining table may be especially helpful in ensuring that the parties are using the same language.

The degree of freedom to participate which is allowed these committee members during negotiation discussions affects integrative bargaining. Assuming that there is some direction maintained to the discussion, the freer the flow of information, views, opinions, and judgments, the better for integrative bargaining.

The level of the organization from which men are drawn to compose the team is important. Using men from lower levels sometimes allows more integrative bargaining because of their access to facts about specific operations affected. By the same reasoning, taking officials from the higher levels of the organization may be necessary for integrative bargaining if the real problem requires awareness of the realities of the external environment. This is one reason why companies sometimes prefer to have an international representative in local negotiations: he can understand the com-

[21] *Ibid.,* pp. 311–312.

pany's problems and can speak management's language. In the following example the right mixture of levels required to produce effective integrative bargaining involved the plant manager and the regional manager:

> The union negotiator had presented a request for increased pay during waiting time under the incentive system. He was able to establish this as a mutual problem by confronting the plant manager and the regional manager jointly with summary figures and recent examples that the union had collected pertaining to waiting time. On the company side, the plant manager also had access to facts and could act on them, but it was the regional manager who was especially motivated to eliminate the waiting time. Without both levels represented, effective integrative bargaining would not have occurred.

Search activities take considerable time. Many management negotiators find themselves anxious to return to their desks and the problems of the business rather than conducting discussions on a day-in-day-out basis with union representatives who may not be equally burdened with organizational responsibilities. One solution is for management to send staff people or assistants who can be released for an extended period of time from their normal duties.

Technical specialists with full comprehension of the problem, who also have information about alternate actions and their consequences, can obviously be helpful. Their usefulness is limited, however, if they do not have any genuine appreciation of the utility functions of the parties and insist upon invoking their own strictly technical preferences. Apparently this was sometimes the case with the technical specialists in the talks preliminary to the 1964 auto negotiations.

The technical specialists, in this case social security analysts, brought a rational orientation to the situation, but they were often out of touch with the real problems. They were oriented more toward their profession of statistics or health information analysis and not toward the workers' needs or toward the institutional realities of the situation.

It is possible that a third party, such as a mediator, may be of some value in providing one or both of the parties information and/or assurances about the probable consequences of some alternative that they are considering based on his wider experience.

The subcommittee is a good technique for integrative bargaining. It facilitates exchange of information and a grappling with the essence of a particular problem. It also enables the people with the most expertise or those who are most affected to be involved in the deliberations.

One limitation to gathering information is that of costs. While in many circumstances this is not the important limitation, in others it does affect the search process. For example, in the 1964 discussions in the automobile industry, the union asked for extensive data about the pattern of medical coverage and costs. This information would have been useful to the union in establishing the level of medical care and the various ways in which it might have been rearranged. Such requests have put the companies to considerable expense in gathering the data. For this reason, the companies have on several occasions refused to supply data because of the cost entailed.

**Trust.** If the problem is important enough that the parties are motivated to work on it and if they have the relevant information and necessary language skills, they still will not engage in problem-solving behavior unless the activity is relatively safe. Both Party and Opponent need to be assured that if they freely and openly acknowledge their problems, if they willingly explore any solution proposed, and if they candidly discuss their own preferences, this information will not somehow be used against them.

The dynamics of distributive bargaining complicate the problem of establishing trust, and we shall explore this problem later in the chapter. Moreover, the building of necessary trust between the parties is a central concern of the attitudinal change process, which is the subject of the next chapter.[22] However, here we are concerned with those factors which—whatever the basic level of trust between the parties—provide greater or fewer safeguards against the violation of the problem solver's trust.

One such safeguard is the degree of privacy of the negotiating proceedings. The use of transcripts or a stenographer may inhibit exploratory and tentative discussions. Large galleries and disclosures to outside persons have the same effect. A liberal policy of going "off the record" somewhat offsets the effect of transcripts.

Returning to the question of size and composition, the larger and more varied committees may achieve a greater flow of relevant information but only at a lower level of trust. For this reason the multiple subcommittee arrangement is an especially apt device for allowing maximum discussion and discussion in a context of somewhat greater trust.

Third parties, such as a mediator, often offer an opportunity for an analysis and comparison of utility functions without either party actually revealing this information to the other committee.

## The Practice of Integrative Bargaining

In our discussion we have talked about the steps or procedures which need to be executed in order to realize the potential joint gain available in a situation. In some cases the process may produce arrangements that

[22] In the next chapter trust will be discussed as an important component of the overall relationship. At that point we shall have more to say about the broader implications of basic attitudes of trust.

increase the joint gain for the parties; in other cases the parties may remain at the *status quo*.

We have attempted to present integrative bargaining as an open-ended process. The parties may get no farther than defining the problem, or they may define the problem and share information about some obvious alternatives but fail to engage in creative search for new alternatives. They may be effective in carrying out all the steps of the problem-solving model and as a result create considerable joint gain. For example, during some recent negotiations in the meat-packing industry the union and the company involved faced a real problem of what to do with high-cost plants. The parties discussed the problem openly and shared considerable information about some of the obvious alternatives: tightening up production standards, laying off employees, making wage reductions, or moving the plant. The degree of integrative bargaining was modest.

Several years later the parties conceived the idea of an automation fund. A tripartite group gradually evolved a number of important arrangements to deal with the problem of high-cost plants. As plants were closed, training problems were initiated, job relocation efforts pressed, etc. Moreover, they inaugurated a long-range personnel planning program so that new plants would be established on a schedule that fitted the displacement of employees from plants being abandoned. The Automation Fund and the programs that have come from it represent innovative solutions and new alternatives that the parties were not considering in their earlier deliberations.

The same point about varying degrees of progress can be made by relating some of the developments in the automobile and steel industries. In the preliminary discussions which preceded the 1964 auto negotiations a degree of integrative bargaining occurred. However, it was limited to the exchange of information about alternatives and the identification of several important problems. No new alternatives were developed nor were any solutions considered. In fact, as soon as a solution emerged, the parties repressed it, or on several occasions they convened the formal bargaining committees, which had the effect of shifting discussions back to distributive bargaining. As the union put the matter, "These are only discussions; we have no authority to bargain an agreement; we have not been sent here by our constituents."

The deliberations in the automobile industry followed many of the guidelines of integrative bargaining: namely, they were off the record, and both sides were free to present whatever ideas they wanted. However, they deviated from integrative bargaining in one respect: minutes were kept of all the deliberations. On balance, one can say that some integrative bargaining took place, but not a great deal.

In the steel industry considerably more integrative bargaining occurred.

Many subcommittees were established: training, medical care, experimental agreement, impact of basic steel agreement on steel service centers and container plants, wage incentives, statistical material for collective bargaining, classifications, subcontracting, and vacations and sabbatical leaves. Some important innovations have come out of these committees. Moreover, the Human Relations Committee in the steel industry has not kept any minutes, and it has generally followed the guidelines of integrative bargaining. The steel committees have also done a better job of handling the dilemma with the rank and file. While deliberations are generally kept quiet, some of the discussions have been reported back on an informal basis, in contrast to the automobile negotiations, about which the union leadership has been supersecret.

It should be clear that the quality of the eventual decision depends upon the performance at each step of the process outlined in this chapter: the accuracy of the formulation of the problem, the imagination in perceiving alternatives, the thoroughness in gathering information about alternatives and their consequences, and the degree of clarity about basic utility functions. When two persons are engaged in joint problem solving, especially in contexts such as negotiations, the nature of the decision is dependent upon a host of behaviors that cannot be evaluated simply in terms of "accuracy," "imagination," "thoroughness," and "clarity." The discussion of integrative tactics above specifies the behaviors and conditions which improve the performance of the participants and allow them to coordinate their problem solving in a setting assumed to be favorable for these behaviors. It is time to add another dimension. Problem-solving performance in the context of labor negotiations depends largely upon how a negotiator handles a series of dilemmas created by the concurrent requirements of the integrative and distributive bargaining processes.

# PART 2 | MIXED DISTRIBUTIVE AND INTEGRATIVE BARGAINING AND ITS DILEMMAS

## Mixed Situations and Strategic Choice

The fact is that labor negotiations present few pure-conflict issues and few problems which individually allow parties direct mutual gain. When the agenda items singularly or in combination involve significant elements of conflict *and* considerable potential for integration, we characterize the situation as mixed.

**Mixed Agenda Item.** This process involves a variable-sum, variable-share payoff structure. Mixed bargaining is really a complex combination of the two bargaining processes. Distributive bargaining assumes little or no variability in the sum available to the parties. Integrative bargaining assumes no problem in allocating shares between them. Mixed bargaining assumes and confronts both these possibilities and recognizes that they are interdependent.

Agenda items can be illustrated in terms of the utility frontiers that describe issues, problems, and mixed items, respectively (see Figure 5-1).

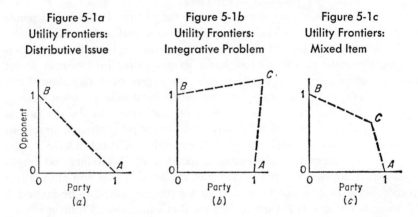

Figure 5-1a
Utility Frontiers:
Distributive Issue

Figure 5-1b
Utility Frontiers:
Integrative Problem

Figure 5-1c
Utility Frontiers:
Mixed Item

For an issue, all points are pure conflict points in the sense that all moves involve corresponding gains and losses. On the other hand, a pure problem contains a maximumly integrative point in the sense that any other point on the curve is clearly a worse position for both parties. Contrastingly, a mixed item is one that contains a trading point in the sense that it maximizes the joint gain; and although either party could gain from moving to other points on the curve, these gains would involve disproportionately large sacrifices for the other party. Thus for mixed items, Party would prefer point *A* (which *might* be achieved through distributive bargaining) over point *C*.

**Levels of Strategic Choice.** In the mixed situation each side has a broad choice between (1) attempting to discover outcomes with larger total values and (2) working toward an outcome which has a smaller total value but which does provide him a relatively high individual payoff. The mixed-game dilemma arises because there are not only several different total values available to the parties, but there are also alternate sharing ratios. A party cannot assume that a larger total value necessarily enhances his individual share.

These choices can be illustrated and elaborated by being presented in matrix form (see Figure 5-2). As the matrix demonstrates, mixed bargaining can be viewed analytically as a complex game involving choices at two levels or along two dimensions.

### Figure 5-2
### Mixed Payoffs in Matrix Form

| | | Opponent Sum strategies | | | |
| | | **D** Fixed sum | | **I** Increase sum | |
| | | Share strategies | | Share strategies | |
| Party Sum strategies | | Soft | Hard | Soft | Hard |
|---|---|---|---|---|---|
| **D** Fixed sum — Share strategies | Soft | 2, 2 | 1, 3 | $2\frac{1}{2}, 2\frac{1}{2}$ | 1, 4 |
| | Hard | 3, 1 | −6, −6 | 4, 1 | −6, −6 |
| **I** Increase sum — Share strategies | Soft | $2\frac{1}{2}, 2\frac{1}{2}$ | 1, 4 | 3, 3 | 1, 5 |
| | Hard | 4, 1 | −6, −6 | 5, 1 | −6, −6 |

First, the parties' choices affect the total sum available. This choice represents the fact that for a mixed situation they may engage in more or less problem solving which may result in more or less integration and joint gain. Thus, the alternate strategies at this level of the game are an integrative, increasing-sum strategy ($I$) and a distributive strategy ($D$), which treats the situation as a fixed-sum issue.

Note that at this sum level of the game, the parties' strategies describe four quadrants of outcomes, each with its own total-sum characteristics. The quadrant described by a pair of $D$, fixed-sum strategies makes available to the parties positive outcomes with a total sum of 4. The quadrant described when Party makes an $I$ choice and Opponent a $D$ choice allows total sums of 5. This is also the amount provided when Opponent chooses $I$ and Party's strategy is $D$. The quadrant resulting from two $I$ choices, that is, when both enter into problem solving, contains outcomes with the greatest total sum of 6. We have ignored for the moment that only three of the cells in each quadrant contain the positive total sums of 4, 5, and 6 respectively, and that the other cell in each case is negative sum. We shall have more to say about this default cell in a moment, when we consider specific strategies for allocating shares.

Choices also occur at a second level in mixed bargaining. The parties must allocate shares of the sum available to them. At some point the parties find themselves in one of the quadrants, and the sum of their joint efforts itself becomes the focus of bargaining. Since the total sum is now assumed to be determined, the bargaining is by definition distributive. The present choice for each is whether to adopt a relatively hard or a relatively soft bargaining strategy. The parties are confronted with essentially the same alternatives regardless of the quadrant. In fact, the submatrix in each quadrant is the one analyzed in the discussion of the distributive bargaining model. Each party must choose between cautious strategy ($S$), which would net some modest payoff, and a bold strategy ($H$), which would lead to either high payoff or default and high cost. Party's efforts to get the most favorable division of payoffs (say, the 5,1 cell in the lower right-hand quadrant) involve the two influence mechanisms also discussed in the distributive model chapter, namely, tactics to influence Opponent's perceived utilities and commitments to change Opponent's perceived probabilities. Ultimately, however, parties must select their share strategies and accept the payoffs which result.

*Complex strategies in mixed bargaining.* If mixed bargaining involves two levels and if at each level Party must choose between strategies, he is confronted with four overall strategic possibilities. The four complex strategies are: (1) Party may select an $I$, integrative strategy to increase the joint gain, accompanied by $S$, a relatively soft strategy in allocating shares. (2) Party may choose $D$, fixed sum, followed by $H$, hard bargaining in allocating the sum; in effect he maintains a consistent distributive or competitive orientation. (3) Party may choose $D$, fixed sum, and then follow with an $S$, soft bargaining strategy in share distribution. (4) Finally, Party may select an $I$, integrative strategy to increase the joint gain, and then select an $H$, hard bargaining strategy to gain the lion's share of the joint gain. Which of these strategic possibilities available to Party are viable and more frequently adopted?

The first and second strategies are easier to understand. Each is internally consistent and presents few tactical dilemmas. Strategy 1, engaging in problem solving to create maximum joint gain and then refraining from any hard bargaining over shares, makes no contradictory demands on Party. He simply behaves as if the mixed item were strictly a problem, virtually avoiding distributive bargaining. Thus, a tactical description of this strategy would consist of those integrative bargaining activities described in Part 1 of this chapter. The primary risk in this strategy is that he can be taken advantage of in the allocation of shares.

In strategy 2 Party ignores the integrative potential. Therefore, the strategy is to treat the situation as an issue throughout, and the tactical implementation is essentially that of distributive bargaining. This distributive bargaining process over mixed items by Party is facilitated to the extent that Opponent approaches the items in a problem-solving way and thus makes himself more vulnerable to Party's strategy. Of course, the drawback to this strategy is the opportunity lost—the failure to realize the integrative potential in the situation. This is especially true if both parties choose the same fixed-sum orientation; and the default outcome is even worse, of course, if both choose hard-share strategies, as they are more likely to do when one has taken this basic approach to the situation.

Strategy 3 is a logical possibility, but there is nothing to recommend first treating the situation as if it were fixed-sum and then adopting a soft strategy in the bargaining over shares. It can result in the lowest possible positive outcome for Party in the matrix. Therefore, there is no reason to believe that this combination would be planned in advance; it may, indeed, turn out that at some point after the first step, the soft strategy over shares is the only alternative to a default outcome.

The fourth complex strategy consists of integrative bargaining to establish the maximum total sum, accompanied by relatively hard distributive bargaining to claim Party's share. This overall strategy faces squarely both realities—the fruits of collaboration and the realities of competition inherent in share allocation. If executed effectively, this strategy appears to be the most attractive; but unfortunately it is the most difficult to implement. An analysis of this fourth strategy follows.

***Difficulties in the preferred complex strategy.*** What is to prevent a party from playing the mixed game in the sequence of first maximizing the sum and then dividing the shares through aggressive distributive bargaining? There are several reasons why this preferred strategy is not easily executed.

First, the designation of shares cannot always be kept separate from the search for additional joint gain. As the bargainers search for alternatives, it may turn out that particular high joint-gain solutions inherently provide one party with a disproportionate share of the total value.

Second, although theoretically the above difficulty can be overcome by using side payments, this is easier said than done. (Side payments are appropriate when the designated solutions do not share the gain according to some standard of equity.) The difficulties in providing a mechanism for side payments are several. For one thing, the disadvantaged person may not have the distributive bargaining power or skill necessary to compel a side payment at the time it becomes appropriate. It is also possible that the advantaged person will not accept the need for this action, arguing that the shares should be allocated according to "where the chips fall." In collective bargaining there tends to be an orientation toward discrete subjects and solutions. It is sometimes hard for the person disadvantaged by a solution on a given subject to establish his claim to benefit elsewhere, let alone agree upon the rate of exchange by which the inequity can be compensated. Agreement in this respect is subject to all the difficulties of distributive bargaining.

A third factor makes it difficult to use any strategy which involves an integrative approach to a mixed situation—the uncertainty about the approach of the other party. Party might be willing to engage in integrative bargaining if he were sure that what appeared as integrative bargaining on the part of Opponent was truly that. Party can never be sure that behind the guise of searching for larger sums, Opponent is not merely introducing the subjects which have "solutions" that give Opponent disproportionate shares. Party cannot be certain that Opponent is not seducing Party into increasing the sum while Opponent maintains a distributive posture—one that will capture the lion's share when the subject of shares is considered.

Fourth and finally, at the very practical level, it is hard for bargainers to shift from an integrative orientation on sum to a hard approach on the distribution of shares. This arises from the contradictory nature of the tactical operations required for integrative bargaining and hard distributive bargaining. The two processes differ in important respects: in terms of the amount of information the parties share with each other at every stage in arriving at decisions and in terms of the amount of consideration each gives to the information about the other's problems. In the integrative process Party makes maximum use of voluntary, open, accurate discussion of any area which affects both groups, and he attempts to avoid consequences that would present new difficulties for Opponent. Just the opposite is involved in the distributive process. Party attempts to gain maximum information from Opponent but makes minimum disclosures himself; in fact, he often tries to manipulate and persuade Opponent. And he explores the implications of actions for possible unfavorable consequences for himself but does not concern himself with the consequences for Opponent.

In brief, integrative bargaining is tentative and exploratory and involves open-communication processes, whereas distributive bargaining involves adamant, directed, and controlled information processes. The shift from integrative to distributive decision processes is difficult because precisely what one has revealed in discussing the item in order to establish the greatest joint gain can weaken his position in bargaining over the shares of that gain. It is in anticipation of this dilemma that he may choose to treat the task of increasing the sum in a cautious distributive way, increasing his chances for effective hard bargaining over shares. Alternatively, Party may choose to throw himself wholeheartedly into the open-exploration process of increasing joint gains and then accept the fact that he will have to be more conciliatory in the share bargaining.

More persuasive support for the statement that certain combinations of strategies for determining joint gains and strategies for determining shares are less compatible than others will have to await our detailed discussion of the tactical dilemmas involved. However, the conclusion is that negotiations cannot be divided neatly into phases and that a bargainer cannot readily shift from an integrative to a hard distributive orientation. Rather, it is easier for him to maintain a more or less consistent orientation throughout negotiations, which from the viewpoint of achieving a minimum level of satisfaction, may be the distributive orientation.

In concluding this conceptual treatment of mixed bargaining, we should underscore the manner in which competitive and cooperative elements are combined in mixed bargaining. It is instructive to contrast it with distributive bargaining in which both elements were also involved.

In distributive bargaining there is pure competition for some limited value; the parties are only motivated to cooperate to the extent of staying within limits. The necessary ingredient in the resolution process required by this type of common interest is caution and moderation in the amount of competition.

In mixed bargaining, on the other hand, cooperation and competition are more inextricably combined throughout the search and consideration of an array of potential outcomes. The parties are motivated to cooperate in an active, creative, problem-solving way in order to create maximum values but are also motivated to take competitive steps in order to ensure themselves of high individual outcomes either as a part of the specific outcome or as a side payment. Therefore, the cooperative elements in a mixed situation require more active and deliberate attention.

Whereas in distributive bargaining the parties cooperate to avoid mutual disaster, in mixed bargaining they cooperate to enlarge the area of interdependency.

**Illustration.** To illustrate the essence of mixed bargaining, we could reintroduce many of the examples used earlier in the chapter. However, all those situations were described in terms of their increased sum potential, and little was said about the shares or how the parties dealt with the inherent conflict. To illustrate mixed bargaining, we need to attend both to the sum and share dimensions, and also to the uncertainty of the Opponent's orientation. The character of the mixed game is not only that the cells specify various combinations of variable share results, but that great uncertainty exists about which choice Opponent will make. Some of this flavor is captured by the following example:

> A large company and a UAW department faced this mixed situation: The area of health insurance had been of concern to both sides for some time. Costs had been mounting for the company, and benefits had been lagging for the employees. Both sides knew that if they sat down to search for better answers, something might come forth that would increase benefits and at the same time lower costs, e.g., getting county medical societies to establish lower fee schedules for doctors,

establishing a comprehensive clinic which the company would supervise, etc.

They both hesitated. The company was afraid that the union would still require it to match the auto pattern which had not yet been established and that, in addition, whatever money was saved on health insurance would have to be spent elsewhere. Consequently the company would end up spending as much money as well as having the headaches of working with county medical societies, running a clinic, etc.

The union also had its fears. The international union feared that if discussions on this problem (and other problems) were successful, the company would be in a position to ask for early settlement. They were aware that such a proposition might be attractive to the rank and file and local leadership who had gotten tired of following the Detroit pattern. The union felt that an early agreement would play into the hands of the company, since its profits were considerably lower than those of the big three. Hence the department leadership wanted a settlement with this company after the auto settlement so they could force the "rich" auto pattern on this company.

The above example can be analyzed in terms of a matrix as follows:

## Figure 5-3

*Company*

|  | Distributive, hard-share bargaining | Integrative, soft-share bargaining |
|---|---|---|
| **Distributive, hard-share bargaining** (Union) | Normal bargaining without preliminary talks, follows the pattern at best and defaults at worst. | All the cost savings are used to add to the pattern. The union uses the savings to increase the level of benefits and also requires the company to match the auto pattern in terms of added costs. |
| **Integrative, soft-share bargaining** | The company achieves cost savings and is able to use these discussions to seduce the union into an early and "cheap" settlement. | The union gains additional benefits, the company gains cost improvements. |

The dilemma, which we shall continue to discuss, can be phrased in terms of a question: How does Party realize the potential of integrative bargaining without being exploited by Opponent's self-interest orientation?

## Dilemmas in the Steps of Problem Solving

We shall attempt to understand the dilemmas presented by distributive and integrative bargaining through a systematic analysis of those points at which we find incompatibilities in the tactics of the two processes. The framework we shall use will be that of integrative bargaining. Our point of departure will be a statement of the ideal behaviors of the participants, given the requirements of the rational problem-solving model. We shall point up the difficulties in pursuing these problem-solving behaviors, given the demands of distributive bargaining. Where possible we shall show how these dilemmas are handled in mixed bargaining in order to allow Party to pursue both processes effectively.

**Identification of the Problem.** Recognition that an issue or some combination of issues has integrative possibilities requires an exchange of information about one's own concerns, stated as accurately and as meaningfully as possible. However, in the negotiation context, certain factors may inhibit such an enthusiastic and candid identification and definition of problems.

For example, to identify a problem may give Opponent the opportunity to work on his own problem instead, under the pretense that he is working on yours. Moreover, presenting a problem may reveal a vulnerability— one which can be exploited by Opponent in some other aspect of distributive bargaining.

A good example of the last point comes from some subcommittee deliberations in a Midwest negotiation.

> Both sides had exchanged considerable information about fringe benefits. From the data the union drew up a report outlining the deficiencies in the dental and psychiatric health areas. The union asked the company representative to join in signing and submitting the statement of the "problems" to higher authorities. The company representative refused, fearing that his signature would place the company in the position of having to take concrete action on these matters.

If we shift to the level of tactics, we can point up the dilemmas even more sharply.

One tactical dilemma involves the use of preconditions to negotiations sometimes invoked by one or both parties. These preconditions serve as commitment tactics in distributive bargaining. For example, during the 1949 steel negotiations the companies refused to negotiate on pensions during a wage reopener, and again they sought to restrict the agenda during the 1955 negotiations when the union desired to talk about SUB during another wage reopener. Frequently a party may notify the other party that it will be willing to engage in negotiations only if the other party makes a preliminary concession. The use of preconditions or prerequisites can also occur in the context of negotiations already underway. A party may insist that one issue be resolved before it will discuss other issues.

These tactics tend to make integrative bargaining more difficult because they preclude or reduce open exploration of the prohibited issue to determine whether it has integrative potential. Further, such a tactic precludes discussing several issues at once to learn if together they may produce integrative possibilities. On the other hand, the linking of one issue to another (i.e., making one a precondition to the other) may reflect the functional interdependence of two issues. Such was the case in the 1946 Ford negotiations, in which the company refused to make its economic offer until the matter of "company security" had been settled, thereby underscoring the functional interdependence of wildcat strikes, productivity, and wage increases.

Another tactical dilemma arises from a requirement of integrative bargaining that Party include only "serious" items. This is often contrary to distributive bargaining, which may call for including items not genuinely of concern to him; including extra items can be a tactic for concealing his true utilities or for creating some "trading horses."

Still another dilemma occurs in deciding the agenda: Whereas in considering several mixed agenda items integrative bargaining is facilitated by giving priority to items whch have a high ratio of gain to sacrifice, distributive bargaining may be more successful if items are chosen according to other criteria such as emotional appeal, which can elicit the most visible commitment from one's own principals.

How can these two dilemmas regarding agenda best be handled? Mixed bargaining on any given item is more effective if there is an effort to balance the total agenda in terms of the amount of integrative potential available to each party. One practical approach is for both sides to limit the number of demands by agreement. Usually the convention in bargaining works like this: the union enters and makes its presentation, and then the company calls for a recess during which time it can decide how many demands of its own to present—it can gear its agenda to the size of the union's. Both sides agree that if a subject area has not been mentioned in the initial presentations, it will not be later introduced.

In our earlier discussion of the agenda question as a part of integrative bargaining, we noted that Party tended to tackle discrete items and develop a pattern of success rather than confront a big problem initially. Now we can add another reason from the perspective of mixed bargaining. By exploring small problems first, the question of share allocation can be handled in manageable terms. The danger with solving a big problem first is that the person with the high benefit may call an end to bargaining, preventing the side with the low sacrifice from introducing agenda items that stand to benefit him.

A quotation from Schelling is pertinent here:

> If each party agrees to send a million dollars to the Red Cross on condition the other does, each may be tempted to cheat if the other contributes first, and each one's anticipation of the other's cheating will inhibit agreement. But if the contribution is divided into consecutive small contributions, each can try the other's good faith for a small price. Furthermore, since each can keep the other on short tether to the finish, no one ever need risk more than one small contribution at a time. Finally, this change in the incentive structure itself takes most of the risk out of the initial contribution; the value of established trust is made obviously visible to both.[23]

One other tactical dilemma in identifying problems deserves attention. For purposes of doing well in exploiting whatever integrative potential exists in an item of mixed character, one would state it as a problem and indicate one's basic concerns. However, to ensure that one does comparatively well in serving his own interests where those of the parties cannot be integrated, he would state the item as an issue, specifying his demands or remedies. Sometimes this dilemma does not hold. Treating a problem area as an issue—by submitting proposals and supporting them vigorously—may be just what is needed to force the other to think seriously and perhaps imaginatively about the problem.

**Search for Alternatives and Their Consequences.** Effective joint problem solving requires that many alternate solutions be identified and mutually and candidly considered. It involves not being satisfied with the available alternatives and searching for new ones by an innovative combination of features from each of these alternatives. However, we recognize that an essential modification of the problem-solving model when applied to mixed agenda items is the addition of risk as an accompaniment to search behavior.

The idea of brainstorming, which is one effective way of getting out alternatives, is that judgment and evaluation be deferred until later. In the context of negotiations, when the atmosphere is typically established by the distributive bargain, behavior is expected to be highly purposeful and is regarded as calculated—just the opposite of that conducive to a free flow of ideas. The mental set of the participants cannot be easily shifted from caution and deliberateness to spontaneity and then back to caution and deliberateness, and so on.

[23] T. C. Schelling, *The Strategy of Conflict* (Cambridge, Mass.: Harvard University Press, 1960), pp. 45–46.

The search processes require a full flow of information which can be used to construct alternate solutions and to explore their probable consequences. However, in distributive bargaining, the parties have an incentive to present only the information that tends to lead to the solution which prior analysis by each of the parties respectively has pointed to and even here to present only that information which will have the intended effect on the other. In the context of distributive bargaining, merely to suggest or mention an alternative carries with it the connotation that the solution is one that is at least minimally acceptable to the mentioning party. In fact, merely to supply information which permits construction of an alternative may be a liability when it comes to choosing among alternatives.

Let us consider the dilemmas at the tactical level suggested by the above discussion.

One such dilemma concerns the time period that should be allowed for negotiation sessions. Typically more time could be used profitably in integrative bargaining, and it would therefore be advisable to have the time period more open-ended. However, a fixed time limit is needed for distributive bargaining. Moreover, dragging out negotiations often dissipates the strength or interest of one or both parties in a way disadvantageous to distributive bargaining.

However, more time does allow commitments to be abandoned. Thus, if one party has already quite firmly committed himself, the other may seek an early opening to encourage and allow for revisions of commitments. If one party typically becomes committed during the period just before the contract opening date, the other may attempt to head off such commitments by an early opening.

Parties have experimented with techniques for gaining the best of both arrangements—open-ended negotiations and deadline negotiations.

> In the 1950 negotiations the UAW and General Motors agreed to a "floater" clause that worked as follows: Negotiations would be put under way by the union's notification to modify the agreement. The modification did not terminate the agreement. This was only done when the union gave a termination notice. The agreement then would be terminated 30 days after the termination notice. Such an approach allowed the union to start negotiations but not to establish a deadline until it was desirable to wrap things up.

A second dilemma involves discussions in conferences without imminent deadlines and sanctions. This can facilitate integrative bargaining. On the other hand, while exploratory discussions in this context involve less risk of being interpreted as a promise to act, the willingness to meet does convey a degree of flexibility which the party may not wish to convey for purposes of distributive bargaining. In this case refusing to meet may be a minimum commitment tactic, for to engage in such discussions may be taken as an indication that the party is willing to accept some aspects of the initiating party's proposal or some of the underlying ideas.

A third type of tactical dilemma arises from the contradictory types of discussion demanded by the two processes. Whereas integrative bargaining requires an exploratory and tentative approach, distributive bargaining often requires firmness and maximal commitments. If an agenda item with mixed characteristics is to be exploited for its integrative potential, the search processes must probe it from every angle and consider every possibility. But if the party is to do comparatively well distributively, he is inclined to invoke any of a number of commitment tactics antithetical to integrative bargaining: argument through repetition, stressing face validity of a particular solution, presenting proposal first and persisting in demand, adjourning meeting without suggesting another, walking out, making further negotiations contingent upon favorable settlement of a particular item, etc.

This general point can be made clearer by analyzing one specific tactic, commitment made credible by face validity. Recall that we have observed that certain demands had more face validity than others, i.e., that the position was more obvious because of a round number, symmetry, patterns, precedents, or other referents visible to both. We have suggested that commitments to positions with more face validity tend to be more credible; therefore this fact was to be exploited in the interest of distributive bargaining. However, it is not clear that this phenomenon has any advantages for integrative bargaining. In the first place, a position easily defended for its symmetry seems more likely to be a compromise rather than an integrative solution. The point is that without the temptation afforded by the uniquely face-valid symmetrical position, the parties might have to look for more underlying validity to their solution. Integrative solutions usually are those which are obvious or natural only in the context of all the particular features of the specific problem, whereas face-valid solutions have an inherent prominence with respect to the more superficial view of the situation.

In brief, most of the commitment tactics described in distributive bargaining would be dysfunctional in searching for integrative potential in mixed items. The distributive tactics that would still be relevant would be those that would *prevent Opponent* from taking a committed position in order to claim a disproportionate share of the joint gain. Here we have a facilitating relationship between certain tactics of distributive and integrative bargaining, specifically some of those distributive tactics which keep Opponent flexible or help him abandon a committed position once it has been taken and those of integrative bargaining which require free and open exploration without preconceived ideas or dogmatic positions.

One way in which parties cope with the tactical dilemmas posed by the search process is to develop a well-understood distinction between "official" and "unofficial," or off-the-record, discussions.

> As a rule, "unofficial" business transpired in the private party caucuses or in "side bar" conferences between mediator and single negotiators. The distinction, however, was not as rigid as joint vs. caucus meetings. In a joint meeting it would be possible for parties, if they chose, to go "off the record" for brief periods. The critical condition was the understood level of operation. "Unofficial" gatherings were given over to strictly exploratory work: to hypothesizing about possible lines of action and probable consequences, to weighing expected advantages and disadvantages, to clarifying uncertainties. Indulgence in spontaneous and speculative talk was confined to these contacts—but here it was the typical approach, and entirely permissible. Indeed, the high point of these meetings was the freedom they provided for talk about points without the implication of any commitment whatsoever. It seems clear that the "unofficial" meetings were always reaching for outlines and boundaries within which agreement could later be nailed down at the "official" level; hence the first understandings to be arrived at—the tentative agreements, that is, on general principles and broad terms of reference— were sought here far ahead of outright commitment in the "official" meetings, where binding concrete details necessarily would have to be hammered out on a vis-à-vis basis.[24]

It is possible to overstate the inherent dilemmas in the search process and the exchange of factual information. In some relationships the parties have demonstrated considerable facility in aggressively pursuing both distributive and integrative potential. General Motors and the UAW is one such relationship.

> While GM has a reputation as a tough bargainer and has been described as rigid, narrow, and restrictive in its approach to labor relations, this has not meant that union demands for new concessions are subject to automatic veto or to offhand and arbitrary treatment. There are, it is true, certain principles which the company feels must not be compromised (especially those relating to management's right to manage); but within the broad framework of objectives and policies which constitute the company's guiding philosophy, GM officials are shrewd, hard-headed pragmatists in their approach to labor issues. They give serious attention and study to union proposals, listen carefully to all supporting arguments, and respond with detailed and

[24] Douglas, *op. cit.*, p. 86.

well-documented explanations of their own position. These replies, moreover, reveal a sophisticated understanding of the problems involved, a firm grasp of the implications and consequences of alternative courses of action, and a thorough knowledge of past experience not only of its own but of others' relations with the union. This patience and ability to marshal evidence and analyze the facts relevant to each issue, together with an insistence that issues be discussed against a background of factual experience rather than "in the abstract," helps account no doubt for Reuther's early advocacy of the need for union research facilities and personnel to accumulate and analyze the facts of actual plant experience.[25]

**Preference Ordering.** Individual problem solving involves the more or less systematic comparison of alternatives, ranking them from "most preferred" to "least preferred" according to the problem solver's function. Joint problem solving involves a jointly constructed utility function, or at least a candid matching process between the functions of the two parties. Thus we ask: "To what extent are the preferences or utility functions of one party candidly reported to the other in choosing alternatives? Do there tend to be overstatements and understatements of the importance of given consequences?"

There is often an incentive for Party to misrepresent his own utilities so as to make one favored "integrative solution" appear to better balance the parties' interest than the other solutions. Consider an extremely integrative situation in which Party can accommodate the solution to Opponent's problem without any cost to himself and possibly with slight benefit. Party may well try to disguise the value he places on the slight benefit, publicly representing his effort to accommodate as having considerable disutility to himself.

Moreover, even if the issue was not partly distributive as inferred above, it may have been based on the same utility functions of Party which underlie other issues which *are* distributive; and to reveal the functions on this issue would jeopardize Party's position on those other issues in the distributive bargain.

Let us consider one tactical dilemma involved in revealing one's true preferences. Inasmuch as integrative bargaining requires a maximum flow of accurate information, including an accurate representation of one's utility functions, Party can use only certain distributive tactics at some cost. Included would be all the tactics related to disguising one's resistance point: single spokesmen, calculated incompetence, low rate of activity, etc. Similarly, since integrative bargaining involves an attempt to understand and take into account the other's utilities, there is no place in this process

[25] R. M. MacDonald, *Collective Bargaining in the Automobile Industry* (New Haven, Conn.: Yale University, 1963), pp. 350–351.

for the distributive tactics designed to change Opponent's utilities, including threats, power plays, etc.

Despite the many forces or considerations in mixed bargaining against revealings one's utilities, the parties do manage to communicate on this level. The parties may naturally sense the appropriate time and place for this type of information exchange. Alternatively, one side may have to take responsibility for enforcing an exploration of both utility functions in mixed bargaining. In the negotiation excerpted below, the company negotiator attempted repeatedly to create a factual basis for the exchange of information about utilities or disutilities connected with various issues. The union negotiator was following a habitual practice of his own of merely starting high and dropping as he revised his own feasibility estimates. The company negotiator's warnings on three occasions were:

> But if you won't agree to read your proposal for a revised agreement clause by clause and *give us your reasons for the changes,* then our answer is "NO." ...

> That is not an answer. We gave you our reasons for the 45-day period: you should give a reason for 15. ...

> There is not a question of 30 cents or 10 cents an hour. It is a question of how much a company can stand.[26]

Paradoxically, the company used threats in order to induce the other to explore the items for integrative potential.

Assuming some mutual understanding about the utilities involved in a mixed agenda, we turn now to the problem of making final choices.

**Decision Making.** Conceptually, the linking of issues and simultaneously increasing the sum and specifying the shares has been termed utility matching. Consider a simplified situation in which four noneconomic items are on the agenda. Management has proposed two changes: union cooperation on job classification and a reduction in wash-up period. The union has proposed two changes: increased seniority rights and strengthened rights to arbitration. We shall assume that these items are discontinuous, they can be either accepted or rejected; there are no intermediate positions on any of the issues. We shall assign hypothetical numerical utilities to each of these items for each party (see Figure 5-4).[27]

Inspection of this table of units of satisfaction attributed to each item by the parties respectively permits us to make certain observations of relevance. Of the two management proposals the first, job reclassification,

---

[26] B. M. Selekman, S. K. Selekman, and S. H. Fuller, *Problems in Labor Relations,* 2d ed. (New York: McGraw-Hill Book Company, 1958), pp. 240–308.

[27] Following some of the operations proposed by L. E. Allen, *op. cit.*

has the better ratio of management gain to union loss. Seniority has the better union-gain–management-loss ratio. Hence transactions which involve these items will represent a better integration of the parties' interests. If management agrees to increased seniority rights and the union agrees to cooperate on job reclassification, the parties have each gained 4 units by this double transaction.

**Figure 5-4**

|  | Labor's evaluation | Management's evaluation |
| --- | --- | --- |
| Cooperation on job reclassification | −3 | +8 |
| Reduction in wash-up period | −6 | +7 |
| Increased seniority rights | +7 | −4 |
| Strengthened rights to arbitration | +8 | −8 |

It is not difficult to cite instances of this type of utility matching taken from actual labor negotiations. Examples are two dramatic innovations in the history of automobile negotiations: (1) the 1950 General Motors negotiations in which there was matching between the five-year agreement and the union-shop issues and (2) the 1961 American Motors negotiations in which the parties coupled certain operating concessions for management and a profit-sharing plan which was of added value to the UAW as a breakthrough on an important front.

In some situations there may be the need for side payments to bring the shares into line with some notion of equity or power reality.

> In a negotiation between a large Wisconsin garment maker and the ILGWU the union agreed to some changes in work rules which involved high benefit for the company and low sacrifice for the union. During the closing hours of bargaining the union demanded a larger wage increase "because of all the money the company was saving."

The convention that "nothing is final until everything is settled" allows for just such an adjustment in shares. If the parties develop a solution that greatly benefits one side, there may be a need to make compensating adjustments in the other areas of bargaining.

The unanswered question in utility matching with or without side payments is: What determines the respective shares? The results of utility matching may not leave the parties even. When one side enjoys a power balance, it is not likely to trade even. The degree of imbalance between the respective gains and losses of the two parties would be determined by the factors important in distributive bargaining.

It is possible that in keeping with distributive bargaining, negotiators distort their actual gains and losses. The tactical use of overevaluation and underevaluation can work to the benefit of one side and to the detriment of the other side. In other words, by giving up something that one says is very costly to him (when it really is not that costly), he may be able to obtain something that is valuable. Either side can force mixed bargaining back to pure distributive bargaining. In other words, Party can threaten to destroy all of the additional joint gain brought about by integrative bargaining if the final share disposition is not within the realm of equity. The approach runs something like this: Both sides have created some additional joint gain because of the integrative bargaining; if Party does not receive an appropriate share of this additional joint gain, he threatens to force bargaining back to the level of joint gain that would have existed if only pure distributive bargaining had occurred. In other words, he refuses to agree on any of the integrative solutions.

We have some empirical evidence for such an approach in a published case study: [28]

> Towards the end of the National Foods case when the parties are close to agreement on the sticky principle of retroactivity, Wagner (union) makes a threat to go back to the union's original proposal if the company will not go the last step with him. By going back to the original proposal, Wagner would be hurting himself, but he would also be hurting the company and it is quite possible for Wagner to make such a threat credible.

The degree to which distributive bargaining enters the share allocation in mixed bargaining is an interesting question. There are certain mixed situations that end up being rather close to pure distributive bargaining. The maximization of joint gain has been accomplished, and now the parties are down to what one negotiator has called "the hard nut cutting." It is very likely that this will be viewed as a distributive process by both sides.

For example, in the final phases of bargaining each side may be trying to find those solutions that minimize the disutility for the other side, particularly if the disutility-matching approach is being used. Now, the question is whether this should be viewed as pure distributive bargaining or as pure integrative bargaining—for it is an important tactic in both processes. In distributive bargaining Party is trying to talk Opponent into a new appreciation of the respective merits and demerits of the situation. In other words, he is trying to change Opponent's utility curve by pointing up new information. In integrative bargaining the altering of disutility comes about by finding new alternatives that create less disutility for Opponent. The tactics are different and the effects are different.

---

[28] Selekman, Selekman, and Fuller, 2d ed., *op. cit.*, pp. 281–283.

The point of all this is that as bargaining comes to a showdown, what is purely integrative bargaining or what is beginning to move more toward distributive bargaining becomes difficult to separate. Both sides are trying to converge on a point, but at the same time they are trying to protect their own self-interests.

## Dilemmas in the Conditions of Problem Solving

We have identified several conditions as essential to the functioning of integrative bargaining. Are different demands placed on motivation, language and information, and trust in the two processes? Do these conditions play different roles in these processes?

**Motivation.** Underlying distributive bargaining are a strict self-interest orientation and a working assumption that the interests of the two parties are in fundamental conflict. For integrative bargaining to be successful, there needs to be considerable motivation to discover and act upon any mutuality or complementarity of interests. Paradoxically, proper motivation sometimes comes only after the parties have been through intense distributive bargaining. As we indicated in earlier chapters, it is possible for distributive bargaining to escalate into a deadly encounter. Both sides become committed to choices in the matrix which involve default. It is at this point when both sides are under some kind of incentive to find new cells in the matrix, in other words to increase the sum of the game, that integrative bargaining may emerge. Such would be the explanation for the innovative solutions that have emerged in crisis situations.

**Information and Language.** Many of the informational conditions conducive to integrative bargaining outlined earlier in this chapter present no particular problems for distributive bargaining. Party may take many steps to structure his own bargaining team in order to increase the problem-solving information without interfering with his distributive bargaining. Nevertheless, tactical dilemmas do arise from certain other steps or procedural issues, namely, the amount of authority vested in the team and the use of bargaining agents, subcommittees, and single spokesmen.

The question of at what level of the organization does one assign authority over the conduct of negotiations contains many possible dilemmas, depending on the specific situation.

Giving real authority to negotiators at lower levels sometimes allows more integrative bargaining because of availability of facts about the specific operation affected and allows more exchange of relevant information. Similarly, reserving real authority above the level of negotiators may be necessary for integrative bargaining if the real problem is one which requires awareness of the realities of external environment. These represent criteria of the integrative process.

Some independent criteria from distributive bargaining are as follows:

Inviting in one's own higher officials may have the advantage of creating credibility to a commitment. Using lower officials without authority sometimes has advantages in disguising one's own resistance point. There is no reason to believe that consideration of the integrative and distributive processes will dictate the same arrangements. In fact, the last distributive tactic mentioned, that of "calculated incompetence," is especially counter to the interests of integrative bargaining as an obstacle to search.

Consider the many facets of the delegated authority issue in one company. The union negotiator contended that his counterpart was "required to fly a kite with ten feet of string."

> The company negotiator did have very limited authority. It is difficult to say what the chief rationale was for this arrangement, but it did serve the company well as a distributive tactic; and in one way it enabled the negotiators to develop a close relationship. But a disadvantage was experienced in integrative bargaining. Items which were largely problems were treated in an unimaginative, stereotyped way according to "company policy."

The use of bargaining agents presents another tactical dilemma. If the company uses an agent to represent it during negotiations, it may be at an advantage in distributive bargaining, since this makes communication asymmetrical, permitting one party greater opportunity to become committed than the other. It is also a way for one to avoid revealing clues about one's true resistance point. However, to the extent that the agent affords this protection because he does not have immediate access to facts and does not know the principal's utility function, the agent arrangement permits less integrative bargaining. Moreover, when the agents are employed, their mandates typically are stated largely in distributive terms; at least they believe that they will be evaluated in these terms. On the other hand, if the relationship between the parties, for instance, management and union leaders, is bad enough, use of an agent by management may improve chances of integrative bargaining.

A third dilemma occurs around the question of subcommittees. Breaking negotiation teams down into subcommittees assigned to certain issues often enhances integrative bargaining. The smaller committees are less tempting as audiences in which to commit oneself. Therefore, any temporary exploration of alternate solutions by one party is less likely to be regarded by the other as compromising any prior commitments the first may have made.

These committees are often specifically charged with fact finding, but in any event, with less emphasis on finding ways to become committed, the members often realize that fact finding and exploring their respective utility functions is something that they can do.

By the same token, the very agreement to assign subcommittees to an issue conveys some flexibility (lack of commitment) on the issue which, considering the distributive bargain, one or both parties may prefer not to communicate.

Whether to use a single spokesman involves a fourth dilemma. Often the requirements of the distributive bargain make it advisable to use only one official spokesman, other members of the committee contributing only if called upon by the spokesman. This limits the risk of betraying the party's resistance point and overstating or understating the party's tactical commitments. On the other hand, this procedure usually works counter to integrative bargaining, in which freer interaction accompanied by a freer flow of information and a wider range of views, opinions, and judgments seems to be called for.

A related question—the size of the committee—provides a many-faceted problem. Larger teams may facilitate integrative bargaining from the point of view of information available but interfere with it in terms of level of trust afforded. Larger teams may facilitate distributive bargaining if a party wishes to increase its commitment but may interfere with it if the party wishes to remain flexible and avoid commitment for the time being.

The clarity of language is essential in integrative bargaining but may be deliberately avoided in distributive bargaining. The ambiguous language used in distributive bargaining sometimes has the effect of obscuring the meaning of messages used in the integrative bargaining process. Moreover, on balance, it is probably in Party's interest to create a reliable language for communicating with Opponent. The most effective commitment is made when a language system has been developed and Opponent believes what Party says about his preferences and intentions. Consequently, in this respect there is a compatibility between the need for full exchange of information in integrative bargaining and the need for a viable system of communication to confirm commitment in distributive bargaining.

Creation of a reliable language system in order that information be exchanged is a disadvantage if Opponent possesses a competitive orientation toward Party. Knowledge on Opponent's part about the relative importance of the problems to Party is essential for integrative bargaining, but it also allows Opponent to punish Party if that is his disposition. Experimental work has documented the fact that lack of information forces Opponent to act indifferently with respect to Party's payoffs, while information enables Opponent to either help or hurt Party.[29]

**Trust.** Trust is necessary to get a party to enter into problem solving,

[29] Sidney Siegel and L. E. Fouraker, *Bargaining and Group Decision Making* (New York: McGraw-Hill Book Company, 1960), p. 102.

and it is essential in order for the parties to believe what the other tells the first in this context. Trust is required in every phase. Trust is required in distributive bargaining in more limited and subtle ways.

The need for trust stems from the complex nature of negotiations. If a minimum system of communication does not exist, no bargaining can take place. Trust provides the mechanism by which the negotiators stay in touch, not necessarily to collaborate, but to provide the basis by which they deal with one another as they seek to reach agreement.

A major contribution of trust is to allow the negotiator some confidence about the current character of the bargaining process. The greatest risk in negotiations is for Party to be engaging in integrative bargaining on the assumption that Opponent is similarly engaged, only to find out that Opponent has been following a distributive strategy all along. Each negotiator needs a sensing device to discern the climate of bargaining.

Sign language enforced by mutual trust performs a vital role in mixed bargaining. It allows a negotiator to suggest a collaborative solution while protecting himself. In many respects the mechanism is the same as tacit communication, which we examined in distributive bargaining. In that context, tacit communication provided the auspices for both sides to abandon commitments and converge on a settlement. The overall atmosphere, however, was still conflict over the shares. In this context we are examining tacit communications as a device that allows the negotiator to choose the collaborative cell of the matrix, one that increases the sum of the game while avoiding the danger that Opponent will act in an exploitive way in order to maximize his share of the settlement.

### A Variation of the Strategy for Mixed Bargaining

Parties engage in mixed bargaining in order to achieve the most from each of the two processes. Generally speaking, the tactics appropriate for pure distributive bargaining conflict with those appropriate for pure integrative bargaining. At virtually every turn the negotiator finds himself in a dilemma: Should he conceal information in order to make his tactical commitment more credible, or should he reveal information in order to pursue integrative bargaining; should be bring militant constituents into the session to affirm feeling, or should he use small subcommittees in which new ideas can be quietly explored; etc.?

Frequently the negotiator's way out of the difficulty is to engage in those tactics which exploit the possibilities of integrative bargaining while guaranteeing a decent share of the larger sum. This strategy of mixed bargaining can be viewed as an effort to increase the sum of the gain while *preventing* Opponent from gaining a disproportionate share of that gain. Refer again to Figure 5-2, which is helpful in identifying this particular complex strategy. Party engages in an increased-sum strategy at that level of the game. Thus he assures that the outcome will be in one of the two lower quadrants, hopefully the lower right-hand quadrant. Moreover, at the level of share strategy, Party assumes a soft bargaining posture coupled with particular efforts to foreclose a hard bargaining strategy on the part of Opponent.

Notice that the competitive element enters in the form of controlling Opponent's distributive behavior. The outright distributive objective of increasing Party's share is not to be held in the same prominence as increasing the sum of the gains; otherwise the conflict of tactics remains. In effect, Party takes the initiative with respect to integrative bargaining and acts defensively with respect to distributive bargaining.

By engaging in those tactics which prevent Opponent from gaining the lion's share of the game, Party guarantees himself a decent share. When the strategy of mixed bargaining is stated in this way, it is often possible to choose tactics that are compatible to both processes.

# CHAPTER VI

# ATTITUDINAL STRUCTURING MODEL

Two parties enter into negotiations. The negotiation process shapes the division of the product of their joint efforts—how much goes to capital, how much to labor. The negotiation process also facilitates the resolution of joint problems and the integration of the interests of the parties. The importance of these economic outputs of negotiations is obvious. A third result of the negotiation process is a maintenance or restructuring of the attitudes of the participants toward each other. The attitudes of each party toward the other, taken together, define the relationship between them.

Why concern ourselves with attitude structuring and the relationship between the parties? We need only recall our discussion in the preface, in which we identified several aspects of labor negotiations. The issues in labor negotiations involve important human values; fulfillment of the contract terms is strongly contingent upon attitudes; instruments in the contest involve social ideologies and psychological tactics as well as economic sanctions; and the relationship between the parties is an exclusive and continuing one. These factors suggest that attitudes and relationship patterns play an important role in labor negotiations. Bargaining theorists ordinarily do not pay attention to the attitudinal dimension of negotiations. It is also fair to say that problem-solving theorists have not attempted to take into account all the above aspects of social or political decision making.

The treatment in this and the next chapter will be social-psychological in orientation. It will focus on the way in which attitudinal variables enter into the conduct of labor negotiations. Part 1 of the present chapter will set forth the various types of attitudes and relationships which are the target areas of attitudinal structuring in collective bargaining. This discussion will include an assessment of both the functional significance of the various relationship patterns and the types of environmental factors which influence the patterns. Part 2 will set forth a model of attitudinal change adapted from the behavioral sciences. The next chapter will then treat the specific tactics which are intended to influence attitudes, and will analyze the ways in which attitudinal structuring interacts with distributive and integrative bargaining.

# PART 1 | RELATIONSHIP PATTERNS: THE GOALS OF ATTITUDINAL STRUCTURING

The parties share a *relationship pattern,* by which we mean a set of reciprocal attitudes salient to the parties in their interaction. We use a classification scheme for differentiating these patterns: conflict, containment-aggression, accommodation, cooperation, and collusion.[1] The classification of an institutional relationship assumes two operations. First, it results from the combination of several specific attitudinal dimensions: (1) *motivational orientation* and *action tendencies* toward each other (competitive-individualistic-cooperative), (2) beliefs about the other's *legitimacy,* (3) feelings of *trust* toward the other, and (4) feelings of *friendliness-hostility* toward the other. These particular attitudinal components are assumed to be crucial to the parties' joint dealings, to be interrelated, and generally to vary together in the labor-management context.

Second, the classification is assigned to reflect the central tendency of the attitudes held by members of the two organizations—the modal attitudes. Thus, the attitude of any particular member of an organization may deviate substantially from this institutional pattern. This becomes important if the deviant attitudes are held by the organization's chief negotiator. However, unless specifically indicated, we shall assume that the attitudes which relate the two negotiators are similar to the central tendencies of the two institutions.

We can elaborate somewhat the distinctions we make regarding motivational orientation, the most general of the attitudinal dimensions. Under

[1] As a point of departure for this scheme, we have used the highly insightful classification of Selekman, Selekman, and Fuller who distinguish among nine patterns of institutional relationship. We use only five patterns and have taken considerable liberty in interpreting and redefining the categories for our purpose. See B. M. Selekman, S. K. Selekman, and S. H. Fuller, *Problems in Labor Relations,* 2d ed. (New York: McGraw-Hill Book Company, 1958), pp. 4–8.

the *competitive* orientation the parties are motivated to defeat or to win over the other. Each side seeks to maximize his relative advantage over the opponent, even though in the process he may incur some sacrifice to his own interests. This is the main attitudinal component of the conflict and containment-aggression patterns. Under the *individualistic* orientation, the parties pursue their own self-interests without motivation to help or hinder the other. This orientation is associated with what is termed the accommodation pattern. Under the *cooperative* orientation, each party is concerned about the other's welfare in addition to his own. Two patterns involve this orientation: cooperation and collusion.

**Conflict.** In this pattern the parties feel extremely competitive. There is essentially a denial of the legitimacy of the other party's ends and means. The company is determined to refuse to deal with unions if at all possible. It recognizes the union only to the extent imposed by law and union power. In the company's pursuance of this policy it is constrained only by the letter of the law (as law enforcement feasibly can be brought to bear by government agencies); it is certainly not constrained by the spirit of the law. Coexistence is not a policy but a temporary state of affairs.

It is not surprising then that the parties have essentially no positive concern for the other's internal affairs. They might, in fact, be inclined to destroy the other organization; they would at least be happy to contribute to the downfall of the officials of the other party, either company management or union leadership, as the case might be.

Other attitudes are extreme distrust and hate. The parties correctly distrust each other's motives and actions; no quarter is asked and none is given. Their disliking for each other frequently assumes irrational proportions. Because of the prospect of irrational and extreme behavior, the relationship is marked by considerable anxiety. The well-known story of the Kohler-UAW strike provides an illustration of such a relationship.

**Containment-Aggression.** The parties are moderately competitively oriented. Recognition of the legitimacy of the other party could be characterized as "grudging acceptance." The union is determined to extend its scope of influence, and the company is insistent on containing the union's scope of action. In their choice of means the parties accept any limits of the law, including a minimum definition of the spirit of the law as they understand it. The actual content of bargaining tends to be confined to the traditional subject matter of wages, hours, and working conditions.

Each has little respect for the other's officials and internal organizational processes, however. Each would gladly weaken the organization or the position of the other's officials if this did not involve significant sacrifices of its own. Each party would not only be interested in gaining the allegiance of the workers but also in detracting from the allegiance enjoyed by the other.

The parties regard each other with suspicion and are mutually antagonistic. Every action is scrutinized. Raw power plays are frankly expected and employed by both sides.

Two well-known philosophies of labor relations reported by Robert McMurry seem to fit this general pattern.[2] The first is "Boulwarism," which is bluntly characterized by an intransigent attitude toward unions.[3]

The institutional strategy of Boulwarism as innovated and practiced by General Electric includes communicating directly with employees rather than through union officials, engaging in activities to compete with the union for employees' allegiance, practicing quite adamantly a final-offer-first bargaining strategy, and communicating the offer directly to employees.

The second, "Crawfordism," after Crawford of Thompson Products, offers a slightly different strategy. It nevertheless embodies the same competitively oriented attitudes toward the union. The strategy of Crawford was to offer employees his own charismatic leadership and a paternalistic program. Management responded to workers' needs, communicated to them in homely parables, and administered extensive welfare schemes.

*Accommodation.* The parties are individualistic in their orientation. Recognition of the legitimacy of the other's means and ends amounts to an "acceptance of the *status quo.*" Neither party is driving hard to change the nature of the agenda of collective bargaining. They have adjusted to each other and have evolved routines for performing functions and settling differences.

Each party has a moderate amount of respect for the officials of the other and pursues a hands-off policy with respect to the other's internal organization. There is little "competition" between union and management for the allegiance of the workers.

The relationship is marked by limited trust. "Although not unduly alarmist about the potential of every demand for encroaching upon managerial prerogatives or every counter-demand for affecting shop rights, the parties to an accommodative pattern maintain a certain alert watchfulness. . . ."[4] The level of affect among the participants is rather low—not strongly positive or negative. They go about their business, interacting in a courteous but informal manner.

Another labor relations philosophy reported by McMurry is an example of the accommodation pattern with some overtones of cooperation. The pattern emerged for a short period between 1952 and 1955 from encounters

[2] R. N. McMurry, "War and Peace in Labor Relations," *Harvard Business Review*, vol. 30 (November–December, 1955), pp. 48–60.

[3] For a more recent account of Boulwarism see H. R. Northrup, *Boulwarism* (Ann Arbor, Mich.: Bureau of Industrial Relations, University of Michigan, 1964).

[4] Selekman, Selekman, and Fuller, 2d ed., *op. cit.*, p. 6.

between Fairless of U.S. Steel and McDonald of the United Steelworkers. For management's part, it recognized union security needs, limited its employee communications to union channels, tackled "problems" without stressing "prerogatives," and recognized the value of building day-to-day relationships with the union. The union reciprocated with a reasonable approach.

*Cooperation.* The motivational orientation is cooperative. There is complete acceptance of the legitimacy of the other. This pattern is characterized by the fact that the parties willingly extend mutual concerns far beyond the familiar matters of wages, hours, and conditions. Productive efficiency, the solvency of the firm, elimination of waste, advance of technology, employment security, and so on are treated as matters of common interest.

There is likewise full respect for the other—its organization and officials. The union accepts managerial success as being of concern to labor; management recognizes its stake in stable, effective unionism. Inasmuch as each has found areas in which the other can be instrumental to its own objectives, it is likely to act in such a way as to strengthen the other organization or its leaders. Finally, there is mutual trust and a friendly attitude between the parties generally.

*Collusion.* The parties go beyond the question of recognizing the legitimacy of the other's ends and means. In certain respects they form a coalition in which they pursue common ends. In contrast to the cooperation pattern, the coalition and the ends it pursues are outside the law. Mutual attention is given to areas not really legitimate within the mandate of their respective principals (they violate the interests of employees or stockholders) or not really legitimate under the law (they violate the public interest). For example, union leaders and employers may combine to freeze out other firms. The parties may collude and agree to irresponsibly high wages in a product market which allows the employer to pass on the full cost to the consumer. In another variation the union leaders may agree to substandard wages for some favor in return.

Close attention may also be given to each other's internal affairs as well, since they have maximum incentive to preserve the mutually profitable relationship designed to exploit some third party.

Trust in the collusion pattern of necessity tends to be complete, since it is based on symmetrical blackmail possibilities. There is a disciplined avoidance of harming the other because of the risk of exposure. Although the parties are not exactly friendly, they do tend to be intimate; hence the appropriateness of the term "sweetheart relationship," which is often used in this connection.

See Figure 6-1 for a recapitulation of the attitudinal components of each of the five relationship patterns distinguished.

**Figure 6-1**

**Attitudinal Components of the Relationship Patterns**

*Pattern of relationship*

| *Attitudinal dimensions* | *Conflict* | *Containment-Aggression* | *Accommodation* | *Cooperation* | *Collusion* |
|---|---|---|---|---|---|
| **Motivational orientation and action tendencies toward other** | Competitive tendencies to destroy or weaken | Competitive tendencies to destroy | Individualistic policy of hands off | Cooperative tendencies to assist or preserve | Cooperative tendencies to assist or preserve |
| **Beliefs about legitimacy of other** | Denial of legitimacy | Grudging acknowledgment | Acceptance of *status quo* | Complete legitimacy | Not applicable |
| **Level of trust in conducting affairs** | Extreme distrust | Distrust | Limited trust | Extended trust | Trust based on mutual blackmail potential |
| **Degree of friendliness** | Hate | Antagonism | Neutralism-Courteousness | Friendliness | Intimacy–"Sweetheart relationship" |

These relationships and the attitudes which define them have implications for the parties and their joint dealings. Consequently, a party's preference for a particular relationship pattern may become an important objective of that party. Some of the above relationship patterns, such as accommodation, will presumably seem more appropriate as a goal than others, such as conflict, but sometimes a party actually will prefer a more conflictful pattern, perhaps for purposes of preserving internal cohesion. We shall turn to this general question, the functional significance of the various relationship patterns, after we have identified some of the basic forces which influence the relationship.

### Determinants of Relationship Patterns

We have observed that there are different relationship patterns. Parties usually develop preferences for a particular pattern, for reasons to be explored later in this chapter. The relationship itself becomes an important goal or constraint on negotiating activities. But can a participant to labor negotiations structure any pattern he chooses? Before we move to consideration of an attitudinal change model and the tactics used to implement change, we should pause and address ourselves to a frank assessment of the many forces which operate to influence the relationship pattern. This will help to distinguish between those contextual factors beyond the control of the negotiators and those factors which can be manipulated during the interaction of the participants in order to bring about change.

Our analysis here extends the type of structural analysis central to Professor Dunlop's theory of industrial relations systems.[5] He explains the web of rules in terms of actors and the various environmental contexts: technology, market and budgetary, and status and power. Dunlop's theory is particularly persuasive in explaining the forces shaping the more substantive aspects of industrial relations. However, a similar question arises in social relationships: How can we explain what relationship pattern will develop in various circumstances? We do not have a thoroughly systematic explanation, but we do find it necessary to include social psychological variables not included in his framework.

Specifically, we view the existing relationship pattern as a product of (1) the technological, market, and power contexts of the parties; (2) the basic personality dispositions of key individuals in the relationship; (3) the social belief systems of these individuals, usually shared in some degree by their respective organizations; and (4) the actual bargaining experiences that they have shared. The above list starts with those factors which usually must be taken as given and proceeds to those which are increasingly sus-

---

[5] J. T. Dunlop, *Industrial Relations Systems* (New York: Holt, Rinehart and Winston, Inc., 1958).

ceptible to change. They are not assumed to be independent of each other in any ultimate sense. Personalities, social beliefs, and experiences are especially closely related.

**Contextual Factors.** There is no doubt that broad environmental forces do play an important role in influencing relationships. Numerous case studies have been developed in an attempt to discern the factors that influence the union-management relationship. The series sponsored by the National Planning Association are the best known.[6] In that study considerable importance was placed on various economic, technological, political, and community aspects of the environment.[7] If a strike as one measure of conflict is in any way indicative of the type of relationship, we have evidence of the influence of such factors. Studies have shown that some industries are more strike prone than others,[8] that there is a correlation between strikes and the business cycle,[9] etc. It has also been suggested that industrial conflict is related to occupational structure.[10] Kornhauser lists other objective conditions which have been used in explanations of peaceful versus conflictful relations: trend in price levels, proportion of labor costs to other costs, labor legislation, company size, age of union, and administrative organization of the plant.[11] Sayles has taken a closer look at the relationship of technology and behavioral styles of work groups at the plant level.[12]

Moreover, it may be that collective bargaining relationships which follow strict patterns negotiated elsewhere can be freer from conflict than those which must establish patterns.[13] In pattern-following situations the content of negotiation might center less on items involving goal conflict, such as wages, and more on items with integrative potential. At least two other environmental factors place limits on the relationship pattern estab-

---

[6] C. S. Golden and V. D. Parker (eds.), *Causes of Industrial Peace under Collective Bargaining* (New York: National Planning Association, Harper & Row, Publishers, Incorporated, 1955).

[7] See Clark Kerr, "The Collective Bargaining Environment" in Golden and Parker, *op. cit.*, pp. 10–18.

[8] Clark Kerr and Abraham Siegel, "The Interindustry Propensity to Strike: An International Comparison," in Arthur Kornhauser, Robert Dubin, and Arthur Ross (eds.), *Industrial Conflict* (New York: McGraw-Hill Book Company, 1954), pp. 189–212.

[9] Albert Rees, "Industrial Conflict and Business Fluctuations," in *Industrial Conflict, op. cit.*, pp. 213–220.

[10] W. E. Moore, "Occupational Structure and Industrial Conflict," in *Industrial Conflict, op. cit.*, pp. 221–239.

[11] Arthur Kornhauser, "Human Motivations Underlying Industrial Conflict," in *Industrial Conflict, op. cit.*, p. 63.

[12] L. R. Sayles, *The Behavior of Industrial Work Groups* (New York: John Wiley & Sons, Inc., 1958).

[13] H. M. Levinson, "Pattern Bargaining by the United Automobile Workers," *Labor Law Review*, vol. 9 (September, 1958), pp. 669–673.

lished. The laws bar certain aspects of the conflict and collusion patterns; and public opinion can limit pursuance of certain aspects of the containment-aggression pattern.

Historically, many relationships have shifted from the cooperative to the competitive side during "tightening-up" programs in response to new market conditions. Consider, for example, the farm equipment and automobile industries. During World War II relationships were generally amicable in these industries, and both sides worked together to maximize production. However, with the shift to peacetime production many of the companies attempted to eliminate loose practices. For instance, in 1946 the Ford Motor Company sought and received guarantees from the union that wildcat strikes would be eliminated. In International Harvester, extensive programs to realign the incentive and classification systems were inaugurated. These attempts to improve plant efficiency resulted in a natural deterioration in labor relations. The tenor of attitudes shifted in the containment direction. However, once these companies regained control of their plant situations, they were able to turn their attention again to improving relationships, and during the last 10 years a high degree of accommodation has occurred at both these companies.

More recent illustrations serve to further emphasize the influence of certain broad economic and technological forces on union-management relationships. The early 1960s found many accommodative patterns moving in the direction of containment, as companies sought to improve their operating position. The 1959–1960 steel strike, the 1962 newspaper strike, and crises in the meat-packing and railroad industries were events which confirmed this trend.

We have suggested that the influence of market competition can shift the relationship toward containment-agression and conflict. Interestingly, a reverse effect may occur if the circumstances take on a crisis character. On many occasions management and labor have entered into cooperative programs to save the company and to save employment. A good measure of the cooperation in the needle trades has been fostered by a crisis atmosphere produced by the instability of the product market.

While we acknowledge the importance of these more or less environmental factors on the particular approach that one or both of the parties will take to collective bargaining and the relationship pattern which results, we also know that there exists a wide variance in the tenor of relationships within similar environments, probably influenced by the personalities and social belief systems of key participants.

Notable examples of quite different relationship patterns can be found in most industries. For example, during the 1940s the Ford Motor Company structured a pattern of accommodation with the UAW in contrast to General Motors' pattern of containment-aggression. In recent years American Motors initiated a cooperative pattern in even sharper contrast to the containment-aggression pattern which continued at Chrysler. In the steel industry, Kaiser's bid for a cooperative relationship set it apart from other steel firms. Similar significant differences exist in the airline industry between United Airlines and Eastern Airlines and in the farm equipment industry between John Deere and Allis Chalmers.

**Personality Factors.** Key leaders in the organizations mentioned above have had an important influence in pointing the direction their institutional relationship will follow. Officials who have primary responsibility for handling the contacts between the organizations also have an important role to play in shaping the relationship.

Anecdotal evidence that personalities are an important factor in this area is abundant. The fact that the labor relations patterns adopted by General Electric, Thompson Products, and U.S. Steel have been referred to as "Boulwarism," "Crawfordism," and "Fairlessness," respectively, is suggestive that the patterns were expressive of the personal styles of their chief architects. Henry Ford's long bitter holdout against any recognition of the UAW, followed by his complete capitulation to the union in 1941 (by granting the union shop, a liberal number of paid committeemen, etc.) in a bid to achieve the best labor relations possible, apparently were extremes characteristic of his manner. Similarly the patterns of labor-management cooperation initiated by Kaiser Steel and American Motors are offered as further evidence. They both seemed to reflect the style of their planners first in the nature of their approach to the union and second in the fact that such an approach represented a pattern deviant from the rest of the industry.

The analysis which follows pertains to the question: What are the personality attributes which influence the level of trust, friendliness-hostility, and the motivational orientation which comprise a relationship?

Authoritarian personality structure, characterized by conservatism, emotional coldness, power seeking, hostility toward minority groups, etc.,[14] has been related to several patterns of behavior pertinent here. The general policy orientation in foreign relations of nationalism versus internationalism correlates with authoritarianism.[15] Nationalism, a facet of ethnocentric thinking, involves a preference for rigid and pervasive distinctions between ingroups and outgroups. Internationalism involves more optimistic assumptions about the potential fruits of collaboration and favors minimizing barriers to a fuller exchange of ideas and mutual assistance. This suggests that a person high on authoritarianism is relatively

[14] Posited by T. W. Adorno et al., *The Authoritarian Personality* (New York: Harper & Row, Publishers, Incorporated, 1950).

[15] D. L. Levinson, "Authoritarian Personality and Foreign Policy," *Journal of Conflict Resolution*, vol. 1 (March, 1957), pp. 37–47.

more likely to initiate a low-trust competitive pattern in collective bargaining as well.

Experimental studies provide further support along these lines. In a non-zero-sum game situation, persons who scored high on authoritarianism (F scale) tended to be less trusting of the other player and tended to be less trustworthy in their own choices.[16] Moreover, those who were untrustworthy seemed to expect to be exploited by others. In a situation requiring problem-solving behavior, those low on F scale were less likely to act in a unilateral manner.[17]

Rokeach has posited a related but more broadly conceived personality structure, "dogmatism," which seems to be even more pertinent to the question of interest here, namely, whether the person will be favorably or unfavorably predisposed to collaborative patterns between labor unions and business management.[18] The *dogmatism scale* measures a relatively closed cognitive orientation of beliefs and disbeliefs about reality organized around a central set of beliefs about absolute authority which, in turn, provides a framework for patterns of intolerance and qualified tolerance toward others. Rokeach presents evidence that dogmatism and the acceptance or rejection of opinionated language are both likely to be found in persons with strong (and presumably exclusive) commitments to religious or political groups. In accordance with the line of argument being developed here, we would strongly expect to find a positive correlation between the dogmatism personality scores of key union and management persons responsible for the development of their institutional relationship and the competitive orientation of the pattern. The correlation might be highly significant if the more important contextual factors mentioned above were controlled.

To consider another personality variable, the amount of self-esteem of key persons in an emergent labor-management system may influence their response to the challenges inherent in the situation. An important aspect of a new institutional relationship is interdependence combined with the implicit threat of power. Cohen found that self-esteem and situational structure interact to determine the perception of threat in the power exercised by other persons.[19] Those low in self-esteem handled threat by bringing still more threat into the situation, were more vulnerable and dependent upon the power-laden situation, and showed a greater need for

[16] William Haythorn et al., "The Behavior of Authoritarian and Equalitarian Personality Groups," *Human Relations*, vol. 9 (February, 1956), pp. 57–74.

[17] Morton Deutsch, "Trust, Trustworthiness, and F-Scale," *Journal of Abnormal and Social Psychology*, vol. 61, no. 1 (1960), pp. 138–140.

[18] Milton Rokeach, "Political and Religious Dogmatism: An Alternative to the Authoritarian Personality," *Psychological Monographs*, vol. 70, no. 18, whole no. 425 (1956), pp. 1–43.

[19] A. R. Cohen, "The Effects of Individual Self-esteem and Situational Structure on Threat-oriented Reactions to Power," *Dissertation Abstracts*, vol. 14 (1954), pp. 727–728.

structure. According to our classification of relationships, conflict and containment patterns incorporate more threat. Hence, we expect persons with low self-esteem to be relatively more likely to structure a competitive pattern.

Sorokin and Lunden present further evidence of personality differences among persons who might be found in decision-making roles in terms of their predispositions to use violence and other forms of extreme sanction.[20]

Certain personality attributes are indicative of a willingness and ability to enter into integrative social processes. In a small group experiment, Haythorn found mature, accepting persons facilitated, while suspicious, nonaccepting persons depressed, group functioning.[21] We suggest that these findings can be generalized to collective bargaining processes.

Dramatic evidence of the influence of personalities sometimes develops when a negotiator who represents a given party is replaced. Ann Douglas reports that the entrance of a new company negotiator into the bargaining room changed the atmosphere—that there was an increase in the frequency of gestures of goodwill.[22] In the Pilgrim Oil Company there was circumstantial evidence that the deadlock of the parties was due in part to the mutual antagonism and resentment between chief negotiators themselves. As the management official said:

> Mr. Arnold (the union official) is referring to statements that are coming to him. I don't mind saying that I have had people tell me: "If Arnold weren't here, it would be easier to reach an agreement." I don't mind saying also that our people in the plant have heard from the outside that if both of us were out, that negotiations would proceed smoothly.[23]

Of course the root of the antagonism may not lie in any basic personality incompatibilities but rather in a continuation of behavioral and attitudinal patterns more appropriate to an earlier period.

Frequently those involved in a conflictful union-management relationship will explain that their own posture is one of response to the other side. They explain that they are merely "fighting fire with fire" and that a competitive approach at least stabilizes the situation. Taking such a person at his word, he responds to what he perceives in the other. It is significant,

[20] P. A. Sorokin and W. A. Lunden, *Power and Morality: Who Should Guard the Guardians?* (Boston: Porter Sargent, 1959).

[21] William Haythorn, "The Influence of Individual Members on the Characteristics of Small Groups," *Journal of Abnormal and Social Psychology*, vol. 48, no. 2 (1953), pp. 276–284.

[22] Ann Douglas, *Industrial Peacemaking* (New York: Columbia University Press, 1962), p. 30.

[23] Selekman, Selekman, and Fuller, 2d ed., *op. cit.*, p. 322.

however, that in the same situation different persons will perceive different things (such as the social intents of the other). The phenomenon of selective perception is observed in everyday affairs and has been demonstrated repeatedly in the laboratory. Some negotiators are predisposed to see competitive or destructive tendencies in the other's behavior.

There is a two-way relation between personalities of negotiators and the institutional pattern in which they operate. The individual may influence the relationship, but the existing relationship also may determine the type of person who gets the job. A type of self-selection process goes on, in which the institutional relationship determines the kind of personality attributes required of the key people to collective bargaining. For example, the International Harvester situation during the late 1940s called forth antagonistic individuals. Rival unionism, lack of central control on the part of both management and the union, the company's tightening-up programs, and the like required union leadership with a competitive orientation. However, eventually the environment changed in such a way that the competitive orientation became less appropriate. Still, union leaders of this type continued to be elected to office. The environment had originally influenced the relationship, which was then perpetuated by the personalities of individuals who filled key leadership positions.

In summary, certain personality attributes are believed to be associated with more conflictful relationships. Persons are less likely to enter into cooperative relationships if they score high on authoritarianism and dogmatism, have low self-esteem, and are inherently suspicious and nonaccepting. In addition, the relationship influences the type of persons selected as negotiators.

**Social Beliefs.** A person's style in interpersonal relations is also suggestive of his social beliefs or ideology. For the individual a distinction between personality and social beliefs may not be fruitful. However, separate treatment is necessary in considering the collectivities of union and management. What was a personal style for Crawford, Boulware, Fairless, or Ford had to be translated into an ideology and accepted in that form by other members of the organization.

Without question the character of the relationship is influenced by the social beliefs of the management and union groups. Management's approach to collective bargaining has typically been characterized by a managerial ideology that places emphasis on "management's mission to manage." The ideology points to business executives as the best equipped and best situated to balance the conflicting interests that impose upon the enterprise—labor, capital, customers.

Given this outlook on the part of management, it is not surprising that they view unions as inimical to the managerial position. The argument over management's rights and prerogatives is evidence of this ideological conflict. In some cases the conflict has gone further than just defending the management domain from the encroachment of aggressive unions. Management's belief system has required that they actively work to weaken and to defeat unions. Such a clash of ideologies dominated the scene during the 1930s.

> Employers did not accept this social revolution without a struggle. From 1936–39, when the union began its assaults on the great redoubts of steel, auto, and rubber, the country got a strong whiff of class warfare. In the Ohio River manufacturing centers, flying squadrons, sitdowns, mass walkouts, and similar techniques of guerilla unionism were employed to keep a factory shut tight and to prevent the entry of scabs. Alarmed by the threat to traditional property rights, many employers struck back. In the small towns of "industrial valley," employers sought to enlist middle-class opinion behind them. The most publicized, and for a while, the most successful method was the so-called Mohawk Valley formula utilized by Remington Rand. In various parts of the country, the formula was repeated. Citizens' committees were launched in a dozen cities. . . . In Hershey, Pennsylvania, irate farmers, barred from selling their milk to the chocolate company, stormed the plant and scattered the strikers. Yet the counter offensive failed. New Deal Governors, such as Murphy in Michigan and Earle in Pennsylvania, kept the state militias neutral. A spotlight on anti-union methods and exposés of company unions by the NLRB put the corps on the defensive. Perhaps most effective was the La Follette Civil Liberties Committee, which, over a 2 year period, documented a black record of labor spies, tear gas purchases, and employment of professional thugs and strikebreakers by the blue-ribbon corps of U.S. industry, among them G.M., Bethlehem Steel, RCA, and others.[24]

Today the ideological conflict is not as open or as intense. One factor which has led to more positive relations over time is the increased agreement about some basic values and issues. Largely through the compliance processes of distributive bargaining, management has at first conceded, later accepted, and finally "valued" [25] many provisions (rights, obligations, conditions) which were originally only union objectives, e.g., restrictions on layoff, seniority, posting requirements, and equal pay for equal work.

[24] Daniel Bell, "Industrial Conflict and Public Opinion," in *Industrial Conflict, op. cit.*, pp. 245–246.

[25] There is experimental evidence that public compliance with some state of affairs, either by reward or by the threat of punishment, exerts a force on one's beliefs in the direction of a change to rationalize what has been done. We shall discuss later further tactical implications of this proposition. J. W. Brehm, "A Dissonance Analysis of Attitude-discrepant Behavior," in M. J. Rosenberg et al. (eds.), *Attitude Organization and Change* (New Haven: Yale University Press, 1960), pp. 164–197.

Yet much of the discussion over union security, right to work, and union monopoly power, illustrates that more than mere remnants of this conflict still persist. Many members of management still hold that trade unionism is not compatible with the free-enterprise system. Much of what is carried on under the label of "Positive Employee Relations" is intended to contain the union's influence. The union is not directly attacked, but it is weakened by limiting its involvement—and management works on strengthening the direct tie between management and the work force. Management is competing for the loyalty and support of the employee organization. This ideology, which strongly emphasizes the leadership mandate of management, has been promulgated by many companies, a notable example being Timken Roller Bearing.

Management is not alone in embracing an ideology that views the interests of management and labor as in basic conflict. Many union leaders are persuaded that the economic and class position of management is in conflict with the best interests of the working man. Social unionism, which has urged basic changes in the society and in the allocation of rewards, has brought union leaders into direct conflict with management. The more extreme unions in this respect were expelled from the CIO for communist domination during the late 1940s, but many of the industrial unions continue to challenge management's rights to unilateral decision making in certain traditional areas, such as pricing.

However, by comparison with other countries the American trade union movement has espoused a minimum of the class-conflict ideology. The statements of trade union leaders in this country reflect relatively little class orientation. The typical American union leader holds a "business" ideology. He is pragmatic; he has a job to get done; he is in office to represent the interests of the rank and file and not to change society. Even union leaders who embrace the uplift doctrine concentrate their energies on achieving social benefits rather than challenging the structure of the economy.

Examples can be found of ideologies that have fostered cooperation. Many members of management see the interests of labor and capital as identical and see the role of union leadership as a helpful intermediary in the process of collaboration. Many profit-sharing and cost-reduction plans established jointly with the union attest to this ideology. In the early 1960s, the Kaiser plan, the Human Relations Committee in the steel industry, and joint study groups in a variety of industries illustrated the fact that certain managers and labor leaders held social beliefs conducive to cooperation.

The change toward closer cooperation is not universal. Some managers feel that joint committees and the cooperative approach result in a sellout. Management loses its position of influence. Similarly, some union leaders view cooperation as a speedup device or as a way of being seduced into accepting mechanization and job elimination.

On balance, however, social beliefs appear to be evolving in a direction making cooperation more feasible. For instance, in the automobile industry, management has always avoided joint study groups during the pre-negotiation period. Yet, for the first time, in 1964 they met in a series of subcommittees to study the problems to be placed on the bargaining table. Management has pointed out that the change has not been just on their side. For the first time the UAW appeared sincere in its desire to collaborate and was not making the proposal merely for publicity purposes.

**Perpetuation Processes and Forces toward Change.** The general story of collective bargaining during the last 20 years in this country has been a general movement from conflict toward accommodation and in some cases cooperation. Yet in some instances relationships have remained static. In general, what have been the forces instrumental in bringing about a change or in perpetuating a given relationship?

Many factors contribute to the stability of an established pattern. Selective perception serves this purpose. Once accustomed to another's patterns and motives, a person tends to perceive only those things which tend to confirm the original view of the other. A related tendency [26] is overrationalizing the other party's position. In the absence of complete information one attributes to the other an "omniscience" he does not necessarily possess: accidents and isolated mistakes are treated as deliberate and tactical. There is pressure to maintain the generalized model of the other's behavior adopted to give cognitive structure to these data.

A second factor is based on the selectivity of personalities appropriate to the current role (which we have already mentioned) followed by a tendency of the occupant to preserve a relationship pattern in which his own personal style is fitting. As one observer put it, "Those who have had long tenure of office . . . have gained and held their power by being fighters, and they are not likely to change." [27] In that connection he cited another study,[28] which indicated that the average length of the international union president's term of office in 10 "representative" unions was 26 years. Also supporting a leader's tendency to preserve a pattern are the traditions and customs held onto by the rank and file of the union.

But change has occurred despite the conservative tendencies just cited. Some of the forces toward change have resulted from changes in the con-

---

[26] R. A. Bauer, "Problems of Perception and Relations between the United States and the Soviet Union," *Journal of Conflict Resolution,* vol. 5 (September, 1961), pp. 223–229.

[27] Ernest Dale, "Union-Management Cooperation," in *Industrial Conflict, op. cit.,* p. 368.

[28] Eli Ginzberg, *The Labor Leader* (New York: The Macmillan Company, 1948), p. 64.

textual factors discussed earlier: legislation which is aimed at limiting the relationship spectrum on both ends (conflict and collusion), public opinion that has shifted back and forth in the last 30 years from management to labor to management whenever evidence has accumulated regarding the abuses by one side or the other, and economic and technological changes. The influence of these changes can be toward either more or less cooperation.

One event that can have a dramatic impact in unfreezing the situation is the onset of a long and intense strike. This was true of some important strikes, such as the 1946 General Motors strike, the 1959 steel strike, and the 1962 strike in New York City newspapers—all of which apparently had a positive effect on their relationships. A type of unfreezing occurs because of the trauma and catharsis associated with the strike and because it brings the parties to a new realization of the costs or deficiencies associated with the previous pattern. In 7 of 13 major firms who bargained with professional engineering unions, drastic changes in the relationship followed a strike or other period of crisis.[29] Again not all changes were in the direction of accommodation, however.

Certain forces associated with the development of the labor movement and union-management relationship may explain the net movement toward accommodation and cooperation. First, there has been a stabilization of jurisdictional patterns enforced by no-raiding agreements among unions and mechanisms for peacefully resolving disputed claims. "*De facto* stabilization of bargaining rights is conducive to more peaceful union-management relations, since interunion rivalry has pronounced unsettling effects." [30] Second, the general social belief systems of both labor leaders and businessmen have changed toward moderation in the period from the middle 1930s to the 1960s. Much of this change has occurred apart from their specific dealings with each other. It is a change experienced by society as a whole. Third, some additional improvement in relationships has resulted from the testing and retesting of the validity of the conceptions they hold about each other. Selective perception only makes this testing difficult, not impossible. A fourth reason for accommodation derives from the fact that labor and business organizations have become increasingly bureaucratic and their officials more professional. The representatives of these organizations tend to measure progress along lines already accepted as legitimate by both. Finally, accommodation has occurred because it has been sought by the leaders of these organizations.

---

[29] R. E. Walton, *Impact of the Professional Engineering Union* (Boston: Division of Research, Graduate School of Business Administration, Harvard University, 1961), pp. 31–32.

[30] Kornhauser, Dubin, and Ross, "Alternative Roads Ahead," in *Industrial Conflict, op. cit.*, p. 508.

## Functional Significance of Relationship Patterns

We have set forth several possible relationship patterns, the particular attitudes which define them, and some of the determinants of these relationships. Before we proceed to deal with the relationship pattern as a more deliberate outcome of the interaction between the parties, we need to ask why the nature of the relationship is important. Just what difference does it make to a party which attitudes are reciprocated between the parties? The status of the relationship can be important to them for various reasons. First, certain patterns of relationships may be valued in their own right by participants. Second, certain relationships are preferred as a means to more effective implementation of the contract terms produced by negotiations. Third, certain relationships are preferred over others as a means to influencing the nature of future bargaining agenda and outcomes. Fourth, the nature of the relationship can affect the internal structure and cohesion of the participating organizations.

Each of the above reasons, especially the last three, refer to certain complex activities which would be especially affected by the nature of the relationship.

**Relationship Valued in Its Own Right.** As mentioned earlier, a company or a union may attempt to strengthen or to weaken the opponent out of personal preference and ideological conviction. Thus a conflict or cooperative relationship might be considered as an end in itself. An organization may have a general preference for a given type of relationship because it is congruent with its dominant social philosophy; and the persons who represent the organizations may prefer a certain kind of relationship because of their own personal outlook. Some people take pride in a positive relationship; they prefer friendly relations, also marked by mutual trust and concern. Others appear basically to like a hostile environment and prefer to deal at arm's length and to ignore the other person's situation.

**Implications for Contract Administration.** Existing attitudes have their influence on many aspects of the total collective bargaining relationship but perhaps especially on contract administration. The parties negotiate a contract periodically, but they must deal with each other almost continuously in handling grievances under the agreement and disputes not covered by the contract.

The relationship pattern influences the manner in which grievances and disputes are handled. Consider three kinds of mechanisms and criteria used for resolving such conflicts as they arise: power, the law, and informal social relations. Parties may employ power to influence the resolution of such disputes, they may resolve them in a strictly legal way according to a rigid interpretation of contract terms, or they may resolve them with reference to the plant social organization, employing less formal concepts of fairness and justice as well as considerations such as compassion and social expediency. Without taking a position here on which are "better" mechanisms, we suggest that there is a tendency for each "mechanism" to be predominant within different relationship patterns: in the conflict pattern power would be dominant; in the containment-aggression pattern power and legal mechanisms would be used; in the accommodation pattern, legal and social relations; and in the cooperation and collusion patterns, informal social relations.

There is more likely to be consensus about the criteria for grievance and dispute settlement under the more cooperative patterns. Therefore, a differential amount of enforcement activity is required in the different patterns, ranging from disciplined observance of contractual obligations under containment-aggression to a relatively unsupervised implementation of the contract during the year under the cooperation pattern. As a result there may be considerable difference in terms of the amount of energy which has to be expended in the activity.

The number of matters of mutual concern not covered in detail by the contract but on which there is nevertheless active consultation or collaborative administration can differ radically depending upon the existing relationship pattern. For example, in cooperative patterns the union might participate in job evaluation, time studies, etc., whereas this would be less likely under the competitive patterns.

Employee relations, morale, and discipline in the plant may well be influenced by the pattern of union-management relations. On the one hand, a containment-aggression pattern, for example, may tend to be accompanied by low morale and low employee trust and confidence in management. On the other hand, the psychological distance associated with competitive patterns may have its advantages. In a series of studies of the quality of relationship between leaders and other members of working groups, Fiedler found that low friendliness rather than high friendliness was associated with task effectiveness.[31] Fiedler's interpretation of these findings lends some support for those managers who argue that there are functional aspects of an "arm's-length" relationship:

> We cannot adequately control and discipline people to whom we have strong emotional ties. If a man is emotionally dependent on another, he cannot afford to antagonize him since this might deprive him of the other man's support.[32]

**Implications for Future Bargaining Agenda and Outcomes.** Attitudinal structuring is not an activity that merely parallels the other negotiation

---

[31] F. E. Fiedler, "The Leader's Psychological Distance and Group Effectiveness," in Dorwin Cartwright and Alvin Zander (eds.), *Group Dynamics,* 2d ed. (New York: Harper & Row, Publishers, Incorporated, 1960), pp. 586–606.

[32] *Ibid.,* p. 596.

processes; rather it interacts with distributive and integrative aspects of negotiations in several vital ways. Perhaps we could preview our discussion of this point by reference to a hypothetical and simplified game situation.

Consider two pairs of adversaries playing in separate but identical mixed games. By that we mean that the objective structures of ground rules, options, and payoffs of the two games are the same and that the games have variable-sum (integrative) and variable-share (distributive) aspects. However, the players in game 1 have mutual positive affect, trust, and a cooperative orientation; whereas the players in game 2 are mutually antagonistic, lack mutual trust, and have a competitive orientation.

The two games would be played out in significantly different ways. Not only is it likely that the parties to game 2 will choose strategies different from those utilized in game 1, but also that the goal structure of the game would have been modified in its interpretation by the players, especially if the situation contains some ambiguities. Finally, we would expect the outcomes to be affected and probably biased in a predictable way.[33]

A general proposition about how the agenda and outcomes of bargaining may be influenced by the relationship pattern in labor negotiations is that as parties move from the competitive end to the cooperative end of the relationship spectrum, they tend to increasingly confine distributive bargaining to the areas of inherent conflict, e.g., economic items, and to expand the number of areas in which integrative bargaining occurs.[34]

Why are fewer agenda items treated as distributive issues as one moves to the right on the spectrum of relationships? The first reason is that some issues are closely related to the attitudes which define relations. One such issue which undergoes redefinition is that of union security provisions. Management's attitude toward the legitimacy of the union largely determines its stance toward union security. Other noninstitutional issues such as layoff security provisions (limiting management flexibility) become more likely to be conceived as problems for integrative bargaining, and there may develop an actual joint sharing of the goal of employee security.

A second reason why the character of agenda items changes with a change in relationship relates to the availability of the appropriate decision process. The parties are better able to enter into the process of integrative bargaining in more cooperatively oriented relationships. Parties do not as readily share information and engage in problem solving until a

[33] Support for these propositions has been produced by several laboratory experiments, e.g., Morton Deutsch, "Trust and Suspicion," *Journal of Conflict Resolution*, vol. 2 (December, 1958), pp. 265–279. However, the tendencies indicated here have not always occurred in bargaining experiments. See Anatol Rapoport and Carol Orwant, "Experimental Games: A Review," *Behavioral Science*, vol. 7 (January, 1962), pp. 1–37.

[34] A similar proposition that there is a relationship between the amount of stress a nation feels and the number of goals it puts forth is advanced by T. W. Milburn, "The Concept of Deterrence: Some Logical and Psychological Considerations," *Journal of Social Issues*, vol. 17 (July, 1961), pp. 3–12.

measure of trust has been established. Additional analysis of the interaction of attitudinal structuring and the other processes at the tactical level is the main topic of the next chapter.

There is no implication that distributive bargaining does not occur in every pattern, from conflict to collusion. None of these arrangements eliminates all conflict of interest. While the parties may have extended joint problem solving to other areas, the distributive issues remain, becoming only relatively less important. Similarly even with collusive arrangements, in which techniques are found for exploiting a third party, the two parties must decide how to divide the fruits of the coalition.

Let us advance a second general proposition about the influence of relationship patterns on distributive bargaining. Quite apart from the number of the items treated as distributive issues, competitive relationships may heighten a party's aspirations on these distributive issues. By definition, a party with a competitive orientation gains additional satisfaction from the losses incurred by the other. Thus, the party has an added incentive to obtain the dominant share of the joint gain associated with the relationship.

Still a third type of phenomenon is operating to raise the minimum demands in a competitive pattern: one needs more in writing to be certain of getting even less in practice. The level of mutual trust at any given point in time affects one's assessment of the value of a given clause. With low mutual trust one must have more guarantees and more provisions limiting the freedom of the other than he would need for the same net benefit in a context of higher mutual trust.

According to our fourth proposition, the relationship may have a most direct influence on the outcome. Attitudes provide a mechanism by which transactions at one point in time can be related to transactions at another point in time. In a situation of recurring negotiations, a type of unwritten balance sheet exists. Should one party drive a hard bargain in a given negotiation, it cannot expect that this will be forgotten in future negotiations. It is through the mechanism of attitudes and the relationship pattern that developments in one negotiation become related to developments in another negotiation. One might think of attitudes in this sense as a type of ledger sheet with debits and credits being added or subtracted, depending upon the type of solutions being reached, and this balance sheet being available for reference in succeeding negotiations.

The fifth proposition is perhaps only a corollary of the one above: there is a *tendency* for the parties in the cooperative or collusive relationships to feel that a negotiation has been successful for both parties if they have settled somewhere near the middle of the distributive bargaining range. In their efforts to ensure that both representatives look good to their respective principals, they may develop evaluations about the settlements that make the results actually deviate substantially from distributive bargaining.

**Implications for Internal Organization.** Some internal aspects of the two organizations may be affected by the nature of the relationship. In a later chapter we shall explore how the attitudinal structuring *activity* between the parties interacts with internal bargaining during the negotiations. Here we are interested in the relationship between the more enduring *structures*—of interorganizational attitudes and of internal organizations. The general idea is that conflict with another group defines group structure and consequent reaction to internal conflict.[35]

Union leadership which keeps its position through elections must be concerned with gaining and keeping members, must ward off rival unions, and must obtain support for its policies, including ratification of the negotiated contract. Labor relations managers retain their positions at the pleasure of top management; they need to make their tasks seem as significant as possible, if not downright difficult; and they too must win support from others for their policies.

An official from either side who feels politically insecure in any of these areas may be motivated to pursue more conflictful strategies and to structure a more conflictful relationship. This permits him to build internal cohesion, to appear to be performing a critical function, and therefore to get the necessary support for him and his policies. In such cases a move to a more cooperative relationship is risky because it might bring charges from within his organization that he is going soft or selling out, and it might make the organization or the official appear to be performing less essential functions.

If in the case of insecure leadership described above, a cooperative interpersonal relationship exists at the outset, the negotiators may find it increasingly difficult to cooperate with each other. Over time it is likely that the conflictful strategy of the one negotiator will have an effect on both the personal relationship between the negotiators and the overall relationship, moving them in a conflictful direction. However, an alternate development in this situation is that the negotiators may help each other deal with internal problems, thereby preserving a cooperative relationship between the two key negotiators. They may even allow the overall relationship to move in the competitive direction but preserve another climate at the person-to-person level.

## Choosing the Optimal Relationship

If one were to focus on distributive bargaining and its content—conflicting objectives—he might conclude that a certain pattern of relationship is most appropriate. But if one were then to focus on the need for integrative bargaining, he might conclude that a quite different type of relationship is

[35] Lewis Coser, *The Functions of Social Conflict* (New York: The Free Press of Glencoe, 1956).

required. If one were to attend strictly to problems of administering the contract according to the mechanism he prefers, he might choose a particular relationship pattern. Exclusive attention to his internal organizational or political problems might suggest the desirability of a contrasting pattern. Similarly, reference to one's social philosophy and to his preferred patterns of interpersonal relations would each present its own recommendation.

The motivations for establishing and preserving a given kind of relationship are often complex. Our analysis of the Jimson negotiation provides an illustration of this point. The union international representative, Watoski, appeared to value his positive relationship with the company's chief negotiator, Scott, for its implications in all four subprocesses of negotiation.

> First, pertinent to the distributive process, he seemed to perceive Scott as a sort of "lawyer inside the house," a person who in some instances might try to convince management to be more generous. Second, his experience was that he could with relatively little risk engage Scott in the frank exchange of information essential to the integrative process. Third, Watoski appeared to place a positive value on the interpersonal relationship itself: he saw Scott as a person who related with him easily and warmly; he seemed to welcome opportunities to be in the presence of high-status management officials, such as Scott; and he and Scott genuinely shared certain interests in sports. Fourth, Watoski knew that Scott, who had been a labor official before he became involved in industrial relations on the management side, had a deep appreciation for the difficulty he (Watoski) sometimes faced in bargaining within his own organization. Scott usually tended to behave in such a way that helped rather than hindered Watoski in handling internal union problems.

It happened that in the above illustration all considerations seemed to point in the same direction. Just as frequently, a situation will call for some balance of these general considerations. The criterion for what constitutes a "constructive relationship" is the one based on full recognition of the mixture of distributive and integrative aspects in negotiations. Therefore such a relationship is one (1) in which the parties do not have attitudes which prevent them from fully exploiting the integrative possibilities but (2) does not make them lose sight of their primary responsibilities to the separate and distinct interests of their respective principals and the need to preserve the strength of these principal organizations.

Many situational factors will influence the party's preference for a particular relationship pattern. The preceding discussion of functional consequences of relationships presented a fairly good case for a cooperatively oriented pattern. In passing, we might quickly examine the conditions that provide little or no incentive to change a competitive or neutral relationship pattern.

Without elaborating our reasoning, we would suggest that the following conditions minimize the advantages of a cooperative pattern: where there is little need or potential for problem solving but considerable need for power bargaining, such as in a pattern-setting industry, and where employee relations are relatively separate from labor relations and the two institutional processes of negotiating and administrating the agreements are themselves quite separate. Two conditions of production technology might make a company less concerned about cooperative relationships: employee performance activities and quality and quantity of output are relatively fixed or controlled by technology, and investment and responsibility per worker are low. Other conditions which might encourage a company to pursue a competitive pattern are: The company sees a chance to get rid of the union; the company is only partly unionized and does not wish to legitimize further extension of unionization; and the company has some plants which are unionized by independents and other plants which are unionized by an international union. Finally, unions tend to be less favorably disposed to cooperative patterns when factionalism is strong and when the union has a strong ideological outlook.

It is with reference to such specific considerations as those listed above that a party chooses its objectives in this area—its preferred relationship pattern. There is an important distinction between the objectives of attitudinal structuring in contrast to those of distributive and integrative bargaining. In the other subprocesses the direction of aspirations was always obvious; a party engaged in distributive bargaining wanted more resources, more flexibility, more security, etc.; likewise a party engaged in integrative bargaining wanted to do a most thorough and effective job of solving mutual problems. However, as we have just indicated, in attitudinal structuring a party may aspire for either a "closer" relationship or for a more "distant" one, for a less formal or a more formal relationship, for a more peaceful or a more militant relationship, and so on. Since we cannot assume a particular direction to the way parties invariably will attempt to evolve their relationship, it also follows that a party may be perfectly satisfied with the present pattern of relationship, in which case their efforts are primarily concerned with preserving it. Moreover, we acknowledge that some parties may be more concerned than others about how the relationship is structured. Generally, however, parties are not indifferent to the status of the relationship.

Although parties have objectives in this area of attitudes and relationships and often engage in behavioral attempts to influence the pattern, these behaviors probably are not as planned or as conscious as those which implement bargaining or problem solving. Moreover, perhaps their objectives regarding attitudes operate most frequently as constraints on the way they pursue their objectives in the other two areas. That is, many behaviors are not chosen in the first instance because they will influence attitudes, rather they are behaviors pursuant to bargaining or problem solving which do not violate the requirements of the relationship.

## Summary of Forces Affecting Relationships

Perhaps a diagram (see Figure 6-2) indicating the relationship among the variables we have discussed thus far will provide an appropriate summary of the material in this part of the chapter. More importantly, it will enable us to sharpen our picture of the task which still remains—explaining the way attitudes are changed during negotiations.

### Figure 6-2
### Model of Forces in Establishing Relationships

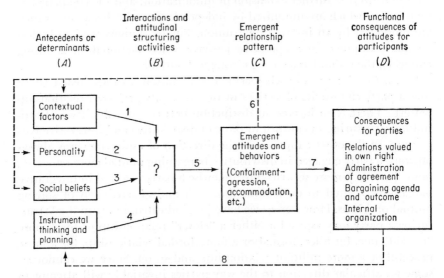

The diagram has four columns: (A) structural determinants, (B) attitudinal structuring activities, (C) emergent relationship patterns, and (D) the consequences of these patterns. The general cause-effect relationships among the variables in these columns are depicted by arrows. Certain contextual factors, personality attributes, and social belief systems influence the actions of Party (arrows 1, 2, and 3), which in turn structure the attitudes of Opponent (arrow 5). What we have not discussed thus far is a fourth factor influencing Party's attitudinal structuring behaviors (arrow 4), namely, the process of deliberately selecting behaviors instrumental to achieving a preferred relationship pattern. Nor have we discussed what the activities are which intervene between these antecedents to the relationship and the emergent relationship; that is, we have not discussed attitudinal structuring tactics (column *B*) and how they work (arrow 5). This is the task for the next part of this chapter and all of the next chapter.

However, let us continue with the summary of what has been done in this section. We have attempted to identify attitudes salient to the interaction between the parties and to develop a classification scheme of relationships along those dimensions. That is the content of column *C*. These relationships, once established, feedback (arrow 6) to influence the contextual factors which become salient (e.g., through selective perception) and the personalities or social beliefs of those who occupy key roles (e.g., through selection of persons to fit the relationship). These relationship patterns in column *C* were also analyzed in terms of their implications or functional consequence for each party. We have discussed a host of propositions under four headings: relations valued in own right, administration of the agreement, bargaining agenda and outcome, and internal organization. Finally, in our discussion of choosing the optimal relationship we meant to suggest that if the consequences of the existing relationship were not regarded as optimal or satisfactory, Party would be induced (arrow 8) to engage in instrumental thinking and planning, the objective of which would be to select (arrow 4) attitudinal structuring tactics.

Now we have set the stage. We have sketched a gross model of total attitudinal structuring factors. But we have left some gaps in our explanation. In particular we have not indicated how attitudes get changed: what activities change them (the empty box in column *B*), and how they change them (the theory of attitudinal change represented by arrow 5).

We turn to the problem of constructing a model of attitudinal change to explain arrow 5. A relationship is the complex of social-psychological consequences of behavior which may or may not have been initiated rationally. We now turn to the possibility of interrupting the less conscious and the self-motivating processes by a more or less purposive intervention to change the level of equilibrium of attitudes or to maintain the equilibrium against some circumstances that threaten to change it in an adverse way. The intervention consciously or intuitively takes into account the principles of attitude change.

# PART 2 | ATTITUDE-CHANGE THEORIES

Part 2 presents a model of the attitudinal-change process. The form of the model needs to be consistent with that of the bargaining and problem-solving models. It must treat attitudinal change as a rational and interpersonal process, specifying how Party more or less purposively goes about changing Opponent's attitudes toward Party. Like the bargaining and problem-solving models, the one presented here will appear to the reader to be overrationalized in the sense that it will seem to attribute too much deliberate purpose to a person's behavior. Our intention is to present a systematic model of the process and then to assert that this is the way persons *tend* to behave. The tactics chapter, which follows, presents the actual behaviors that we believe are consistent with the propositions of the model.

Our treatment of the problem of attitude change will be limited in several respects, which we should clarify at the outset. First, as already indicated, we are interested in attitudes toward a person or an organization. The parties' attitudes toward other objects—issues, events, and third parties—are of interest here only when they become instrumental in changing the interpersonal (interorganizational) attitudes. Recall also that the several attitudinal components that define a relationship are assumed to be closely correlated. Opponent's attitudes of trust and friendliness, beliefs about the legitimacy of Party, and motivational orientation and action tendencies toward Party all tend in the same direction and toward the same intensity.[36] Thus, a change in any given component will set up pressures for like change in the other components.

Second, we recognize that a party may prefer to change the relationship in the direction of *either* more cooperation, friendliness, and trust or less of these qualities. However, in order to simplify the exposition of the model and tactical material, we assume that Party wishes to modify Opponent's attitudes in the direction of more trust, friendliness, and cooperation, or at least wishes to maintain the current level of the relationship. We also believe that it is more difficult to move a relationship toward cooperation than toward conflict.

Third, we assume for purposes of giving focus to our analysis that Party directs his efforts at attitudinal change toward Opponent, the negotiator

[36] There are at least two types of explanations for this clustering. First there is the possibility that the configuration of Party's many behaviors toward Opponent might actually make it appropriate for Opponent to react to Party with trust, friendliness, and cooperativeness in similar degrees. Second, there is the well-documented psychological phenomenon of the *halo effect:* Opponent's perceptions and judgments of Party will exaggerate the unity or homogeneity of the latter's personality and behavior.

Some experimental evidence supporting this tendency is especially to the point. Experiments by Morton Deutsch have demonstrated the relation between motivational orientation and trust. See, for example, "The Effect of Motivational Orientation upon Trust and Suspicion," *Human Relations,* vol. 13 (May, 1960), pp. 123–140. An earlier experiment tended to confirm the relation between friendliness and motivational orientation—Morton Deutsch, "An Experimental Study of the Effects of Cooperation and Competition upon Group Process," *Human Relations,* vol. 2, no. 3 (1949), pp. 199–231.

of the other organization. It is true that for a change to occur in the institutional relationship pattern as we have defined it there must be more widespread change in the attitude of members of the other organization. However, we focus on the problem of changing the attitude of the other chief negotiator (and others directly involved in negotiations) for two reasons. The first is that this is an important step toward a change in the institutional relations and may create the desired chain reaction. The opponent negotiator may have an interest in bringing the attitudes of others in his organization in line with his own, and he is in a fairly strategic position to exert such influence. Second, even if the opponent negotiator cannot or does not wish to change the institutional pattern, many of the benefits of a more collaborative relationship may accrue to Party by changing only the attitude of the negotiator and perhaps the negotiator's team.

Finally, Party has certain explicit or implicit assumptions about Opponent's current attitudes and their structure, i.e., which attitudes are more controlling of the behavior relevant to Party and which are more accessible to influence. On the basis of this information, Party makes certain judgments about the particular attitudes of Opponent which are promising targets for Party's change-induction efforts and about the particular behavior patterns which might be influenced directly.

In brief, Party wants to modify Opponent's attitude and behavior toward him—in the direction of friendliness, trust, respect, or legitimacy. He wants him to be more cooperatively oriented in their interactions. How does Party actually go about modifying Opponent's attitudes and behavior? What principles underlie Party's influence attempts and govern the effectiveness of these efforts?

Our explanation of attitude change which occurs during negotiations is based primarily on two theories: cognitive balance theory and reinforcement theory. An introductory statement about each follows:

The cornerstone of balance theory is the idea that a person will prefer consistency (or balance) among his cognitions, i.e., his perceptions and beliefs. We have already stated that there is a tendency to hold feelings toward a person and beliefs about the person which are consistent with each other. Here the point is that he also will tend to eliminate the inconsistency among sets of beliefs and feelings toward two or more persons and objects. There apparently is a psychological cost associated with holding discrepant cognitions, and hence there is a strain toward balance. This presents an influence opportunity: by introducing a new and discrepant cognition into another person's awareness (a perception or belief which is not congruent with his present perceptions and beliefs), one creates forces toward modification of the existing cognitions. A change in the target attitude will tend to be followed by a change in behavior.

The essence of reinforcement theory is that a person will behave in ways that are rewarded. Behavior which is rewarded is repeated, and behavior which is not rewarded or seems to lead to punishment is not repeated. A party to negotiations has distinct preferences about how the other enters into the interaction; he also has control of things of value to the other, ranging from compliments to economic concessions, and as one might expect, he tends to use these rewards to influence the tone and pattern of interaction.

Party tends to administer rewards and punishments to shape aspects of Opponent's behavior directly and apart from the immediate set of attitudes which relate the parties. Party "trains" Opponent to engage in particular cooperative behaviors and to avoid specific destructive behaviors. Then, when Opponent finds himself engaging in more accommodative or cooperative patterns, he will tend to develop more positive attitudes toward Party consistent with his new behavior. The influence of reinforcement is on behavior patterns first and attitudes second.

The important distinction we wish to make here between the influence attempts explained by these two theories is in terms of whether the more immediate effect is on attitudes or behavior. Balance theory focuses on how Opponent's *attitudes* toward Party are changed and how Opponent's behavior is assumed to change accordingly. Reinforcement theory explains how Opponent's *behavior* toward Party is shaped and how attitude change is assumed to follow.[37]

## Balance Theory

Balance theory as developed by Heider [38] and elaborated by Newcomb,[39] Rosenberg et al.,[40] and others provides a way of understanding something about internal organization of the attitudes held by Opponent and the conditions under which change in these attitudes takes place. The theory is concerned with the relationship among certain aspects of a person's cognitive field. The basic unit of analysis focuses upon what Heider calls the P-O-X unit. If P and O are persons and X is an impersonal object, idea, or

---

[37] We can only assert a tendency for attitudinal change to accompany behavioral change. An important body of theoretical and experimental work is aimed at understanding the conditions under which a person's public behavior is contrary to his private attitudes. See, for example, Herbert Kelman's treatment of the compliance process: "Compliance, Identification, and Internalization: Three Processes of Attitude Change," *Journal of Conflict Resolution*, vol. 2 (March, 1958), pp. 51–60.

[38] Fritz Heider, *The Psychology of Interpersonal Relations* (New York: John Wiley & Sons, Inc., 1958).

[39] T. M. Newcomb, "An Approach to the Study of Communicative Acts," *Psychological Review*, vol. 60 (September, 1953), pp. 393–404.

[40] M. J. Rosenberg et al., *Attitude Organization and Change* (New Haven, Conn.: Yale University Press, 1960).

event, the problem is how $O$'s [41] cognitions of the relations of $O$, $P$, and $X$ are organized. The three relations are conceived of as interdependent. The unit may be in a state of balance or imbalance.

Balance occurs if given one positive bond, the remaining bonds are of like sign, either positive or negative. In other words a balanced system will contain three positive bonds or two negative bonds and one positive bond. A positive bond is either positive evaluation (+), such as liking, and/or association ($a$), such as belonging to or responsible for. The negative relations are negative evaluation (−) and dissociation ($d$). If $O$ approves of event $X$ and $P$ is seen as responsible for $X$, then there will be a tendency for $O$ to like $P$ (Figure 6-3). All three relations are positive. If $O$ disapproves of $X$ and $P$ is seen as responsible for $X$, the system is in balance if $O$ dislikes $P$ (Figure 6-4). The unit contains two negative relations and one positive relation.

### Figure 6-3

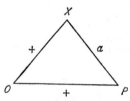

$O$ approves of $X$. $P$ is seen as responsible for event $X$ (a positive relationship). $O$ likes $P$. System is balanced.

### Figure 6-4

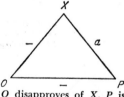

$O$ disapproves of $X$. $P$ is associated with $X$. $O$ dislikes $P$. System is balanced.

Now assume that $O$ dislikes $P$, who is responsible for event $X$, which would normally be evaluated by $O$ as good or helpful (Figure 6-5a). If $O$ feels negatively about $P$ but positively about $P$'s actions, the system is in a state of imbalance and contains pressures to restore balance.[42]

$O$ can restore balance by revising any of several aspects of his cognitive structure as described in Figure 6-5a. First, $O$ can change his attitude

---

[41] We deliberately switch from Heider's analysis, which focuses upon the cognitive field of $P$, since we shall continue with our treatment of $O$ (for us, Opponent) as the *target* of tactical behaviors. We are interested in explaining $O$'s response.

[42] Considerable experimental evidence has been accumulated to support the generalization that states of balance as defined by Heider tend to be preferred over imbalance and tend to replace imbalanced states: N. Jordan, "Behavioral Forces That Are a Function of Attitudes and of Cognitive Organization," *Human Relations*, vol. 6 (August, 1953), pp. 273–287; and N. Kogan and R. Tagiuri, "International Preference and Cognitive Organization," *Journal of Abnormal and Social Psychology*, vol. 56 (January, 1958), pp. 113–116.

toward $P$, feeling that $P$ is not really such a "bad guy" (Figure 6-5$b$). Second, $O$ can change his evaluation of the meaning of $X$ for himself, now believing that $X$ is not so good after all or at least does not affect him; he may achieve the same effect by suppressing recognition of $X$ (Figure 6-5$c$). Third, $O$ can change his assumption about the responsibility of $P$ for $X$, i.e., by dissociating these two elements, e.g., by adopting the view that $P$ did not intend nor want to cause $X$ (Figure 6-5$d$). Fourth, $O$ can gain a more differentiated picture of the situation, particularly of $P$, preserving his negative evaluation of $P$'s bad parts but now recognizing $P$'s better qualities which were responsible for event $X$ (Figure 6-5$e$).

## Figure 6-5

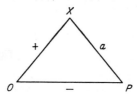

Figure 6-5$a$. $O$ dislikes $P$. $P$ is associated with $X$. $O$ approves of $X$. System imbalanced.

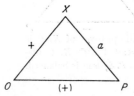

Figure 6-5$b$. $O$ eliminates imbalance experienced in Figure 6-5$a$ by developing a liking for $P$. System is balanced.

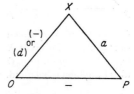

Figure 6-5$c$. Alternative way for restoring imbalance of Figure 6-5$a$. $O$ changes his attitude toward $X$ to disapproval. Or $O$ disassociates $X$ from himself: he decides it doesn't affect him. Or $X$ suppresses any thoughts of $X$

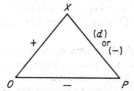

Figure 6-5$d$. Referring again to Figure 6-5$a$, $O$ can restore balance by disassociating $P$ from event $X$; e.g., by assuming $P$ did not really intend $X$.

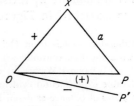

Figure 6-5$e$. $O$ can restore balance to the $P$-$O$-$X$ cognitive unit by differentiating certain aspects of $P$ which he does not like from those he does approve.

**Figure 6-6**          **Figure 6-7**          **Figure 6-8**

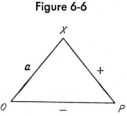          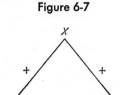          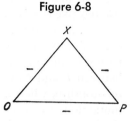

*O* dislikes *P*. *O* is associated with *X*. *X* benefits *P*. The situation is imbalanced.

At least one other possibility exists—that *O* will suffer continued imbalance in this particular *P-O-X* system. It is not always possible to reduce imbalance. If each of the alternate ways of restoring balance indicated above would result in imbalance in some other cognitive unit salient for *O*, say *P-O-X'*, then imbalance may persist in one or the other cognitive units. Assume, for example, that *O* disapproves of another object salient to the *P-O* relationship, namely *X'*, and that *P* approves of *X'*; if *O* should now adopt a favorable attitude toward *P*, he places this unit in imbalance. The theory states only that there is a strain toward balance, not that it will automatically occur.

Consider another basic way in which strain is placed on *O*'s cognitive structure. Above we portrayed *P* as behaving in a way which was not consistent with *O*'s attitude toward him. *P* may be able to structure the situation in such a way that *O* finds he has behaved (or is behaving) toward *P* in a way not consistent with his own attitudes. *O* dislikes *P*; *O* is associated with event *X*; event *X* benefits *P* or is approved of by *P* (Figure 6-6). This situation is imbalanced in a way similar to Figure 6-5*a*. Similar basic alternatives are again available to *O*. Basically, he can look more favorably on *P*, dissociate himself from activity *X*, somehow minimize in his own mind the extent to which *P* benefits from *X*, or differentiate that part of *P* which he likes or which is benefited from those he does not like. We assume that he cannot dissociate himself from *P* completely; he cannot leave the relationship.

The third and fourth basic ways that *P* can place strain on *O*'s cognitive structure, such that it may lead to a change in the *O-P* bond, is to establish or identify an object *X* which both *P* and *O* like or dislike (Figures 6-7 and 6-8, respectively). Again changing his attitude toward *P* is only one of several ways for *O* to balance these cognitions. A fifth way involves the establishment of common bonds of association, even though the evaluations are neutral.

In the first two situations of imbalance (Figures 6-5*a* and 6-6) one of the two positive bonds between *O-X* and between *P-X* was an associative bond, whereas in the third and fourth situations (Figures 6-7 and 6-8) both bonds are evaluative. Is this an important distinction? It can be argued that the nature of these linkages with *X* influences the nature of the relationship between *P* and *O*. Common evaluations toward *X* produce a consensual relationship, whereas the presence of an associative bond implies a symbiotic tie between *P* and *O*. Gross, who studied natural groups in an Air Force setting, concluded that both symbiosis and consensus may operate as cohesive ties in small groups but that symbiosis seems to be a more powerful tie than consensus does.[43] We would expect this to be especially true in the task-oriented setting provided by labor negotiations.[44] Thus, we assume that symbiotic imbalance is more stressful and more likely to lead to change than evaluative imbalance.

**Conditions Affecting Restoration of Balance.** The fact that there are alternate ways by which *O* may restore balance is of utmost importance to *P*. Assume that *P* brought about event *X* (such as a gesture of assistance toward *O*) in order to improve *O*'s attitude toward *P*. In that case only a change in attitude toward *P* is a successful outcome. The other ways of eliminating imbalance as well as continued imbalance itself represent failures in the bid by *P*.

Under what conditions is imbalance more likely to persist without change in attitudes? Under what conditions is *O* more likely to restore balance by changing his attitude toward *P*? The following propositions are derived by extending the logics of the theory and/or are supported by the findings of experimental studies:

1. *The more inconsistent O's cognitions of P and X are, the more likely there will be modification of attitude toward P.* *O*'s cognitions of *P* and *X* may be only slightly inconsistent with each other, or they might be quite inconsistent. The greater the discrepancy, the greater the strain, and therefore the greater the likelihood of change.

2. *The more central for O the attitude object X and the attitude object P are, the less likely is some change in O's attitudes.* By "centrality" here we mean the relative importance of the attitude to the person.

Each person has a limited number of ideals, e.g., religious values or key aspects of his self-concept (such as individualism, egalitarianism, competence, and integrity), which serve as anchor points for his attitude organ-

---

[43] Edward Gross, "Symbiosis and Consensus as Integrative Factors in Small Groups," *American Sociological Review*, vol. 21 (April, 1956), pp. 174–179.

[44] Also consider Newcomb's discussion of complementarity and similarity in T. M. Newcomb, "The Prediction of Interpersonal Attraction," *The American Psychologist*, vol. 11 (November, 1956), pp. 575–586.

ization. When both $X$ and $P$ involve highly central attitudes and become part of an imbalanced system for $O$, it should be apparent that $O$ will experience relatively great discomfort. But attitudes tied to central values are usually very resistant to change through the introduction of discrepant information.[45]

In net effect, we would predict that the more central the attitude objects (where both are central in about the same degree), the more likely is imbalance to persist. Moreover, where balance is achieved, it will be through the mechanisms of dissociation ($X$ from $P$ or $X$ from $O$) rather than reversing evaluation.

3. *The more central for $O$ the attitude object $X$ is, the more likely $O$ is to change his attitude toward $P$.* For $O$, $X$ is more rather than less resistant to change. This resistance to change of $X$ serves to increase the probability that restoring the balance will involve a change in attitude toward $P$.

4. *The more central the attitude toward $P$ is, the less likely $O$ is to change his attitude toward $P$* (reasoning similar to that in proposition 3 above).

5. *The more salient for $O$ are simultaneously both the attitude objects $P$ and $X$, the more likely is some change in $O$'s attitudes.* Salience is a temporal concept referring to a psychological state of immediate awareness, brought about by situational variables. An individual may have many attitudes and beliefs which are not consistent with each other but which cause him little or no discomfort until something occurs to make them all salient at the same time.[46]

6. Assuming an imbalanced state and a salient *P-O* relationship, *the more salient for $O$ attitude object $X$ is in particular, the more likely $O$ is to change attitude toward $P$.* If $X$ is salient, $O$ cannot suppress $X$. It is also more difficult for $O$ to distort $X$ in such a way as to dissociate himself from $X$ or reverse his evaluation of $X$.

7. *The more information possessed by Opponent about both $P$ and $X$, the more likely the imbalanced unit is to be differentiated into several balanced units and involve no change in the prevailing attitudes.* Newcomb has suggested that a large storage of information about the attitude object "equips the individual to make minor (and hairsplitting) adjustments which minimize the degree of change in generalized affect toward the object" which must occur and hence the amount of change in attitudes

---

[45] Marc Pilisuk, "Cognitive Balance and Self-relevant Attitudes," *Journal of Abnormal and Social Psychology*, vol. 65 (August, 1962), pp. 95–103.

[46] W. A. Scott, in "Rationality and Non-rationality of International Attitudes," *Journal of Conflict Resolution*, vol. 2 (March, 1958), pp. 8–16, points out that in the area of international relations the incompleteness and remoteness of the information and the lack of pressures on the individual to defend his views result in inconsistencies which are under no pressure to be resolved.

toward other related objects as well. "Upon receipt of new information, a person is more agile in producing 'Yes, but . . .' responses when he is well-informed about an object than when he is poorly informed." [47]

8. *The more information O has about X compared with P, the more likely O is to change his attitude toward P.* Prior information and an abundance of props in the situation which confirm the true nature of X make it more difficult for O to change his evaluation toward X or to dissociate X from either P or himself.[48]

9. *The more information O has about P compared with X, the less likely there will be any attitude change toward P.* Thus, if O has little prior information about P upon which to base his evaluations, O will more readily change his attitude toward P. Of course, the credibility of the information about P can vary from being accepted as fact to being discounted completely.

It is significant that creating imbalance by an overt act or by a communication which implies something about P contrary to O's beliefs makes O more receptive to still additional information about P.[49] There may also be a tendency for O to seek information which agrees with his prior opinion, but presumably any relevant information already available will be given more attention.

10. *The more tolerance O has for imbalance, the less likely there is to be any attitude change.* Tolerance for apparent inconsistency varies among individuals. Indeed it may be a generalized personality attribute.

11. *There are individual differences in preferences for ways of restoring balance.*[50]

Most of the above propositions indicate some aspect of the attitude objects or relations between attitude objects which influences how an instance of imbalance will be resolved. For example, assume that object X, which is the source of the strain, has the following characteristics: it is significantly discrepant with P; it relates to an important value of O; it is salient in the present P-O situation; and it is an object familiar to O. Such an object should be relatively potent in producing a change in O's attitude toward P. This would be especially true should O's attitude toward P be related to peripheral rather than central aspects of O's attitude organization and should P be relatively unfamiliar to O.

---

[47] T. M. Newcomb, unpublished manuscript, draft: October, 1962.

[48] R. P. Abelson, "Modes of Resolution of Belief Dilemmas," *Journal of Conflict Resolution,* vol. 3 (December, 1959), p. 349.

[49] J. S. Adams, "The Reduction of Cognitive Dissonance by Seeking Consonant Information," *Journal of Abnormal and Social Psychology,* vol. 62 (January, 1961), pp. 74–78.

[50] I. D. Steiner and E. D. Rogers, "Alternative Response to Dissonance," *Journal of Abnormal and Social Psychology,* vol. 66 (February, 1963), pp. 128–136.

We shall keep in mind the facilitating and resisting factors listed in the propositions above when we analyze the tactical operations actually used by negotiators in an effort to change attitudes.

## Reinforcement Theory

Balance theory indicates one route to attitude and behavioral change. P can create imbalance in O's cognitive structure. Sometimes O will reduce the tension by changing his attitude toward P and concomitantly his behavior toward P. The balance model suggests how new attitudes directly and behaviors indirectly are elicited from O. Balance theory analyzes P's efforts which occur *before* an instance of the changed attitudes and behaviors from O.

Reinforcement theory will yield further insight into the process of bringing about change.[51] It deals with a process which is implemented *after* the occurrence of a desired behavior. Simply, certain activities by Opponent become more likely to recur in the future if they are followed by a reward.

The propositions embodied in reinforcement theory which are of interest to us have been adequately tested in animal experimentation. In fact, they have been elaborated in considerably more detail than we can use in our analysis. The propositions are supported by a lesser amount of experimentation with human subjects.[52]

1. *The more frequently Party's activity rewards the behavior of Opponent, the more often the latter will emit the behavior.* Experimental studies raise many questions about what constitutes an optimum schedule of reinforcement. For example, intermittent reinforcement has been demonstrated to be more effective than regular reinforcement. However, in general Party can strengthen a behavior pattern by Opponent by more frequent reinforcement.

2. *The more valuable to Opponent the reward activity of Party is, the more often Opponent will emit the behavior rewarded by Party.* Simply, Party's ability to strengthen appropriate behavior patterns by Opponent

[51] B. F. Skinner, *Science and Human Behavior* (New York: The Macmillan Company, 1953). Also, G. C. Homans, *Social Behavior: Its Elementary Forms* (New York: Harcourt, Brace & World, Inc., 1961).

[52] Some relevant studies are E. H. Schein, "The Effect of Reward on Adult Imitative Behavior," *Journal of Abnormal and Social Psychology*, vol. 49 (July, 1954), pp. 389–395; D. C. Hildum and R. W. Brown, "Verbal Reinforcement and Interviewer Bias," *Journal of Abnormal and Social Psychology*, vol. 53 (January, 1956), pp. 108–111; W. S. Verplank, "The Control of the Content of Conversation: Reinforcement of Statements of Opinion," *Journal of Abnormal and Social Psychology*, vol. 51 (November, 1955), pp. 668–676; G. Mander and W. K. Kaplan, "Subjective Evaluation and Reinforcement Effect of a Verbal Stimulus," *Science*, vol. 124 (1956), pp. 582–583.

will depend upon how much Opponent values the potential reinforcers. If, for example, Opponent dislikes and disrespects Party, the latter's compliments are not likely to be prized highly by Opponent and are consequently poor reinforcers. This underscores the advantage for Party of being perceptive about the needs and preferences of Opponent at all times.

3. *If Party's activity punishes the behavior of Opponent, the punished behavior will probably be temporarily suppressed.* Punishment does not eliminate the particular behavior from Opponent's repertoire of behavior, however. The dynamics of punishment are often misunderstood.

> In everyday personal contact we control through censure, snubbing, disapproval, or banishment . . . all of this is done with the intention of reducing tendencies to behave in certain ways. Reinforcement builds up these tendencies; punishment is designed to tear them down.[53]
>
> The technique has often been analyzed, and many familiar questions continue to be asked. Must punishment be closely contingent upon the punished behavior? Must the individual know what he is being punished for? What forms of punishment are most effective under what circumstances? This concern may be due to the realization that the technique has unfortunate by-products. In the long run, punishment, unlike reinforcement, works to the disadvantage of both the punished organism and the punishing agency. The aversive stimuli which are needed generate emotions, including predispositions to escape or retaliate, and disabling anxieties.[54]

Nevertheless, the experimental finding of studies conducted under the direction of Skinner do suggest that punishment may have some useful purpose in learning situations. There are several "rules" which serve to show when and how punishment may be useful.

1. Punishment may be used to hold a response at low strength. Under these circumstances, punishment has to continue indefinitely as it does not eliminate the response. The continuing punishment is equally or more effective if administered occasionally than if it is given every time the objectionable behavior occurs.

2. It is possible to take advantage of the period of suppressed response following punishment in order to strengthen some other response by reinforcement.

3. It is important that punishment be given in the presence of discriminative cues for the response. Delayed punishment is likely to

[53] Skinner, *op. cit.,* pp. 182–183.
[54] *Ibid.,* p. 186.

prove ineffective because it is given at a time when the discriminative stimuli leading to the undesired conduct are absent.[55]

The main alternative to punishment is to condition desired behavior through positive reinforcement. And even if a case can be made that punishment is sometimes effective, the evidence is that rewards represent the superior alternative.

[55] E. R. Hilgard, *Introduction to Psychology*, 3d ed. (New York: Harcourt, Brace & World, Inc., 1962), p. 113.

# CHAPTER VII

# ATTITUDINAL STRUCTURING TACTICS

Negotiating a labor agreement provides union and management personnel with a unique opportunity to strengthen or to change the prevailing attitudes of each toward the other. Several characteristics of negotiating sessions serve to increase the likelihood of attitude change—changes which may be beneficial or harmful depending upon the skill and sensitivity of each negotiator. Perhaps the most vital of such characteristics is that during contract negotiations, interpersonal interaction between ranking officials of the two organizations is frequent and intense; hence, the increased salience of each party's attitudes. We can cite many cases in which skillful handling of contract negotiation led to more cooperative relations and other cases in which ineptness resulted in a deterioration of union-management relations.[1]

Perhaps Professor B. M. Selekman has been one of the most emphatic expositors about negotiations as a setting and an opportunity for the reduction of intergroup tensions. In 1947 he urged negotiators to view the negotiating process "as a social and psychological device for actually beginning to liquidate rather than merely continuing the hostilities." In this way the negotiators may "remain aware from the moment the conference opens that not only the formal terms but also the fundamental quality of their evolving relations must now be determined." [2]

[1] B. M. Selekman, S. K. Selekman, and S. H. Fuller, *Problems in Labor Relations*, 1st and 2d eds. (New York: McGraw-Hill Book Company, 1950 and 1958). Also Sidney Garfield and W. F. Whyte, "The Collective Bargaining Process: A Human Relations Analysis," parts I, II, III, and IV, *Human Organization*, vol. 9 (Summer, 1950), pp. 5–10; vol. 9 (Fall, 1950), pp. 10–16; vol. 9 (Winter, 1950), pp. 25–29; vol. 10 (Spring, 1951), pp. 28–32.

[2] B. M. Selekman, *Labor Relations and Human Relations* (New York: McGraw-Hill Book Company, 1947), p. 30.

In the preceding chapter we suggested several reasons why a negotiator might prefer one pattern of relationship over another: A more cooperative pattern might lead to more expeditious handling of problems which arise under the contract throughout the year. A more cooperative pattern might result in more integrative bargaining in future negotiations. A more competitive pattern might be preferred because it would contribute to internal cohesion within one or both of the organizations. Either a cooperative or a competitive relationship might be valued in its own right by one or both of the parties. A negotiator will take into account these general considerations when he decides whether to improve a relationship, preserve the current pattern, or allow it to deteriorate.

Assuming a negotiator decides to move the relationship toward the more cooperative end of the spectrum of possible relationships and given the opportunity to do so during the course of negotiations, how does the negotiator proceed? The necessary steps in structuring new attitudes can be described and illustrated in terms of the model developed in the previous chapter.

Before attitudes of trust, friendliness, and respect can be changed, one is advised to learn of their origin, content, and utility with respect to the given individual. Hence, one of the important assignments the negotiator accepts for himself is that of analyzing the situation in terms of prevailing attitudes. Since attitudes are not something that can be observed directly, each negotiator is constantly making inferences about the basic orientation of his opponent based on his verbal behavior, actions, and other sorts of cues. Actually, the negotiator may go through an analytical process that would parallel the previous chapter. He may review the history of the relationship and the impact of the environment, personalities, etc., on the shaping of that relationship. He will pay particular attention to all facets of the union-management situation that are operating currently to preserve that relationship.

With some sense of the constraints within which he must work as well as the possibilities for changing Opponent's attitudes, Party is ready to utilize the appropriate techniques for the structuring of new attitudes. The tactics suggested by balance theory aim at changing Opponent's attitudes directly and his behavior indirectly. Once a key attitude is changed, then a wide spectrum of behavioral change can be expected to occur. In reinforcement theory, attention is focused on Opponent's behavior, assuming the attitudes will change accordingly. By being applied to specific behaviors of Opponent, the reinforcements tend to influence a narrow spectrum of behavior, at least initially.

This chapter will be developed as follows: The first part will deal with the tactics implied by balance theory. The second part will present tactics associated with reinforcement theory. This part will also include a review of the preconditions to purposive attitude change. Part 3 will analyze the dilemmas between the tactical requirements of attitudinal structuring and the other subprocesses of negotiations.

## PART 1 | INFLUENCING OPPONENT'S COGNITIONS IN ORDER TO CHANGE ATTITUDES

**Implications of Balance Theory for Tactical Assignments.** In our discussion of the balance theory model we assumed a negative relationship between Opponent and Party at the outset. Party could create some inconsistency in the cognitive structure of Opponent so that balance would be restored if Opponent improved his attitude toward Party. There are a variety of ways for creating this inconsistency, ranging from relatively active to relatively passive tactics.

Party attempts to influence the cognitions of Opponent in order that:

1. Opponent perceives the parties as having common preferences (either likes or dislikes) for goals, behavior, third persons, ideas, etc.

2. Opponent perceives the parties as having common associations, such as problems, experiences, etc.

3. Opponent perceives Party as associated with some object (or event or idea) which benefits Opponent.

4. Opponent perceives himself as associated with some object which benefits Party.

5. Opponent perceives Party as dissociated from an object which harms Opponent.

6. Opponent perceives himself as dissociated from an object which harms Party.

Thus, Party attempts to create in Opponent's mind the particular configurations of evaluations and associations [3] which tend to produce the desired changes in attitudes.

Producing these patterns can be thought of as the tactical operation facing Party. The first four configurations are balanced when Opponent adopts a positive attitude toward Party. Therefore these configurations *tend* to produce such an outcome. If we assume a negative relation be-

---

[3] The diagrams which will be presented throughout the discussion will take note of these distinctions. A positive evaluation will be indicated by $+$, a negative evaluation by $-$, a neutral evaluation by $o$, a positive association by $a$, and a negative association or dissociation by $d$. Where the valence of the bond is not given but is only inferred from the others, it will be included within parentheses, e.g., $(+)$.

tween Opponent and Party at the outset, we should say that Party creates an imbalance in the cognitive structure of Opponent, so that one way in which the balance can be restored is by Opponent improving his attitude toward Party.

Therefore, it is clear that Party may take supplementary steps to reduce the availability to Opponent of alternate methods for restoring balance. Recall for example that Opponent may tend to ignore or distort a positive overture by Party rather than change his attitude toward Party. Our analysis will note the circumstances or tactical efforts which have the effect of increasing or decreasing the likelihood that Opponent will achieve balance via the route of adopting a more favorable attitude toward Party.

The tactical assignments of dissociation and differentiation (5 and 6) have been separated from the rest since they do not in themselves set up forces for more positive attitudes. Rather, they tend to neutralize situations otherwise potentially damaging to the attitudes between the parties. In effect, they tend to preserve the existing relationship.

### Party Shares Opponent's Likes and Dislikes

Similar attitudes toward an object (event, idea, third person) set up forces toward attraction between persons.[4] In Figure 7-1 we consider both common likes and dislikes.

**Figure 7-1**

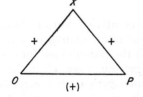 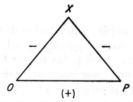

Both Opponent and Party have positive or negative evaluations toward an object in the situation. Given these evaluations, the cognitive system of Opponent can be balanced by adopting a more positive attitude toward Party. To create this result, Party can establish or emphasize the *O-X* bond or the *P-X* bond. This means that Party may emphasize his own attraction or aversion to *X*, which Opponent had not been fully aware of

---

[4] In support of this hypothesis, Riecken and Homans have collated the findings of many experiments: H. W. Riecken and G. C. Homans, "Psychological Aspects of Social Structure," in G. Lindzey (ed.), *Handbook of Social Psychology* (Reading, Mass.: Addison-Wesley Publishing Company, Inc., 1954). See also T. M. Newcomb, *The Acquaintance Process* (New York: Holt, Rinehart and Winston, Inc., 1961).

previously. Alternatively, it may be the attraction or aversion of Opponent toward X which Party creates or emphasizes anew.

We shall first discuss some situations which fall within the "common like" paradigm and then some which fall within the "common dislike" paradigm.

The most straightforward of these efforts to promote positive interpersonal attitudes is to discover and stress preexisting characteristics common to both parties.

*Location of personal points in common.* Negotiating situations, like most interpersonal situations, offer many opportunities for locating personal points in common. In the Jimson case, informal discussion between the two negotiating teams invariably preceded each negotiating session and centered on one of their three favorite topics—baseball, fishing, and Hoffa. Presumably baseball and fishing were common preferences, and Hoffa a common dislike. In any event, this conversation usually served to create a congenial atmosphere in which to begin work. In a case reported by Whyte the common ground was hunting and fishing—"whenever you run into a real sportsman, you'll find he is a regular fellow." [5] In still another case, the two negotiators were influenced by their common Jewish ethnic background.

*Use of similar language.* Another tactic of this type to gain the confidence and acceptance of the other negotiator is to use familiar language and arguments—language the other negotiator is accustomed to and reasoning that he trusts. This calls attention to similarities and plays down differences.

> For example, international representative Sutton found himself dealing with a peculiarly adamant plant manager. Sutton and his committee took pains to put forth the union's case for each demand in reasoned, unemotional language; but it was clear that they were making no progress. The plant manager's replies suggested that he considered these arguments simply an attractive cloak for personal ambitions. He seemed to feel that the men across the table just wanted what they wanted for personal reasons and were out to take him for all they could get.

> Sutton then tried another tack. He placed the demands in the institutional framework of the union. He began talking about "the policy of our organization" and "the decisions of our executive board." He used words that had a familiar and pleasant ring to the executive. He suggested, by implication, that there were many similarities between the two organizations represented in that room.

[5] W. F. Whyte, *Men at Work* (Homewood, Ill.: The Dorsey Press and Richard D. Irwin, Inc., 1961), p. 334.

At last the manager began to warm up, and it became possible for the parties to work out a contract that was a realistic adjustment to the problems of both organizations. The approach was twofold. Sutton avoided red-flag words and used those that would not only sound familiar but safe and respectable to the executive. And then he used these words to place himself in the institutional structure of the union so as to make clear the limitations within which he acted. Management can apply the same principles in presenting its case to the union.[6]

To the extent that Party can honestly indicate an affinity for language and reasoning processes similar to those of Opponent, he not only increases the likelihood of communicating the thoughts intended but also underscores a common preference.

**Definition of a common problem.** A more direct means for involving the common preference is to define a common problem. This refers to what we had in mind in our discussion of integrative bargaining. Thus, identification and solving of joint problems, such as safety, job evaluation, or reducing the backlog of grievances, may result in more positive attitudes between Party and Opponent, because both have a common evaluation of a given object.

When the common problem is of sufficient magnitude, this operation amounts to introducing superordinate goals, which Sherif defines as "goals which are compelling for all and cannot be ignored, but which cannot be achieved by the efforts and resources of one group alone."[7] Sherif has demonstrated experimentally the effect of superordinate goals in reducing the conflict between warring gangs in a study conducted at a boy's camp in 1954.[8]

**Focus on mutual successes.** Common evaluations can relate to success experiences. Occasionally the outcome regarding a specific agenda item is highly satisfactory to both parties. If a negotiator achieves his target settlement on an issue, or at least substantially exceeds his original resistance point, he will have positive feelings about the outcome. Some issues are easier to resolve than others; a few actually allow both negotiators to approximate their targets and therefore to feel quite positive about that particular result.

A company spokesman of the Marathon Company, studied by Ann Douglas, commented on the need to have an area in which progress would be made in order for the meeting not to have a deteriorating effect on

---

[6] Garfield and Whyte, *op. cit.* (Summer, 1950), p. 9.

[7] Muzafer Sherif (ed.), *Intergroup Relations and Leadership* (New York: John Wiley & Sons, Inc., 1962), p. 11.

[8] Muzafer Sherif et al., *Intergroup Conflict and Cooperation: the Robbers Cave Experiment* (Norman, Okla.: University Book Exchange, 1961).

relationships and perhaps to solidify the parties more in their respective (current) positions:

> Well, we've got two weeks. I'm wondering whether a meeting is going to do anything but stir up tempers and recriminations unless we have a ground on which to meet, an area of discussion described for us.[9]

The Pilgrim Oil Company negotiations demonstrate another instance of avoiding a certain kind of provocative discussion that does not promise to be fruitful.[10] In order to prevent further deterioration in the relationship, during the session in which the parties were negotiating a shutdown of the refinery management avoided discussion of issues on which they had failed to make progress and focused instead on technical factors about which there was a common objective—a safe shutdown of equipment.

If common evaluation of results during negotiations has potential for attitude change, Party may deliberately sequence issues so that there will be a success experience for Opponent early in negotiations. By addressing and settling relatively easy issues first, the negotiators can tackle tough issues in a positive and collaborative atmosphere. The management negotiator in the Utility manufacturing case arranged that in each session the parties take up an issue that he was quite certain could be partially or totally resolved in a mutually satisfactory way. Then at the beginning of each session he reviewed the success of the preceding session and stressed the implications of this progress for the negotiations as a whole and for the new relationship which was emerging.

*View toward outsiders.* Rather often the parties are drawn closer together because of their common dislike of an object. Interestingly, the common dislike can be directed at a technician or staff member from one of the organizations who brings a set of values and standards of judgment incompatible with those used by the two chief negotiators. In effect, the "outsider" becomes a contrast that permits the two negotiators to better appreciate the extent to which they share the same language and reasoning. For example,

> During the final weeks as the parties spent increasing time on fringe matters, the union's technicians from Detroit and the company's technicians from the personnel staff played a more dominant role in bargaining. But they brought the line negotiators closer together out of antipathy to these technicians. The company negotiator kidded the union: "Why did you bring these fellows in from Detroit

[9] Ann Douglas, *Industrial Peacemaking* (New York: Columbia University Press, 1962), p. 23.

[10] Selekman, Selekman, and Fuller, 2d ed., *op. cit.*, p. 309.

—we were getting along so well before they came?" Or similarly the union ribbed the company: "Can't you handle these fringe items on your own without calling in all of these staff fellows?"

Another study provides an interesting illustration of the common aversion to an outsider.

In previous negotiations top management had relied upon a labor relations consultant to "fix things up" if the union began to present the company with difficulties. The consultant's approach was to contact the vice-president of the international union. Quite understandably, the union negotiator (a subordinate to the vice-president) disliked the consultant since occasionally he found his position undercut by his own superior as a result of the intervention of the consultant. The local official was extremely resentful of the consultant and of the fact that he was used by management. When the issue was raised by the union negotiator, the company negotiator also expressed disapproval.

It should be noted in the immediately preceding example that the company negotiator went further than merely dissociating himself from the consultant. The act of dissociation (which is involved in another tactical assignment discussed below) would have merely neutralized a potentially negative attitude between the union and the company negotiators. By actively expressing dislike for the methods used by his own superiors, the company negotiator encouraged a positive bond with the union negotiator. Of course the company negotiator was only effective in producing the desired result to the extent that his purported dislike for the consultant was convincing. His sympathetic position on the emotionally charged issue of the "fix-it-up" consultant was more credible because other common attitudes of dislike also entered into the relationship. It happened that the company negotiator had disagreed with his superiors on several matters raised during the current negotiations, including their refusal to allow a referendum in the shop and their decision not to provide the union with insurance costs.

*Deemphasis of differences.* When the two parties actually have radically different evalutions of the settlement (or some other object common to both parties), a negotiator cannot point to either common preferences or common aversions. However, a negotiator who wishes to structure positive attitudes at least does not exaggerate the differences between the parties.

Consider the effect in a case in which a union negotiator chose to boast about a victory:

During the 1946 negotiations between Allis Chalmers and the UAW a union security clause was worked out after the intervention of the government. Historically, Allis Chalmers had opposed any form of union security and only gave it grudgingly under the pressure of the Federal government. The UAW official returned to Milwaukee and boasted to his followers that "union security" had been won and constituted, according to his interpretation an advancement toward a closed shop. No sooner had he publicized his victory than the company refuted its concession in anger.

In terms of our model, the union official emphasized the dissimilarities between the two organizations' attitudes toward a provision and consequently produced strain which tended to produce a more negative relationship bond. If the union were interested in structuring more favorable attitudes, it would have been better for the union leader to have played down his victory, taking cognizance of the internal predicament facing some of the key company officials.

A good contrast to the "We won! We won!" tactic illustrated above was the approach taken by Reuther and Bugas of the UAW and Ford Motor Company as they announced the results of their 1955 negotiations.

> "Who won?" was the question as the two parties proceeded to the next room for the formal announcement and picture taking. "We both won," Reuther replied. "We are extremely happy to announce that we have arrived at an agreement. . . . Both the Company and the Union have worked very hard and very sincerely at the bargaining table." [11]

Bugas responded in the same vein, indicating equally positive approval of the historic settlement which provided for supplementary unemployment benefits, generally regarded as an important breakthrough for organized labor.

*Effectiveness of tactics.* In summary, Party can refer to personal interests shared with Opponent, adopt similar language in negotiations, introduce mutual problems or goals, refer to mutual successes, note similar dislike toward an outsider, and deemphasize those differences which do exist between Party and Opponent. We assume that Opponent feels inconsistent about the fact that both he and Party have similar preference(s) and yet he dislikes Party. These actions, then, create some strain in Opponent in the direction of a more favorable attitude toward Party.

Whether the inconsistencies presented Opponent will actually have the desired effect depends upon several circumstances. According to the theory we outlined in the model chapter, these tactics will be effective only to the extent that the specific common interests and language, the mutual successes, etc., are important to Opponent and appear to be pertinent to

[11] Selekman, Selekman, and Fuller, 2d ed., *op. cit.*, pp. 428–429.

the current setting. Recall also that Opponent may achieve some consistency in his perceptual world without changing his attitude toward Party—by denying or distorting the nature of these ideas or events or by actually modifying his attitude toward them; therefore, the similarity in preferences implied by Party must be credible to Opponent and the ideas and events themselves relatively unambiguous.

## Parties Have Common Associations

In this case the important influence on the attitudes of the parties is their common association with an object. The object may be certain experiences or activities shared by the parties. In balance terminology, the situation may be characterized by Figure 7-2, in which $a$ is an associative bond and $o$ indicates a neutral evaluative bond.

**Figure 7-2**

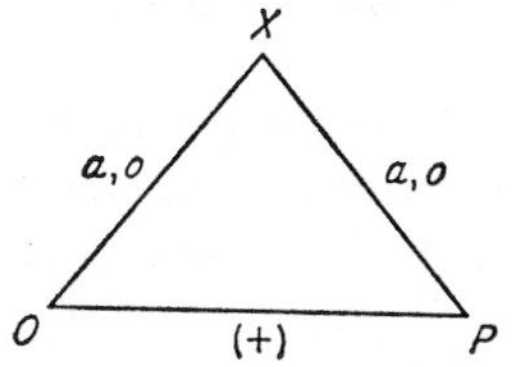

It is quite possible that the common association with the object may eventually turn into common benefits or feelings of attraction of the type we described in the first tactical assignment. Here we are more interested in the association with the object even though the persons have no particular evaluative attitude toward it. An awareness of a common experience or fate, even when the evaluative component of the cognition is relatively neutral, produces positive feelings between participants.[12] As the change agent, Party produces or emphasizes the common experiences or other similarities. Our discussion will focus on experiences shared by the parties and will proceed from some of the more central to the more incidental shared activities.

*Increase of interaction.* Party may structure the situation in a way that increases the rate of interaction. For example, problem-centered interaction was required when Utility Company management shared administrative responsibilities for allocating overtime with the union. Management also defined the problem of explaining the union shop to the nonmembers as a common one, requiring the joint effort of union and management. This worked toward accommodation in two ways: (1) by establishing discussions which are separate from negotiations and (2) by structuring these interactions between union officials and line management. Here we are interested in the fact that they engaged in common *activity*, in contrast to the earlier focus on the *goals* held in common.

How does interaction tend to produce positive sentiments? The proposition itself has been advanced in many forms. It has been especially cen-

[12] Fritz Heider, *The Psychology of Interpersonal Relations* (New York: John Wiley & Sons, Inc., 1958), p. 184.

tral to Homans's theory of small groups.[13] One of Gandhi's tactics incorporates the idea.[14] Johan Galtung and others have identified the tactic as "creating a network of primary relations between groups." [15] In the terms of balance theory: given their negative attitudes toward management officials, union officials would not expect to be in collaborative interaction with them; the union officials can either discontinue the interaction or restore balance by feeling more positive toward management. However, the relation between interaction and interpersonal attitudes is hardly unequivocal: if fundamentally different attitudes toward objects exist between the persons, interaction may lead to greater dislike.[16] The effectiveness of increasing contact may therefore depend on whether in the process the parties discover similarities and potential interdependencies about which they were previously unaware.

*Emphasize common fate.* Party may call Opponent's attention to their common fate. The recognition by the negotiators of their common fate may be an important force on attitudes, whether this fate be potential (e.g., the prospect of a work stoppage) or actually experienced (e.g., the sweat and tears involved in hard bargaining).

It is paradoxical that certain experiences inherent in conflict bargaining can foster positive attitudes. The approach of the strike deadline and the possibility that both sides may undergo severe costs emphasize what the negotiators have in common:

> One observer tells a story of a negotiation in a shoe company in New Hampshire. The atmosphere was tense, and bargaining was definitely an adversary affair until the lights went out. Their common fate was dramatized by this incident, and the parties quickly reached settlement.

Certain social processes involved in bargaining around the clock prior to a strike deadline influence interpersonal attitudes: the common need to get some sleep and the common desire to finish what has been started.

> *Management* The company would like a caucus. You want to get breakfast and then come back?
>
> *Union* It's early, isn't it, for breakfast? Oh, it's seven o'clock.

[13] G. C. Homans, *The Human Group* (New York: Harcourt, Brace & World, Inc., 1950).

[14] I. L. Janis and Daniel Katz, "The Reduction of Intergroup Hostility: Research Problems and Hypotheses," *Journal of Conflict Resolution*, vol. 3 (March, 1959), p. 86.

[15] Johan Galtung, "Pacifism from a Sociological Point of View," *Journal of Conflict Resolution*, vol. 3 (March, 1959), pp. 67–84.

[16] Heider, *op. cit.*, pp. 180–190.

*Management* It's seven o'clock.

*Mediator* We'll be awfully hungry by breakfast time.

*Management* Well, we can eat another one then.

*Mediator* If anybody goes home for a clean shirt, we're going to lose about half of you.

*Management* The guy that goes home for a clean shirt pays for all the breakfasts.

*Union* All right. Who needs another shirt here—white, blue? (Considerable discussion follows regarding police tickets for parking overnight. Discussion ensues about places open at this hour for breakfast. The mediator compliments someone because his hair isn't mussed, but accuses him of not having worked. As recording ends someone remarks that it's getting daylight.) [17]

Another example of what people have in common is the statistical summary that General Motors tabulated for several negotiations showing how many cups of coffee were consumed. Just the fact that they would tabulate these figures and that both sides took a certain whimsical satisfaction out of publicizing them is evidence of the importance of common experience, however neutral it may be as an attitude object.

*Emphasize common background.* Negotiations are replete with examples of common experiences that are background to the negotiating meetings. The Barrington Oil negotiations [18] provide an interesting illustration of a negotiator attempting to invoke a common association.

The president of the international union, Mr. Knight, had just entered a local negotiation where management had pretty much had matters their own way. In a bid to generate positive feelings, the management negotiator said, "I am very glad to have Mr. Knight here. We are old fellow workers."

It should be noted that Knight did not respond to the attitudinal tactic but rather immediately introduced the threat of economic sanctions. Given the basic attitudinal set on Knight's part, namely, one of suspicion and hostility toward the company, it is not surprising that Knight ignored the gesture aimed at establishing common association. It is also possible that Knight held negative feelings toward his experience as a worker in the company. More probably, he managed his perception so as to ignore the gesture of the management official.

[17] Douglas, *op. cit.*, p. 174.
[18] Selekman, Selekman, and Fuller, 2d ed., *op. cit.*, p. 288.

This brief exploration of why the tactic did not have the intended effect should help us keep in proper perspective the potential of this type of tactical operation.

## Party Associated with Objects Opponent Likes

In this paradigm Party becomes associated with something which is approved by Opponent (see Figure 7-3a).

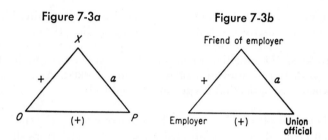

Figure 7-3a          Figure 7-3b

Opponent likes an object with which Party is associated. Given these cognitions, Opponent can achieve balance by feeling more favorable toward Party. Party may contribute to this situation either by creating or emphasizing the O-X evaluation or the P-X association, whichever was not previously apparent to Opponent. It is not necessary for Party to indicate approval for the object in question!

For the most part, this paradigm occurs when Party produces a substantive benefit for Opponent, such as progress on a problem of Opponent which strengthens his position within his own organization, recognition of the institutional legitimacy of Opponent's organization, or enhancement of the personal status of Opponent. In each case Party is associated with a situation beneficial to Opponent. We shall turn to these possibilities as well as to a fourth in which Party is associated with a person Opponent likes.

**Work on a substantive problem of Opponent.** This is a fundamental way of eliciting a more favorable response from the other. It goes to the heart of what is meant by a more positive working relationship. "By being responsive to [Opponent] in the present and making relatively minor sacrifices of short-term interest, [Party] can succeed in building and maintaining the sort of good will which will pay off in the longer term." [19]

The types of proposals submitted for the bargaining agenda can have important attitudinal consequences in this respect. They can signal either

[19] D. G. Pruitt, "An Analysis of Responsiveness between Nations," *Journal of Conflict Resolution*, vol. 6 (March, 1962), p. 8.

a desire for a more collaborative or a more antagonistic basis for the relationship. Party may take the initiative in including on the agenda a proposal for a change, the substance of which is obviously of more benefit to Opponent. An example is Romney's voluntary offer to hold prebargaining conferences between American Motors and the UAW, an arrangement similar to that which Reuther previously had requested of General Motors and Ford without success.

Unions are in an especially good position to take the initiative and exercise a leadership role in the solution of some of management's problems. Garfield and Whyte report a case in which the union leadership went before the membership urging that the latter cooperate in reducing the level of absenteeism, which had become a serious problem for management. The members responded, and the absenteeism record improved substantially.[20]

The industrial relations people in one company sought to affect attitudes by settling many grievances preliminary to negotiations, not on their merits and not because they were forced to, but merely to promote "good feeling." The divisional industrial relations personnel wanted to convey to the union the impression that the company was trying to meet them more than halfway. Similarly, in the Jimson case the chief negotiator for the company decided to volunteer to improve the language of the contract to conform to a more liberal plant practice. He reasoned that "that would show the union that the company would do the correct thing when it was necessary."

Providing a substantive benefit for Opponent sometimes assumes a more personal character. Some participants create informal interchanges which can influence formal patterns between union and management negotiators. One UAW official said that until 1952 he received his autos for dealer's cost plus $75 and that they were loaded down with extras. These were sent out at a vice-president's personal request.

When an important concession is to be made, Party has a choice regarding with whom in his organization the benefit is to be associated. The Labor relations manager in the Utility company would often let the line manager announce the company's concession of a benefit. This tended to focus favorable attitudes toward the person or group within his own organization whom he deemed most important to the relationship at the moment.

Each of the above are ways in which Party can take voluntary steps to benefit the principal represented by Opponent in order to place a strain toward more favorable attitudes.

[20] Garfield and Whyte, *op. cit.* (Winter, 1950), p. 28.

***Strengthening of Opponent's position.*** Another way of structuring more favorable attitudes is to assist Opponent in strengthening his position within his organization. A management which has acknowledged a union leader's internal problems and has assisted him in strengthening his own position has taken an important step in building an accommodative relationship with him. The whole matter of a relationship between a negotiator and his organization will be considered in the next chapter. At that point, we shall explore rather elaborately the way in which one negotiator can facilitate the intraorganizational bargaining of the other negotiator. Here we might take note of several examples which suggest how Party can act to benefit Opponent:

> Management at International Harvester actively pursued a policy of helping the union leadership to strengthen its own internal position. For example, during the 1955 negotiations, management proposed the establishment of a screening procedure wherein all grievances appealed to arbitration would be processed by the Harvester Department of the union. The company also encouraged discussions with top union officials over unresolved grievances and policy problems.

In other instances management has voluntarily granted the union shop in an effort to encourage and strengthen responsible leadership. Such would be the explanation for the action of Henry Ford in granting the union shop to the UAW in 1941. In some cases management will actually help build the power of a potentially cooperative leader by giving him credit for certain improvements. In one case the management negotiator allowed a particular union official to take credit for winning the union shop.

Another tactic is to alert Opponent about major maneuvers one must take during the forthcoming session, so that he is not caught by surprise and embarrassed before his own team. Thus, Opponent will associate Party with the fact that he has information which helps him perform his role. Jimson negotiations contain many examples of this. For example,

> Scott advised his team that there would probably be further discussion on insurance. His expectations actually grew out of informal discussions with Watoski. These discussions enabled him to make a prediction which he was almost certain would be accurate. The same thing may have been true for Watoski with his committee. Thus, their informal discussions positively structured their attitudes toward one another, since it enabled them to give a further impression of competence to their teams, and through the teams, to their superiors.

Party may confide in Opponent about his plans and intentions even when such a disclosure contains bad news for Opponent. In one case management confided in the union about a major modernization program.[21] Presumably management took this step assuming that the act of giving advance information would strengthen the union leadership in its internal dealings. It was also hoped that the leadership would recognize that management was responsible for this gratuitous advantage. Thus, Party would be associated with a procedure which benefited Opponent. However, the procedural overture was not successful in eliciting a favorable response; instead the union responded with a strong challenge to management's right to initiate the program. The overture failed because the content of the communication was too adverse. While the act of confidence may have had positive value, the consequences of the modernization program were too damaging to the work force for the union to respond in a positive way to management. It is also possible that the union viewed the action of management as an attempt to manipulate it; in this sense, even the symbolic value of the overture would have been negative.

*Conferring status on Opponent.* Another way for Party to be identified with an event which benefits Opponent is to structure a situation which confers legitimacy, respect, or status on Opponent and perhaps members of his bargaining team.

In one case the management negotiator was responsible for creating an atmosphere of dignity and status by several moves. He obtained the use of the conference room belonging to the chairman of the board. He also brought to the negotiating conference members of top management who by their presence could attest to the importance of the proceedings.

It must be emphasized that the steps taken to confer status upon the opponent must be genuine and not ritualistic. Cordiality which is officious and not genuine can provoke a hostile response. Moreover, conferring legitimacy and respect for Opponent's organization goes beyond mere formal recognition. It involves a respect for the ability and vitality of the other institution. It involves a respect for the central power position of the other side.

There are many things that management can do to signal its respect for the union. One step is to allow the union to present its position with care and deliberateness. Many companies refrain from presenting their own proposals or even attempting to respond to the union's proposals until the union has been given an adequate opportunity to present its story and until management has had adequate time to analyze the situation. For example, during the 1950 negotiations between the UAW and General Motors, the company did not make its presentation until almost a month had passed in the negotiations. By contrast, the technique of

[21] Selekman, Selekman, and Fuller, 2d ed., *op. cit.*, pp. 105–126.

General Electric in presenting its proposals early in negotiations conveys a lack of respect for the ability of the union to represent the needs of the workers. The opposition on the part of unions to Boulwarism rests on the fact that this strategy represents an attack on the legitimacy of unions.

Management can convey respect or acceptance of the union through mere tolerance of some of the actions of the union, as the following example illustrates:

> *Management* They love to have these things (negotiations) go on till say 12 o'clock Saturday and then have a meeting in union hall at 12:15 Saturday. And they stroll in there and get up on stage, you know, all sleepy-eyed from being up late that night. They were really pooped, and they looked worse than they were. These people just ate it up. "Those stalwarts in there, struggling for us."
>
> *Mediator* This man doesn't appreciate all those dramatics, does he?
>
> *Management* I understand good theater, and I'm willing to do all I can to set the stage as long as I don't tangle with the scenery.
>
> *Mediator* You know, it might be said that we ought to be paying dues to the Actors Guild.[22]

The records of negotiations are replete with examples of how management failed to recognize the legitimacy of the opponent. Hence, they become associated with situations which the union has disapproved. The union achieves balance by adopting a less favorable attitude toward the company. Garfield and Whyte cite a dramatic example of how a company provided for a settlement which was mutually satisfactory in substantive terms but did it in a way that discredited the union as an effective force in the determination of hours, wages, and working conditions.

> They went in and argued for that wage increase all afternoon long. Finally the representative of top management stepped in and cut off the discussion with these words:
>
> "Well, you fellows have done a lot of talking, and I must say I haven't found your arguments very convincing. Still, I think you're a good bunch of fellows, and I tell you what I'll do. I'll give you 10 cents." [23]

The offer was in line with the best around the country, and they accepted. But as a consequence, antimanagement feeling ran high and made the union more adamant in the next negotiation.

In another negotiation, management failed to display adequate con-

22 Douglas, *op. cit.*, p. 331.
23 Garfield and Whyte, *op. cit.* (Summer, 1950), p. 9.

cern for the position of the union. Its cavalier response evoked considerable hostility.

> *Management* Based on the cost of living, and the cost of living, according to government, has still not reached the 1937 level, there is no justification on that basis for a general increase.

> *Union* Alright. We'll show that to our wives on Saturday—and maybe they will show the butcher and the baker who don't seem to read the same books Mr. Malcolm does. My wife tells me after shopping, "Last week I spent $10 and this week I spent $13 for the same things, *those* are *my* actual statistics." [24]

Expressions of cynicism probably represent the most severe attack on the legitimacy of the opponent and his position.

> *Management* (Responding to a union request for a 15% wage hike.) I would like to have a rake-off myself.

> *Union* We don't feel like it is a rake-off at all. It is earned.[25]

The use of company letters to inform employees about bargaining developments can indicate a lack of concern for the internal status of the union officials. The following is a quote from such a letter:

> I am hopeful we can negotiate a new contract before July 31. But it is a short time. Ordinarily, contract negotiations begin their meetings 30 to 60 days before the old contract expires. The company preferred to begin the discussions during the week of June 16, and we suggested this to the union. That would have allowed at least 40 days to complete a new contract. However, the union has said that they do not believe it should take more than two weeks to negotiate a new contract.[26]

This letter carries a veiled criticism of the union leadership and its ability to conduct negotiations. It is not surprising that the union committee recommended against acceptance of the company's final offer.

The above are illustrations of how management became associated with situations which harmed the union—belittlement, cavalier disrespect, cynicism, and criticism. The union official's cognitive system can incorporate each such indication of management's disapproval by adopting or strengthening a negative attitude toward management. We would not

[24] Selekman, Selekman, and Fuller, 1st ed., *op. cit.*, p. 382.
[25] *Ibid.*, p. 376.
[26] *Ibid.*, p. 599.

suggest that management was unaware of these consequences and that these represented errors in judgment, although this might have been partly true. However, we do want to point out the consequences of such actions, consequences which are not always anticipated by management.

*Party's association with friend of Opponent.* Party may be associated with a person whom Opponent likes, regardless of whether the person in question tenders any benefits to Opponent. Whyte cites a case in which an employer felt antagonistic toward union officials in general and refused to confer with one in particular whom he had never actually met.[27] The employer held a stereotype of union officials as racketeers. However, the employer also had a friend who assured him that the union leader was actually a quite acceptable fellow: he could be counted upon to keep his word, he disliked fights, and he liked opera! The friend (rather than the union official directly) had created imbalance for the employer.

From Figure 7-3b, which represents the employer's cognitive imbalance, it becomes apparent that the employer could respond in one of three ways to reduce strain. First, he could change his evaluation of his informant to a negative. Note, however, the crucial role of friendship in preventing the employer's use of this alternative as a means of restoring balance. Second, the employer could attempt to dissociate his friend from the union official: "I'm not sure my friend really feels that way"; or, "He didn't have much of a basis for his tentative conclusions"; etc. These are also unlikely alternatives, in this case, because the friend had not only associated himself with the union official in some general sense but had attributed to the official some specific attributes (keeps word, likes opera) which happened to appeal to both the friend and the employer. Thus, the friend's association with the union official became more credible and less ambiguous. The third alternative was for the employer to look more favorably upon the union official. This is what apparently happened.

Note that the original antagonism was partly a consequence of the employer's stereotype of union officials. His subsequent acceptance of the union official was probably accommodated by some degree of differentiation of this official from union officials in general. Thus, the employer's more central structure of attitudes toward unions did not necessarily have to undergo serious modification.

## Opponent Associated with Objects Party Likes

We are still interested in Opponent's cognitions as influenced by Party. Thus, Party attempts to have Opponent see himself as associated with objects which benefit Party. This involves a somewhat more subtle proposi-

[27] Whyte, *op. cit.,* p. 334.

tion than those which underlie the three tactical assignments discussed above (see Figure 7-4).

Party is benefited by object $X$, and Opponent perceives himself as associated with $X$. Given these cognitions, Opponent balances his cognitive system by feeling more favorable toward Party. The proposition is that people tend to like those whom they have benefited [28] and to trust those who place themselves in a position of future dependency.[29]

**Figure 7-4**

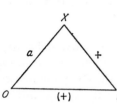

There are several negotiation tactics that seem to have their effect in a way explained by this paradigm. In its simplest form Party merely expresses appreciation for what Opponent has done. In so doing he establishes the fact that he has a positive feeling toward the object for which Opponent is responsible. Later in the chapter we shall present material on the subject of appreciation in which the main message is one of reward. At this point we want to note that the expression of appreciation can be viewed as an attempt to influence cognitions in a way explained by balance theory.

By identifying an object as beneficial to himself (object for which Opponent is responsible), Party may communicate to Opponent that the latter has some control over Party's fate. By this action—placing himself in a position of dependency—Party is taking the first and important step of eliciting trust from Opponent. Party gives Opponent the option of acting in either a helpful or a harmful way toward Party.

Consider an example from negotiations in the food industry: [30]

> In one of the negotiations reported by Selekman, the company negotiator allowed the union to "write the seniority clause." In effect, the company allowed the union to structure the seniority system as it best saw fit, trusting that it would take into account the interests of the company. Clearly, the company was exposing itself to potential harm, but the union responded in a responsible way and the act of the company in giving the opportunity to write the seniority clause strengthened attitudes between the union and the company.

[28] Leon Festinger, "Cognitive Dissonance," *Scientific American*, vol. 207 (October, 1962), pp. 93–106. Sorokin, also, notes the effect of the "technique of good deeds" in producing favorable attitudes in both parties: P. A. Sorokin, "Some Activities of The Harvard Research Center in Creative Altruism," *Journal of Human Relations*, vol. 2 (Spring, 1954), pp. 12–17.

[29] See Morton Deutsch, "Trust and Suspicion," *Journal of Conflict Resolution*, vol. 2 (December, 1958), pp. 265–279; and Festinger, *op. cit.*

[30] Selekman, Selekman, and Fuller, 2d ed., *op. cit.*, p. 262.

A second illustration is taken from negotiations in a leading manu-facturing industry:

> In another situation a company negotiator used the practice of set-tling small issues "on a without precedent basis." Both sides realized that the union could use these concessions as leverage for obtaining comparable changes in other situations. Clearly, the company ex-posed itself by making these settlements. However, the union com-pleted the overture of trust by agreeing that these cases would not stand as precedent and that the union would not use them against the company.

The dynamics of the trust-building process can be analyzed by steps. The first step is the association that Party helps to establish between Op-ponent and the given object. In the first illustration the company negotia-tor permitted the union to write the seniority clause; the second instance was the association between the union and its promise not to use the set-tlements as precedent for future action. The second step is the choice made by Opponent between helping and harming Party. By writing the seniority clause in a responsible way and by not using the special settlements against the company in comparable situations, the two unions established a strong positive bond with their respective companies. The positive attitude was reciprocal, since the union liked the company because it had helped the company and the company liked the union for its help.

The second step involves the question of whether the bid for trust is actually successful and thereby rewarded—a matter which we take up in detail later in the chapter.

### Party Dissociated from Objects Opponent Dislikes

Without particularly committing himself about his like or dislike for an object which Opponent disapproves, Party does take steps to dissociate himself from the objects: the idea does not belong to him, the action was not his responsibility, etc. (see Figure 7-5).

**Figure 7-5**

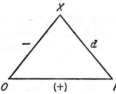

In the diagram shown, Opponent dislikes an object and Party is dissociated from the object. Given these cognitions, Opponent can also ac-commodate a feeling favorable to Party. These cognitions by themselves do not set up a force toward positive attitude. Thus, in contrast to the tactical assignment of stressing common dislikes, the step of dissociation is defensive: it protects positive feelings if they exist for other reasons.

*Dissociation of self from others.* Perhaps the most common tactic of this type is for Party to place the blame for certain matters on members of his own organization not present at the bargaining table. This tends to safeguard the relationship between negotiators, although one cannot escape some strain on this bond. Consider an exchange between the negotiators in the Jimson study:

> **Union** I'm not happy at all about the company's refusal to let us hold the referendum at the plant. You might be interested to know that Evans Containers is permitting a vote to be held on their premises.
>
> **Management** Well, that's one of the things the company decided; I don't feel that there's any reason to get into that here.

We note that the management negotiator not only avoided accepting any personal responsibility for what "the company" decided but tried to avoid getting involved in any discussion of the matter. He was trying to divorce himself as completely as possible from the attitude object which irritated the union.

*Dissociation of present from past.* In another instance the same negotiator dissociated himself from his own past behavior which had provoked an outburst from his union counterpart.

> **Management** Shall we go to work?
>
> **Union** Go ahead.
>
> **Management** I don't know quite what to do. We didn't accomplish much last time. There seem to be several issues that we're far apart on. . . . (Pause.) Today, I do have a letter of understanding on the waiting time issue. You gave us a pretty hard time last time because we didn't have the letter. I think we were wrong by not having the letter the last time, Jim, and I don't blame you for getting rough with us.

The effect of apologizing ("we were wrong . . . and I don't blame you . . .") was to allow both negotiators to dissociate their present selves from their earlier action.

*Dissociation of self from circumstances.* Dissociation may involve placing the blame on circumstances not related to the present situation. Party may have to admit that he must initiate an action which Opponent disapproves and yet maintain that the action is not intentional in its effect on Opponent. Consider the following example:

*Union* Well, I quite agree that time is running out and I'm conscious of it. While I indicated that I was willing to sit and listen to 1 o'clock tomorrow afternoon, unfortunately that is not going to work that way. I've got a staff meeting to attend tomorrow morning at the District office, and I want time enough to prepare my report for the membership meeting at 1 o'clock. Now as far as I'm concerned about today, I have a personal problem, and I may as well make it clear right now that I'm not going to stay here after six thirty tonite. My youngster is making his communion next week and I need to take him to buy one of the white suits that you pay money for and get nothing out of, but that's it.[31]

In the above example the union negotiator was calling off the session—an action which management disliked since it had hoped to reach agreement that evening. By providing considerable information about his personal predicament, the union negotiator made credible his assertion that his action in abruptly calling off the scheduled session was not personal, even though management disapproved of it.

Several excerpts show how various management negotiators attempt to avoid personal responsibility for their companies' position.

*Management* We feel we are in line with our competitors and regret very much we are not prepared at present to grant your request for increase. I hope you will take it in the spirit I am saying it. There is nothing personal whatsoever.[32]

*Management* I regret that Barrington cannot agree to the arbitration of wages . . . that is our belief right or wrong, but I am explaining how the company feels about it—and feels very strongly. I am under instructions of my headquarters never to put into an agreement a clause which would permit the arbitration of wages. I am sorry to tell you that, but it is my duty to do so.[33]

*Management* (Commenting on the company's refusal to improve the wage offer.) Well, to summarize the whole thing, as I said before and I wish you would realize this, it is not a personal issue. . . . On certain things, administrative matters, I am given certain freedom. On certain cardinal principles I have to take instructions given me.[34]

*Management* They like me, George?

*Mediator* Well, yea, I think they do. They don't like your bargaining position, but I don't think they dislike you.[35]

[31] Douglas, *op. cit.*, p. 388.
[32] Selekman, Selekman, and Fuller, 2d ed., *op. cit.*, p. 220.
[33] *Ibid.*, pp. 225–226.
[34] *Ibid.*, p. 228.
[35] Douglas, *op. cit.*, pp. 377–378.

A good question can be raised about the effectiveness of some of the above protestations that there is "nothing personal in my actions." Opponent may be rather skeptical of Party's constant repetition that all of his actions are not designed to hurt Opponent personally. There is reason to doubt when he "doth protest too much." Again, to be convincing, Party's disclaimers must be accompanied by sufficient information about himself and his role position so that Opponent can make the appropriate differentiations.

## Opponent Dissociated from Objects Party Dislikes

In this case Party attempts to dissociate Opponent from those objects which Party dislikes or is harmed by (see Figure 7-6a). Party dislikes an item and Opponent is dissociated from it. These cognitions allow Opponent to have favorable attitudes toward Party. Again, this tactical assignment only protects the current attitudes, whatever they may be, from a potentially deteriorating influence.

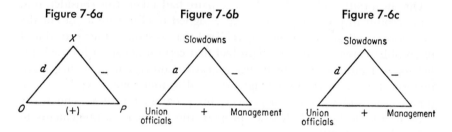

| Figure 7-6a | Figure 7-6b | Figure 7-6c |

The proposition is a relatively subtle one: "We dislike those we harm." If Opponent were to see himself as somehow associated with events that harmed Party, he would like Party less. Thus, Party attempts to dissociate Opponent from such events. Hence, the importance of saying to Opponent, "I don't blame you or hold you responsible," and meaning it! A person may say this and not mean it. In fact, he may not really want to convince the other person completely; instead, he wants the other person to see his gesture as being somewhat gratuitous. However, this subtle form of punishment of the other is self-defeating, because according to this proposition, unless Opponent is completely dissociated from the harmful event, there will be forces toward negative feelings about Party.[36]

In this tactical assignment we are primarily interested in examining

[36] We shall have more to say about the tactic of holding the opponent responsible for the negative effect of the object. This form of punishment may have a stablizing effect if certain conditions are present. We shall turn to this subject later in the chapter when we consider the whole matter of reward-punishment.

the steps that Party can take to help Opponent dissociate himself from the object, assuming that the object remains and Party continues to dislike it.

*Avoidance of direct accusations.* One tactic is for Party to avoid direct accusations when calling attention to unfavorable situations largely within Opponent's control. In his study of dramatic change in union-management relations at Inland Steel Container Company's Chicago Plant, W. F. Whyte noted that in negotiations management repeatedly expressed its concern regarding slowdowns and work stoppages and other evidences of what management considered irresponsible actions. Despite the fact that union leaders had indeed instigated some of these activities (see Figure 7-6b), management was careful to state that they were not accusing any union official of being involved.[37] Thus they dissociated Opponent from acts which harmed them (see Figure 7-6c).

Garfield and Whyte cite another case in which a union official detailed the mismanagement of a methods engineering program in the plant but then carefully placed the blame on an outside engineering firm, despite the fact that the laxness of management was an important factor.[38] In effect, Party says to Opponent, "I don't blame you for my misfortune."

One negotiator related how his company had taken this consideration into account in preparing a proposal designed to eliminate abuses of the sick-leave privilege. The company realized that as soon as they introduced the problem area, the union might feel that certain persons who used this sick leave legitimately were being attacked. Consequently, management prefaced their remarks by saying: "We realize that some have been genuinely sick, and we want to protect this program for those who really need it. In the light of this, we propose the following arrangements to police this program. . . ."

## Joint Dissociation Techniques

The two preceding tactical assignments involved first dissociating Party and second Opponent from an object disliked by the other. Certain tactical operations can affect both parties simultaneously—some aspect of the situation is differentiated from other aspects of the conflict between the parties. The result is that the two negotiators preserve a degree of positive affect, trust, and concern for each other, even though other aspects of the relationship are negative. They seek to insulate the Party-Opponent bond from the other aspects of the situation.

*Fighting the antagonism, not the antagonist.* Certain measures can be taken which permit some positive sentiment to characterize the relations

[37] W. F. Whyte, *Pattern for Industrial Peace* (New York: Harper & Row, Publishers, Incorporated, 1951).

[38] Garfield and Whyte, *op. cit.* (Winter, 1950), p. 27.

between individual participants, even though the two organizations remain in disagreement and in an antagonistic relationship generally. The differentiation required here is the one implicit in the Gandhian norm to fight the antagonism, not the antagonist.

> This norm has many facets, one of which is an expression of Gandhi's insight into what frequently happens in the earlier phases of a group conflict: the conflict is no longer seen in terms of conflicting values and issues, but the persons behind the values are seen as the causes of the conflict. The disagreement with the value is correspondingly transformed to a depreciation of the whole person.
>
> If the resented actions of the antagonist group are regarded as status actions (e.g., of the status of "occupant," status of "employer," status of "white") more than as parts of the personality of the actor, a redefinition of the situation becomes possible. Instead of putting the blame on the individual racist or occupant, the blame may be put on his definition of his status and the whole status network, thus making it possible to criticize and even impede or fight the actions while at the same time supporting or sustaining the status holder.
>
> A great deal of "permissiveness" and direct "support" can thus be expressed toward the individual enemy, while at the same time complete "denial of reciprocity" can be made use of with regard to the status actions, e.g., by refusing to interact.[39]

In some instances the attempts are to separate pleasant attributes of personality from unpleasant attributes. This is nothing more than "emphasizing the positive," by seeking to preserve a Party-Opponent bond, however slim the basis. Consider the following example:

> *Management* I have found that your union representatives, even when they were angry and sore and mean—and they get that way just the way we get that way, because we are all human—even their worse moments, they were all men whose word could be trusted.[40]

*Invoking institutional sanction rather than personal aggression.* Douglas indicates that the parties to the four negotiations she studied frequently discounted role behavior appropriately, not letting it affect the established person-to-person relationship. ". . . while the parties are busily engaged in depreciating each other, at the level of interpersonal relationships there flow warm currents of personal goodwill and friendly respect between and among individual negotiators." [41]

[39] Johan Galtung, *op. cit.,* pp. 78–79.
[40] Selekman, Selekman, and Fuller, 2d ed., *op. cit.,* p. 550.
[41] Douglas, *op. cit.,* pp. 17–18.

When there is not merely potential goal conflict but the Party actually begins to employ power tactics against Opponent in the pursuit of opposed goals, the differentiation just referred to becomes crucial. Several steps can be taken to minimize the negative impact on attitudes of power tactics, such as a work stoppage, by clarifying the action as institutionalized sanctions rather than personal aggressions.[42] Dissociating *both* union and management officials from the institutional action protects their relationship. Action is taken in behalf of one's organization, without any reflection of personal animosity. It is in part for this reason that many companies in recent years have provided comfort and convenience items to strikers: shelter, hot lunches, loudspeakers playing music, and the like. Moreover, permissive arrangements have been provided by unions allowing management to carry on some work and move through the picket line without loss of dignity. These are in line with an earlier war tradition of "wage no battle before breakfast and none after dusk."

There is a danger in completely separating institutional sanctions and personal aggression. When the line between these meanings remains blurred and a favorable personal relationship exists, the relationship provides a helpful constraint on the use of institutional sanctions. If the differentiation is carried too far, however, then the positive personal relationships built between members of the parties become less of a constraint on their recourse to economic sanctions. Eventually the use of sanctions may mar the relationship. For example, in the 1959 steel strike there was at the outset little need for the representatives to concern themselves with the impact of a stoppage on the relationships, because the strike had become such a neutral and institutionalized phenomenon. However, this situation changed with the injection of the emotional work-rules issue and with the prolonged nature of the stoppage.

### Supplementary Balance Tactics

A word needs to be said about private meetings between negotiators. Although such a conversation may itself be an attitudinal structuring tactic, it also does facilitate many of the types of behaviors or activities discussed above. Private meetings enable a negotiator to differentiate himself from the actions or ideas of his organization with a minimum of risk of negative sanctions from his own group. These private encounters increase the flexibility of Party in giving aid and assistance or otherwise associating himself with something Opponent likes. Moreover, it should be stressed that these contacts outside negotiations allow the negotiators to discover and emphasize the personal interests they have in common.

[42] I. L. Janis and Daniel Katz, "The Reduction of Intergroup Hostility: Research Problems and Hypotheses," *Journal of Conflict Resolution*, vol. 3 (March, 1959), p. 86.

A second all-purpose tactic of a supplementary nature is the simple momentary diversion from the business at hand: a well-timed joke, the introduction of casual conversation about nonrelevant issues, etc. As we noted in an earlier chapter, such diversions may be intended to head off a statement which would constitute a commitment for distributive bargaining. They may also be designed to avoid antagonism at the table damaging to the continuing relationship. They may be thought of as releasing tension. Pertinent to the terms of the present analysis we suggest that they are "all-purpose dissociation techniques." The diversion comes at a time when there is strain in Opponent's cognitive structure, because unfortunately Party has become associated with an object $X$ which harms Opponent. If Opponent is allowed to consider this harm against his otherwise positive feelings toward Party, he might resolve the inconsistency by feeling less favorably toward Party. Therefore, Party diverts Opponent's thinking away from these three elements in imbalance and helps Opponent suppress the associative bond between Party and object $X$.

We should acknowledge one additional facilitating condition for the other attitudinal structuring tactics, namely, empathy for Opponent. Empathy with respect to the motives, affects, expectations, and attitudes of members of the rival group and the possession of knowledge about the other's situation permit Party to respond when it is least costly to himself and maximally beneficial to Opponent.

**Concluding Remark about Balance Tactics.** The six tactical assignments presented in Part 1 cover the major implications of balance theory for understanding the negotiator's instrumental efforts to change attitudes and achieve new patterns of relationship. We believe that the range of behaviors discussed as tactics in the foregoing analysis are best understood by balance theory and its specific propositions.

There are, however, other behaviors and behavioral sequences with apparent implications for attitude change for which balance theory is not as analytically helpful. We shall turn to a discussion of the tactics of reinforcement.

# PART 2 | SHIFTING REWARDS AND PUNISHMENTS TO CHANGE BEHAVIOR

Let us continue with our assumption that Party wishes to establish a more positive or constructive pattern than the one which currently exists.

There are two reasons why (or occasions for which) Party might deviate from the present pattern in a more gratuitous direction: to elicit attitudes from Opponent in the same direction or to reinforce any preceding behavior by Opponent. There is one occasion for which Party would deviate from the established pattern in the negative direction: to punish Opponent if he has recently violated the established pattern.

Having discussed the eliciting power of certain Party behavior, we now turn to the rewarding and punishing rationale for Party's behavior.

### Rewarding Opponent's Behavior

In this section we consider the tactics which are especially appropriate for rewarding behavior. We shall consider three categories: compliments, expressions of appreciation, and acts of favor.

*Extending compliments.* In many instances a negotiator is observed complimenting the other regarding some preferred behavior or some achievement: taking a problem rather than an issue orientation to an area such as job evaluation, being well prepared for the session, making a balanced presentation, etc. Consider a typical complimentary statement:

> *Management* I might inquire as to the job evaluation committee. I want to say that you people have gone along in pretty fine style there. It is new to you and the reason you are doing well is because you have an open mind.[43]

It should be noted that the compliment tactic could be handled within balance theory, but it seems particularly pertinent to reinforcement theory. The reinforcement interpretation of the compliment emphasizes the particular timing of Party's act. For the compliment to have the proper rewarding effect, it has to be directly related both in time and meaning to a preferred behavior of Opponent. On the other hand, in balance theory the compliment or favorable gesture can have its effect without being associated with a preceding behavior by Opponent.

In addition, it should be noted that for the compliment to be viewed as a reward by Opponent, there needs to exist some positive relationship between Opponent and Party. The compliment will be rewarding only if Opponent has some attraction to, or respect for, Party.

More importantly, however, even in the context of a slightly positive relationship, if Party does nothing more than personally compliment Opponent, he may not be very successful at his attempts to shape behavior. Verbal compliments (which may be appreciated by the person) without substantive benefits (which are facilitative of *role* performance) have limited reward value. They may even appear to be vacuous and insincere.

[43] Douglas, *op. cit.*, p. 255.

Nevertheless, some negotiators find themselves in the difficult position of possessing a limited array of rewards—compliments may represent the only important reward which they can tender Opponent. For one reason or another they have become so constrained by their own organization that they possess very little latitude with which to substantively reward Opponent. In this case a compliment is used as the only available form of reward.

Even though compliments may have limited value because they cannot be coupled with substantive benefits or because Opponent does not value an expression of gratitude, they still have communication value. In certain respects a compliment is the statement of a standard, the violation of which may evoke punishment on the part of Party. When management is complimenting the behavior of the union, it is, in effect, saying something about the appropriate role which it envisions for the union. These statements may have the effect of placing the union on notice that management might initiate punishment should the union's behavior deviate from these norms of conduct. (At the very least, of course, management would withdraw the compliment.) We shall discuss punishment tactics later in this chapter, but at this point we want to indicate that the compliment can be a forewarning of possible punishment in the sense that it is an effective way of underscoring Party's role expectations for Opponent.

*Expressing appreciation.* Beyond mere compliment, a party can show an attitude of appreciation. Now the focus of the statement is on Party and his own feelings. The following example is a typical statement of appreciation:

> *Management* Gentlemen, I think that you will be pleased to learn that we are unanimously of the opinion that your last proposition is a fair one.
>
> *Union* We are very much pleased that we have come to this kind of a conclusion, and hope this year we will continue the very satisfactory relationship which has existed in the past. I want to express my own appreciation to each of these men who represent our people. It seems to me that too often their efforts are not fully recognized by their members. I also want to thank you, Austin, and the company for the sincere method with which you have dealt with us. We really appreciate it.
>
> *Management* Thank you, Lou. I am sure you know that we hold all of you in the highest personal esteem. I should also like to pay the very highest tribute to all of the men on the Management side.[44]

It is worth noting that an expression of appreciation could be handled as "Party likes object associated with Opponent" in balance terms. In other words, the expression of appreciation can be nothing more than

[44] Selekman, Selekman, and Fuller, 2d ed., *op. cit.*, pp. 556–557.

Party's statement about the bond between himself and the object. He says to Opponent, "I like the object for which you are responsible." But to the extent that the statement does not provide Opponent with new information about Party and his preferences but rather simply enhances Opponent's self-respect and self-confidence, it would have its effect mainly through reinforcement of Opponent's preceding behavior.

**Returning the favor.** The most powerful reward is for Party to tender a favor to Opponent. This is similar to Party becoming associated with something that benefits Opponent. But it is also appropriately considered at this point if the act of doing something substantively beneficial for Opponent is a reward for a specific behavior on his part.

An excellent illustration of the tactic of returning a favor is taken from the Jimson negotiations. Here we see management taking a step to solve a problem (management drafted a letter "with teeth in it" committing the company to take certain steps within its own organization) and the union returning the favor since it wanted to reinforce the sincere effort made by the company.

> **Watoski (U)** The way the letter is written up is a real compliment to the bargaining committee. . . . The committee has already seen some improvement with the foremen. There's been a real spirit of co-operation on this, and we feel a good job has been done by the company on the letter.
>
> I have a couple of points to mention. (Pause.) The general foremen should not bypass the foremen and tell the employees what to do. They should use the chain of command.
>
> **Scott (M)** That's right, it's not good for a general foreman to bypass his own foreman.
>
> **Watoski (U)** On communications, a foreman should tell a crew what they have to do and when—instead of asking them if they'll do something when they can. A foreman should set guidelines for the people, so they know what they're supposed to do. (Scott nods.)
>
> **Scott (M)** Jim, those are real good points to bring out. I think you're right on both of them. Did you want something on this in the letter?
>
> **Watoski (U)** No, I just wanted to mention a couple of problems that you have in the plant. (Pause.) The committee will recommend acceptance of the letter to the membership.

Not only did Watoski compliment the company team, but he also promised that the union committee would recommend acceptance. The latter was an especially significant reward tactic because Scott had just previously indicated that he wanted this matter settled before proceeding, whereas

Watoski had preferred to learn more about the company's position on other matters before responding on this one item. Watoski was further rewarding the company negotiator for his genuine efforts when he indicated that it was not necessary to get further commitments in writing from the company on the additional problems that he (Watoski) had raised.

Let us consider an instance in another company in which both officials apparently shared a desire for closer cooperation and used a pattern of returning favors to achieve it:

> During early meetings of the classification subcommittee of the negotiations, the company spokesman volunteered to show the union spokesman letters that he was sending out to plant management. These letters requested information on classifications which the union had protested. In letting the union representative see internal company correspondence, the company's spokesman was seeking to develop a relationship of confidence between himself and the union spokesman. When shown the letters, the union spokesman indicated that certain classifications did not need to be explored further.

This was an important concession. Viewed from the point of view of the manager, his own act may be seen as an attempt to elicit such behavior from the union spokesman. However, what we are interested in here is the response of the union representative who shared a desire for a closer relationship. One can view his reduction in the union's position as an attempt to reinforce the manager's behavior. The sequence is repeated again and again—that is precisely how a relationship can develop through a history of preferred behaviors and reinforcements.

### Punishing Opponent's Behavior

An established pattern of behavior is the manifestation of what we call a relationship. Interaction behavior is stabilized and governed by a set of norms, that is, do's and don't's. Presumably these norms represent the most productive set of ground rules which occur to the parties or on which they can concur. Such norms are usually well supported by the basic attitudes of the participants, but in a particular instance a person may not feel constrained by the norm or established pattern. He may perceive an advantage in deviating from that pattern—by failing to meet some particular obligation. Deviation probably does yield a temporary gain. And it may not be harmful to him in the long run, unless it affects the relationship in a way that he regards as adverse or unless he is somehow punished for the deviation.

Pursuing the above reasoning, Party will often consider punishment as a way of coping with an instance of deviation by Opponent. The extent to which it may achieve the intended effect is a matter for analysis. In any event it should be clear that punishment is not useful in structuring a more positive relationship. It is impractical to punish all behavior that flows from a negative relationship. Punishment then is employed effectively only in a defensive way—in order to preserve a preferred relationship once achieved.

Very often the punishment being used for behavior which deviates from the preferred pattern is the threat or act to deteriorate the relationship further. Naturally, if a valued relationship does not exist at present, then this punishment is without meaning. Generally, punishment is more effective if it is directed at conscious and tactical rather than spontaneous behavior. That is, punishment can focus on nonconforming behavior, but not on sentiments and feelings.

Punishing behaviors are usually quite distinct because Party wants to make it unmistakable that the sanction is for a limited and specific purpose rather than an act initiating a new and more destructive pattern of relationship.

The problem can be stated another way. How Opponent responds will depend upon how he views the behavior. In particular, the question is whether he will view it in a past or future context. If a negative sanction by Party is viewed by Opponent as resulting from his own past deviant behavior, the negative gesture may have the intended effect of restoring a more collaborative relationship; but if Opponent views it with a future orientation, he will regard Party as acting in bad faith and is likely to respond with negative gestures himself.[45]

The inherent problem in punishment is that in punishing Opponent for what Party regards as some default in the role performance required by the relationship, he may simply induce Opponent to respond in measure. Consider the following example:

> The delegate from Springfield deplored the fact that the company had not yet come up with an offer. "We have been very reasonable this year; if the company does not take advantage of it, *things will be different*. It appears to me that the company is not sincere, General Motors has settled, John Deere has settled, and yet the company has done nothing." He was accusing the company of bad faith.

Implicit in the delegate's accusation was his threat to behave differently at the local level. He implied that he could hurt the company during contract administration. Presumably he was driven to emphasize the attitudinal side of negotiations by the company's lack of movement. In reality,

[45] Anatol Rapoport, "Lewis F. Richardson's Mathematical Theory of War," *Journal of Conflict Resolution*, vol. 1 (September, 1957), pp. 249–299.

considering the larger context, other developments had probably triggered this statement. In one of the sessions between him and the divisional industrial relations manager, he himself had been punished for behavior regarded as deviant from the relationship. He had been accused of double-dealing, in other words, of taking one position at the local level and another position in the negotiations at the central level. The delegate objected, "There is no one who has worked harder than me to settle these grievances." He may have been still smarting from this punishment when he found occasion to call management to task later.

The point is that these attempts to punish the other may build up tensions that find their outlet through still other responses of the same kind, snowballing and resulting in a deterioration of the relationship. Punishment becomes an increasingly "legitimate" technique for expressing hostility and aggression. Unfortunately punishment attempts also become increasingly destructive to the relationship itself.

In order to avoid the self-perpetuating cycle (each reaction to the other's punishment being a further return of punishment), the parties need a method of restoring the *status quo*. There is a need for retaliation followed by a method of absolution. In a lab experiment Deutsch provided for retaliation and then absolution by allowing the subject the following statement: "If you don't cooperate, then I will choose so that you can't win; and if you decided to cooperate and make a cooperative choice after not doing so first, then I will cooperate." [46] The key elements in absolution are first that the punishment is directly related to the deviant behavior and second that it is clear to Opponent that the punishment will stop, and in fact, will not even be initiated if the undesired behavior is changed.

There are various ways in which this absolution can be tactically executed. Party can state the punishment as a contingency on a certain form of deviant behavior of Opponent.

> In one negotiation the management negotiator at one point said to his union counterpart, "if you continue in this fashion, then all is no." The effect of the statement was to put the union on notice that if its conduct continued, then management would retaliate.

Opponent then realizes that the punishment is a direct response to his deviant behavior. Such a statement also suggests that the punishment will be withdrawn as soon as the deviant behavior is adjusted.

Punishment can take several forms: reminder of role obligations, the manipulation of self-concepts, and the use of open threats or retaliations— the invoking of specific sanctions.

*Reminding Opponent of role obligations.* In this and the next section

[46] Deutsch, *op. cit.*, p. 274.

(manipulation of self-concepts) we examine how Party punishes Opponent by telling him how Party's expectations about the role or personal behavior of Opponent have not been fulfilled. This tactic has more impact if Opponent needs to have his conception of his role or self reinforced by the viewpoint of Party. To the extent that this is not true, Opponent's response may be, "Well, I don't give a darn about what you think of what I am doing." Nevertheless, although he may not care about Party in particular, he may not like to hear from anyone that he is not living up to his own expectations. Such information is experienced as aversive whatever its source.

Our division of the tactical material into categories that emphasize the role and personal integrity of Opponent is somewhat arbitrary. As we have already noted, in some situations the person is indistinguishable from the role, while in others the separation can be made.

Let us first consider some examples of how negotiators remind each other of their roles. Negotiations abound with this tactic.

During the Jimson negotiations an instance of punishment occurred in a private conversation between the union negotiator and two company officials. The former, Watoski, appeared to try to induce some shame in the latter—for treatment not consistent with the relationship.

> Watoski declared that the company's position of not permitting the union shop referendum to be held on company premises had been a real "slap in the face" for him. He said that he would have expected that from other companies, but not from Jimson. Scott and Givens of the company listened, looked at their drinks, and made no reply.

In the same case the union called an unusual postnegotiation meeting in which several significant punishments were administered. The union committee was still resentful about what they regarded as reneging on the part of the company. The reneging act itself was somewhat ambiguous. Therefore, rather than raise the question of trust about this particular act, the union team chose this occasion to comment on some language that allegedly had been added without the union's knowledge to one provision in the previous contract.

> *Watoski (U)* Well, the point on the temporary assignment thing is the company put in something without getting the membership's agreement. (Pause.) Your promise on job evaluation is no good if you do the same thing here you do at the other plants.
>
> *Scott (M)* That's not my worry. I'd rather not get into that.
>
> *Watoski (U)* You're not supposed to put anything extra in the contract.

> **Scott (M)** The only part that's different is the first sentence. Besides, it's been in a year, and we haven't had any problems on it. This is something we've always done in the past. We haven't done anything to change things.

Reminding Opponent that he has not fulfilled his role obligation usually carries with it the implication that he should make good in the future, either through changed behavior or some substantive benefit. In the following example we see the Ford Motor Company reminding the UAW about an agreement made in 1941. The company had certain expectations about what would flow from that agreement. The company is calling for the union to make amends for its failure to comply with the essence of the agreement.

> The Company agreed in 1941 to the Union shop and check-off provisions. Its purpose in so doing was not only to give the Union the benefit of membership and financial security, but to eliminate a great deal of friction, dispute and downright industrial strife.
>
> In return, the Company was assured by Union representatives that it would receive greater security and that disturbances of the type then prevalent in other plants would be avoided.
>
> Our experiences in the last four years have substantially dispelled this hope. The peaceful relations have not materialized. The experiment has been an unhappy one. The record shows, for example, 773 work stoppages since the signing of the contract in 1941.[47]

In some instances the expectations enforced upon Opponent contain the implication that Party's sanctions include withholding a future benefit. Consider the following example:

> In one negotiation studied, the two chief negotiators repeatedly reminded each other of the historical ongoing relationship. In effect, they said to each other, "Look, if you persist in this particular behavior, then you are going to damage a potentially beneficial relationship." The two negotiators had to live with each other in the future, particularly during a long contract administration period. Thus, each was in a position to withhold benefits if the other did not behave with reasonableness and maturity.

Sometimes the use of role reminder is aimed at reinterpreting Opponent's behavior—behavior which Opponent would like to have Party view beyond the call of duty. Presumably, if Opponent could get Party to view it as an unrewarded gesture, then Party would be under some obligation

[47] Selekman, Selekman, and Fuller, 2d ed., *op. cit.*, p. 362.

to respond with a *quid pro quo*. However, if Party is able to convince Opponent that Opponent's behavior was merely what it should have been under the circumstances, Party has gained a tactical advantage. Consider the following illustration:

> *Management* Now, you say to us that you have cooperated. That's right, you have. You say to us that you have given us good productivity. That's right, you have. You say to us that you upheld the disciplinary system in the plant, you have corrected the drunks. That's right, you have. But, by God, that's what you ought to do. *You're not doing us any favors when you do that; you're doing what you're supposed to do in terms of being mature trade union leaders and men of responsibility.*[48]

**Threatening Opponent's self-concept.** Quite apart from the desire to be seen as complying with his role obligation, a negotiator has a certain image of himself which he would like to preserve. A threat to one's self-concept, like being reminded of one's role obligations, is experienced as aversive. Therefore, Party often tries to suggest a connection between Opponent's failure to behave according to Party's expectations and a deficiency in a personality trait or professional competence of Opponent. Each negotiator has his own sensitive area: the manager's self-image may emphasize trustworthiness, while an important aspect of the self-concept of the union official may be his status.[49] One is frequently impressed by the need of union leaders to preserve an image of the "man in charge." An illustration of how this concept can be manipulated follows:

> During several of the sessions held between a large company and its union, the company made this comment to several of its delegates: "Can't you take care of your local, why do you have more grievances than your associates?"

> Later the company expressed annoyance about the extremely large number of demands that several members of the union committee had brought to the master table. The company said something to the effect, "I don't think you are in control of your local or you wouldn't bring in all of this stuff."

Let us examine the messages contained in the second of these two similar statements. Management may have been conveying that it did not take the union's demands seriously—for purposes of distributive bargaining—and may have been indicating that until the union has placed priorities on its demands, they could not engage in integrative bargaining. However, pertinent to the present discussion, management's message was that it did not

[48] Italics supplied. Selekman, Selekman, and Fuller, 2d ed., *op. cit.*, p. 551.
[49] Mason Haire, "Role Perceptions in Labor-Management Relations: An Experimental Approach," *Industrial and Labor Relations Review*, vol. 8 (January, 1955), pp. 204–216.

regard the union official's behavior as consistent with the images that the union leaders presumably desired to maintain. Implicit, too, was the idea that management might act outside the established pattern in a way that would be disadvantageous to the union.

In the following example the company negotiator calls upon the union negotiator to act in a manner consistent with his experience and competence:

> *Management* It's pretty hard for you fellows to wash your hands of the thing. You are party to it. The retroactive pay should have been set up in a separate stipulation. *I cannot understand seasoned labor men, Tom, on your side not seeing that.*[50]

The overall result appeared effective; at any rate, as negotiations unfolded, the union negotiator displayed more conciliatory behavior toward the company.

It appears that it is less risky to manipulate the concept of competence and the qualities of job performance than it is to manipulate the more sensitive concept of honesty. When the challenge involves a charge of duplicity, there is more chance that the result will be anger rather than cooperative behavior. In a recent discussion in the meat-packing industry, a mediator commented over the phone to the union negotiator, "Sam, the company negotiator thought he had an agreement." While this simple statement carried a lot of meaning, for it said that the company believed that the union had gone back on its word, it was not effective, since it raised the dangerous and explosive issue of bargaining in bad faith.

Generally, it is dangerous for a negotiator to manipulate a sensitive self-concept of the opponent. When the challenge involves a condescending posture, the result is likely to be even worse. Thus, in the following example, the company's attempt to manipulate the self-concept of the union negotiator backfired because the company conveyed an air of scolding and engendered resentment toward the person administering the punishment:

> *Management* We have tried not to create for ourselves too much of a bargaining position and have confined ourselves to a reasonable number of points. Frankly, you made some proposals that I don't think any of you, in your wildest dreams, expect to get. *So cut out the clowning and get down to business.*[51]

*Uses of direct threats and tangible sanctions.* Party may resort to more concrete punishment, ranging from mild behavioral sanctions to major economic sanctions such as a work stoppage itself. In all cases the object is to modify the behavior of Opponent. The range of possible economic

---

[50] Italics supplied. Selekman, Selekman, and Fuller, 2d ed., *op. cit.*, p. 281.

[51] Italics supplied. *Ibid.*, p. 536.

sanctions is unlimited and really parallels our discussion in the distributive chapter. We shall not take time to reproduce all those tactics (we shall introduce only several); however, we need to know that the intended result is different. In distributive bargaining the economic sanction is being used to gain an advantage in the settlement, whereas in this instance it is being used to affect the relationship pattern.

Let us first consider a few examples in which behavioral punishment is being used to discourage certain actions on the part of the opponent.

A dramatic instance of a procedural sanction occurred during the 1960 negotiations between General Electric Company and the International Union of Electrical Workers.

> General Electric Company negotiators indignantly walked out of contract talks with the International Union of Electrical Workers over the propriety of the union president's language.
>
> The GE manager of employee relations declared that his team was forced to leave the room rather than allow the IUE president to continue an outburst of obscene language.
>
> However, according to the union officials the outburst itself was a response to management's failure to uphold its role obligations as viewed by the union. They charged management with "inane questions and time-wasting tactics."

In one other negotiation in which relations were bad and could not get worse, the management negotiator complained about the union's propaganda attack on the company and himself. In the response below, the union negotiator is assuring him that these attacks are intended to be punishment for his own actions:

> *Union* This question of undermining works two ways: and since we are all adults we are going to have to face it on that basis. If you put out propaganda and instruct your foreman to do certain things, then we are going to retaliate. When the local Management dabbles in the affairs of the local Union, then you are going to get reaction from us.[52]

Sometimes the tactic is a mixture of behavioral and economic sanctions.

> *Union* The company hasn't given us anything to take back to the people yet.
>
> *Management* You didn't give us an answer on the job-evaluation plan.
>
> *Union* I'm not giving until the company gives.

[52] *Ibid.*, p. 216.

*Management* I don't think that's the right attitude, Jim.

*Union* Saying you won't give something because of company policy is not good. [Referring to the company's position on another issue.]

In the above illustration the two negotiators are exchanging their respective expectations about what are legitimate reasons for refusing to make the next move in distributive bargaining. Although this exchange in itself is an instance of role reminding, the exchange also illustrates an overt punishment, namely, the union's refusal to make the next concession as a penalty for the company's use of "company policy" as a reason for rejecting a certain proposal.

In another episode in the same negotiations, the penalty being invoked was directly economic.

Early in the negotiation, top management became very annoyed with the official who represented the union in negotiations at that plant. The local newspapers carried an item reporting the company's refusal to allow a union shop referendum (required by law) to be held on company premises. Management officials believed that the article which showed the company in a bad light was initiated by the union official. The firm's chief spokesman in the negotiations repeatedly referred to the fact that his superior was "teed off" with the union official and that this fact in turn was in part responsible for the harsh bargain he was instructed to achieve. The company withheld something from the package to teach the union official a lesson and told him as much. Ironically, and yet significantly, this official swore he was *not* responsible for the news item.

In the same negotiation, the union official was smarting under the disappointment of an "inadequate settlement." In a postnegotiation meeting he threatened to retaliate—to punish the company (for its punishment of him). He underscored how disappointed the committee was in both the "meager settlement" and the company's attitude.

Word has gone around in the plant and in the papers on the way the meetings have gone. The company didn't like it either.

We can promise you that *next year . . . will be a rough negotiation.* The company has to change policy. They have to look at the Benner City situation. (Pause.) *It's going to be rough in job evaluation, too, if the company doesn't change its way of thinking.*

We don't have any hard feelings toward the company committee, *but we want you to go back and tell the executives they have just put some wood on the fire for next year.* We give you a fair warning—be prepared next year. We think the employees got a poor deal this year, and we expect it to be better next year. We've forgotten about this year, and we don't have any hard feelings. (Pause.) I hope this settlement won't be reported in the union paper—I'm still ashamed of it. The people here are a determined group, and they work hard. The company shouldn't be so backward. You say Chicago has problems, well so does Benner City.

In one case reported by Peters, management's attempt to bypass the union leaders was sharply disapproved by the union negotiating team. Prior to making its offer to the union, management had spread the word through its supervisors that the company's offer would be 8 cents. The union was annoyed at this blatant attempt by management to build its own prestige among workers at the expense of the union leaders. In the following excerpt from Peters we see the union punishing management's behavior for a second violation of the union's role expectations. The union leaders obtained a "surprise" rejection of the company's offer after they had indicated to management that they would not take this position.

"You can blame yourselves for what happened. You left us no choice but to ask for a rejection of your offer."

Oppenshaw (company) glared at him. "I'm not questioning your right to oppose any proposal we make," he rasped, "but you owed us the courtesy of making known your intent to oppose our offer, instead of pretending to be neutral."

The placid expression on Monte's face turned into a scowl. "All right, I'll tell you why we changed our minds," he said belligerently. "We were neutral when we left the meeting the other day. But in no time at all your foremen had it all over the plant that you were offering two more paid holidays. How did we look? Or did you even think about us? What did you expect us to do—ask the membership to ratify a proposal made directly by the foremen to the workers? Speaking of courtesy, you could have shown us the courtesy of letting us bring the company offer to the membership ourselves."

Oppenshaw tried to interrupt, but Monte brushed him off. "Look, Mr. Oppenshaw," he continued, "as long as this company insists on negotiating directly with the membership and keeps bypassing the committee, you're going to have trouble. When you start dealing with the union instead of just going through the motions of negotiating, then maybe we'll get somewhere." [53]

Management is in a similar position to retaliate for objectionable behavior on the part of the union.

---

[53] Edward Peters, *Strategy and Tactics in Labor Negotiations* (New London, Conn.: National Foremen's Institute, 1955), p. 92.

During one of the negotiations at Allis-Chalmers a rash of wildcat strikes broke out after the company had made its offer. Immediately, the company revised the proposal saying, "It is perfectly plain that no agreement was entered into by your union in good faith. Your union is guilty of flagrant irresponsibility, and it is evident that you have no serious intention of honoring this proposed agreement. For those reasons, the company will now withdraw from this proposed agreement. We have not signed and will not sign such an agreement, even though the locals may ratify and desire to sign it."

## Precondition to Purposive Attitude Change

Our discussions of cognitive balance and of reinforcement suggest several lines of purposive behavior which tend to lead to attitude and behavioral change. We turn here to a different kind of experience—the "working through" of deep feelings. This process is often a precondition to purposive attitude change, for two reasons. First, to the extent that Party's *own* personal and private feelings remain antagonistic, he will neither see the tactical possibilities presented above nor be able to implement them effectively. Second, to the extent that Opponent's attitudes are ego defensive, they will be little affected by the tactical operations of balance theory or reinforcement theory.[54] The phenomenon in both cases involves self-oriented needs and behavior.

**Self-oriented Needs and Behavior.** When examining all the behavior at the negotiating table, it becomes clear that some actions can be explained only as expressions of the personal feelings of the negotiator. These are actions which do not in any way conform to the role requirements of the particular negotiator.

Within the present theory of negotiations a behavior is regarded as instrumental to the extent that it contributes to the establishment of a preferred pattern of relationship (or facilitates one of the other three subprocesses of negotiation). A behavior may be instrumental for objectives pursued by the negotiators through distributive bargaining or through problem solving; it may be instrumental to the negotiator in achieving a desired relationship pattern across the table or in achieving consensus within his own organization. As we have indicated before, a behavior may facilitate one subprocess but interfere with the others. It is nevertheless instrumental because it has some task or role rationale. Behaviors which are not consistent with any of the subprocesses occur either because of an error in judgment or because they have expressive value for the negotiator. Those which have expressive but not instrumental value we call self-

[54] Daniel Katz, Irving Sarnoff, and Charles McClintock, "Ego-defense and Attitude Change," *Human Relations*, vol. 9 (February, 1956), pp. 27–45.

oriented behaviors.[55] They arise from strong attitudes and in turn can have profoundly adverse effects on attitudes.

As a result of somewhat objective analysis, the negotiator gains an idea about which type of relationship pattern would be better for the organization—a preferred pattern. The negotiator also has personal emotions stimulated by basic attitudes toward the other party, its goals, its means, and its members. Often the enduring personal feelings are more antagonistic than the more rationally preferred pattern of relationship is. Personal feelings also get involved as a result of events which occur during bargaining—the negotiator's sensitivities are violated by certain behaviors directed toward him. There is considerable evidence that people react emotionally to "irresponsible" behavior or to people who are seen as perpetrating frustration. In any event, the negotiator's conception of the requirements of the task (including attitude change) and his psychological needs lead to different behaviors. Moreover, the competing tendencies may exist without the negotiator being fully aware of them.

Numerous examples could be given of the kind of behavior that is not instrumental to any role requirement or organizational goal but is purely a personal feeling or response. Many of the illustrations that were discussed earlier as contrasts with effective tactics must be understood as self-oriented behaviors. Negotiations abound with expressions of sarcasm, petulance, and exasperation. These feelings get in the way of the role requirements and prevent a party from negotiating effectively.

Certain self-oriented behaviors are apt to trigger personal reactions on the part of Opponent. Emphasizing status differentials, belittlement, and rudeness usually go far beyond anything that might be conceivably functional for bargaining and would directly attack the personal integrity and word of Opponent.

> But the angry, resentful (and therefore immaturely reacting) administrator uses the techniques of negotiation for other purposes than achieving a bargain. He converts them into instruments of continuing conflict; he utilizes them to keep the union in its place, a grudging, narrow place where the workers will find how little the new organization can do.[56]

Before we turn to the methods of working through the negative feelings, let us present two specific illustrations of the forms in which verbal hostility appears in labor negotiations. The first is a management statement:

[55] The emotional need of the negotiator to aggress, to express hostility, to punish the other party also may be shared by members of his own organization. Of course, to the extent that the negotiator and other members of his organization actually are *seeking* a pattern marked by mutual hostility and aggression, then the antagonistic behaviors are in some sense instrumental as well as expressive.

[56] B. M. Selekman, *Labor Relations and Human Relations, op. cit.*, p. 162.

*Management* Some of your people in their overzealousness for propaganda are distributing statements in public whereby they insinuate management is making a handsome profit and is unfair. . . . So far as I am personally concerned, I have the same reaction if I see a little old mangy dog barking in the moonlight.[57]

The second is a statement by a union official:

*Union* Let's start going, Bill. I'm gonna start listening to you from now until 1:00 on Saturday. And very frankly I don't give a crap what you do.[58]

A note of caution is needed here. Much of what appears to the naive observer to be personal aggression is in reality instrumental behavior intended to impress Opponent (commitment tactic) or members of Party's organization (fulfilling their expectations for purposes of internal bargaining). We agree with Douglas:

Some of the most misleading interpretations of the behavior . . . have been contributed by psychologists. Having gone into this field with the idea that a negotiating conference is merely another example of the small, autonomous problem-solving group which has engaged so much social science attention in recent years, they have pointed to the donnybrook of outbursts and denunciations as evidence of anxiety, hostility, and aggression as clinicians are accustomed to deal with these. In their haste to extrapolate in a straight line from clinical observation of troubled persons to relationships between modern-day power aggregates, they have mistaken purposive social action for individual *re*-action. . . .[59]

Hence, we stress that we refer to only those instances where the larger context in which the instances occur supports the interpretation of behavior as self-oriented.

**Party's "Working through" of His Own Feelings.** Party may take certain steps to work through his own feelings in order to improve his ability to behave according to the requirements of the situation. The steps outlined below are reported by Blake to have been used successfully in several union-management "warfare" situations.[60]

[57] Selekman, Selekman, and Fuller, 2d ed., *op. cit.*, p. 215.

[58] Douglas, *op. cit.*, p. 357.

[59] *Ibid.*, p. 15.

[60] R. R. Blake and J. S. Mouton, "The Intergroup Dynamics of Win-Lose Conflict and Problem-solving Collaborations in Union-Management Relations," in Muzafer Sherif (ed.), *Intergroup Relations and Leadership* (New York: John Wiley & Sons, Inc., 1962), pp. 94–140.

First, the members of Party's negotiating team learn to recognize the consequences associated with extremely negative attitudes and the win-lose conflict which results. This is sometimes accomplished through a laboratory training program, in which participants experience directly, through the involvement of their own actions and emotions, the conditions and consequences of intergroup hostility. These sensitivity training workshops enable the participants to better understand the bases of their own negative feelings generally and to recognize the situations which trigger destructive behavior on their part.[61]

Second, Party's team conducts a norm-setting conference for achieving unanimity of attitudes. Participants talk through their own attitudes toward Opponent, including their reservations, doubts, hopes, and so on. In this way the negotiator can receive social support for his newly adopted behavior and need not rely upon his individual determination alone.

Third, if other approaches fail, Party may choose to invite Opponent to join their two teams for a "leveling conference."

> Rather than convening for an accusation and counter accusation session, the warring factions explore with one another the attitudes, feelings, and emotions that undergird disrespect, distrust, and the motivation to frustrate and destroy. Amazing though it is, once leveling starts, the tension in the situation is reduced. People are telling one another the very attitudes they ordinarily withhold—the underlying ones which "explain" the mutually destructive surface actions.
>
> With leveling started, usually through a behavioral science intervention, the way is opened for much more extensive joint exploration of history leading to the present situation. An historical review, say over a decade, offers the advantages of placing present conflict in perspective, providing diagnostic cues to account for the present dilemma, and offering suggestions for the kinds of altered thinking necessary to achieve success against a background of failure.[62]

**Party's Assistance of Opponent's "Working Through."** Party is in a position to stimulate and support efforts by Opponent to work through his

---

[61] Additional evidence that similar techniques can be used effectively in labor relations is offered by B. J. Speroff, "Group Psychotherapy in Labor Relations: A Case Study," *Personnel Journal*, vol. 39 (1960), pp. 14–17. This study reports on a six-month training program in a large steel mill. Ten labor relations supervisors met in series of two-hour meetings, all tape-recorded. Problems were presented by any of the supervisors, and questions were asked by remaining supervisors. Results of this "group therapy" and role playing helped supervisors to understand themselves and empathize more effectively with workers. Grievances were reduced considerably, and grievance disposition was doubled over an eight-month period.

[62] R. R. Blake and J. S. Mouton, *Group Dynamics: Key to Decision-making* (Houston: Gulf Publishing Company, 1961), p. 111.

more destructive attitudes toward Party. In particular, he establishes conditions which evoke self-oriented behavior, and he allows catharsis, provides emotional support, and occasionally offers implicit direction for new insight and self-awareness on the part of Opponent.

Party may induce and encourage catharsis by Opponent.[63] In many situations, Opponent is ready to "blow off steam" at a moment's notice. In other situations, more deliberate evocation is needed. Opponent may be directly encouraged to verbalize deep feelings and begin to develop new attitudes.

> *Management* I might say this—the fact that I, or any of us, do not give our reaction, does not mean we haven't one. We feel this is a good opportunity for your fellows to clear the air.[64]

In the Jimson negotiations, the management negotiator was aware of the need for catharsis as well as its limitations.

> Scott explained that Watoski was a "pretty nice guy," but also a "damned stubborn Polack." Frequently Watoski did not collect and analyze the facts before deciding to take a certain position. He would often become angry and cling to a position that he had reached too hastily.
>
> In the process Watoski would get "pretty worked up" and "blow off a lot of steam." Scott acknowledged the need to "let the record run out." He said that it was "not good" to interrupt a person before he had finished presenting an idea. On the other hand, Scott had to work constantly to prevent Watoski from becoming committed to a position too quickly. Moreover, Scott believed that if Watoski became too abusive, he would then have to "get pretty tough" himself.

In the act of "letting off steam," Opponent may become more entrenched in his beliefs, particularly in his negative attitudes toward Party. This is the danger in uncontrolled catharsis. There may be something about the manner and presence of Party that serves to reinforce Opponent in his beliefs and behavior.

In one case, exactly this happened. The union entered the bargaining room and immediately began attacking management. For the most part, management sat and "took it." Rather than draining the hostility, the passive behavior seemed to reinforce the union belief that management

---

[63] An experiment by J. W. Thibaut and John Coules has demonstrated that hostility is reduced when persons can communicate and act freely in response to their hostility: "The Role of Communications in the Reduction of Interpersonal Hostility," *Journal of Abnormal and Social Psychology*, vol. 47 (October, 1952), pp. 770–777.

[64] Selekman, Selekman, and Fuller, 2d ed., *op. cit.*, p. 525.

was "weak." The result was that the union became more and more abusive.[65]

It must be added, however, that it is unlikely that any posture on the part of management would have been successful in taming this particular union. Given the amount of hostility harbored by the union, any response might have triggered a further outpouring of the accumulated ill will.

We have assumed that Party is capable of exercising self-control in order not to become emotionally involved himself. If personal attacks and counterattacks go too far, the only solution may be to remove a key personality. It has been reported that during the final weeks of the 1959 steel negotiation, MacDonald and Cooper were kept on the sidelines because they had become very hostile toward one another personally.


## PART 3 | DILEMMAS OF ATTITUDINAL STRUCTURING

### Dilemmas within the Process of Attitudinal Structuring

A variety of dilemmas exists within the process of attitudinal structuring. Some of them have been alluded to in discussion of the tactical material. At this point we can present a selected sample of the kind of difficulties inherent in the attitudinal structuring process.

*Balance tactics.* Assume that Opponent behaves in a way Party disapproves of. Assume also that Party subsequently helps Opponent in some way. Now, what is Opponent's response? Does Opponent view his original behavior as reinforced? Or does he experience imbalance because Party's new actions are inconsistent with Opponent's earlier conception? The theories appear to predict different responses. The actual response by Opponent depends upon supplementary cues available to him.

Let us consider a case in which Party is associated with some object that benefits Opponent. It is quite possible that Opponent feels more negative toward Party as a result of the initiative taken by Party. The overture of Party is looked upon with suspicion. Opponent says to himself, "I wonder what the trick is?" Or Opponent may view Party as naive and weak to have given something away for nothing.

Consider another example of the boomerang effect wherein Opponent is associated with something that benefits Party. We have reasoned that Opponent might increase his liking for Party on the assumption that "people

---

[65] *Ibid.,* pp. 334–349.

like those whom they benefit." But if Opponent is in a reward frame of mind when he discovers that an act of his benefited Party, he may expect to be rewarded. In other words, his act carries an expectation with it—not meeting this expectation may produce resentment and hostility. Parenthetically, it might be noted that the reinforcement paradigm carries with it the necessity of continuing in this vein. Once Opponent becomes conditioned to view all behavior on the part of Party as part of the reward approach, it is difficult to get Opponent to view something in a way that creates imbalance.

The above dilemmas could be avoided if the negotiator had complete knowledge about his opponent and about the total context, but negotiators are not so endowed, and consequently these dilemmas develop and present real problems.

*Reinforcement tactics.* In our discussion of punishment we pointed to the many pitfalls. Party may aim his punishment at a specific behavior of Opponent, but the effect on Opponent may be to create inconsistent perceptions, and he solves his imbalance by feeling more negative toward Party. As we noted, this unintended result comes about because Party's time perspective connects past behavior with present punishment, whereas Opponent's time perspective is the present.

Punishment is most effective when it can be clearly linked both in time and meaning to the undesired behavior. In this sense the act of punishment must be quickly, consistently, and impartially administered. The punishment must be consistent in the sense that Party generally responds in a similar way to Opponent's erring ways. This consistency helps Opponent establish the linkage between the punishment and the undesired behavior. It is also helpful for Party to be impartial in the sense that he also punishes others who behave accordingly. Again, the effect is that Opponent realizes that the punishment is not directed at him personally but at a type of behavior.

It is also clear that Party needs to have sufficient power in order to thwart undesired behavior. If Opponent views the punishment of Party as weak and indecisive, he may be perplexed about the real intention of Party. At the least he will not be compelled to honor the wishes of Party. Consequently, it is necessary for Party to possess gradations of punishment. He needs to choose the appropriate punishment for the given behavior.

While it is important to choose punishment which is big enough for the job, it is also important not to choose punishment which is too overwhelming. If Party makes the mistake of administering a very unpleasant sanction for a minor behavioral deficiency of Opponent, it is possible that Opponent will conclude that party really dislikes him.

*"Working through."* As we indicated in our discussion of "working through," it is possible that in the process of giving vent to attitudes and

discharging hostility, the two parties may become more resolute in their negative feelings toward each other. This is understandable by referring to the balance framework: each party may be behaving in a way which presents him in an unfavorable light.

The matter of authenticity is also crucial here. The mere presence of Party and his demeanor in the face of catharsis can prompt Opponent to feel even more negative about Party if the latter's behavior is not viewed as authentic. Opponent may view the behavior of Party as condescending, overly charitable, etc. What from Party's viewpoint is intended to be supportive and friendly behavior, is from Opponent's viewpoint "sickening and pretentious."

### Attitudinal Structuring versus Other Subprocesses

The following discussion will analyze the various ways in which the attitudinal structuring process interacts with integrative and distributive bargaining. We shall be interested in behaviors selected for their tactical value in attitudinal structuring which also have consequences for the other subprocesses. Of interest also are the tactics instrumental in distributive bargaining and integrative bargaining which have unintended consequences for attitudinal structuring. We shall turn to the various possible functional relationships between pairs.

**Attitudinal and Distributive Processes Mutually Interfering.** For any given negotiation, the tactics of attitudinal structuring may tend to conflict with the process of distributive bargaining. A tactic designed to promote a better relationship frequently entails a sacrifice of the substance of distributive bargaining; and conversely a tactic designed to achieve a distributive gain often adversely affects the relationship. Occasionally this connection is rather deliberate, as a negotiator manipulates one process in order to achieve gains in the other.

*Trading distributive gains for attitudinal progress.* There is no question that the task of structuring more positive attitudes often entails substantive sacrifices. Earlier in the chapter we discussed the various ways in which party can develop a more positive relationship with Opponent. Tactics which involved "working on the problem of Opponent," "making gestures of good faith," etc. entailed certain substantive sacrifices on the part of Party. Of course, when the initiative for structuring a new relationship is shared, or at least when a party's efforts are quickly reciprocated, the concessions granted voluntarily for purposes of shaping attitudes may, in fact, constitute a mutually profitable trade in substantive terms.

*Exploiting the relationship for distributive gains.* It is also possible for the connection to be turned around, for distributive gains to be achieved at the expense of attitudinal losses. A class of such behaviors falls into the category of exploitation. In these instances a distributive gain is sought by trading on the existing relationship. Recall that we have discussed role reminders and other punishing acts which were appropriate and genuinely in the interest of the relationship. There is, however, a point at which the act of threatening the relationship in order to induce Opponent to abandon a position or a type of negotiating behavior is in reality trading on the relationship rather than trying to preserve it.

Such tactical use of attitudinal structuring works only if the other party is interested in maintaining or in improving the relationship. Of course, there is a limit to how far one can go in exploiting the attitudinal preferences of the other negotiator. In one negotiation studied, the company negotiator desired to bring about a more positive relationship and, in particular, desired to avoid a strike for fear such action would weaken the relationship. The union negotiator was quite aware of this outlook and pressed for concessions right up to the strike deadline. However, he could press only so far, for if he precipitated a strike or if he forced too many costly concessions on the company, he might find himself facing a new counterpart across the bargaining table at some point in the future. Consequently, he was under some constraint not to behave completely distributively but to preserve the relationship that he had developed with his counterpart.

In the above example the restraints happened to be symmetrical. The union negotiator had been striving to develop better attitudes under contract administration. He had fostered a more mature approach to grievance handling. The company negotiator was in a position to remind the union negotiator that if all did not work out well at the bargaining table, matters might not work out well in contract administration either. At one point during negotiations, the company negotiator went so far as to remind the union negotiator of his role requirement to act decisively and to cut back on unnecessary union demands. However, the company negotiator was on dangerous ground, since he could push his counterpart only so far—if he went too far in constraining his opponent, he, too, was likely to be facing a new counterpart across the bargaining table in the future. Thus, a relationship can be manipulated only to the extent that it is not in danger of being terminated, and the possibility that it might be terminated acts as a real restraint on the tactical exploitation of a relationship.

Within the limits in which the relationship may be terminated or the position of a particular negotiator jeopardized, room exists for the tactical use of attitudes. For example, in the International Harvester negotiations, a number of people sought to exploit the good feelings engendered under the "new look" [66] for the purposes of a distributive gain.

[66] The "new look" is described in some detail in Chapter X.

> During the 1961 negotiations, one of the delegates threatened to end the "new look" unless he received satisfaction on certain local matters. He used this tactic until he got complete satisfaction.

> Another delegate gained some ground for his local by reminding the divisional industrial relations personnel about the "good working relationship that we have at this plant," and adding "you wouldn't want to see it sour."

> Toward the end of negotiations one of the union's international representatives commented that in view of the company's "poor" offer he was convinced that the "new look" had not amounted to very much.

The net effect of tactics by which Party exploits a relationship by partaking too liberally of its beneficial aspects is a deterioration of the relationship. The relationship can become more costly than Opponent had previously assumed. Moreover, the question of trust is raised. What starts out as a trading situation may backfire. In the last example mentioned above, the company responded rather angrily to the union's suggestion that the new look was in jeopardy.

> The company negotiator took the initiative and delivered a long talk about the "new look." In essence he told the union that they should not continue the "new look" unless they saw an advantage in the program. He also emphasized that the program was not a means for forcing capitulation on the company's part but was an attempt to seek mutually satisfying solutions. The company negotiator went on to emphasize that some of the union people did not understand the new relationship, as evidenced by their statements.

Of course, it is quite possible that, over a period of time, the union could take some advantage of the relationship without causing the company to alter the nature of the relationship. Whether they could or could not would depend upon how important that particular pattern of relationship is to the company relative to its importance to the union. Waller and Hill propound the principle of least interest: "That person is able to dictate the conditions of association whose interest in the continuation of the affair is least." [67]

If the pattern of relationship and the specific attitudinal bonds which relate the parties is of more importance to Opponent than to Party, then Party may be able to successfully extract some advantage in the distributive bargaining outcomes. Indeed this may well have been what was hap-

[67] W. W. Waller and R. Hill, *The Family: A Dynamic Interpretation* (New York: Holt, Rinehart and Winston, Inc., 1951), p. 191.

pening in International Harvester, where management may have cared somewhat more about the "new look" than the union did. Such asymmetry appeared to exist in the Jimson case, in which the union official received more personal gratification from his relationship with the company official than vice versa. Let us present another illustration:

> **Union** If we are ever to develop good faith, management just ought to say, "All right, boys, we are willing to take the chance and go along on certain things." There is much at stake here because it involves your employees, their relatives, your potential labor market. Your employees are going to have bitter feelings and so forth. We are drifting back to where we were, or even to something worse.[68]

The above illustration demonstrates how the union may implicitly threaten a deterioration of attitudes if the company does not come across with substantive gains. Thus, if management does not meet the union's demands, the union may feel obliged to fulfill the threat and deliberately foster discontent and disappointment. We need only footnote again, however, that the extra tolerance of Opponent has limits which Party risks overrunning.

The above discussion concerned a conscious tradeoff between distributive bargaining and attitudinal structuring. We now turn to some dilemmas between attitudinal structuring and distributive bargaining which occur because in emphasizing one subprocess, a party must accept the losses incurred in the other subprocess as an inadvertent by-product.

*Dilemmas in developing friendly attitudes.* There are a number of points at which the tactics designed to create positive affect can conflict with the dictates of distributive bargaining. Given the reality of certain differences in preferences before a settlement, distributive bargaining involves overstatement of the area of disagreement (Party overstates his resistance point); whereas attitudinal structuring is aided by understatement of differences (Party deemphasizes differences).

To develop affect, Party must treat Opponent with respect. He must listen to the arguments of Opponent and consider them carefully. But such an approach conflicts with the requirements of the early-firm-commitment strategy which may otherwise be quite effective for distributive bargaining. The final-offer-first tactic can be implemented only by ignoring the arguments of Opponent, with an obvious cost to the relationship between the negotiators.

The development of a positive feeling toward Opponent is inimical to the use of power tactics which are quite functional for distributive bargaining. For example, emphasizing a basic power advantage over Oppo-

---

[68] Selekman, Selekman, and Fuller, 1st ed., *op. cit.*, p. 459.

nent is rather helpful in distributive bargaining, but such an approach may induce Opponent to act emotionally and attempt to even the score eventually.

Power tactics also require developing membership commitment to particular objectives and to the necessity of fighting for these objectives. Arousing the membership and its will to fight is usually essential for distributive bargaining, but the disadvantage for attitudinal structuring is that the arousal may leave a residue of antagonisms and negative feelings on both sides.

Again, power bargaining envisions such tactics as identifying Opponent as "the enemy," impugning his motives, questioning his rationality, challenging his competence, etc.—these moves develop increased internal support for Party's bargaining position and hence increase the likelihood of success. But by their very nature these tactics foster stereotyped thinking, and they have an undesirable effect on attitudes.

Stressing status differentials often has implications for both attitudinal structuring and distributive bargaining. Status is communicated by dress or casual conversation, about leisure-time activities, expense-account living, "old school ties," educational plans for children, personal investments, etc. Management officials may stress these differences in order to awe, impress, or elicit deference on the part of union committeemen, when it is to management's advantage in dictating the terms of distributive bargaining. (Of course this tactic runs a risk even within distributive bargaining of inducing extremely rebellious actions.) However, such a tactic conflicts with the attitudinal objective of developing collaborative relations based on friendly feelings.

In another area the efforts at building a positive relationship may lead to a disadvantage in distributive bargaining. By assisting Opponent in gaining strength internally, Party may enable Opponent to turn his full energies to pursuing his organization's objectives, with the consequence that Opponent may then represent a more formidable bargainer. This is a commonly held assumption, but on balance allowing Opponent to obtain a more secure position internally, probably results in more moderate demands and bargaining behavior by Opponent.

Whereas attitudinal structuring stressed the value of congeniality and acts of assistance, distributive bargaining may involve more antisocial behavior. In some cases a negotiator will figuratively assault the other negotiator in the interest of achieving a distributive advantage.

We might question the wisdom of such a maneuver, and we shall have more to say about it later, but for the moment we need to deal with it since it does occur in the bargaining room. Douglas presents several examples in which a negotiator hoped to change the position of his opponent by getting him so upset and discouraged that he revealed his minimum position. A cynical management negotiator reported his reasoning:

I think U2 needs some of that, myself. I mean really nasty stuff right across the board. I think he needs it. Because if I judge U2 rightly, you can break him because he has a tremendous desire to be loved (AD: Yeah), to be a—a—well—well, to (AD: He thinks that he—) —to have approval, see, and I think a direct personal attack—a vicious personal attack on U2 would break him. Just—he—he'd— he'd just break under the thing (AD: Uh-huh). And I have had a feel- ing all along—C2 held me back, the vice president held me back, M held me back, so I dropped it finally. But I was itching to make a direct personal attack on U2. I felt sure I could blow him higher'n a kite. Didn't dare do it in the last few days, but if I could have done it a week ago, or two weeks ago before ready—U2 was ready to take the strike, he would have had to gather himself together again and come back into the bargaining. And at that point U2 would have been whipped psychologically and we could have gotten almost any kind of a contract we wanted. Now, that was my theory.[69]

In another case a management negotiator created antagonism in order to elicit clues about the other's true utilities.

As he (the company spokesman) verbalized his conscious desire in all this, if his blows failed to elicit personal annoyance, he interpreted this to say that the point was not significant to the opponent; on the other hand, when he "drew blood" with one of his attacks, he took it as a sign that he had hit sensitive ground, a fact which he noted mentally for future use in trading off negotiable points. When asked what cues he utilized to distinguish bonafide from synthetic emo- tional reaction on the union side, he replied: "I don't think it is anything that is said, but I notice flushing of the face, and mainly watch the neck muscles in the other fellows." [70]

There was no evidence to indicate that the negotiator was cognizant of the impact of his behavior on the continuing relationship. Moreover, perhaps we are giving him too much credit to assume that his behavior is purposive in any way. It is quite possible that the behavior illustrated above can only be explained in terms of the individual's own psycho- logical needs. These may be instances of self-oriented behavior, not instru- mental or functional for any subprocess, even for distributive bargaining. Indeed, the effect of the above behavior may be to have Opponent take a firmer or perhaps more extreme bargaining position rather than reveal himself.

**Dilemmas in the development of trust.** The requirements of trust are such that Party must keep his word and deal in a good-faith manner with his Opponent. However, for the purposes of distributive bargaining it

[69] Douglas, *op. cit.,* p. 26.
[70] *Ibid.,* p. 24.

may be advantageous for Party to renege on an implied concession. In one case it appeared as if the negotiator used tentative movement toward the other's position in order to determine the other's flexibility. Such a tactical use of one's bargaining position may have a short-run gain, but it would also have an adverse effect on the relationship over the long run.

It is a distributive tactic for the company to include a man on the bargaining team who could be helpful in picking up and analyzing clues on the behavior of the union team. However, such a step might antagonize the union team and undermine the relationship.

In our earlier discussion of the gesture of placing one's self in a position of potential harm we alluded to the distributive losses that might be involved. Indeed, as we explained the dynamics of trust building, Opponent is induced to change his attitudes toward Party because Party shows his sincerity by assuming a position that could redound to Party's disadvantage. In one of the examples cited earlier, management revealed its modernization plans; in effect, it took the union into the company's confidence, only to find itself at a disadvantage because the union chose to use the information against the company.

*Dilemmas in the development of concern or mutual acceptance.* There are numerous instances in which a feeling of concern for Opponent conflicts with what Party would like to do under the directives of distributive bargaining. Consider several examples of this conflict. To show concern means that Party is aware of Opponent's predicament and is willing to help Opponent deal with this predicament. This means that Party should refrain from activities that make life more difficult for Opponent. Such tactics as systematically studying the workers' attitudes, locating the workers' resistance points, etc. might be useful to distributive bargaining, but these very tactics produce resentment on the part of the union leaders and consequently foster a more negative relationship. The same point could be made about direct communications to workers. These communications, which are intended to weaken rank-and-file expectations as well as to commit the company, will have an adverse effect on attitudes. Similarly, direct communications on the part of union officials to members of management may serve the purposes of distributive bargaining but have a negative effect on attitudinal structuring. For example, members of the professional engineering union at RCA picketed outside the company's headquarters at Radio City Music Hall in New York in an effort to communicate directly with the top executives, much to the consternation of the management officials with whom the union had to deal back at the research lab in Camden, New Jersey.

A concern for Opponent carries with it the recognition that Opponent must justify himself to his own organization. Opponent must be able to say to his organization that bargaining produced something which Party was not willing to concede prior to bargaining. Again, we see how the early-firm-commitment strategy conflicts with the dictates of attitudinal structuring. The company that takes a firm position early in negotiations may win at a distributive level, but it loses at the attitudinal level: the opponent is frustrated and forced to act vindictively when the opportunity presents itself.

There are many other tactical situations in which distributive bargaining and attitudinal structuring make opposite demands on the negotiator. Whereas in the discussion of distributive bargaining we explored the sometimes tactical advantages of secret plans and obscure objectives, in the context of attitudinal structuring these tactics are dysfunctional. They violate Gandhian norms:

> Do not use secret plans or moves or keep objectives secret.
>
> Announce your case and the goal of your campaign explicitly and clearly, distinguishing essentials and non-essentials.[71]

Similarly, in distributive bargaining Party's targets and resistance points are influenced by the aspirations and power of Opponent. Thus, soft spots in Opponent's position automatically lead to an enlargement in Party expectations. Gandhi disapproved of expanding an objective at a moment of weakness in the opponent because of its effect on attitudes:

> During a campaign, change of its declared objective makes it difficult for opponents to trust your sincerity.[72]

**Attitudinal and Distributive Processes Mutually Facilitating.** Above we suggested ways in which tactical assignments involved in attitudinal structuring are not compatible with those involved in distributive bargaining. However, there are circumstances in which these two subprocesses are or can be mutually facilitating. Thus, our discussion will include some observations about how dilemmas earlier described can be resolved.

There are at least three areas in which there is a facilitating interaction between the attitudinal and distributive subprocesses. The first has to do with developing a minimum language and degree of trust. The second concerns commitment tactics. The third has to do with the participants' recognition of their common fate.

Like attitudinal structuring, distributive bargaining also requires that minimum understanding be reached between the parties, in order to avoid mutual destruction. Without a minimum level of trust and accept-

[71] Arne Naess, "A Systematization of Gandhian Ethics of Conflict Resolution," *Journal of Conflict Resolution*, vol. 2 (June, 1958), p. 146.
[72] *Ibid.*, p. 147.

ance of the other as a legitimate force, it is possible for them to pursue a course of action in which neither of them gains from their interdependency. Both lose because pathological hostility creates a relationship in which each side's objective is to destroy the other. The minimum attitudinal structuring required to avoid this difficulty is moving from attitudes of conflict to those of containment-aggression.

The parties may arrive at mutual losses through another route. Although the parties do not place a positive value on hurting the other, they pursue mutually destructive tactics through miscalculation. The remedy here is to establish sufficient trust and common sign language to engage in tacit bargaining in order to avoid untenable positions and the costs of a mutually devastating strike. The "hot line" between the Kremlin and the White House is an example of what we have in mind in the collective bargaining sphere.

An important element in trust is a predictability or consistency in behavior. In carrying out a commitment strategy, Party needs to have his word believed; in other words, he needs to have his actions and intentions accurately predicted by Opponent. Consistency and believability are important if untenable bargaining positions and unwanted strikes are to be avoided.

Second, a minimum acceptance of the other is a precondition to accurately assessing his utilities and commitment tactics. When Party completely denies the legitimacy of Opponent, he probably does not and cannot comprehend Opponent's real interests and intentions.

Before Party can sensibly pin himself down to a hard position, he needs to have a good picture of Opponent's bargaining position and all the circumstances internal to Opponent's organization that influence that position. If Party is to take a committed position that has some chance of being realized, then he needs to have some empathy for Opponent. Moreover, if Party hopes to have his own commitment believed, then he must assume that Opponent has sufficient understanding to conclude that Party's position is credible.

One means for taking a committed position without destroying the relationship is to focus attention on specific issues. Party develops a "will to fight" on the part of his organization in favor of specific demands and not in opposition to Opponent. Thus, it is possible to indicate commitment without getting the organization aroused in a general way—which contains more risk for undermining the relationship.

The third way in which these two subprocesses are compatible is illustrated by some of the tactics which emphasize commonness. For example, an awareness of their common fate not only allows the parties to stay within the area of joint dependency in distributive bargaining but also contributes to more positive attitudes. One event which serves to heighten joint feeling, both in terms of attitudinal structuring and distributive bargaining, is the strike deadline. It is not surprising that mediators constantly focus attention on the strike deadline and the chain of consequences that follow the onset of a strike.

There are other ways in which a given tactic serves both the attitudinal and distributive requirements simultaneously. One tactic is not to say "no" too quickly. One way to prevent the other side from becoming committed is to delay in answering his demands. The thoughtful and careful consideration of Opponent's position also can affect attitudes if such deliberation is regarded as "taking the Opponent seriously."

Certainly the private discussions between negotiators can have such a dual function. We have already cited some of the practices of the negotiators of the Jimson company which helped preserve their favorable relationship. The dinners, drinking, and telephone conversations between them were an integral part of the bargaining which occurred. Their relationship seems to have been a necessary prelude to such informal bargaining. The informal bargaining in turn seems to have aided the men in their attempts to identify bargaining paths and bargaining cues. It also helped the negotiators avoid miscalculation in distributive bargaining.

**Attitudinal and Integrative Processes Mutually Facilitating.** Attitudinal structuring and integrative bargaining are generally mutually enhancing. There are few, if any, dilemmas. This particular interaction between two subprocesses is not only the most important one but it is undoubtedly the most obvious. It will require little elaboration. Before integrative bargaining can take place, the two organizations need to develop a good measure of trust and friendliness. The activities of talking frankly about one's needs, sharing information, jointly formulating solutions, etc. cannot be undertaken unless trust is present. The problem-solving activity serves to improve the relationship even further. In fact, many of the tactics which emphasize Party's helping to solve Opponent's problems are nothing more than integrative tactics presented in this chapter in terms of their attitudinal components.

Integrative bargaining is a cognitive task, while attitudinal structuring is a socioemotional process. The process of integrative bargaining brings the parties together to solve specific problems and search for other areas of common interest.

During integrative bargaining the parties move closer both substantively and attitudinally. First, because the demands of integrative bargaining require that the parties approach the agenda items from an objective point of view, the interaction can serve to structure positive attitudes between the participants. Under such neutral interactions (as far as attitudinal content is concerned), interaction leads to positive sentiments. Second, to the extent that the parties do more than engage in the interaction and succeed in identifying (or underscoring the salience of) areas of common interest, the participants will tend even more to be positively disposed toward each other.

# CHAPTER VIII

# INTRAORGANIZATIONAL BARGAINING MODEL

This chapter discusses still another process which we believe is useful to abstract from the total behavior which constitutes contract negotiations. Whereas the processes discussed earlier were concerned with the resolution of conflict between organizations, the process we refer to as intra-organizational bargaining deals with conflict which occurs within each organization. Thus far, for purposes of exposition, we have assumed that each organization acted with single purpose in a manner which was generally acceptable internally and with perfect coordination. As a result, in our still somewhat simplified version of negotiations the chief negotiator had to deal purposively only with respect to the other organization. It is time to drop these assumptions and add the final complication to our overall model of negotiations.

The organizations participating in labor negotiations usually lack internal consensus about the objectives they will attempt to obtain from negotiations, and this is especially true for labor organizations. Different elements of the organization may have different ideas about the priorities assigned to various objectives being pursued, or they may disagree on what should be minimally acceptable for the total contract. Disagreement can also exist around strategies and tactics and around such questions as which items are distributive issues and which are problems with potentially integrative solutions. Similarly, there may be a lack of consensus about what type of relationship should be developed with the other party. These are only illustrative of the internal differences which can exist over ends and/or means. They point up the need to look directly at the problems involved in achieving internal consensus.[1]

[1] The importance of this subject is attested to in an important study of unions. See L. R. Sayles and George Strauss, *The Local Union: Its Place in the Industrial Plant* (New York: Harper & Row, Publishers, Incorporated, 1953), especially pp. 43–58.

Generally these internal conflicts must be resolved *during* the process of negotiation with the other party. Of course, some differences of opinion can and are worked out before negotiations, but there are reasons why some differences persist into the period of negotiations. First, the real nature and implications of some issues on the agenda and the relative strength of the parties can be learned only during negotiations. Second, the negotiation process itself may offer one element of the organization an opportunity to induce another element to adopt the first's point of view. Thus, the internal consensus process is concurrent with the intergroup processes, in part, because this cannot be avoided, and, in part, because the latter may facilitate the internal consensus process.

These two processes—intergroup and internal consensus—are not always mutually facilitative. In fact, more often they are the opposite: a tactic which brings about internal consensus may not be instrumental for distributive bargaining; behavior which helps resolve internal conflict may not be consistent with the requirements of integrative bargaining; and so on. One of the purposes of this and the next chapter will be to show how this fourth process interacts with the other three processes analyzed in earlier chapters.

Upon whom does the job of achieving internal consensus fall? In examining the functions required in each of the three processes previously considered, we have focused on the actions and thinking of a person with primary responsibility for negotiations. As a matter of convenience we have usually assumed a focal position in each party, namely, the chief negotiator, who makes decisions about strategy and tactics and who exercises influence regarding the objectives pursued but who ultimately must account to his principals (the membership in the case of the union negotiator and top management in the case of the company negotiator).

In this present chapter we shall continue to center on the problems of the person who occupies the focal position of chief negotiator. We shall preserve the assumption that this is a position which has influence and is instrumental in achieving results. Now, however, we shall be more interested in the fact that the activities and influence of the chief negotiator are constrained and shaped by internal organizational forces. The chief negotiator is seen as a target of attempts at influence which originate with various sources within the organization. Moreover, even with respect to the potential influence he does possess, he must choose and time his tactics wisely.

The decision to center on the activities of the chief negotiator has an important implication for the range of conflict phenomena we ultimately deal with in our tactical analysis. In our discussion we shall set forth the many types of organizational conflict relevant to negotiations, but it is primarily the resolution of differences in viewpoints and preferences between the negotiator, on the one hand, and elements of his organization, on the other hand, that we shall attempt to explain. It is the emergence and dissolution of this conflict, in particular, which impinge upon behavior at the bargaining table.

The subject of this chapter will be developed as follows: The first section discusses the constraints under which the negotiator operates—it is because of limitations placed upon the settlement terms by distributive and integrative bargaining and the pressures placed upon the negotiator by attitudinal structuring that he must turn to deal with his own organization. This section also explores the nature of the other differences that exist within each organization. In the second section, we shall attempt to identify the conditions under which internal conflict is likely to be more pronounced, and in the third section, we indicate how these bear on the position of chief negotiator. The fourth section presents a rudimentary model of the internal-bargaining process. This model provides a framework for exploring the dynamics involved in resolving internal conflict, and in the next chapter we turn to the various tactics which a negotiator can use in dealing with his own organization. In the next chapter we shall also explore dilemmas by introducing this question: What implications do these tactics have for the conduct of the other subprocesses?

# PART 1 | THE NATURE OF INTERNAL CONFLICT

In previous chapters we have focused on the distributive and integrative bargaining by which agreement is reached by changing Opponent's position. But the chief negotiator operates within limits. First, the bargaining position of Opponent and the behavioral expectations of Opponent (which grow out of their relationship) place real restraints on what is substantively attainable and behaviorally possible. Second, the contradictory demands which sometimes originate from within Party's own organization present complications. Thus, we need to reverse the emphasis and take Opponent's position and behavior as given in order to examine the process by which the Party deals with his own organization.

We turn to a preliminary examination of two forms of internal conflict —boundary conflict and factional conflict.

**Boundary Role: Two Sets of Expectations.** *Role concepts.* A role is defined by a set of complementary expectations. Deviations from the role bring disapproval and negative sanction; conformity brings approval and positive rewards. Whether formal or informal, each role is prescribed by someone or some group. In effect, a role is sent from a particular direction, and it constitutes a bid for the role occupant to orient himself in that direction.

A negotiator can be seen as occupying several roles simultaneously. The primary role of the negotiator is that which is sent from within his own organization. (Later we shall note that he may receive more than one set of internal expectations.) Another role exists because of the relationship that links him with his opponent.

Thus, the boundary role [2] occupied by the chief negotiator is the target of two sets of prescriptions about what the negotiator ought to do and how he should behave. That role expectations should originate from within his own organization should be obvious. In addition, a negotiator is often expected to behave with understanding and to act in a way that accommodates the needs of his opponent. This role usually carries with it a set of prescriptions for the role occupant, e.g., the negotiator should not behave in a way that undermines the long-run interest of the relationship. Let us continue to explore the role expectations which originate outside the negotiator's own organization.

There are several reasons why negotiators for the two parties have a relationship with each other not shared or valued by their respective principals. The relationship develops naturally out of the interaction between the two men and their joint responsibility for hammering out an agreement.[3] They also sometimes have unique responsibilities for administering that agreement. These factors may lead to positive sentiments toward each other. The relationship also grows out of a need that they feel for some limits to the contest and for some predictability of the outcome. Since the two chief negotiators have to live together during the course of the ensuing contract, they both desire some predictability in the behavior of the other person.[4] Often the result is a sense of mutual obligation in certain areas. The importance of friendliness and trust and the ways in which they can be achieved were discussed in detail in the previous chapters on attitudinal structuring.

These constraints inherent in the relationship must be taken seriously by the negotiator.[5] Important sanctions are associated with Party's viola-

---

[2] The apt concept of boundary role has been used in a similar way by others. In particular, R. L. Kahn, D. M. Wolfe, R. P. Quinn, J. D. Snoek, and R. A. Rosenthal, *Organizational Stress: Studies in Role Conflict and Ambiguity* (New York: John Wiley and Sons, Inc., 1964) study the role conflict inherent in boundary positions of organizations.

[3] S. H. Slichter, J. J. Healy, and E. R. Livernash, *The Impact of Collective Bargaining on Management* (Washington, D.C.: The Brookings Institution, 1960), p. 921.

[4] Sayles and Strauss, *op. cit.*, pp. 71–72.

[5] We need to clarify that we are not referring to collusion between the negotiators where one or both sacrifices the interests of their respective organizations for selfish reasons. Although this may be involved in some of the cases contemplated, it is not the

tions of Opponent's role expectations. For example, if Party violates these expectations, (1) negotiations themselves may be more difficult, producing retaliation (such as that explored as punishment in the analysis of attitudinal structuring tactics), (2) administration of the contract may be more difficult, and (3) Opponent may be less helpful in maintaining Party's internal position and strength.

The retaliation for violating Opponent's role expectations may net Party nothing more than verbal criticism.

> In the Jimson negotiations the company spokesman, Scott, was given very little authority to negotiate with the union. As negotiations progressed, he had to make increasingly frequent phone calls to his superior in another city. As this practice continued, Watoski, his union counterpart, began to tease him about having to make "another telephone call." This verbal needling bothered Scott since he valued the opinion and respect of Watoski.

However, violating Opponent's role expectations may lead to deterioration in attitudes and place in jeopardy a mutually beneficial relationship such as the one implied in the following statement by a union official:

> I say to Claude, "I'll fight hard for my union, and you do the best job possible for your company." But within those limits we try to help each other out personally. There are all kinds of little things we do for each other—and without sacrificing the interests of the people we represent. Little things—sometimes big ones—that help keep us in solid with our people.[6]

What is really of interest is not that these constraints and sanctions exist but that Party takes them more seriously than the other members of the organization do. He does so because he occupies a boundary position between his organization and Opponent. The negotiator occupies a position that encompasses more than just a leadership role with his own organization; it includes a role relationship with the other negotiator.

*Boundary-role expectations: conflicting or compatible?* The negotiator is forced to reckon with the positions and expectations of the Opponent.

---

typical case. Rather our differentiation of the two sets of demands that are involved in boundary conflict approximates that made by Thibaut and Kelly in defining *prescribed roles* versus *functionally requisite roles*. "Prescribed roles" are comprised of those norms of the group which members actually apply to the person behaving in their behalf. "Functionally requisite roles" are those norms which, if the group is to deal successfully with the problems and tasks confronting it, *should* be applied. The latter role conception assumes a better understanding of means-ends relations. J. W. Thibaut and H. H. Kelly, *The Social Psychology of Groups* (New York: John Wiley & Sons, Inc., 1959), p. 144.

[6] Edward Peters, *Strategy and Tactics in Labor Negotiations* (New London, Conn.: National Foremen's Institute, 1955), p. 107.

This may or may not cause him any internal difficulty. Party's own organization may be less ambitious with respect to the terms of the settlement and more conciliatory with respect to negotiating behavior than the expectations of Opponent. In this instance Party does not experience role conflict. The demands of the two roles are compatible. However, it is also possible for these role demands to be in conflict.

Are these role demands usually compatible or not? Certainly, as Ross points out below, there are contract negotiations in which the negotiator's net influence is to raise the principal's aspiration and other negotiations in which his influence is the opposite. He poses this as a strategic decision for the negotiator.

> Knowing what seems attainable, sensing the temper of the membership, and bearing in mind the strategic possibilities of the situation (from the standpoint of the union's institutional objectives), the officials must decide whether to "play it up" or "play it down." They can emphasize the employer's exorbitant profits, or his high cost of production and difficult marketing problems. They can point to the rapid advance in the cost of living, or they can argue that the price level shows definite signs of receding. In calling attention to the wages, and wage increases, of other groups of workers, they have a wide field of selection. They can praise the employer's cooperative attitude or condemn his lack of good faith.[7]

We believe that the negotiator is often the man in the middle, experiencing role conflict because his position is less ambitious than that of his principals. This is the case of interest to us in intraorganizational bargaining. Our first reason for stressing this situation is that it appears to be the most common one. This is not to say that negotiators do not engage in whipping up interest and enlisting support. This activity is a standard part of most labor negotiations, especially in early stages of negotiations for reasons associated with distributive bargaining. But on balance we believe that the negotiator acts as a subduing influence; and certainly during the crucial stages when an agreement is being hammered out, his part is usually that of moderating the views of his own organization.[8]

This impression tends to be confirmed by the work of other investigators

[7] A. M. Ross, *Trade Union Wage Policy* (Berkeley, Calif.: University of California Press, 1948), p. 41.

[8] This assumption is contrary to the position taken by many students of intergroup conflict, e.g., Daniel Katz, "Consistent Reactive Participation of Group Members and Reduction of Intergroup Conflict," *Journal of Conflict Resolution*, vol. 3 (March, 1959), pp. 28–40. This is a critical matter because Katz's assumption leads him to conclude that more member involvement in decision making facilitates the resolution of intergroup conflict, whereas we shall develop the opposite point that negotiators may on occasion be effective in achieving intergroup resolution by employing various tactics for limiting the role of group members in intergroup decision making.

of labor relations. Jack Barbash suggests that the business agent in the construction industry characteristically regards himself as the man "in the middle between the contractor and the union," seeking some common ground.[9] Rosen and Rosen further stress that the boundary role of the business agent involves making some assessment of the legitimacy of the demands of both the company and his own organization.[10] According to Blum, moderating internal pressures actually dominates a large part of what we regard as the total process of collective bargaining.[11]

Parnes, who conducted a major investigation on this subject, concluded that "in the majority of cases the rank and file is more, rather than less, 'extreme' than the leadership in pressing for contract demands." [12] He noted that the problem is less often one of arousing the membership and convincing them of the righteousness of the demands, than it is one of restraining the rank and file "from pressing for terms which the leaders' wider experience and greater knowledge tell them are either unwise or undefensible. . . ." [13]

There is also some evidence that the trend is in the direction of increasing militancy on the part of the principals, who are not satisfied with the job being done by their more moderate negotiators:

> A rising defiance among union rank and filers is making life on the collective bargaining front increasingly perilous for labor chieftains as well as management officials.

> More and more frequently, angry and well organized union dissidents are mustering enough votes to reject contract settlements painstakingly worked out and approved by their own negotiators. . . .

> While a great majority of the turndowns involve union rejection of contracts, some represent management dissatisfaction. Not long ago, the executive committee of Philadelphia Transportation Company disapproved an agreement drawn up by the union and Robert H. Stier, company president and chief negotiator. Mr. Stier resigned as a result. Too, there have been several recent instances of contract agreements being approved only by narrow margins.[14]

[9] Jack Barbash, *Labor's Grass Roots: A Study of the Local Union* (New York: Harper & Row, Publishers, Incorporated, 1961).

[10] H. M. Rosen and R. A. H. Rosen, "The Union Business Agent Looks at Collective Bargaining," *Personnel*, vol. 33 (May, 1957), pp. 539–545.

[11] A. A. Blum, "Collective Bargaining: Ritual or Reality?" *Harvard Business Review*, vol. 39 (November–December, 1961), p. 64.

[12] H. S. Parnes, *Union Strike Votes: Current Practice and Proposed Controls* (Princeton, N.J.: Industrial Relations Section, Department of Economics and Sociology, Princeton University, 1956), p. 61.

[13] *Ibid.*, p. 62.

[14] "Union Workers Rising Rejection of Pacts Imperils Labor Leaders and Management," *The Wall Street Journal* (June 3, 1963).

Our second reason for emphasizing the situation which requires a reduction of the principals' expectations is that it presents the more interesting tactical assignment. Parnes reports that union officers themselves regard this as the more difficult of the two possible problems. They assert that "the problem of selling what they believed to be an acceptable contract to the rank and file almost always posed greater difficulties than the problem of attaining strike authorization when a satisfactory contract had not been obtained." [15]

Finally, raising the principal's expectations is less interesting for our analysis here because it is basically equivalent to the internal activity that accompanies distributive bargaining. It is in the boundary conflict situation that the internal-consensus process interacts with and complicates intergroup bargaining, a point to be stressed again later.

**Factional Conflict.** Internal conflict may develop quite apart from the particular position taken by Opponent. Two elements of Party's own organization may send him incompatible demands or roles. Some of these internal conflicts center on negotiating objectives; some focus on the means used to achieve these objectives.

*Objectives.* The most serious type of conflict over objectives involves basic disagreement over purpose. In some instances various groups will hold opposing views about what is good and desirable. This occurs when one group can gain only at the expense of another. Wage inequity adjustments frequently take on this character for the union. Seniority provisions also involve choices among the competing claims or interests of several employee groups. Differences in objectives arise simply because different people sometimes have contrary needs.

Even when people share many of the same needs, they may assign radically different priorities to the objectives under consideration. None of the elements of the organization would disagree about the desirability of a particular proposal, but some groups would stand to gain more, while others would be less directly benefited. For example, such benefits as shift differentials and free clothing affect only part of the work force. Similarly, money issues may be relatively more important to the membership, and institutional issues such as union security of more interest to the union leadership.

Perhaps the most common difference over negotiating objectives involves nothing more than differing aspiration levels. That is, the several elements of the organization would agree generally on what to strive for but would each define substantially different targets and/or resistance points. The chapter on the distributive model discussed the factors that influence these levels. It is rather common for these factors to have a differential impact on various parts of the organization. For example,

[15] Parnes, *op. cit.*, pp. 61–62.

every group within the union may support the demand for a "generous wage increase," but they might disagree on what is minimally acceptable. Different groups within the organization are sensitive to different standards, e.g., wages in the local labor market versus industry wage comparisons. As a result, they develop different targets and resistance points.

*Means.* Conflicting expectations often exist about appropriate negotiating behavior. The rank and file, who place the union negotiator in his position and give him the objective of obtaining a good settlement, also impose upon him certain expectations about how he will behave during the course of negotiations. For instance, some may expect him to behave reasonably and maturely; others may expect him to act militantly and aggressively. But even when agreement has been reached about the general emphasis, many conflicts can exist around the particular tactics to be employed. For instance, even though all persons within the organization agree that distributive bargaining is the appropriate approach, they may not agree upon the emphasis to be given to strike action or on the timing of specific concessions.

## Conditions of Internal Conflict

The boundary-role conflict experienced by the negotiator results from two forces—those which pull him in the direction of Opponent's expectations and those which pull him in the direction of internal expectations. Factional conflict may involve any of several types of differences in outlook within the organization. Boundary and factional conflict are two forms of internal conflict. The discussion now turns to the conditions which underlie internal conflict generally.

The discussion of distributive bargaining indicated that what a party expects from negotiations is a function of both utilities and estimates of feasibility. Why do various groups within an organization develop different expectations? "Expectations" is a proxy for all the differences that may exist regarding objectives, priorities, aspirations, and behavior. These differences can have as their basis rational motivational forces, perceptual factors, or emotional forces.[16]

**Motivational Forces.** Intraorganizational conflict may occur because of differences in underlying goal structures among persons or groups within the organization. Differences in goal structure are more likely, the greater the organizational distance between groups. Some potential for internal conflict arises because of the vertical differentiation, and some relates to the heterogeneity of membership groups or departments.

*Vertical differentiation.* First let us look at the problems on the union

[16] J. G. March and H. A. Simon, *Organizations* (New York: John Wiley & Sons, Inc., 1958), pp. 121–129.

side. The main interest of the rank and file centers around employment issues. They are concerned about work rules, disciplinary action, and the like. As one moves higher in the organization, attention focuses more on issues of an institutional character. For the top officers in the union, considerations of precedent, policy, public image, size of the membership, etc. become dominant. Proposals for union security, superseniority for union officials, the right to distribute literature on company premises, grievance-handling procedures, and pay for released time are likely to be fundamentally more important to union officials than to members. Here then, we could list all the factors which influence the extent to which there is a lack of coincidence between employee and institutional interest. The list might include total size, size of administrative staff, degree of present institutional security, competition for leadership, etc.

Differences within the company can also be identified with different positions in the hierarchy. Top management normally feels strongest about matters involving principle or large sums of money. Central labor-relations personnel (including the chief negotiator) focus on policies and matters that have chain-wide importance. Plant management and local industrial relations people worry more about matters of convenience and administrative simplicity.

These general points can be illustrated with several examples. In some instances the conflict focuses more on objectives and in other cases more on priorities. More of the examples come from the union side—this is not accidental since intraorganizational bargaining is a much more serious problem for the union negotiator.

A major concern presented the following demands to the union during the 1958 negotiations: superseniority for all supervisory personnel, elimination of shift differentials, establishment of a vacation shutdown period and a reduction in the period for which disability payments could be received. None of these demands was accepted by the union in the final agreement. The company negotiator confided that the demands represented a fixation of top management on principles and on practices which were above those existing elsewhere. He personally did not think that they should have been pursued because they raised such a vehement response on the part of the union.

In a negotiation between a group of symphony musicians and the management of a summer music festival the local negotiating committee was anxious to gain acceptance of certain demands: consecutive days off and rotation of personnel for ballet music (the ballet orchestra was half the size of a normal symphony orchestra). The negotiating committee from the orchestra placed high priority on these items, since they were directly affected by them and since they had recently been elected to office with these items as part of their platform. The international union subscribed to the wisdom of these changes, but it did not want to press too adamantly for them. The international was more worried about finding employment for additional musicians and avoiding a showdown which might have a bad public relations effect.

During 1962 and 1963 several meat-packing companies sought wage concessions in order to compete with nonunion plants. One of the international unions involved steadfastly refused to sanction any break in the wage schedule embodied in the master contract. On the other hand, local employees and their representatives pressed for permission to roll back wages as a way of keeping their plants in operation.

In a negotiation conducted in 1963 in the garment industry, the international union pushed for inclusion of the following items on the bargaining agenda: union label and contributions to an area-wide medical plan. The membership placed higher priority on inequity adjustments and equality of benefits between men and women.

During the 1963 steel negotiations it was reported that the international union requested the curtailment of overtime in order to provide more employment. The issue was never pressed—the district directors and subordinate officials expressed little enthusiasm for the idea. The workers liked the overtime and the big paychecks.

***Heterogeneity of groups.*** The greatest horizontal distance comes when the bargaining group is made up of different entities. A bargaining team drawn from several unions would probably have more internal dissension than one drawn from only one local union. Similarly a bargaining team comprised of several companies would tend to have more internal conflict than a team representing one company. However, the analysis will also apply to a single union dealing with a single company.

Again, let us first examine the union side and then turn to the company side. Some issues have differential impact on several employee groups. Job-security or wage classification proposals may favor one class of employees, but primarily at the expense of another class. The same point can be made regarding agreements on the introduction of automated machinery. To develop this idea we could list all the factors which result in diversity of interests among the membership: heterogeneity of employee occupations, skills, age groupings, seniority, sex, etc. These factors are likely to lead them to prefer different wage structures, seniority arrangements, and plans and benefits programs.

As Sayles and Strauss point out, a worker is not only a company employee and a union member, "he is also a member of countless other special interest groups: he may be a mill operator, on the night shift, with low seniority, paid on an 'incentive rate,' and so forth. The members who work in each of these groups may have bargaining objectives which conflict with those of other union 'brothers.' " [17]

In the following example the locals representing new versus old plants were at odds over a proposal of the international union:

> The subject of company-wide seniority had been a bone of contention within a large CIO type of union. The company had closed several plants during the postwar period. The international union, aware of the problems associated with plant shutdown and realizing that other plants would be closed, decided to institute an arrangement by which long service employees would enjoy bumping rights at other plants in the company. Representatives from some of the older plants agreed and supported the international. However, representatives from the newer plants objected strenuously. They did not want displaced employees taking jobs from their constituents. In discussing this situation, the company negotiator was accurate when he said, "Seniority is more of an internal union problem than a company problem."

On the management side differences also exist between departments, especially between line and staff personnel.[18] For example, staff people are more attuned to matters of principle and contract language. They consider the implications of prior arbitration decisions and future contract negotiations. In contrast, the line people worry more about getting the present job done. These differences in outlook are well illustrated by a management meeting attended by one of the authors.

> First, the labor relations manager who was responsible for administering the contract was most concerned about the chain-wide implications of certain union proposals. The request to institute a job-posting procedure particularly caught his attention. He was concerned that the job-posting arrangement would once again raise an old problem of selection of personnel and make it difficult to achieve company-wide uniformity on matters of seniority.

> Other central personnel people were concerned about the policy implications of certain union demands. They were especially insistent

---

[17] Sayles and Strauss, op. cit., p. 43. See also L. H. Fisher and Grant McConnell, "Internal Conflict and Labor-Union Solidarity," in Arthur Kornhauser et al. (eds.), Industrial Conflict (New York: McGraw-Hill Book Company, 1954), pp. 132–143.

[18] This is similar to the proposition advanced by many people that compartmentalization and cleavages increase as the complexity and the division of labor in an organization increase. See for example, Robert Dubin, "Leadership in Union-Management Relations as an Intergroup System," in Muzafer Sherif (ed.), Intergroup Relations and Leadership (New York: John Wiley & Sons, Inc., 1962), p. 80.

that the union effort to scuttle a testing program be repulsed. They had developed the testing program for strengthening local management in its task of selecting personnel, in which heavy emphasis was placed on ability factors. The testing program had represented the personnel staff's solution to the demand of top management that qualified personnel be selected and the demand of local management that some practical technique be available. As a result, the testing program was very important to the personnel people.

Finally, the orientation of the chief negotiator, who was cognizant of the various expectations, was directed at formulating a company position that would have a chance of acceptance with the union. He wanted a contract rather than a substantiation of certain principles. Of all the people present he seemed the most realistic about what the union might accept or reject.

Consider another example taken from the Brookings study:

In one plant the line and staff representatives were at odds over "foremen working." The contract provided that foremen should work only in emergencies and to train other workers. The plant manager could not emotionally accept this concept. In his eyes a good foreman stepped in and helped out in any kind of production difficulty. The staff representative accepted the contract provision as stating appropriate foremen activity....[19]

Interestingly, this cleavage between staff and operating personnel also obtains on the union side, as the following example illustrates:

Towards the end of bargaining, the negotiators focused their attention on incentive and time study issues. The union brought a time study specialist from international headquarters into the negotiations. He presented the union's case in a very sophisticated way loaded with scientific accuracy and principles. The local representative of the union was quite embarrassed since his orientation was quite different from that of the industrial engineering expert. He tended to be more flexible and more anxious to work things out on a practical basis rather than adhering to policy positions of the international.[20]

*The influence of disutility.* As we indicated in the chapter on the distributive model, basic preferences are directly influenced by potential costs associated with striving for specific objectives. Different groups will experience different disutilities in the event of a strike.

[19] Slichter, Healy, and Livernash, *op. cit.,* p. 890.
[20] Ann Douglas, *Industrial Peacemaking* (New York: Columbia University Press, 1962), p. 31.

Top leaders are more calculating and appreciate the full range of sanctions that can be impressed upon them should they fail. Despite the prevalent notion that workers have few reserves and are reluctant to take chances, they actually may be more willing to gamble than the union leadership is.

The difference between top and bottom groups within the organization is illustrated by the following example:

> It was reported during the recent newspaper strike in New York City that Local 6 of the ITU was in no hurry to end the strike since all its members were drawing handsome strike benefits. The international, however, from whose treasury the benefits were coming, was anxious to settle the strike.

On the company side differences also exist over the disutilities associated with a strike. Generally, the operating people weigh the cost of a strike more heavily than staff people, as the following example illustrates:

> Time after time labor relations officials recounted instances where they felt that the line, under pressure for production and quick resolution of problems, wanted to make concessions detrimental to long term efficiency, to get the question resolved quickly and not interfere with production.[21]

**Perceptual Factors.** Often the basis of conflict does not really have anything to do with differences in goal structures. The problem is that different parts of the organization receive different information. Since one will define the bargaining situation in terms of the information he has, there is a possibility of quite different perceptions.

Several types of perceptions have an influence on the level of aspirations. What a member knows or assumes about a proposal (for example, a seniority clause, about the characteristics of the related problem (for example, potential layoffs), about the position of the employer and his willingness to invoke sanctions (for example, strike action), and about the related probabilities for these events will all influence the member's interest in the proposal and the degree of support that he will give to it.

Differences in perceptions and expectations in turn result from several factors. The propositions presented below are that there is greater diversity of expectations where there is relatively more compartmentalization of information, relatively more complexity in the decision situation, and relatively more novelty in the proposal.

*Compartmentalization.* One can imagine, theoretically, the condition that all information is equally available to all members and officials. In

[21] Slichter, Healy, and Livernash, *op. cit.*, p. 893.

reality this condition never obtains: we can speak of information in organizations being compartmentalized and reaching certain parts of the organizations but not others. Information is channeled in this sense whether deliberately or not. Factors which result in greater compartmentalizing include size, geographical separation, amount and nature of communication media, frequency and attendance at meetings, diversity within employee population, etc.

Often there is a considerable disparity in the amount of information that the organizational members take into account compared with that of the negotiator. First, the negotiator is in more direct contact with the opponent. He is exposed to more clues about the nature of the other's preferences and his power. Second, the negotiator is more experienced and more skillful in appraising the eventual meeting ground. Recall the discussion of symmetry and focal-point solutions discussed in the chapter on distributive bargaining tactics. For example, settlements reached in other negotiations can provide clues for assessing the situation. Like two people who have to meet without communicating to each other, a certain pattern becomes a convenient meeting spot. Generally, negotiators who have bargained together regularly learn the natural sequence of negotiations and the variety of clues that can provide indications of the eventual outcome. Consider the following illustration:

> The contract was due to expire on August 31. When one of the authors visited the negotiating teams on that day, a visible difference was noted in the composure of the lower-level delegates and officials and that of the two chief negotiators. The divisional personnel from the company and the delegates from the union were actively meeting in subcommittees, attempting to resolve all the differences before expiration. The chief negotiators appeared calm. As it turned out, the contract was extended for several weeks. Both of the chief negotiators anticipated this development before the proposal to extend the contract was even discussed. This had not happened through private discussions, but through the symmetry (or natural sequence) of the situation. Both of the negotiators knew that bargaining could not come to a showdown until the pattern settlement had been signed in Detroit.

In brief, the negotiator usually gains a realistic view of the situation considerably in advance of other members of his organization.

*Complexity.* A second informational factor influences perceptions and hence expectations, namely, the complexity of the decision situation. The more complex the decision situation, the more ambiguous is related information and the more subject it is to differing interpretations. Many proposals relating to supplementary unemployment-benefit plans and provisions for limiting transfer of work or subcontracting, to mention but a few illustrative issues, are too complex to be understood by most members of the union.

> The UAW leadership experienced difficulty in gaining acceptance for the profit-sharing idea among rank and file workers at American Motors. After the contract had been rejected by the workers at the Kenosha plant, the UAW leadership directed that another vote be taken. During the interim it conducted an intensive educational campaign. The difference in outlook on the part of the membership stemmed primarily from the fear of getting into a complicated wage payment plan. After the plan had been explained and the safeguards outlined, they were more favorably disposed to the agreement.

*Novelty.* A third type of informational factor is the novelty of the decision situation. Novelty can inhere in the problem itself or in the proposed solution. If the environment presents problems which are rapidly changing, perceptions of the situation are likely to be dissimilar. Shifts in relative importance of various employee skills, changing technologies and administrative techniques, etc. are examples of forces that tend to have such influence. The decision can be novel for another reason: The proposed solution to a continuing problem may be an innovation. Thus, there is less past experience as a basis for developing common assumptions and meanings. Certain aspects of supplementary unemployment benefits, profit sharing (previously illustrated), more broadly defined crafts, etc. have been seen in widely differing ways because they were unfamiliar.

> The 1947 negotiations between Ford Motor and the UAW illustrate the difficulties that come from a new idea. During those negotiations the union leadership had pressed hard for a pension agreement. They were successful and obtained from Ford one of the first negotiated pension proposals in American industry. When the matter was put to ratification, the membership chose the alternative embodying a substantial raise increase, rather than the pension program, despite the advice of the union leadership. A Ford official interpreted the rejection of the pension plan as evidence that union leaders were definitely out of touch with the thinking and desires of rank-and-file union members. Part of the disparity arose from different needs (the rank and file was more interested in keeping up with the spiraling cost of living), but it came mostly from differences in appraising the complex pension plan and from the newness of the pension idea.

**Emotional Forces.** Conflicting expectations may develop primarily out of differences in emotional states. Groups within the organization may

hold radically different assumptions about appropriate negotiating behavior or the desired relationship to be structured with the other organization. One group may have a greater need than the other to "defeat" the
company or at least to "hit out at" the company. The range of factors that
influence the emotional state held and the relationship desired by a person
were outlined in the chapter on attitudinal structuring. It is not necessary
to review all of those influences except to suggest that they could have a
differential impact on various groups within an organization.

On the union side many individuals transmit strong feelings to their
bargaining committees.[22] Some of this may grow out of tradition, for
example, forge shops and foundries often pride themselves on being "dead
end kids." Presumably the unpleasant character of the work has fostered
a certain spirit which leads to aggressiveness in bargaining outlook. Sometimes the emotional state may go deeper, as the following statement of a
union leader illustrates:

> We've got a lot of hotheads we have to hold down. They are ready
> to strike at the drop of a button. We don't like that. Fellows who are
> so anxious to strike are generally one of two types. First, there's the
> guy whose wife is working and maybe making as much as he is. Being
> on the bricks for a while doesn't worry him, and he is always ready
> to fight for more money. Then there are the hammer throwers. There
> aren't too many of them, but they would like to run for (union) office
> sometimes and think they can get some support by showing how
> tough they are and by yelling that the union could do a lot better if
> the leaders were willing to fight.[23]

In some instances the differences in emotional states can be explained by
recent experiences. Some parts of the organization may be smarting under
an unpleasant memory, while others are moving toward a different relationship. The point is that when relationships are changing, there is
bound to be a disparity between the part of the organization that is holding to the old outlook and the part of the organization that is adopting
a new outlook. Consider the following interesting example:

> During the 1955 negotiations at International Harvester, the leader-
> ship of the union thought a settlement was possible without a strike.
> Indeed, at the expiration of the contract few important issues re-

---

[22] Militant behavorial expectations is apparently a more important factor with unions,
taken as a group, than with management. For example, Haire found that the use of
divisive pronouns ("We," "They") is significantly more common in labor's statements
than it is in management's. Mason Haire, "Role Perceptions in Labor-Management
Relations: An Experimental Approach," *Industrial and Labor Relations Review*, vol. 8
(January, 1955), pp. 204–216.

[23] Parnes, *op. cit.*, p. 62.

mained unresolved. The local leaders, however, demanded strike action as a way of getting even with the company. Their emotional state had been affected by the company's unwillingness to reopen the 1950 contract under the living-document philosophy, the turbulence created by the company's tightening-up program in the area of production standards, the tense jurisdictional warfare between the former FE union and the UAW, etc. On the other hand, the top leadership had developed respect for the company as a result of the many discussions with top company officials on problems of mutual concern.

As a step toward stating an overall model, let us diagram the hypothesized relationships discussed above (see Figure 8-1).

## Figure 8-1
### Sources of Internal Conflict

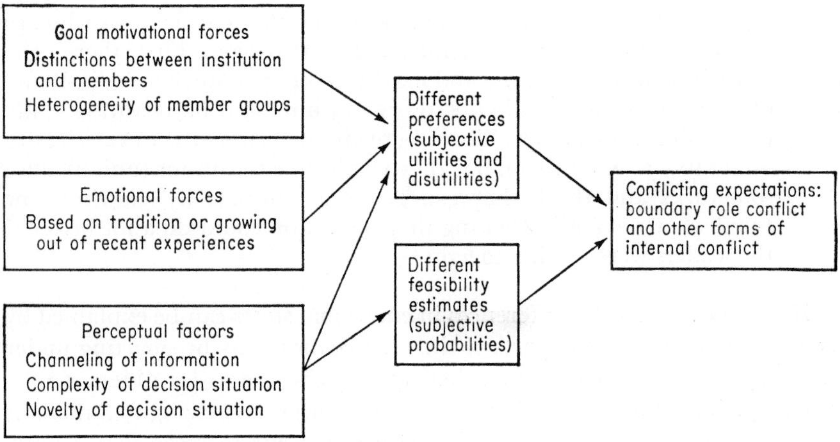

## Internal Conflict and the Negotiator

A negotiator frequently experiences role conflict. This may occur in either of two forms. First, the negotiator occupies a boundary role which may induce him to adopt expectations different from those of his organization. Second, the negotiator may find himself aligned with one of two or more conflicting factions within his own organization.

Both types of conflict produce a cleavage between the negotiator and all or part of his own organization. With respect to factional conflict the negotiator, at some point, becomes a participant to the conflict. He himself comes to prefer (or sees a necessity for) a position which differs from that of some elements of the organization. Actually, if factional conflict persists, the negotiator becomes involved whether or not he develops any particular preference, since he is at the point at which the actual decisions are eventually made. This is apparent to those who represent competing interests within the organization. Therefore, he experiences pressures from that element and may elect to exert more or less counterpressure. At any rate, this aspect of intraorganizational conflict is one for which the negotiating table sometimes becomes an arena and the negotiator a direct participant.

In boundary conflict the negotiator comes into conflict with his own organization because he cannot, or prefers not to, ignore the demands and expectations of his opponent. Again, he cannot escape the situation, because he is at the point at which the relevant decisions are made. He can resolve the conflict, but he cannot avoid the conflict situation.

These two types of conflict are similar in some respects and dissimilar in others. First, both types involve the negotiator in conflict with his organization (or an element of it). But the reasons are different: In one case, he is in conflict with parts of his organization because he identifies with the position of another organizational faction, such as the leadership. In the other, he is in conflict with his organization because of his position in the *inter*organizational conflict and because inherent in this position are different preferences and different considerations which must be taken into account. His job in either event is to influence some small or large group of his own principals to reduce their attachment to some issue or to otherwise modify their expectations.

Second, both types of conflict may involve delibrate pressures upon the negotiator, originating from within the organization. And while he usually cannot completely ignore pressure in either case, conflict which is strictly internal is more likely to pit the negotiator against a minority element of his organization. In contrast, in boundary conflict the negotiator is often isolated from his entire organization (isolated in terms of his outlook and the positions he takes). The pressures he receives in boundary conflict to conform to certain expectations and the sanctions he is threatened with for failing to conform probably differ, in magnitude if not in kind, from those in factional conflict.

Third, both types of conflict may occur during negotiations, but boundary conflict is almost a certainty. A related point of difference, and the most important one for our purposes, is that in the case of boundary conflict the opponent becomes an ally of sorts. While the resolution of both types of intraorganizational conflict do sometimes impinge upon the activities at the bargaining table, boundary conflict is much more significant in this respect.

As a way of illustrating both the factional and the boundary dimensions of role conflict, it might be helpful to present some examples that illustrate the predicament faced by a negotiator. Consider the example of a district union official.[24] He operated at the juncture of three competing roles as follows:

> In the course of negotiating an agreement, Hill was sensitive to three criterion groups. He was responsive to the role prescribed by district level officials inasmuch as "both in terms of age and tenure, Hill was still a bit insecure in the district hierarchy. That is, he was still striving to make his mark and gain full acceptance . . . on an equal footing with the other business representatives." Another criterion group was the local bargaining committee and through them, the rank and file from the local union. This orientation was important to Hill because he was "striving for full acceptance by the men in the shop." He needed the support of the men in order to effectively administer the agreement. A third criterion group was the company. He desired to get the best possible contract under the circumstances; and he also felt the necessity of reaching a quick agreement. As it happened, each of these three roles contained elements incompatible with the other two.

Normally the conflict involves only two axes, one representing the wishes of the principals and the other representing the wishes of the opponent. The following example, which is taken from the 1961 negotiations in the farm equipment industry, illustrates the type of conflict that occurred on both sides of the bargaining table. On the union side:

> The union spokesman faced this situation. Classification inequities had been a historical problem, and he knew the issue would receive close attention in the forthcoming negotiations. If past negotiations were any indication, he could expect to receive thousands of inequity demands from the various locals. On the other hand, he knew that the company had never spent more than a few cents in any negotiation on inequity problems.

> At the behavioral level an equally difficult situation existed for the union official. The locals expected aggressive bargaining and were not afraid of a strike, indeed, they had frequently resorted to strike action in support of their demands. However, the company negotiator expected that this negotiation would be conducted without resort to a strike. During the preceding year a new tone had entered labor-management relations. Contract administration had been characterized by a much more constructive and responsible approach on the part of top officials from both sides.

[24] A. R. Weber, *Union Decision-making in Collective Bargaining* (Urbana, Ill.: Institute of Labor and Industrial Relations, University of Illinois, 1951).

And on the company side:

> The subject of classification inequities also placed the company nego-
> tiator in definite role conflict. On the one hand, he was guided by
> firm commands from top management to avoid costly concessions
> and from his colleagues in wage administration to avoid any con-
> cessions on principle which might have company-wide implications.
> On the other hand, he knew that the union would be seeking relief
> on a larger number of inequities than the company could find justi-
> fiable on wage administration criteria, and that the form of the relief
> would normally be the most expensive, in other words, the job would
> invariably be upgraded.
>
> The company negotiator also experienced conflict at the behavioral
> level. In terms of his relationship across the bargaining table, he
> knew that the union negotiator shared his desire to avoid a strike
> as a way of cementing the new relationship. On the other hand, top
> and staff management were not as interested in avoiding a strike.
> They were more interested in avoiding costly concessions on both
> money and principle.

Both of these examples highlight the conflict that takes place over bargaining behavior in general. But considerable conflict also can take place
between the negotiator and his organization over the matter of specific
bargaining tactics, as the following example from the Jimson negotiations
illustrates:

> The union negotiator, Watoski, had brought a representative of an
> insurance firm to the negotiation table as a tactic in support of the
> union's position. Although Scott had not been consulted on this
> move in advance, he decided against objecting or otherwise making
> an issue of it.
>
> Rand, Scott's superior, believed that decision was a mistake. Scott,
> of course, wanted Rand's approval. But if he had done what Rand
> had preferred, he probably would have antagonized Watoski. The
> situation, therefore, made it difficult for him to maintain his rela-
> tions with both Rand and Watoski.

By this point we should have demonstrated that the negotiator frequently faces a difficult situation; he is boxed in between the pressures
stemming from his own organization and those from his opponent's. Such
a predicament presents considerable stress for the negotiator, and he is
under considerable incentive to resolve the competing pressures. The following example portrays some of the frustration that goes with occupying
a position of role conflict:

Negotiations were reaching a climax. Scott's superior had indicated that he could use a benefit if he needed it to settle. Scott had communicated tacitly to Watoski that this was in the offing, provided it would settle things. Watoski, who had generally been unsuccessful during these negotiations, readily agreed—he needed something like this benefit to save face with his committee.

In the final maneuvering, Scott's boss decided against the extra benefit since it was probably not really required to settle. Scott's reaction to this decision of his boss was depression and defeat.

# PART 2 | A MODEL FOR ROLE-CONFLICT RESOLUTION

Role-conflict theory provides a way of thinking about the predicament faced by the negotiators, but it does not prescribe methods for coping with role conflict. Sociologists and social psychologists have been interested in role conflict and in studying the various ways in which the role occupant copes with it. None of the ways in which these writers formulated the alternate coping responses proved to be suitable for role conflict in the context of labor negotiations, especially given the type of analysis required here. One study,[25] for example, which researched role conflict among industrial executives focused on coping responses but described responses primarily in psychological terms—rejection or withdrawal, tension, avoidance, hostility, apathy, and distortion. In contrast to this, we are interested in picking up behavior at a higher level of social analysis—interactions between the negotiator and the groups involved. Moreover, we are interested in spelling out the responses first in more rational and instrumental terms.

Another role-conflict study is relevant but still not quite comparable. Gross et al.,[26] in a study of school superintendents, abstracted responses to role conflict at a level comparable to our analysis. They found that superintendents made four alternate responses: (1) to step out of the role and in a sense pass the buck, (2) to sell both ways or negotiate with each side, (3) to take a middle position, not as a compromise, but as a result of an independent analysis, and (4) to take one side or the other, identifying completely with its position.

[25] D. M. Wolfe and J. D. Snoek, "A Study of Tensions and Adjustments under Role Conflict," *Journal of Social Issues,* vol. 18 (July, 1962), pp. 102–221.

[26] Neal Gross, W. S. Mason, and Alexander McEachern, *Explorations in Role Analysis: Studies of the School Superintendency Role* (New York: John Wiley & Sons, Inc., 1957).

Because of the way in which we have stated the problem, these are not particularly meaningful distinctions for our analysis. For example, we assume that the negotiator has explored all the possibilities for changing the expectations of the opponent, and we focus here on his mechanisms for dealing with only one source of pressure—his own organization. He must find some means by which he can eliminate the divergence in expectations between his own organization and himself. The task for the model is to identify meaningful alternate responses and to specify the factors which influence his selection of responses.

**Alternate Methods of Resolution.** At this point we need to conceive of alternate methods by which a negotiator can bring the expectations of his constituent group into alignment with his own. Instead of the opposing negotiator being the focus for his tactics, the principal group becomes the focus. Instead of taking the wishes of his organization as a given and seeking to change the position of his opponent, he takes the position of his opponent as a given and seeks to change the wishes of his organization. This is essentially what happens, but with one important consideration. The negotiator usually has to carry out the activities of internal bargaining while he appears to be doing the best possible job for his organization. For instance, he may need to give the appearance of engaging in unrestrained distributive bargaining with his opponent, while in fact he is seeking to modify the wishes of his own organization. To accomplish this internal change, he does not simply engage in distributive bargaining *with* his own organization, because he cannot overtly take a committed position vis-à-vis his organization in hopes of forcing it to change its aspiration. In getting his own organization to change position, he has to do it by different and often more subtle means.

Anticipating one subtle aspect of this process in bringing about an adjustment of the thinking of his organization, we can note that the negotiator may be able to utilize the active cooperation of his opponent. Naturally, Opponent has every reason to help Party deal with his constituent group, since any change in the thinking of the constituent group will be to the advantage of Opponent. Thus, we may have a situation in which, in effect, Party is sensitive to the expectations of Opponent while carrying through in some sense the expectations of his constituent group (or at least giving the impression that he is doing so).

To return to the task at hand, there are two basic ways in which the negotiator's problem can be solved. His problem is that there is a potential or existing gap between the expectations of his principals and his own projections about actual achievement. The problem is resolved if expectations are brought into alignment with achievement, either *before the fact* of settlement or *afterward,* or if *perceived* achievement is brought into alignment with expectations.

These constitute statements of what must be accomplished in order to eliminate the discrepancy. How does the negotiator accomplish these feats? What actions lead to these results? We shall attempt to construct Party's alternate courses of action in terms of how he responds to, first, the *behavioral* expectations of members of his organization, and, second, their *substantive* expectations (both of which we assume are in conflict with those of Opponent).

Logically, Party can respond to the behavioral expectations of his organization in one of three ways: he can *conform* to them, *ignore* but not challenge them, or *modify* them to bring them into alignment with those of his other role sender. He has the same choices with respect to the substantive expectations or aspirations of his organization. As we shall develop, the alternatives of whether to conform versus ignore versus modify expectations in the two areas are at least partly independent. He may, for example, conform to behavioral expectations but seek to modify substantive expectations. We hope to show that some of the nine possible combinations make interesting strategies which could be reasonably expected to be utilized under specified conditions (see Figure 8-2). Our approach is process of elimination.

### Figure 8-2

|  |  | Party's alternate responses *to* substantive expectations of own organization | | |
|---|---|---|---|---|
|  |  | Modify | Ignore | Conform |
| Party's alternate responses to *behavioral* expectations of own organization | Modify | * | * | *† |
|  | Ignore | Option 1 | Nothing to recommend it | † |
|  | Conform | Option 2 | Option 3 | † |

* Modifying the behavioral expectations of his own organization is not feasible in the short run.

† Conforming to the substantive expectations of his own organization fails to resolve the interorganizational conflict.

***Modifying behavioral expectations.*** First we consider all alternatives which involve Party's attempts at modification of the behavioral expectations of his organization. Behavioral expectations specify the mechanism by which the principal group seeks to reach its objectives. Since the principals cannot always be directly involved in the negotiations, they prescribe certain behavior for their agent, the negotiator, as a way of ensuring the achievement of their objectives.

In actual fact, the behavioral expectations of the primary group become so important that it is very difficult for a negotiator to manipulate them within the context of a given negotiation. This point about the difficulty of changing behavioral expectations of the primary group can be made in terms of the concepts introduced in Chapter VI. Typically the negotiator finds himself in the situation depicted in Figure 8-3.

**Figure 8-3**

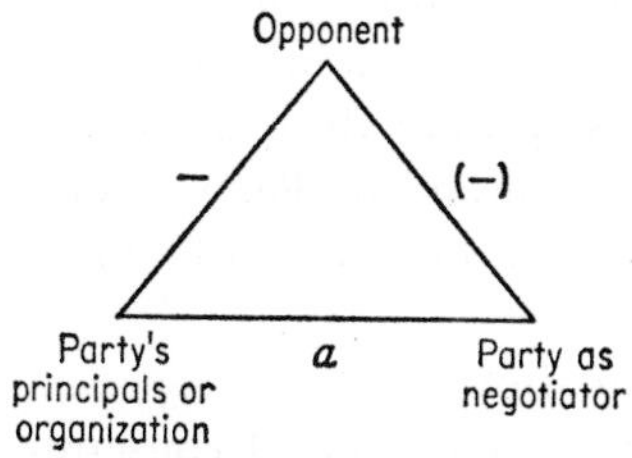

Opponent

$-$        $(-)$

Party's     $a$     Party as
principals or          negotiator
organization

The negative bond between Party's principals and Opponent indicates the former's feelings of dislike and distrust toward Opponent. The associative bond between the principal group and Party represents the primary role relationship. The negative bond in parentheses indicates the principals' expectations that Party will behave toward Opponent in an aggressive manner.

From the viewpoint of the principal group the triangular situation is in balance: it holds beliefs about the opponent and about the behavior of its own negotiator which are compatible. If the negotiator actually behaves in the expected way toward the opponent, aspects of the situation as viewed by Party's organization are in harmony.

Now let us assume that the negotiator desires to behave in a positive manner toward the opponent. If he attempts to do this without altering the attitudes of his organization, he takes certain risks. The principal group may dissociate the negotiator and itself or at least disapprove his actions; in short, the negotiator risks severe sanctions.

The ideal solution to this problem is for the negotiator to induce his organization to adopt positive attitudes toward the opponent. The dynamics of the change are those discussed in previous chapters on attitudinal structuring in which we examined how the linkage between the negotiators might be changed. Now we ask the question of whether the negotiators possess as much influence within their respective organizations. They do have the capacity to influence, but probably not as effectively during negotiations as during the period of contract administration. In fact, the negotiator is most vulnerable to censure by his principals if he attempts to alter their assumptions and attitudes about the opponent during negotiations. The principals expect him to represent their feelings vis-à-vis the opponent and not attempt to alter them. If he seeks to alter the feelings of the principal group about the opponent, then the group may maintain those negative feelings and match them with similar feelings directed toward the negotiator. Therefore, we conclude that a modification of the principals' basic behavioral expectations is impractical when the negotiator is confronted with important intraorganizational conflict. This eliminates certain theoretical options from our consideration. The only options for coping with internal conflict which are practical are those which take behavioral expectations of the organization as given and either conform to them or discreetly ignore them. (We cite an exception in the discussion of dilemmas.)

*Conforming to substantive expectations.* Options involving complete acceptance of the substantive expectations present one important draw-back—they fail to reach resolution of the *inter*organizational conflict. By definition of boundary conflict on substantive matters, acceptance of the organization's position will lead to a strike with Opponent. This is certainly an available alternative, although in effect it means abandoning the objective of achieving internal consensus on terms acceptable to the opponent. The choice of alternatives involving this option will be influenced by the cost of a strike to Party and his organization and by Party's assessment of the degree to which his organization's aspirations could be modified if he tried.

*The viable options.* Three of the four remaining options represent those which are both feasible and intended to reach internal consensus consistent with the limitations imposed by the opponent.

First, Party can attempt to modify his organization's aspirations and ignore at least some of the behavioral expectations. This approach involves directly confronting the divergent aspirations and seeking to change them. The negotiator attempts to bring the aspiration of the organization into line with the position of the opponent early in negotiations. In doing this, he can utilize arguments and pressures that work on perceptions of utility of the issues, feasibility of achieving them, or the potential strike costs associated with certain bargaining positions.

In seeking to directly change the aspiration of his own organization before the fact of achievement, he often must ignore the behavioral expectations of his own organization. His ignoring of these expectations may be discreet, but he disregards them nevertheless. The main factors influencing whether Party will choose this approach can again be stated in terms of opportunities and costs. If Party is in a good position to directly persuade his principals, he is more likely to prefer this approach. Moreover, if his principals are unlikely to notice or disapprove of his deviant behavior, this option is a more viable one.

Second, Party can attempt to modify his organization's substantive expectations but at the same time conform to behavioral expectations. This can be done by having the pressure to change the aspiration emanate from the environment and the bargaining process itself rather than from the negotiator. The techniques are fairly specific and must be available and effective in their impact.

Third, Party can in the final analysis ignore his organization's substantive expectations but comply with its behavioral expectations. This approach involves doing nothing about the divergent aspiration and letting the "situation take care of itself." The negotiator carries through on the behavior expected of him by his organization and allows the aspiration to remain unchallenged but in the final analysis acts on the basis of his own judgment. The hope is that the aspiration will change once achievement is a *fait accompli*. Of course, when agreement is reached, discontent may well develop.

Whereas in the first option the costs to the negotiator are those entailed in not fulfilling behavioral expectations, in the third option they are the costs entailed in not fulfilling aspirations on matters of substance. The negotiator needs to "get off the hook" for the less-than-expected achievement. There are several devices which he can exploit in his efforts to help the organization rationalize its sense of failure. One of these is what can be called "going through the motions." The very act of complying with behavioral expectations serves as a type of trade off, wherein the negotiator convinces the organization that it obtained all that was humanly possible.

There are also other ways in which the negotiator can help the principals reduce their displeasure about the gap between expectations and actual achievement. For example, he can influence the perception concerning the magnitude of the discrepancy by not communicating results or by misrepresenting the level of actual achievement.

Another cost inherent in the third option is that Party violates the behavioral expectations of Opponent when there is an understanding between the negotiators that they take responsibility for their respective organizations. By taking a passive role, Party runs the risk of angering Opponent. One way of dealing with this problem is through the mechanism of tacit communication. The function of tacit communication is to apprise Opponent that what appears like distributive bargaining behavior (and this is the impression that Party hopes his principals will gain) should be viewed by Opponent as a technique by Party for exhausting his organization and convincing it that it achieved the most that was attainable under the circumstances.

The fourth option, ignoring both aspirations and behavioral expectations, appears to be an empty cell. There is nothing to recommend it logically, nor does it appear to be one actually utilized by negotiators.

To summarize, in the first option, the focus is on directly changing aspiration. The second option also involves changing aspiration, but avoiding the risks caused by not fulfilling the behavioral expectations of the organization. In the third option, the behavioral expectations become the guidepost, and the negotiator uses them to first ignore substantive aspiration and then bring about a change in aspiration after the fact of achievement. In none of the cases does the negotiator attempt to change the behavioral expectations of his own organization. In none of these options does he, in the final analysis, accept the organization's aspirations on substantive issues as given.

**Factors Influencing Choice of Options.** Figure 8-4 sets forth a gross model of the types of variables we see operating in the internal conflict resolution process. The arrows indicate the ways in which we believe the several types of variables enter into the process.

### Figure 8-4
### Internal-conflict Resolution Process

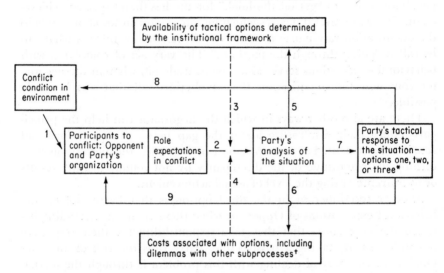

\* The tactical assignments which correspond to these three options are developed in the next chapter.

† Costs include institutional economic costs, organizational sanctions, Opponent's disapproval, and personal discomfort.

"Role expectations in conflict" is intended to correspond to an objective statement of the incompatibilities in the expectations bearing on Party. The next variable, "Party's analysis of the situation," refers to the rational analytic response by the negotiator. We see institutional factors influencing this response (arrows 3 and 4) through their affect on availability of options and risks or costs associated with each option. Arrows 5 and 6 indicate the adjustive or supplementary responses of Party to make options more available or less costly.

By the next type of variable, "Party's tactical response to the situation," we have in mind all of the adaptive responses the negotiator can make to resolve or cope with the conflict. The responses act back on the conflict-producing conditions (arrow 8) or on the role senders themselves (arrow 9): they either reduce expectations or enhance perceived achievement to eliminate the discrepancy.

In the next chapter, after we have specified the tactical operations involved, we shall return to our discussion of how particular tactical and strategic choices are influenced by specific cost and availability factors.

# CHAPTER IX

# INTRAORGANIZATIONAL
# BARGAINING TACTICS

The previous chapter discussed the problem which the negotiator often faces with respect to his own organization; namely, the principal group (or a portion of it) holds expectations which are not compatible with the negotiator's own projections about the outcome and judgments about the best way to bargain. How the negotiator copes with the resulting conflict was explained in terms of a general model. He makes strategic choices about whether to modify, ignore, or comply with the substantive and behavioral expectations of his principals. Three broad options are especially viable:

First, he may directly attempt to modify the aspirations of his principals, ignoring their behavioral expectations. Tactical assignments 1 and 2 listed below are central to this option. This option represents the most active strategy for achieving intraorganizational consensus.

Second, he may attempt to modify his principals' aspirations, but less directly and by managing to comply with their behavioral expectations. Tactical assignment 3 is essential to this option. This is a moderately active strategy.

Third, he may ignore, rather than change, his principals' aspirations, but meanwhile conscientiously comply with their behavioral expectations. Tactical assignments 4 and 5 implement this option. This is a passive strategy.

The actual strategy a negotiator uses for achieving intraorganizational consensus involves one or more of the six tactical assignments listed below. Most of our discussion will be stated in terms appropriate to the union side, primarily for convenience but also because of the greater importance of this activity on the union side.

1. The negotiator can avoid incompatible expectations from the beginning. That is, he can prevent the principals' expectations from becoming firm until after the opponent's position is apparent to him.

2. The negotiator can attempt to persuade the principals to revise their expectations after they have been developed.

3. The negotiator can structure or manipulate the bargaining situation in a way that the inducement to alter expectations arises out of the situation rather than from his own arguments or analysis.

4. The negotiator can rationalize the discrepancy. That is, he can acknowledge the discrepancy between expected and actual achievement by accurately revealing the lower level of achievement and attempting to modify the principals' expectations after the fact.

5. The negotiator can attempt to obscure or misrepresent the discrepancy by not accurately revealing the level of achievement. In other words, the negotiator would disguise or exaggerate the actual level of achievement in order to minimize the dissatisfaction experienced by the principal group.

6. A tactical assignment supplementary to some of those described above is tacit bargaining. The negotiator can engage in tacit bargaining as a way of explaining to his opponent that his behavior is not to be taken seriously.

The arrangement of the tactical assignments generally parallels the sequence through which bargaining naturally progresses. Considering the total time span available between prenegotiations and postsettlement, we shall be analyzing the steps available to the negotiator during different stages of negotiation. The first assignment, preventing incompatible expectations from crystallizing, normally takes place during the prenegotiation period. The second and third assignments, directly changing the aspiration of the organization, normally occur during the bargaining process itself. The steps of rationalizing and misrepresenting the discrepancy occur toward the final stages of bargaining and after the contract has been signed.

Each of the first five ways of coping with internal conflict is a tactical alternative independent of the others, independent in the sense that it may, but need not be, used by itself. After we have explored each of these approaches, we shall review them in terms of the extent to which each of them represents an active versus passive attack on the basic problem. Many specific institutional factors influence the choice of tactical methods, some being more appropriate to one situation than another. We shall discuss this matter after we more fully understand what is involved in each tactical assignment.

# PART 1 | TACTICS FOR ACHIEVING INTERNAL CONSENSUS

### Avoiding Incompatible Expectations from the Beginning

Even before proposals are exchanged and any negotiating meetings are held, Party has been analyzing the situation from the point of view of Opponent. However, during this same prebargaining period Party's principals are likely to be developing exaggerated notions about what they want and what is attainable.

Party, the chief negotiator, is aware of such differences, even before they develop, and is cognizant of the forces operating to create differences, even before they occur. And since he will regard his own expectations as more realistic than those of the principals, he will draw the obvious conclusion —that he must deal with this real or potential conflict sooner or later. The union negotiator may decide to avoid the conflict by deliberate effort to keep the expectations of the membership quite tentative or structure them in such a way that they are probably compatible with those of the management.

What tactics are used to avoid internal conflict from the outset? In the long run a large number of tactics are available to the negotiator. He can help into office those who will have a similar outlook, he can design the organization so that more information flows to the membership, and he can modify emotional influences which bring about differences in outlook —all these steps and more are available to the negotiator and are helpful in achieving an early consensus between the principals and the negotiator.

The negotiator can take other steps in a given negotiation to avoid the development of incompatible expectations. First, he can adopt an exploratory approach in order to keep preferences tentative. He can communicate information about the feasibility of obtaining any given objective. Merely emphasizing the exploratory approach and conveying information about feasibility may not produce a realistic agenda. If so, the negotiator may act to limit the participation of active and outspoken individuals.

**Adopting an Exploratory Approach.** The chapter on integrative bargaining outlined many of the tactics that can be used to develop tentativeness rather than commitment. Many of these tactics are also appropriate here. The expectations of the primary group are kept both vague and conservative in order not to conflict with the demands of the opponent. In general, the negotiator provides himself as much flexibility as possible.

In passing, it should be noted that management shares the desire to avoid commitment on the part of the union membership. Obviously, there are many things that it can do to prevent the membership from adopting a committed position. The chapter on distributive bargaining tactics outlined the steps that can be taken to prevent the opponent or his organization from taking a committed position. Again many of these tactics are also appropriate here.

By way of contrast, in the following case the actions of the opponent negotiator were not coordinated toward helping the first negotiator maintain an exploratory approach on the part of his organization:

> After the long newspaper strike in New York City ended, a leader of local 6 of the ITU complained that the employers, by focusing attention on the wage demand of $38, had got the membership so aroused to the achievement of a $38 package that he found his hands tied. By their very action the employers had made it difficult for him to move his organization away from its stated bargaining position.

**Conveying Early Information about Feasibility.** The negotiator is in a better position to judge the feasibility of each issue, and consequently he can direct attention toward those issues which are more likely to be achieved. The negotiator can direct attention toward those issues which will mean a lot to his organization but which will probably not cost the other party very much.

In communicating information about feasibility, the negotiator may be direct and take a stand on feasibility of the issue when it is first urged upon the negotiator. The following is an example of modest success in this endeavor:

> A union over the objection of its business agent voted to demand a three dollar wage increase of an employer. The business agent then refused to negotiate on this basis. He told the rank and file that the representatives of the employer would consider him guilty of irresponsibility were he to make such a demand. That it "would have impaired the satisfactory working relationships with the employers' association which had been built up over a period of years. Moreover, there was always a possibility of arbitration. The three dollar demand would have seemed unreasonable to an arbitrator and would have reduced the value of the union's arguments." After consideration of the business agent's position, the union voted to reduce its demands to an increase of two dollars.[1]

---

[1] A. T. Jacobs, "Some Significant Factors Influencing the Range of Indeterminateness in Collective Bargaining Negotiations," unpublished Ph.D. thesis, Ann Arbor, Mich., University of Michigan, 1951.

Another illustration provides further insight into how a negotiator can prevent an idea from crystallizing into a demand. He merely asked suggestive questions.

A union negotiator from the ILGWU related his experiences in dealing with an adamant membership and bargaining committee. During the session devoted to developing the bargaining agenda he adopted the posture of asking questions: "Why do you want an increase in the death benefit when you turned down the union's plan? Should we place small items on the agenda and confuse the company about what we really want? Will the company be able to afford a longer sick leave program for the women employees?"

The 1958 automobile negotiations provide a good illustration of how Reuther gained flexibility by substituting one objective for another.

During 1956 and 1957 Reuther had established the shorter work week objective as his number one bargaining item for the 1958 negotiations. But as the time to enter negotiations arrived, he realized the inappropriateness of this objective: the space race with the Russians had just got under way, the 1958 recession made it difficult to strike, and he knew that such an important demand might not be obtained without a strike. Consequently, he sought to divert the attention of the membership to an issue which he knew he could not get but for which the membership would not automatically strike. He substituted the profit-sharing idea.

**Limiting Participation in Formulating Proposals.** The negotiator may define a limited role for other members of the organization in the formulating of negotiating proposals and objectives. One possible tactic for the negotiating committee is to take the initiative in the crystallizing of the bargaining agenda. Garfield and Whyte believe it "inadvisable to have the actual formulation of contract demands come out in the membership meeting, because there people are likely to be overenthusiastic and commit the union to things that are totally unobtainable." [2]

Consider the practice in the steel industry:

The Wage Policy Committee's first job is to issue a written set of instructions to the union's negotiators. These instructions reflect the substance of hundreds of local union resolutions. The latter, as we know, are not considered individually by the policy committee; instead, they reach the committee in distilled form and frequently with some additions which have been injected in the course of a one-

[2] Sidney Garfield and W. F. Whyte, "The Collective Bargaining Process: A Human Relations Analysis," *Human Organization*, vol. 9 (Summer, 1950), p. 7.

stage or two-stage process of condensation. Some of the resolutions are submitted by the locals to their annual district conferences, which then in effect replace them with a smaller number of their own more comprehensive resolutions. The resolutions adopted by the district conferences are then forwarded to International headquarters at Pittsburgh where, together with the wage policy resolutions submitted by the locals to the constitutional convention, they are analyzed, classified, and screened by such staff departments as research, wage inequities, insurance, pensions and unemployment benefits, salaries, office and technical, international affairs, and others. Then the International officers and key staff members, for example, the research director and chief counsel, draft a lengthy document for consideration by the policy committee. Thus the committee acts on the basis of a paper that has been drawn up in advance by the International's technical staff. The latter, of course, pay close attention to the resolutions submitted by district conferences and local unions, but they are not bound by these resolutions, nor are they prevented from introducing suggestions of their own.

As a result of the discussion in the policy committee, the draft paper may be reworked in the sense that its emphasis might be altered or additional demands inserted. But the policy committee never imposes its will upon the International executive.[3]

Note what happened in one situation in which a company negotiator did not exercise caution in the way in which he consulted his management organization about negotiating proposals.

During the 1958 negotiations in the farm-equipment industry, one company negotiator solicited other management personnel for their suggestions. As a result, he received a strong demand that the company obtain superseniority for all its foremen. The proponents thought that they had a moral obligation to protect the job security of a person who had joined the foreman ranks, should it become necessary because of a falloff in business to return these individuals to the bargaining unit. The issue was seized upon by the union and made the subject of their resistance—they characterized the claim as giving the company "the right to take away your job." The company negotiator found himself between these two adamant positions. He was frank to say that he would never ask for recommendations from management again.

Sometimes the limited-role idea applies even within the negotiating committee itself. In a recent negotiation the union leader took the initia-

---

[3] Lloyd Ulman, *The Government of the Steel Worker's Union* (New York: John Wiley & Sons, Inc., 1962), pp. 62–63.

tive for making several important decisions, thereby shaping the outlook of the organization in a more realistic direction.

> During the prenegotiation period, the union leader gained acceptance of the idea that the key objective of the union should be progress toward a master book in the classification area. By emphasizing the concept of progress toward the uniform book, he focused attention away from inequities per se. Previously, the locals had submitted hundreds of inequities claims, and they had fought hard to have each one granted by the company. The union leader realized that such an approach would only provoke a deadlock and possibly a strike.

> The union leader took the initiative and drew up the initial list of classification inequities, a list which was considerably smaller than that presented in previous negotiations.

In the situation just cited, many delegates were happy to have been pushed aside. They avoided having to make a decision on bargaining objectives. Although they knew that the expectations of the rank and file were exaggerated, if they had been put on the spot, they would have had to press for the rank-and-file demands. Publicly, they complained about the modest size and limited nature of the union's demands, but privately, they were aware that the best course of action had been followed.

**Countertactics.** The above tactics represent ways in which negotiators attempt to gain flexibility for themselves in order to facilitate their dual task of achieving intraorganizational and interorganizational consensus. The tactics are used by both union and management negotiators. Principal groups within their respective organizations often take steps to counteract these tactics—to limit the flexibility of the chief negotiators and to encourage them to place maximum pressure on the opponent.

One such countertactic is for top management to withhold information from their chief negotiator. In a negotiation observed by one of the authors, top management kept its chief negotiator in the dark about the resistance point in order to offset any tendency the chief negotiator might have had in being too "soft" with the union. The fear existed that the company negotiator, who had to live with the union over the long run, might lean too much in the union's direction.

The following example demonstrates that this tactic can also be used by peer groups, particularly staff groups.

> The issue under discussion involved the use of written tests in the selection of clerical personnel. During the negotiations the union had taken a strong stand against these tests. The company negotiator defended the tests. Most of the arguments that he used had been

funneled to him by the personnel people who had been responsible for developing and administering the test program. The issue remained unresolved and went down to the strike deadline as a key item on the agenda.

During the final hours, the personnel group came up with a suggestion, namely, to include seniority by adding a number of points to the test score on the basis of a person's service. The idea was immediately accepted by the union as a way of marrying the interests of ability with seniority. After the agreement, the chief negotiator complained about "being kept in the dark by these personnel fellows —they had this idea up their sleeves all the time—my job would have been a lot easier if they had told me about the idea earlier in the negotiation."

## Revising Expectations through Logic and Power

For reasons discussed earlier, the principals often develop aspirations divergent from those of the negotiator. Sometimes these differences develop despite his efforts to avoid them. Then too, he may deliberately allow them to develop as a part of his commitment strategy in distributive bargaining with the other party. This is especially likely for the union, which can have its strength more easily monitored by the other party. If the union wants to convey commitment, it is almost necessary to have had this commitment already reflected in the behavior of the members.

For whatever reasons these incompatibilities develop, the negotiator must turn to resolving them at some point. In order to persuade his principals to reduce their expectation, he can advance rational arguments, rely upon personal prestige, or invoke organizational power.

**Invoking Rational Arguments.** The chief negotiator often revises internal aspirations through the use of rational criteria. He attempts to discuss issues on their merits or to cast new light on the question of feasibility. The position of the chief negotiator usually allows him to be persuasive. He has the advantage of specific information and general expertise, especially on matters such as seniority and welfare arrangements, in which the programs are rather complicated.

The rational criteria may come from traditional job evaluation and work-measurement techniques. When agreement exists about the principles to be used in the area of wage administration, it is possible for each negotiator to judge the appropriateness of a given demand in the light of the accepted guidelines.

In one situation the principles of job evaluation were helpful to the union negotiator in bringing about a modification of internal demands. By viewing each inequity claim against a structure that was best for the total organization, he was able to secure a substantial reduction in the number of requests.

Another argument, related to the feasibility of achieving a certain objective, involves an analysis of patterns. Settlements during previous negotiations; settlements in other negotiations during the current year; or limits imposed by government, such as wage stabilization, can provide the negotiator with ammunition for dealing with his organization.

> The union negotiator used a 10 per cent limit imposed by the government to counter a question from the membership meeting, "Since when does the company give everything on the first round?" By indicating that the company's offer was at the 10 per cent level, the union negotiator could persuade the rank and file that they should accept the agreement.[4]

It should be unnecessary to detail completely the rational arguments used by a negotiator to convince his principals that they need to reassess the value of a proposal or the feasibility of obtaining it. In fact, what he presents to his principals is often precisely what the other party has already confronted him with. The following two examples illustrate how these arguments are used internally:

> At the conclusion of a negotiation in a small electronics firm, the company negotiator commented to an outsider, "I am certainly glad we had you prepare that wage survey. The union made more use of it in slowing down their boys than we did in defending our position."

> In another negotiation, the union leader had worked himself into the untenable position of demanding 4 weeks vacation after 20 years. Only when the company was able to demonstrate that no firm in either the immediate area or the given industry had granted the arrangement, was the union negotiator able to convince his organization that the demand should be dropped.

An exchange excerpted from the Jimson negotiations furnishes an example of the company providing the union with a rationale for revising its expectations.

> *Watoski (U)* I've been averaging a package of 10 cents per hour in my other negotiations with the smaller companies.

> *Scott (M)* You haven't been dealing with the other companies as long as with us. You've already gotten most of the 10 cents in the

---

[4] A. R. Weber, *Union Decision-making in Collective Bargaining* (Urbana, Ill.: Institute of Labor and Industrial Relations, University of Illinois, 1951).

past from Jimson. It's also hard to compare figures between companies; not all figures are accurate.

*Watoski (U)* Well, that is true. Not all companies are honest about reporting their costs.

Scott offered Watoski a convenient way to rationalize the fact that he was not obtaining as large a package from Jimson as he was from the other companies with which he had negotiated when he noted the inaccuracy of settlement figures. Watoski did not refuse this explanation. Apparently this exchange was primarily for the consumption of the union committee, because there was other evidence that the union negotiator himself had more realistic expectations.

The illustrations above focus on the union negotiator. The company negotiator makes equally as much use of arguments internally. It is usually difficult for top management to appraise the union's position merely in terms of the intrinsic quality of the demands. Some referent is needed. Settlements in comparable industries can provide this measure. Top management's main concern is staying competitive in the industry. Therefore, as long as the company negotiator can demonstrate that a union's request is not above competition, he usually enjoys additional bargaining freedom.

**Invoking Personal or Political Power.** The negotiator who must influence his organization's position may depend more upon his personal prestige and power than upon the inherent logic of his arguments. This is especially effective in the judgment of feasibility but also applies to questions of value about certain demands.

> In attending several conferences held by the UAW in preparing for the 1958 automobile negotiations, the authors heard many expressions of doubt about the profit-sharing plan but considerable confidence about the leadership of Walter Reuther. In effect, many of the delegates expressed the feelings, "I don't understand or agree with this profit-sharing idea, but if the Red Head wants it, I will go along."

Usually the negotiator has to find informal means for invoking his personal prestige. It is dangerous to lay his authority on the line. As the following sample illustrates, there are other ways of bringing about influence:

> During the recess, members of the executive board unostentatiously circulated among the members and suggested in private conversations that it was unlikely that a better contract could be obtained. The business agent pointed out during the interview that while this was a fairly safe procedure, it would have been foolhardy from a

political point of view for the executive board formally to have urged the acceptance of the offer.[5]

If arguments are not handy, or effective, the negotiator may use another form of influence. The negotiator can promise to dispense rewards, threaten to withhold favors, or otherwise bring political or organizational pressure to bear on dissenting groups.

> Hill used his political power by indicating to the bargaining committee that he intended to push for their reelection if they would support his program. The trade was not made explicitly, but it was clear to all concerned that political power was being used. At another point, Hill suggested to one of the delegates that his constituent group was overpaid. After this suggestion, the delegate was quite happy to drop the demand for additional relief for his group.[6]

In general, the union negotiator is in a good position to trade such items as advice on technical aspects of the labor agreement, preparation of news releases, help in the processing of grievances, etc. in an effort to bring a recalcitrant member into line.

Before a negotiator can invoke personal prestige, he needs to gain that prestige. Since a negotiator's credibility with his own organization is such an important part of his effectiveness in intraorganizational bargaining, he may utilize the bargaining situation to enhance that credibility. For instance, in Jimson negotiations, each of the two negotiators usually gave the other in private some advance warning about the position they would take in the next negotiating session. Members of the management committee were visibly impressed by their spokesman's ability to predict the union's next move. He used the tips from his counterpart to increase his own influence internally within the company.

Whyte's study of Inland Steel Container provides another pertinent illustration:

> Now here was a point that was of only minor importance to management. Nevertheless, the effect upon the union was highly important. Up until now, the committee members were just hoping for the best but were not at all confident that Shafer would be able to meet management on even terms. Shafer had to prove himself to his own group. When that was accomplished, he gained much greater

---

[5] H. S. Parnes, *Union Strike Votes: Current Practice and Proposed Controls* (Princeton, N.J.: Industrial Relations Section, Department of Economics and Sociology, Princeton University, 1956), p. 64.

[6] Paraphrased from Weber, *op. cit.*

security in his dealings with management and increased his influence with the union committee.[7]

In the above example, management's concession on a particular issue
helped enhance the internal status or credibility of the union negotiator,
which in turn aided him in restructuring the expectations of his own organization. In other instances management has given the union negotiator
an inequity fund to be distributed to various groups by the union negotiating team, presumably in a way which plays a key role in achieving
internal consensus. A similar tactic is often used in master contract negotiations in which the parties consider some of the unresolved grievances
at the various plants. The settlements of these grievances are often acts
of selected leniency consistent with the need of the chief union negotiator
to gain the support of the various committee members. It is a mild form
of payoff in advance.

We could extend the number of examples by restating the material presented in the chapter on attitudinal structuring. All the devices that give
status and stature to the opponent help the opponent evolve the kind of
personal prestige that can be used to reckon with his own group—all
these are important in revising internal expectations.

### Revising Expectations through Experience

The purpose of the tactics discussed in this section is the same as the
purpose of those of the preceding section, namely, to revise the principals'
expectations during negotiations. However, instead of taking responsibility for directly persuading the principals to reduce their expectations,
Party structures the situation so that they (or their more immediate representatives) will persuade themselves. These tactical steps cause more members of the organization to actually experience the essence of the situation.
The negotiator finds ways to get them to revise their utility and feasibility
estimates without being too actively involved himself.

There are at least two reasons why Party employs these tactics instead
of his own persuasion efforts or as a supplement to them. The first is simply that Party might not be persuasive enough—his logic and his power
might not do the job. The second is that direct persuasive attempts involve risks. In particular, as the negotiator attempts to gain a more realistic
outlook on the part of his principals, he runs the risk of betraying their
expectations about behavior. Therefore, in this section we shall be especially interested in how he can minimize this risk.

**Directly Confronting Principals with Reality.** Sometimes it is possible

---

[7] W. F. Whyte, *Pattern for Industrial Peace* (New York: Harper & Row, Publishers,
Incorporated, 1951), p. 83.

to bring the principal group into a more direct confrontation with the realities of the situation.[8]

One form of this approach is to tell the delegate to go it alone. Rather than rebuff the demands of the delegate, the chief negotiator permits the delegate to deal directly with the company. The delegate himself encounters the resistance of the company. The negotiator may avoid violating behavioral expectations if he suggests: "I think these demands are so important that you should present them to the company."

He has not rejected the demands of the delegate, which would constitute a direct default on the behavioral expectations that he fight aggressively for all demands. Moreover, by not personally presenting the demands to the company, he may dissociate himself from a demand which management would view as irresponsible. However, this tactic does not in every case comply with the behavioral expectation of both parties. It is quite possible that the principals expect the negotiator to "carry the ball" personally and not dodge his responsibility to fight for all interests. Similarly, the company negotiator may be annoyed to have individual delegates "unleashed" against him and may view the permission of such action by the union negotiator as a violation of their relationship.

Usually the negotiator cannot step aside and let the constituents deal directly with the opponent on their own. He discovers other ways of bringing the adamant members of his organization into contact with the bargaining situation.

> During the negotiations over a master contract for a large multiplant firm, one of the delegates who was having difficulty gaining acceptance for his local's needs decided to call to town several representatives from his local. By bringing them into the negotiations and having them confront other delegates, he achieved two results: the local representatives softened their position when they realized how difficult it would be to achieve all their demands, and the other delegates agreed to give more consideration to the needs of this particular local.

Peters provides us with an excellent illustration from his experience as a mediator. An experienced union negotiator is talking:

> "I'll tell you about one instance, just to show you: I went through a real tough negotiation—how we made it, I don't know. So, finally, we brought back a package I didn't hesitate to recommend. Sure, we

<hr>

[8] R. R. Blake and J. S. Morton, "The Intergroup Dynamics of Win-Lose Conflict and Problem-solving Collaboration in Union-Management Relations," in Muzafer Sherif (ed.), *Intergroup Relations and Leadership* (New York: John Wiley & Sons, Inc., 1962), pp. 117–118.

gave up a lot of our demands—but we made some real gains, too—that's bargaining, and I was satisfied. So, some guys with more mouth than brains—nobody's kidding me, they were put up to it—raised the roof about the things we conceded, and got the membership so stirred up that in spite of my recommendations the package was rejected.

"Do you think I folded? Not me. I just asked the membership to put the two super dupers on the committee, so they could try their luck."

He chuckled: "Yup, I just leaned back and let them go under the gun for a change. Hah! It was something to watch. When the management sailed into them at the next session, they found out: Speeches in union hall are one thing: being on the firing line is something else. They had it! And from then on I had no more trouble from that bunch—not since then."

I asked him, "Did the rejection of your recommendation by the membership damage your effectiveness with the management?"

"Not a bit—not after the way I handled it. In fact, I came through with the membership and management." [9]

Bringing the organization face to face with a strike decision is another procedural maneuver.

When the local negotiating committee in management finally reached an impasse, the international representative came in for these meetings. Each time he argued the union's case vigorously—with no real hope of success.

Finally, in his third meeting, the international representative called a recess and announced to his committee: "Look, I'm tired. I don't think we can get any further. The company refuses to budge. I think you ought to go back and recommend a strike to the people. Let's break off negotiations, call a special meeting, and call for a strike. I will clear it with the international union. You already have strike sanction. I say it's OK—go ahead, call a strike." The committee members argued back: "No, no, let's not break off negotiations . . . let's keep it going. We don't want to take a strike vote . . . let's keep talking." . . . The local people still wanted to keep the negotiations going and kept arguing until the international representative came forth with a new proposal: "I would suggest that we go back and negotiate now and say that we will accept the same contract, but with a thirty day wage opener. And I am willing to go to the membership and sell that." The local officers accepted this proposal immediately.[10]

[9] Edward Peters, *Strategy and Tactics in Labor Negotiations* (New London, Conn.: National Foremen's Institute, 1955), p. 189.

[10] Garfield and Whyte, *op. cit.*, vol. 9 (Fall, 1950), p. 11.

In certain instances, the union negotiator may allow the rank and file to vote on a strike authorization, even though he knows that the international union would not allow a strike. He wants the local to think seriously about the strike. In so doing, it may weigh more realistically the value of its demands vis-à-vis the cost of striking for them. One negotiator of a multiplant system has called this a process of education—educating a delegate who has the limited perspective of one local about the costs involved in obtaining his demands.

The effect of structuring the situation may go beyond that of bringing the principal group face to face with the realities of the main table. Recalcitrant individuals may be caused to experience considerable personal cost if they continue to hold on to their demands.

Consider some interesting examples of this tactic:

> In one negotiation, bargaining sessions were purposely stretched out over a long time period. The delegates had been assembled from various parts of the country. As the negotiations dragged on, they became anxious to return home. They began to drop their demands, not because they responded to the persuasion of the chief negotiators, but because the act of continuing to press their local demands carried with it some personal cost. These costs took the form of lack of sleep, lack of food, and just boredom.

The marathon talks discussed in the section on distributive tactics are also a device for internal bargaining. This is reflected in Peters's description at the conclusion of one such session. The respective committees had put in an exhausting night climaxed by off-the-record discussion between the two chief negotiators.

> Taylor and Hite closeted themselves . . . for about an hour and a half. Upon emerging, they looked the freshest of the negotiators, some of whom had been dozing in their chairs, while others had been engaging in occasional listless conversations. Neither Hite nor Taylor had any difficulty in obtaining from their weary committees approval of the tentative understanding on wages that had been worked out in their private discussions. . . .
>
> It was a pleasure to abandon the disordered conference room, where even the furniture seemed to reek of stale tobacco, and to inhale the cool night air outside. . . .[11]

Consider another illustration from Ulman's research on the Steelworkers' Union. The example refers to a meeting of the wage-policy committee

[11] Peters, *op. cit.*, pp. 18–19.

within the United Steelworkers, drawing up the demands for a forth-coming negotiation.

> A story is told about a sizable group of committeemen who on one occasion were determined to pass a resolution over President Murray's opposition. This attempt was spoiled by a judicious use of executive filibuster, as a result of which the luncheon recess was delayed until the opposition, exhausted by hunger and talk, capitulated late in the afternoon.[12]

**Ensuring Cooperation of Opponent.** The above tactics bring those who need to be persuaded closer to the reality of the situation. However, the negotiator needs to ensure that these persons are going to learn the right lesson—get the correct picture of the feasibility of certain targets. This often requires the tacit cooperation of the opponent negotiator. By maintaining a firm position for a considerable period of time, Opponent may be able to help Party get the idea across to his organization that their target is unrealistic. In effect, Opponent maintains a firm position and says tacitly to Party, "Look, I'm maintaining a firm position for the present time so that you can use it internally as a basis against which you can modify your own position. At some later point, I'll move my explicit position in the direction of the settlement."

If the opponent abandons his initial position too early, it may give people within the first party's organization false hope. While Party may publicly attack the rigidity of Opponent's position, privately he may be pleased, since it enables him to bring about an adjustment in his own organization's position. An illustrative statement to this effect was made by a business agent: "If we didn't have effective opposition [from the employer], the membership would drive me to the wall with unreasonable demands." [13] The dynamics involved are reported in the following discussion:

> Some companies will come in and let's say they are going to use 6 cents and they know that's their maximum. They will start off with 2 and jump to 3. That's wrong. . . . They are making it difficult for the union. Now, the union wants to come down. I know that. But if you made it easy for him (by moving too quickly to the 6 cents), he'd have to stay up. You are making him come down, and he wants you to do that because he's already said to me that he has to come down.[14]

[12] Ulman, *op. cit.*, p. 63.

[13] Jack Barbash, *Labor's Grass Roots: A Study of the Local Union* (New York: Harper & Row, Publishers, Incorporated, 1961), p. 79.

[14] Ann Douglas, *Industrial Peacemaking* (New York: Columbia University Press, 1962), p. 492.

The matter of Opponent maintaining a firm position until the proper moment and then moving in the direction of the settlement point is not easily executed. Once Party reaches a tacit understanding with Opponent about the settlement point and structures the expectation of his own bargaining team accordingly, he can be as embarrassed by a higher settlement as by a lower one.

> A negotiator experienced in bargaining confided to one of the authors the following incident: He had made a deal with a union negotiator to settle at a certain point. The union negotiator opened up after the recess and blasted away at the company. In order not to seem negative, the company negotiator asked these questions: "Is this what you mean by your demands, well let me see if I can restate what you want, etc." As the company negotiator proceeded to do this, the union negotiator was visibly shaken. After the contract had been signed at the agreed point, he came to the company negotiator and said, "You scared me; I thought you were going to give us more than we had originally agreed upon."

There could be several reasons why this negotiator was "scared" that he might get more than he planned for. For instance, he might have feared contributing to unrealistic aspirations of this membership in the future. Moreover, there is the difficulty of extending overly generous settlements to other companies. However, the consideration most pertinent here is that it would reduce his prestige internally. Since the union had obtained more in this case than he had said was possible, that would reduce the credibility of his feasibility estimates in the future.

### Rationalizing the Discrepancy

Let us assume that the discrepancy persists and that the negotiator must anticipate the dissatisfaction, discontent, or feelings of failure that accompany less than expected achievement. At the very least, in his own interest he must lessen the propensity of the principals to sanction him.

The objective of this tactical assignment is to encourage an after-the-fact reduction in expectations. The principals are induced to acknowledge to themselves, "Well, maybe this is all we should have expected under the circumstances." The tactical assignment shifts the blame away from such targets as negotiating skill and/or earnestness of the leadership and places the blame, if any, on circumstances beyond their control, such as the inherent power realities, superordinate and controlling policies, or the failures of the membership themselves.

**Complying with Behavioral Expectations: At the Bargaining Table.** What the negotiator could not persuade his principals to accept before the fact of achievement he may be able to get them to acknowledge after the fact, particularly if they are convinced that he did all he could. Recall that the principals not only have opinions about what the outcome ought to be but also about how the objectives ought to be pursued. If the principals believe that the negotiator, in his strategies and tactics, conformed to their behavioral expectations and pursued their preferred objectives, the disappointment with the actual outcome may be somewhat diminished —at least it is deflected away from the negotiator. The principals may even accept more responsibility themselves for the outcome.

"Going through the motions" may have an additional function in reducing the discrepancy between expectation and achievement to the extent that emotional forces of resentment or hostility underlaid the original demands made of the other party. Evidence that the other party has been given a hard time may make the unfulfilled demands themselves less important.

In some instances, going through the motions is nothing more than stalling until the pressure subsides. "If the cross-pressures are of a temporary nature, it may be possible for the individual to postpone making a decision until one or both the groups relax their demands . . . it involves placating and promising while competing obligations are not being fulfilled." [15]

For the union negotiator going through the motions may involve arguing vociferously and at length about a given proposal, or it may mean merely keeping it on the agenda for a certain length of time. It may require pressing for a certain minimum package, or it may necessitate telling off the bosses. Usually these tactics are observed by the bargaining committee, which is sometimes enlarged strictly for this purpose.

In the extreme, fulfilling behavioral expectations may involve taking negotiations "down to the wire." By bargaining hard and aggressively and giving the company no quarter, the union negotiator can convince the rank and file that they got all that was in the offing. Often the moderates within an organization cannot exercise influence unless the agitators are calmed by having the bargaining reach a dramatic climax. Peters cites a case in which the union negotiator was able to keep control of the situation by carrying through on the assumptions of the activists.[16]

An interesting instance of going through the motions occurred in the Jimson negotiations.

> The company had persisted for some time in its refusal to supply information on insurance costs, and the union committee had evidenced increasing frustration. The union spokesman interrupted the session to instruct one of his committee members to phone the lawyer

[15] Jackson Toby, "Some Variables in Role Conflict Analysis," *Social Forces*, vol. 30 (March, 1952), p. 327.
[16] Peters, *op. cit.*, p. 135.

and ask him to file an unfair labor practice charge against the company for its stand on this issue. The committeemen left and later returned. During the next caucus members of the management team all agreed that his threat to file an UFLP actually had not been fulfilled and was not sincere. It turned out their reading was correct.

Viewed in the context of the total negotiation, it would appear that the union negotiator had staged this incident primarily for the benefit of the union committee, who expected management to be convinced of its authenticity. For his own part, the union spokesman probably wanted the acting to be sufficiently transparent that the company would not mistake it for a real threat that he might need to make on another occasion but not so superficial that it would lose its expressive value for the union committee itself. The union negotiator reported privately that he had become angry in another meeting during those negotiations, in part for the benefit of his own committee.[17]

**Complying with Behavioral Expectations: Other Circumstances.** Carrying out of behavioral expectations needs to be done at the main bargaining table; however, some way needs to be found to acquaint the various levels of the union with this fact. There are people lower in the organization, namely, the rank and file, who need to be convinced that the union negotiator and the union negotiating committee have done all that they could. The following episode illustrates one way of achieving this result through a report to a membership meeting:

> We sold a contract that the membership of this local did not want by telling the members how I—an outsider representing them—"told off" the vice president of the company during negotiations. . . . My highly dramatic description of how I rubbed these executives' noses in the dirt gave the membership the vicarious thrill of talking back to management, something all of them had wanted but none dared to do. . . . So pleased were they that, without any discussion, they unanimously voted acceptance of the contract.[18]

Garfield and Whyte report a case in which there was considerable discontent among the workers and hostility toward management generated by a methods engineering program in the plant. The membership had rejected an economic settlement which the union committee regarded as adequate, even generous. The chief negotiator, Shaw, realized that while

---

[17] These observations raise serious questions about the validity of the findings of content analysis of statements between parties, unless one discounts for hostile statements motivated by internal considerations. See, for example, M. G. Zaninovich, "Pattern Analysis of Variables within the International System: The Sino-Soviet Example," *Journal of Conflict Resolution*, vol. 6 (September, 1962), pp. 253–268.

[18] Jacobs, *op. cit.*, p. 270.

the committee members had worked out some of their hostility toward management during the face-to-face encounters of negotiations, this did not extend to the rest of the members who must now ratify the agreement. Shaw's tactic for overcoming this emotional source of resistance was to allow the members to share vicariously the experiences of the committee during the negotiations.

> Shaw began by describing the lecture he had given the management people on the engineering and methods changes. Not only did he repeat what he had said to management, but he described which management people had been present, how they had looked and how they had reacted. He was particularly careful to describe the vice president who had become so upset. As he told his story, he found the crowd coming with him. They tittered and laughed at certain spots, and he could hear them saying, "That's telling them," or "That's what I tried to tell them, but they wouldn't listen!" and similar remarks that indicated that he was really expressing what they felt.[19]

Convincing the membership that the union negotiator has "given it his best" is often aided by the physical condition with which the union negotiator greets the membership. Often, he has bargained into the late hours, and as he appears at the membership meeting, he obviously gives the impression of one who has tried his "darndest."

Sometimes going through the motions may involve taking a strike. After a strike has been under way for several weeks, people may be more willing to revise their expectations because they feel they have "given it a good try." But this is extremely risky, because as we have noted previously, strike action is likely to result in more, not less, commitment to the issues in dispute.

During the 1949 negotiations with the Ford Motor Company, Reuther was under considerable pressure from the membership for favorable action on a production standards issue. Rather than directly repulsing the membership, he allowed strike action to occur, and then he moved to modify expectations. This pattern was repeated during the 1961 automobile negotiations. After signing the master agreement with General Motors, the local sought relief on many of their individual problems. Reuther let the locals go out on strike. Through skillful timing, after the strike had been under way for several days, he was able to induce the locals to scale down their demands.

The negotiator who must terminate the strike that has been started for purposes of carrying out behavioral expectations often ends it with a battle cry.

[19] Garfield and Whyte, *op. cit.*, vol. 9 (Winter, 1950), p. 27.

He makes a flaming speech on the fighting traditions of organized labor—tries to inspire them. Then he says, "The conditions are no longer favorable to carry on the strike. We shall continue the fight for right and justice, but through other means. We will end the strike, and carry the fight to the labor board. We demand that the labor board put a stop to this brazen flouting of the law of the land —that it order the company to bargain with its employees in good faith. We will go on fighting, etc., etc." [20]

**Shifting the Blame.** The negotiator can explain and justify a disappointing outcome in terms of higher authority, policies, or rules. He attempts to convey the idea that the organization achieved what was inherent in the situation and that he personally could not have improved on the result.

Sometimes the negotiator cites a policy of the organization as the reason behind particular settlement terms. The rank and file may be unhappy with a particular contract, but the negotiator can say, "It follows the policy of the international and is in the best interest of the organization." Sometimes a mediator provides the function of a scapegoat—he can be blamed for a party's failure to achieve all its objectives. Vice President Nixon served such a function for the steel firms when they acted to end the 1959–1960 steel strike by abandoning their work-rule demands.

Finally, the principals themselves may be assigned responsibility for a disappointing settlement.

Every single person in this hall and every single person within management knew, number one, that you weren't going to strike, that you didn't want to strike, and number two, that you felt you would be lucky to get the same contract. Whenever you talked about the negotiations, inside the plant or outside, you blabbed, every one of you. You said: "We'll be lucky if we get the same damn contract." The management knew it. You gave guns to your committee, and then you forgot to give them the ammunition.

You were fighting a losing battle from the beginning, but you do have a 30-day wage opener. I don't know if it's going to do you any good, but if conditions change, and you fellows really mean business, then you have a chance to redeem yourselves. You can't blame anybody but yourselves for what has happened. . . .[21]

### Obscuring and Misrepresenting the Discrepancy

Another approach is for the negotiator to modify the principals' perceptions of achievement—he attempts to exaggerate, disguise, or create ambiguity about the actual level of achievement in order to minimize the

---

[20] Peters, *op. cit.*, p. 58.
[21] Garfield and Whyte, *op. cit.*, vol. 9 (Fall, 1950), p. 11.

dissatisfaction experienced by the principal group. The general idea is that "What they don't know won't hurt them." At the least, this is a technique for avoiding or minimizing the sanctions that might be applied by the principals. Retaliation can take place, should the facts become known, but often it is too late or the desire to retaliate has lessened after the heat of negotiations subsides.

This tactical alternative is employed during the critical period when a settlement is being reached and after the settlement has taken place. We shall consider the steps which can be taken to obscure the real nature of the current progress or lack of it and later the actual terms or implications of the final outcome. Several types of tactics implement this tactical assignment.[22] The negotiator may exclude certain persons who would object most, select spatial facilities that make communication difficult, keep some issues too technical for anyone but the specialist, lose an issue in the shuffle, resort to oral understandings which are not reported to the principals, or actually misrepresent the level of achievement.

**Limiting Opportunity for Surveillance.** There are various ways by which the negotiator can restructure the bargaining teams to exclude persons or groups whose expectations are most extreme.[23] For example, the negotiator may restructure the situation so that delegates or the persons under direct influence of the membership are removed from the dilemma.

The leadership of the Teamsters has tended to insulate itself from lower groups. Consider an observation made in the Brookings study:

> The Teamsters in negotiating with one association wanted to hold closed sessions, with only one or two people on each side rather than with a full union committee as the association preferred. The Teamsters wanted commitments for future use without making these commitments known to anyone but negotiators. In the judgment of the employers, the union did not want active interest or participation by members.[24]

We can make the point a bit more colorfully by quoting some language attributed to Jimmy Hoffa. This statement was made to members of his negotiating committee in the Central states:

[22] Robert Dubin, "Leadership in Union-Management Relations as an Intergroup System," in Muzafer Sherif (ed.), *Intergroup Relations in Leadership* (New York: John Wiley & Sons, Inc., 1962), p. 84.

[23] We should note the similarity between this tactic and the one introduced earlier, excluding key persons. Both tactics are similar in their execution but different in their intent. The first tactic aims at keeping inappropriate items from crystallizing into demands, or at least not reaching the bargaining table. The second tactic aims at obscuring the level of achievement, assuming the aspirations of the organization are clearly formulated.

[24] S. H. Slichter, J. J. Healy, and E. R. Livernash, *The Impact of Collective Bargaining on Management* (Washington, D.C.: The Brookings Institution, 1960), p. 937.

I'm not going to tell you guys what we've done, because you'd have it all over the street before I left the hotel.

While in many cases the principal is held aloof without his consent, he may be excluded by his tacit acceptance of the organizational restructuring. As we mentioned earlier, the individual who finds himself in a role-conflict predicament may welcome the opportunity of disclaiming knowledge of what went on. By sensing the role-conflict predicament of a subordinate, the negotiator can exercise initiative and help both himself and the subordinate. In effect the technique enables the subordinate to place the blame on someone else and "ties his hands" in a helpful way. Publicly the individual may attack the exclusion, but he welcomes the arrangement since it removes him from a situation in which he would receive information upon which he would feel obliged to act.

In fact, sometimes the convenient "out" is masterminded by the subordinate himself. Consider the following interesting example:

> In one negotiation, the chief negotiator for the union took a contract over the heads of the delegates to the larger group of the union called the council. The delegates voted in favor of this move, even though they refused to ratify the agreement. The council approved the agreement. This left the delegates in the flexible position of being able to say to a disgruntled member that they had voted against the contract but also left the chief negotiator in a position to bring about the end of the strike.

One manager of labor relations purposely keeps his plant personnel out of the negotiations in order to keep them in the dark about developments. He feels that if the local line or staff personnel were in negotiations, his hands would be tied. This same manager of labor relations avoids other management personnel as much as possible. To the extent that these other management personnel hold rigid beliefs based on principle, he is avoiding difficulties.

The use of small bargaining committees also helps. Often as negotiations go down to the wire, negotiating teams are made smaller. Those who are not represented in the bargaining room cannot exert pressure nor can they intelligently assess the nature of concessions. Of course, they may get restless, and one technique is to keep them busy on subcommittee work while the main decisions are hammered out in sessions between small groups from the respective sides.

> Classification inequities had proved a troublesome issue. Until the final days of the negotiation, these matters had been discussed in a subcommittee. Deliberations had been rational and professional in

tone. As the expiration date of the contract approached, the discussion of classification problems shifted to the main table, to the arena of the chief negotiators. From this point on, the subcommittee which had been handling the work lost contact with developments. Positions which they had so carefully developed on the basis of factual information gave way in the rush to sign a contract. People who had been bargaining on the basis of "what is right" had to be isolated from a process which was aimed at getting an agreement.

Sometimes a negotiator will call a recess until a recalcitrant member of his group leaves the scene. The opposition may leave town for some reason or become occupied with other business. By biding his time carefully, the chief negotiator eliminates the opposition from the scene or effectively keeps them in the dark about developments.

Certain special arrangements make it easier to obscure the nature of the settlement. In one negotiation it was interesting to observe the differences in communication when bargaining took place in a building of few rooms and when bargaining occurred in a hotel. In the hotel, people were scattered throughout the building. The hotel facilitated caucuses and small meetings between different groups both within the organization and between the organizations. In particular, it allowed key people to meet together without the presence of watchful eyes.

Insulating the bargaining committee from the principal group throughout negotiations is a common tactic employed by unions. Consider the following example of how an international representative implemented this idea:

> Shafer also persuaded the committee to agree that the development of negotiations would be kept strictly confidential until there was definite progress to report to the membership or else they had gone into a deadlock. He argued that in a situation such as this the committee needed a maximum freedom of action and should not be hampered by the pressures that would come from a membership stirred up by fragmentary reports of developments.[25]

**Keeping Issues Complicated.** The inability of constituent groups to exercise surveillance also stems from the truly or apparently complicated nature of the issues. Fringe benefits with their involved clauses are difficult for rank-and-file personnel to evaluate. They literally are in the dark about whether interests are being represented or jeopardized.

Shortly after one company had made an elaborate proposal on fringe benefits, a delegate was asked what his reaction was. He said, "I just don't know; I'll have to get the advice of the international." Often the inter-

[25] W. F. Whyte, *op. cit.*, p. 73.

national does not know and needs the advice of its technicians and specialists. The complexity of issues gives the union leadership tremendous control and flexibility. The rank and file know whether they have won SUB or a breakthrough on disability pay, but they do not really know the value of these benefits in economic or other terms. The union leadership possesses great flexibility in claiming success on these complicated matters.

**Silently Dropping an Issue.** Another way of keeping people in the dark is just to "silently drop" an issue. A negotiator will accept a demand early in the negotiation, when it would be awkward to object. As negotiations unfold and the pressure develops, he says nothing more about the matter, and everyone is too busy to inquire. By the time someone wakes up and inquires, the negotiations may be over. Similarly, the issue may be lost in the shuffle during the final rush to an agreement which often takes place at the eleventh hour.

> One delegate spoke of the technique in this way, "We never sign a contract until 4 o'clock in the morning. Things happen so quickly that we do not know what we are agreeing to." In the last-minute rush to achieve agreement, things are dropped or lost sight of, and none of the delegates really knows what is happening to his special needs.

In effect, the negotiator often needs a final hurly-burly to obscure the nature of key concessions.

> In a negotiation conducted by an international representative the local committee complained that "things were being done too quickly." The negotiator squelched the feeling by asking, "Don't you trust me?"

**Keeping Agreements Quiet.** Some unions refuse to commit to writing some of the matters on which the parties had reached agreement. By keeping an understanding oral or in some type of side letter, the membership does not receive reliable information about these understandings reached during contract negotiations. Many contracts are like the top of an iceberg. These supplementary agreements never reach the rank and file, nor the plant management, for that matter.

Other groups within the organization may counter with tactics of surveillance that are intended to offset the exclusion techniques just described. For instance, in one negotiation, the international union required that minutes be made of all discussions between the local committee and management. The international feared that the local union would not carry through on certain policy commitments.

**Exaggerating the Level of Achievement.** A common deception tactic is exaggerating the value of some minor or false issue. This was also discussed as a rationalization tactic in distributive bargaining—a way of abandoning a commitment. If a negotiator sees that he is going to fall short of the minimum expectations of his principals, he may decide to make a big fuss about some minor issue, one which the other party could readily concede. In this way he can enhance the subjective value of what he *can* get—he manipulates the subjective criteria of success.

Peters cites an instance of creating a completely false issue.

> The negotiator finally decided to offer the union committee a package which included an "additional item"—equal pay for women—when this condition already existed in fact. He knew that the union committee needed one more item to sell it to the membership. At first the company negotiator was reluctant to play the game this way, but as his consultant said, "Look, Harry, we need one more item to sell the package, that's my considered judgment. Which would you rather give? Something they already have or something they don't have?" [26]

Garfield and Whyte describe a case in which the union committee had managed to get a larger package from the company than the union negotiator or the committee had expected; nevertheless, it did not meet the expectations of the membership, which refused to accept it.

> In a joint meeting, Shaw (chief negotiator) told the union . . . and company executives that he still felt the contract offer was a fair one. However, he would have to insist that the company make a new offer, an offer to be made in a way that would not hurt the company financially. He suggested a cost of living adjustment, and told the company to pick out the points of the cost of living index beyond which the cost of living would have to rise in order for the adjustment to go in effect. He suggested that they should not choose a ridiculously high figure, but one on which they could count on not having to pay anything. Since the cost of living at that time appeared to have leveled out and was beginning to decline, this seemed to offer no practical difficulties.[27]

In the Jimson negotiations the union negotiator feigned surprise when the management spokesman announced that he was prepared to disclose certain cost figures on insurance—a tactic apparently for the benefit of his own committee. The union negotiator had become committed to obtaining cost figures from the company, and the top management steadfastly re-

[26] Paraphrased from Peters, *op. cit.*, p. 98.
[27] Garfield and Whyte, *op. cit.*, vol. 9 (Winter, 1950), p. 26.

fused them. The few figures which were about to be disclosed were not actually important ones, but the union negotiator behaved as if he had actually achieved an important concession.

Often the activity of enhancing the perceived value of a settlement takes place at the membership meeting. The union negotiator is in a strategic position to "sell" the agreement and to convince the rank and file about its value. One negotiator observed, "I usually start with the small items, run quickly over the items we did not get, and then build to a climax on the big things we gained." In the study by Weber, Hill created an exaggerated sense of value by telling the membership "the welfare plan is so important, that the company would not even put it in the main agreement. They have reserved it for a side-letter of understanding." [28]

As with many other aspects of internal bargaining, there is much that Opponent can do to help Party mislead the latter's organization. Specifically, Opponent must not dispute Party's attempts to exaggerate the value of the new agreement. Beyond merely keeping quiet, Opponent can actively help Party exaggerate the value of the actual gains. For example, by giving up on a minor issue very hesitantly and grudgingly, Opponent creates the impression that the issue is of real importance.

## A Supplementary Tactical Assignment: Tacit Communication

The two preceding tactical assignments—which constitute a passive strategy of achieving internal consensus—assume that Party, the chief negotiator, complies with the behavioral expectations of his principals. Therefore these factors often either mislead Opponent or annoy him. Opponent is apt to be misled regarding the true level of Party's aspirations. He is apt to be annoyed because Party's actions appear to be violating the norms of the relationship with Opponent.

The negotiator needs to communicate to the other side that certain of his actions should not be taken seriously. Tacit communication may be used for this delicate task.

The negotiator can choose language which has different meanings to different audiences. He can evidence continued interest in an item which was included to satisfy a segment of his own organization at the same time that he signals concession to the other party. A union negotiator made this statement to management: "You know our position on that subject." While he was seemingly indicating to management that the union's position had not changed, he was not taking the trouble to elaborate it or state it with intensity—facts that management did not overlook or fail to attribute the appropriate significance to. To the delegate sitting in the

[28] Weber, *op. cit.*

room it appeared as if the issue were still on the table, but the union negotiator was just allowing time to run its course until the moment when the
pressure of the strike would allow him to actually drop the issue.

Consider an instance from another negotiation: After a tough bargaining session on grievance problems, the union negotiator remarked, "Well,
it's too early yet." Such a deceptively simple statement conveyed considerable information to the company. In effect he said, "We may be bargaining aggressively, but a movement in position will take place subsequently."

The technique of presenting a demand late in the negotiations can indicate that it is really not important and that it is being aired only to
release steam.

> In a subcommittee that was discussing inequities, the union nego-
> tiator presented piecework problems late in the negotiations. Up to
> that point, the union's position had centered on day-work inequities.
> The company spokesman was certain that these demands were not
> important, not because they had not been discussed with intensity by
> the union and not because he had learned of their unimportance in
> any *sub rosa* way, but merely because he had interpreted the timing
> of their presentation to indicate their relative unimportance.

Thus, in tacit communication, both sides know what the other side
knows, but it has never been stated explicitly. It cannot be stated explicitly without risk of severe censure from the respective constituent groups.

An article on collective bargaining by Blum cites an example of going
through the motions, apparently accompanied by tacit bargaining.

> During negotiations, management offers 8 cents; the union persists in
> demanding 9 cents. As has happened nearly always in the past, the
> end of the week draws near and it is time to arrive at a settlement.
> The union representative slams down his papers, shouts that he has
> had enough, that he will call his men out Monday if they don't get
> the 9 cents, and stalks toward the door. Each year he does something
> like this, and each year this is a signal for the manager to get up,
> calm him down, offer 8½ cents, and sign an agreement; then every-
> one can rush home to their families for the weekend.[29]

We have assumed thus far that the valid communications—those which
one party wishes the other to take seriously—occurred at the bargaining
table. There is an alternative to tacit communication, namely, on-the-side
discussions. There are various ways in which such encounters may occur
and allow for covert bargaining meetings in the bar or in the coffee shop;

[29] A. A. Blum, "Collective Bargaining: Ritual or Reality," *Harvard Business Review,*
vol. 39 (November-December, 1961), pp. 65–67.

telephone conversations often serve such a purpose. Whether the negotiator will rely on tacit communication or engage in covert discussion will depend on his weighting of several factors. Each contains its own type of risk of being discovered by the principals. Of course, the more sophisticated the principals or constituent groups are about tacit communication, the more necessary it is to resort to covert discussions.

### Strategic Question for the Negotiator: Active or Passive Role?

We have reviewed the tactical assignments for reducing the discrepancy between the principals' expectations and the negotiator's own expectations. Each of these represents a set of tactical operations available to the negotiator who wishes to take some responsibility for reducing this discrepancy. For the negotiator, the strategical question associated with the process of achieving internal consensus is: How much responsibility will be assumed for reducing this discrepancy? Or stated another way: How active versus passive a role will be assumed in this process?

Our distinctions regarding active-passive roles correspond to the timing and method of the negotiator's attempts to cope with the role conflict. The five basic tactical assignments have been presented in a sequence reflecting more to less initiative.

On the one hand, an active strategy would rely upon avoiding the incompatible expectations or reducing them through persuasion during negotiations. It might be supplemented with tactics which brought the principals into direct contact with the opponent in order to let this direct experience persuade them.

On the other hand, a passive strategy would rely partly upon attempts to rationalize disappointing outcomes after the fact and partly upon efforts to disguise or exaggerate results which fell below expectations.

In practice, it is seldom a question of these two alternative approaches: assuming complete initiative *or* merely responding to the expectations of the principals and allowing them to define the mandate as they will. It is rather a question of the degree of initiative and therefore of the appropriate combination of techniques selected from the tactical assignments described above.

The strategy—even a mixed one—is not necessarily well laid out in advance and then adhered to throughout negotiations. The negotiator often must shift his strategy and tactics in order to maintain his effectiveness— his influence and control.

At times maintaining control of one's own organization means actually going along with the fervor of the organization and leading the organization into a strike (in other words, following the dictates of the passive strategy to their ultimate extreme), as the following example illustrates:

A union leader can have a good relationship with the company and go along for years and years, *up to a point.* . . . So he gets himself into position, sometimes, where he must have his face saved or strike the company, because the pressure gets greater. Sometimes he will be accused of not getting enough, too easy with the company, and this grows and grows and grows. Actually he doesn't want a strike, but it would be political suicide, after a certain span of time, if he doesn't do it.[30]

On the other hand, a negotiator may make a mistake in letting a strike occur. In many instances, it would have been better to have pursued a more active strategy in order to prevent the onset of a strike. Consider the following example:

A strike was actually voted by the membership despite the recommendation of the business agent and the executive board that the employer's offer be accepted. According to the business agent, the membership was demanding a pension and welfare plan and a wage increase during the 1949 negotiations, although the executive board felt that economic conditions did not warrant higher wages. . . . The union leaders recommended at a membership meeting that the employer's offer of a pension and welfare plan be accepted. According to the business agent, one of the members jumped to his feet and shouted, "Who in the hell do you think we are? We want money now, not when we are 65." This sentiment prevailed, and the members voted a strike which lasted five weeks and was ultimately settled without the wage increase.[31]

During any given negotiation, the negotiator may find it necessary to mix his strategies. The central theme may be one of maintaining control and effectiveness, as the following two examples illustrate:

As bargaining moved toward the deadline, the union negotiator was uncertain whether to seek strike authorization from the membership. Top officials from both sides hoped to negotiate the new agreement without resort to a strike, and the hope went even further—that they could conclude negotiations without the *threat* of a strike. Accordingly, the inclination of the union negotiator was to avoid taking a strike vote unless forced to do so by the "militants." During the week leading into contract expiration, the activists forced the chief negotiator to hold a strike referendum. He responded to their pressure and established the machinery for the taking of a strike vote. In preparing the membership for a strike vote, the chief negotiator wrote a

---

[30] Douglas, *op. cit.,* p. 381.
[31] Parnes, *op. cit.,* p. 63.

long letter in which he castigated the company's position and asked for membership support.

In the above example, we see the sequential postures of first ignoring and then conforming to the role sendings of the membership. Initially, the negotiator attempted to direct events by postponing the strike vote. Eventually he had to respond to the pressure of the negotiating committee, and he agreed to conduct a strike vote. Whereupon he reassumed the posture of active leadership by making sure that the strike vote would be an overwhelming success.

A somewhat similar pattern developed for Reuther in the 1961 auto negotiations.

> During the 1961 automobile negotiations, Reuther had to go along with local pressure for action on production standards, relief time, and the like. When Reuther and Seaton reached a meeting of the minds on the national issues, everyone thought the negotiations were finished. However, locals felt rebuffed on their own problems and demanded the right to strike. Reuther reacted by permitting the locals to take the necessary action to solve their own problems. However, in the process he angered the company by what they thought was a lack of direction.

In a general sense the discussion is about leadership style. In many ways the leadership problem facing the negotiator is no different from that facing any leader. He is simultaneously striving to increase the productivity of the group (in this case, the gains from a new contract), maintain some degree of internal stability, and preserve his own effectiveness.

# PART 2 | DILEMMAS OF INTRAORGANIZATIONAL BARGAINING

As in earlier chapters, we shall explore major issues within intraorganizational bargaining and then examine the connection between this subprocess and the other three subprocesses.

**Tactical Dilemmas Arising within the Subprocess.** The six tactical assignments do not present many dilemmas within the subprocess of intraorganizational bargaining. The categories can be differentiated along a time span running from prenegotiating to postnegotiating activity. As we have also indicated, the tactical assignments range from active to passive posture on the part of the negotiator. Moreover, the tactical assignments can be differentiated in terms of the concepts of aspiration level, achievement level, and the gap between the two. In effect, the tactical assignments represent a sequence of options. An early option can be chosen (such as the tactic of directly changing aspiration) without foreclosing the use of a later option (such as distorting achievement). Indeed, a negotiator may employ passive tactics because he has not been successful with the more active tactics.

However, when two of the tactical assignments involve activities which are opposite in some sense, certain problems do arise. Consider the two activities of bringing the constituent group into a direct confrontation with the realities of the bargaining situation (involved in the active strategy) and keeping various parts of the organization in the dark (involved in the passive strategy). Here we have an example of specific tactics which appear to be in conflict.

As we have indicated, the problem is minimized by the differences in timing. The tactic of bringing the organization face to face with the opponent takes place earlier in negotiations and is aimed at modifying the aspiration of the organization. On the other hand, keeping people in the dark takes place later in the negotiations and is aimed at manipulating their perception of achievement. Nevertheless, in actual practice a negotiation cannot be neatly separated into early and late phases and into periods in which the most concern is with aspiration and periods in which it is with achievement. For example, confronting the organization with the essence of the situation may also give the constituents information about the actual level of achievement. By the same token, keeping the organization in the dark about achievement may also keep the organization uninformed about the power realities of the situation and thus allow an untenable aspiration to persist.

The point is that while the tactical assignments are compatible conceptually, the negotiator may experience considerable difficulty in using certain combinations of these tactical assignments effectively.

**Factors Influencing Intraorganizational Strategies.** We have identified the tactical assignment associated with relatively active and relatively passive strategies for achieving internal consensus. The following is a discussion of the factors that influence the negotiator's choice of strategy.

The negotiator faced with role conflict must contend with various possible costs or side effects. These costs fall into several categories: institutional economic costs (such as a strike), organizational sanctions (such as being voted out of office), Opponent's disapproval (leading to such responses as an uncooperative approach to contract administration), and personal discomfort (such as strain from not fulfilling beliefs about one's own behavior). Consequently, the two strategies can be differentiated on the basis of the various potential side effects which they minimize. Usually, the negotiator must weigh one set of costs against another—this is the nature of the important dilemmas within intraorganizational bargaining. Moreover, obviously the negotiator will be influenced by the availability of a given tactic in the specific institutional setting.

Viewing the strategic choice as an attempt to minimize unfortunate consequences implies certain hypotheses which can be spelled out in some detail. We should expect the active strategy to be used by Party under certain circumstances discussed below and the passive strategy under opposite circumstances.

*Hypothesis 1 The greater the expected institutional costs which result from a failure of the two parties to agree, the more likely it is that Party will adopt an active strategy.* The active strategy of reducing the principal expectations is regarded as a more cautious one in the sense that it decreases the risk of a strike at the wrong time and over the wrong issue.

Institutional costs take many forms. For the purpose of deciding between alternate strategies, the rate of strike costs, should a breakdown occur, is a prime consideration. But other institutional costs are involved in negotiations. For example, it is possible that integrative potential is yet to be exploited from the negotiation. If such is the case, it may be necessary for the negotiator to adopt an active strategy in order to prepare his organization for integrative bargaining, specifically, avoiding commitments and securing acceptance of the problem-solving method.

*Hypothesis 2 The higher the probability that Party will be able to actually modify the expectations of his organization, the more likely it is that Party will adopt an active strategy.* The first proposition expressed the anticipated costs of a strike that would stem from continued divergence in expectations. This proposition expresses the probability that the negotiator can modify the outlook of his own organization if he tries. The question is whether he has sufficient skill or influence to modify their expectations.

Some negotiators find it easy to manipulate the outlook of their organization because they possess the requisite skill or political influence. In our discussion we indicated that certain institutional issues, such as union security, lend themselves to leadership control. In such circumstances we should expect a negotiator to adopt an active strategy. Also important here is the psychological makeup of the constituent group. Clearly, if the members are more influenceable by use of reason and persuasion, then the active strategy is more available to the negotiator. When the negotiator has relatively few means of influence available, when the issues are simple and unambiguous, and when the members are adamant and close-minded, then the negotiator may have to rely on the technique of evasion employed in the passive strategy.

*Hypothesis 3 The smaller the sanctions associated with not fulfilling the behavioral expectations of the organization, the more likely Party is to pursue an active strategy.* Closely related is *Hypothesis 4 The larger the sanctions associated with not fulfilling the substantive expectations of the organization, the more likely Party is to pursue an active strategy.*

Considerable disapproval from the principal group can be encountered under either strategy. In the first, the disappointment of members of the organization comes because the negotiator has not fulfilled their behavioral expectations; and in the second, because he has not delivered according to their aspirations. Organizational sanctions may involve censure and loss of job. It may be expressed through such actions as a wildcat strike, a slowdown, or a general disruption of the bargaining process. Disruptive and demoralizing tactics are available to constituent groups on both union and management sides. For example, during the 1961 negotiations between General Electric and the IUE, local groups chose to ignore the directives of the union leader. Similarly, during the 1959 steel strike negotiations, Kaiser broke ranks to settle with the union. It happened that in both of these instances the principal groups were less ambitious than the negotiators whose leadership they were rejecting.

Some negotiators are secure in their position and are able to minimize any sanctions which the organization might impose upon them for not behaving as "good negotiators." [32] Probably the less secure the negotiator is in his organizational position, the more reluctant he will be to take an active strategy which risks violating behavioral expectations. He may adopt passive coping techniques late in negotiations, because by this time he has no alternative,[33] not necessarily because the disappointment in substantive results is accompanied by weaker sanctions.

*Hypothesis 5 The larger Party's costs associated with not fulfilling the behavioral expectations of Opponent, the more likely Party is to utilize an active strategy.* The opponent can inflict costs in terms of the relationship between the two negotiators. For the reasons given earlier in this chapter, a negotiator can be sensitive to the relationship that connects him to his opponent. To the extent that the negotiator is sensitive to this dimension, he will tend toward an active strategy. We would expect

---

[32] The study of role conflict among school superintendents indicated that a high status member of a group is not only more immune to sanctions but may be allowed a greater degree of role freedom in his task accomplishment in the first instance. Neal Gross, W. S. Mason, and Alexander McEachern, *Explorations in Role Analysis: Studies of the School Superintendency Role* (New York: John Wiley & Sons, Inc., 1957).

[33] In fact, the representative who does not enjoy high status may be more comfortable with explicit behavioral and substantive role expectations from his organization, according to experimental findings of H. B. Gerard, "Some Effects of Status, Role Clarity, and Group Goal Clarity upon the Individual's Relations to Group Process," *Journal of Personality*, vol. 25 (1957), pp. 475–488.

these costs to be particularly acute when the relationship, at least between the two negotiators, is "improving," i.e., moving in the direction of accommodation and cooperation.

If the negotiator is not as concerned about his opponent and what he thinks, he is more likely to use a passive strategy. Moreover, inasmuch as it is possible for the negotiator to avoid some of this disapproval through the mechanism of tacit bargaining or covert discussions, we would expect the availability of these mechanisms to increase the use of a passive strategy.

*Hypothesis 6* *The greater the costs to Party in terms of loss of personal esteem from not assuming the initiative, the more likely Party is to adopt the active strategy.* A fourth source of discomfort comes from matching behavior against self-image [34] or preferred leadership style. More broadly, we identify action tendencies with certain unions which specify the appropriate image for their leaders. For example, craft unions lean more to active intraorganizational strategy, while industrial unions tend more toward the passive strategy. The industrial union adheres to a tradition of rank-and-file participation and grass roots democracy, while the craft union adheres more to a tradition of businesslike efficiency and direction by business agents.[35]

However, there are marked differences among unions within these two broad categories. By tradition and preference some industrial unions place more emphasis on initiation and others more on reaction. Consider two industrial unions: the United Steelworkers illustrates the active strategy and the United Automobile Workers a more passive strategy.

Recall Ulman's description of the Steelworkers' Wage Policy Committee. In that statement we see a picture of control and direction on the part of the International. The International signs the contract, and there is no requirement for endorsement at the district or local level. On the other hand, the UAW is more responsive to the sentiment of rank-and-file members. The UAW has developed a series of departments organized along company or industry lines. Within these departments separate councils hammer out bargaining demands. During the course of contract negotiations, there is continual feedback between the chief negotiator and his respective group. The contract becomes official only after the ratification by the membership.

**Intraorganizational and Distributive Bargaining Interfering.** Almost by definition the two processes of intraorganizational bargaining and dis-

---

[34] See, e.g., S. A. Stouffer and J. Toby, "Role Conflict and Personality," *Journal of Sociology*, vol. 56 (March, 1951), pp. 395–406; and J. W. Getzels and E. G. Guba, "Role, Role Conflict and Effectiveness: An Empirical Study," *American Sociological Review*, vol. 19 (April, 1954), pp. 164–175.

[35] See Peters, *op. cit.*, pp. 12–32.

tributive bargaining are in conflict. In distributive bargaining the negotiator attempts to modify the opponent's position toward the expectations
of his principals. In internal bargaining the negotiator endeavors to bring
the expectations of his principals into alignment with those of the opponent. In this sense, the purposes of these two activities are diametrically
opposed. The two processes also frequently interfere with each other at the
tactical level.

Distributive bargaining involves tactical attempts to crystallize internal
feeling and increase the willingness to fight. These and other steps are
helpful in conveying strong commitment and increasing the power position of the party. All these activities conflict with intraorganizational
bargaining, in which the negotiator reduces feeling, divests the membership of ambitious objectives, and generally strives to prevent the membership from developing too great an attachment to any particular proposal.

A particularly important limitation is placed on effective distributive
bargaining in which the negotiator is unsure of his ability to revise his
own organization's position. He is foreclosed, for example, from making
a timely concession—one which might lead to the best overall distributive
results—when his own organization is not yet convinced of the need for
a concession.

Considered together, the two processes also make Party ambivalent
about whether he prefers a firm or a flexible statement from Opponent
during bargaining. In distributive bargaining Party keeps Opponent uncommitted and ready to change position, yet this makes it more difficult
for Party to modify the position of his own organization. A firm commitment by Opponent or some other demonstration of strength may be just
what is needed for Party to bring his organization to an appreciation of
the realities of the situation. The analysis above is only illustrative of the
way in which the tactical assignments for intraorganizational bargaining
directly conflict with those of distributive bargaining. This generally
interfering relationship between these processes is relatively obvious.

A few of the less obvious ways in which the two processes are mutually
interfering takes into account the fact that both negotiators are simultaneously engaged in intraorganizational bargaining. Considering Party's
task in distributive bargaining, he wants to assist Opponent's intraorganizational efforts at reducing expectations. However, the more successful
Opponent is in toning down his organization, the more difficult it will be
for Party to tone down his organization. In other words, once the members of Party's organization get signals that Opponent is not so ambitious
after all, they will be inclined to want still more out of negotiations; and
the task of intraorganizational bargaining for Party will become more
difficult. The same point could be made in connection with the tactical
assignment of distorting the level of achievement. To the extent that

Party is successful in convincing his organization that they have achieved more than really was the case, he tends to foreclose the possibility of Opponent doing the same thing with his organization.

**Facilitation of Intraorganizational and Distributive Bargaining.** The relationship between these two processes is not always interfering. We turn to a discussion of the ways in which they are either mutually facilitating or in which their conflicting effects can be neutralized.

Intraorganizational bargaining by Party and distributive bargaining by Opponent are certainly compatible, since any reduction that Party brings about in his own internal position is an accommodation of Opponent. Actually this is nothing more than what was implied in the discussion of distributive bargaining. In that chapter it was assumed that the person being forced to change position had the necessary authority and freedom. Our discussion of intraorganizational bargaining is an intensive look at the dynamics by which the negotiator gains this freedom and flexibility. Obviously the compatibility of processes works in the other direction, namely, the intraorganizational bargaining of Opponent facilitates the distributive bargaining of Party. Thus, we have an exchange situation. The compatibility between these two processes can be illustrated by recalling some of the tactical assignments. For example, by maintaining a firm position (distributive tactic), Opponent can help Party revise the position of his own organization. Similarly, by giving up on an issue very grudgingly and making a big issue over a small point (distributive tactic), Party can help Opponent distort the level of achievement as perceived by Party's organization. In both cases, the distributive tactics of one assisted the other in achieving internal consensus.

However, the potential exchange contains an important weakness: the possibility of a double cross. It may not be easy for either negotiator to make the correct interpretation about his opponent's behavior. What Party viewed as helpful "distributive" bargaining by Opponent may turn out to be strictly serious power bargaining designed to maximize Opponent's gain and not designed merely to help Party deal with his own organization. Stated differently, it is quite possible for Party to have engaged in intraorganizational bargaining, assuming that Opponent was doing likewise, only to find out that Opponent had not carried through on his side of the assumed understanding.

These points can be illustrated. Let us assume that Opponent has been acting in a militant manner. This helps Party convince his own organization that they are up against a tough situation and that they had better revise their outlook. But the militant behavior of Opponent may have more impact than Party would like. His organization becomes willing to settle for less than Party himself regards as "fair" and possible. In this instance, Opponent has gone beyond the limits of what is facilitating for Party in his intraorganizational bargaining activity.

The risks that this misunderstanding might occur are minimized by tacit bargaining. This mechanism assumes a level of familiarity and trust. Therefore, prior attitudinal structuring provides the basic understanding by which each side can ascertain the true intentions of the other side. Tacit bargaining enables the negotiators to be sure about the real meanings of the various bargaining activities. Since these processes occur simultaneously, and since they are reciprocally related, it is difficult for each negotiator to make accurate inferences without the mechanism of tacit bargaining.

Tacit bargaining enables the interwoven processes to be separated in the following manner: While Opponent is maintaining an aggressive posture, he communicates to Party that his behavior is aimed at allowing Party to handle his intraorganizational bargaining and that it can be discounted by Party for purposes of his own calculations. If Party is successful in revising expectations within his organization, he communicates this fact to Opponent but does his best to keep the information away from the other members of Opponent's organization. In other words, both sides give the appearance of distributive behavior around the *explicit* bargaining position (which helps the opposite negotiator in his intraorganizational bargaining), and as movement takes place in the *silent* position of each organization, this fact is communicated to the opposite negotiator but not to members in the opposite organization. Thus, the negotiators gradually work themselves into positions of greater flexibility.

Information needs to be communicated about the actual modification of the internal position in order to convince the other negotiator that the first negotiator is meeting his side of the bargain. It is designed to avoid the situation in which Party, having engaged in intraorganizational bargaining, senses that there has been no modification in the internal position of Opponent. This is the double cross. Thus, one way of interpreting the true intent behind militant behavior on the part of the opponent is to ascertain what has happened to the silent position of the opponent's organization while this behavior was taking place. If the position has hardened, then the behavior can be interpreted as purely distributive; if it has softened, then the behavior is in part facilitative to intraorganizational bargaining within Opponent's organization and complimentary to distributive bargaining by Party.

We have come to the point of being able to qualify some conclusions of an earlier discussion. It will be recalled that we saw the intraorganizational activity of one negotiator conflicting with that of the other negotiator. Such can be the case but does not need to be in the light of our discussion about tacit communication and the careful handling of information about explicit and silent bargaining positions. In other words, the modification of the internal position of Opponent's organization will not make life more difficult for Party if Party's organization has no knowledge of the fact.

Thus, it is quite possible for a given tactic to be facilitating for intra-organizational bargaining on both sides of the table, providing both negotiators are clear on what is happening. Returning to the example of militant behavior, it can be seen that aggressive behavior by Opponent can facilitate the active strategy of Party (by giving him the anvil against which he can hammer out a more moderate aspiration) and at the same time be part of a passive strategy on the part of Opponent (going through the motions in order to convince the organization that the level of achievement represents the maximum attainable under the circumstances).

An interesting question can be raised about this tactic: Is the amount of movement brought about within Party's organization equal to or different from that brought about within Opponent's organization? The difficulty is that in one case the aspiration of Party's organization is being directly modified; in the other case, the potential achievement of Opponent is being rationalized. At the point in time when the tactic takes place, Party may feel a little uneasy since he has lessened his stake in the negotiations by modifying the internal position of his organization while Opponent is only preparing to rationalize achievement and has not yet directly changed the expectations of his own organization. The uneasiness of Party can be assuaged if he is certain that Opponent will, at the predetermined point, deal directly with the discrepancy between the high expectations of his organization and the presumed settlement position. However, the possibility exists that Opponent will say at some point toward the end of negotiations, "I cannot sell the package; I need more." Given this possibility, Party must be cautious, as the company negotiator is in the following example:

> As negotiations went down to the wire, the two chief negotiators knew that the contract would be extended pending developments elsewhere. Rather than disclose this fact to their respective organizations, the two chief negotiators kept their committees in direct confrontation with each other in order to exert as much pressure on them to revise positions and come up with a more realistic approach. In the process, however, the company negotiator sensed a danger. The members of his organization were under such pressure (believing they were facing a strike deadline), that they tended to give in on issues which the union should have been expected to eventually concede. Consequently, the company negotiator confided to one of his subordinates, "Look, don't give a horse and only receive a pony. We

are interested in wrapping things up but not in giving the company away."

Again, we need to note that what is clear at the conceptual level may not be too easy to execute in the bargaining room. Tacit bargaining is difficult to conduct when many people are involved. The negotiator finds himself in great difficulty in handling the complex ramifications of the two processes as well as his relationship with the other negotiator. The following example points up some of the problems of coordination:

The union leader presented numerous grievances for action by the company. He argued hard and vigorously for these grievances in the early meetings with the company. In effect, it was "going through the motions." As negotiations proceeded to the final week, the union negotiator remarked to the company negotiator, "Not all the grievances should be taken seriously." In other words, he was engaged in tacit communication, suggesting to the company that his behavior was not distributive bargaining per se but distributive bargaining modified by the dictates of his internal organization. So far, so good. The difficulty developed when the company negotiator told other members of his organization that the union would be dropping most of the grievances. He felt obliged to do this in order to acquaint his organization with the true nature of the union's behavior. The company negotiator was afraid that some of his subordinates would grant many of these grievances after the "show" which the union had put on. Eventually the word leaked to the union that the company was waiting for the union to drop all the grievances. Whereupon, the union negotiator came into negotiations and vehemently attacked the company and demanded action on all the grievances. In effect, he reverted to the distributive posture since the company had made it difficult for him in his activity of intraorganizational bargaining.

**Intraorganizational Bargaining and Attitudinal Structuring.** The relationship between the two negotiators is sometimes a constraint on the behavior one negotiator might use to comply with the expectations of members of his own organization. At other times, the relationship bond actually enables the negotiator to be more effective in achieving internal consensus. In fact, these interactions between the two processes are so fundamental that it was not possible to elaborate the intraorganizational bargaining process without mentioning them.

Thus, we have already noted the important role that attitudinal structuring plays as a facilitating element in the complex interaction of intraorganizational bargaining and distributive bargaining. Recall, also, that many of the attitudinal structuring tactics involved helping Opponent, sometimes in ways that strengthened his position internally. If handled skillfully, the negotiators can work on their relationship bond and at the same time increase their abilities to actively influence their respective organizations.

The main conflict between the two processes occurs when Party must violate the norms of his relationship with Opponent in order to fulfill the expectations of his own organization. There are two ways out of this dilemma: (1) tacit bargaining during negotiations, which we have discussed at length; and (2) modifying the organization's behavioral expectations, which we have not yet discussed because it usually requires work over a longer period of time.

When the members' behavioral expectations are based as much on strategy considerations as on underlying emotions, the dilemma may be resolved. Lincoln Fairley, research director of the International Longshoremen's and Warehousemen's Union, describes how the union embraced a new outlook toward management and technological change. The result was the historic West Coast Longshore Fund.

> Had a vote been taken the first day, the decision might easily have been to continue to use the union's muscle to preserve the *status quo.* "We've gotten along all right so far, so why not continue?" But as the discussion proceeded, the view gradually prevailed that the continuance of gorilla persistence meant fighting a losing battle, a delaying or holding action at best. . . .
>
> The decision was therefore made, by unanimous action of the delegates, to accept the recommendation to explore further with the P.M.A. the possibilities of some sort of *quid pro quo,* some specific benefits to the longshoremen, as our "share of the machine" in return for what the employers were seeking; namely, a chance to adopt new methods and relaxation of such working rules as required multiple handling, set a limit on the size of sling loads, or call for unnecessarily large gangs.[36]

**Intraorganizational Bargaining and Integrative Bargaining.** Very often integrative bargaining is impeded by intraorganizational pressures which require the negotiator to act in a specified way. His constituents may not tolerate off-the-record discussions, subcommittees, and the other tactics necessary for integrative bargaining. Nor may the constituents be satisfied with an agreement that had been reached via problem solving. As one negotiator pointed out, "The boys will only accept a contract when they are convinced I have taken a 'pound of flesh' from the company."

It is precisely because of these intraorganizational pressures on the ne-

[36] Thomas Kennedy, *Automation Funds and Displaced Workers* (Boston: Division of Research, Graduate School of Business Administration, Harvard University, 1962), pp. 76–77.

gotiator that integrative bargaining is so difficult. These pressures have operated on top officials in the UAW, who have consequently found it difficult to pursue the exploratory talks (preliminary to the 1964 auto negotiations) in a completely integrative fashion. Other examples could be given. During the 1960–1961 negotiations in meat-packing, one of the major firms declined to grant a 5-week vacation after 25 years, a proposal which would have benefited the union because of its symbolic quality and the company because it cost less than the alternative of 3 weeks after 10 years and 4 after 20. The company accepted the latter arrangement instead of the 5 after 25, stating, "The rest of American industry would kill us for making this kind of breakthrough."

Intraorganizational bargaining aims at developing flexibility in one's position. To the extent that the organization takes a more flexible position, the purposes of integrative bargaining can *also* be served.

Consider the tactic of bringing the constituents face to face with the realities of the situation. Such a move can serve the purposes of intra-organizational bargaining by forcing the constituents to revise their aspiration and the purposes of integrative bargaining by making available more viewpoints and problem solvers (assuming that their energies are harnessed through subcommittees, etc.).

Even the alternate tactic of isolating the membership serves the same double purpose. Such a move is functional for intraorganizational bargaining in that it prevents them from perceiving the actual level of achievement until it is too late; and it is functional for integrative bargaining in that it removes constraining influences from the bargaining room, thereby allowing the key participants to increase joint achievement through problem solving.

# CHAPTER X

# SYNTHESIS OF
# THE SUBPROCESSES

In this and the next chapter we attempt to gain further synthesis of the subprocesses of negotiations and to extend the total theory to other instances of social interaction. The discussion which follows first attempts to clarify our assumptions about the rationality of the negotiator as he copes with stringent demands of one subprocess and the complications of interacting subprocesses. Then we attempt to highlight certain key aspects of each subprocess and consider them in relation to each of the others. Finally, this chapter concludes with a discussion of how these key dimensions are being handled in the 1960s. To do this, we review the changing practices of collective bargaining in the electrical equipment, automobile, steel, agricultural implement, meat-packing, and longshoring industries.

### Note on the Rationality of Negotiating Behavior

We have described how negotiators tend to behave; that is, we have specified the types of procedures they adopt and activities they engage in when certain types of objectives have prominence for them. However, we have also been implying that the systems of activities and procedures are generally instrumental to the negotiator's objectives. In doing this, we have started with one class of goals—those economic and work-rule objectives which the parties hold in conflict—and have specified the types of activities—distributive tactics—which are instrumental in that situation. These distributive tactics then are rational behaviors for pursuing conflicting ends. And if negotiations constituted nothing more, these would be rational negotiating behaviors.

But as we have stressed continuously throughout the manuscript, there are other types of goals or constraints, each of which has its own rational behavior. We have considered three other subprocesses of negotiations: integrative bargaining, attitudinal structuring, and intraorganizational bargaining. Each of these was viewed first as a rational system of activities in its own right and then as a complicating factor in the operation of other processes previously discussed. Since there is at least as much conflict as compatibility among the sets of activities which are instrumental to the several types of goals held by the same negotiator, the definition of rational behavior in total negotiating context becomes difficult to determine.

We would, nevertheless, continue to contend that the negotiator in this admittedly complex context behaves purposefully, attending in some balanced way to conflicting goals, integrative potential, desired relationship patterns, and the need for intraorganizational consensus. Implicit in our framework is the assumption that these four processes both encompass the objectives that a chief negotiator attends to and include the significant functions that he performs.

The meaning of the concept of rationality, which is a central point here, should be clarified. Herbert Simon's distinctions are helpful. "Roughly speaking, rationality is concerned with the selection of preferred behavior alternatives in terms of some system of values, whereby the consequences of behavior can be evaluated." [1] In order to distinguish among the many meanings possible within that definition, he suggests:

> Perhaps the only way to avoid, or clarify, these complexities is to use the term "rational" in conjunction with appropriate adverbs. Then a decision may be called "objectively" rational if *in fact* it is correct behavior for maximizing given values in a given situation. It is "subjectively" rational if it maximizes attainment relative to the actual knowledge of the subject. It is "consciously" rational to the degree that the adjustment of means to ends is a conscious process. It is "deliberately" rational to the degree that the adjustment of means to ends has been deliberately brought about (by the individual or by the organization). A decision is "organizationally" rational if it is oriented to the organization's goals; it is "personally" rational if it is oriented to the individual's goals. [2]

Employing the above distinctions, our first question might be: "Rational for whom?" We have described negotiating behavior appropriate from the point of view of the chief negotiator, who is primarily oriented to organizational goals modified only somewhat by his own personal psychological needs (especially in attitudinal structuring) and by his personal career goals (especially in intraorganizational bargaining).

[1] Herbert Simon, *Administrative Behavior* (New York: The Macmillan Company, 1959), pp. 75–76.
[2] *Ibid.*, pp. 76–77.

The second question might be: "What are the limits of rationality?" Taking our elaborate specification of tactics for pursuing each type of goal situation as the beginning of a normative theory of tactical and strategical choice, we obviously think in terms of objective rationality. However, taking these same hypothesized relationships for descriptive and predictive purposes, we must deal with behavior as subjectively rational [3] and treat knowledge as an important parameter. The behavior may or may not be consciously rational and may or may not be deliberately rational.

As researchers we were continuously amazed at how much of the total behavior produced in a negotiating session was appropriate tactically when we analyzed the interactions in terms of the four-process framework. Notwithstanding this apparent rationality, the action-reaction behaviors came so rapidly and instinctively that the participants simply could not be selecting their behaviors consciously. Like a skilled boxer or basketball player a skilled negotiator produces many types of appropriate behavior on the basis of minimal cues from the situation and with virtually no mental processing. Thus while much of negotiating behavior is not consciously or deliberately rational, it must still be viewed as subjectively rational.

Negotiators may not think through the operations in the way presented in the various subprocesses, and even when they adopt such an analytic approach, it certainly would not be as formal as the models in this study are. Nevertheless, we would contend that skilled and sophisticated negotiators are conscious of most and responsive at some level to almost all the factors encompassed in this theory of labor negotiations.

## Key Issues in the Negotiation Process

The development of theory involves analysis and synthesis. We have attempted both in some degree in the preceding chapters. Within each of the subprocesses we have tried to analyze the process into its component operations and to relate these to one another in terms of their chronological sequence, functional interdependency, and degree of consistency. Synthesis at a higher level was achieved in some degree by examining the points at which the activities of one process facilitated or interfered with the other processes. Here we extend this synthesis by selecting a key aspect of each process and considering it in relation to the other processes.

The key questions for the negotiator in the four processes, respectively, are: What commitment pattern should be employed in distributive bargaining? What degree of open communication should be used in inte-

[3] An individual cannot take into consideration all the factors relevant to his choice. There are limits to knowledge at hand and to his ability to incorporate into a decision framework all the information within his grasp. Time constraints are especially limiting.

grative bargaining? What level of trust should be sought in attitudinal structuring? What degree of control should be exercised over the organization in intraorganizational bargaining? Then, how are these four questions interrelated?

**Degree of Commitment.** In distributive bargaining a key question is: What commitment pattern should the negotiator adopt? Should he start high and execute gradually increasing commitments as the bargaining position approaches his resistance point? Or should he adopt an early-firm-commitment strategy involving essentially no further concessions, on the assumption that he can force a settlement at some preferred point near the resistance point of the opponent?

In our discussion of distributive tactics, we concluded that a negotiator attempts to use as early and firm a commitment pattern as is permitted by his present knowledge about his own and his opponent's resistance point and by the available means for communicating and confirming tactical commitments and rationalizing them, if necessary, etc. Thus, we viewed the choice of commitment strategy strictly from the point of view of the requirements and constraints of distributive bargaining.

The early-firm-commitment pattern involves further considerations when viewed in the light of integrative bargaining. Integrative bargaining requires that Party set forth problems, not specify outcomes or final solutions. Moreover, the joint gain is most likely to be increased when he brings to the table more rather than fewer agenda items. Thus, for whatever tactical advantage it has in strengthening the bargaining position of Party, a commitment pattern which unilaterally preselects the agenda items for which change will be made and for which the solutions are specified certainly frustrates effective integrative bargaining.

Similarly, from the viewpoint of attitudinal structuring, there are problems with the early-firm-commitment strategy that appears to determine terms unilaterally ahead of effective bargaining. One of the important elements in a cooperative relationship is the degree of concern shown by Party for the role requirements impinging upon Opponent. To the extent that Opponent will be evaluated by his principals according to the amount of concessions actively obtained from Party in the course of bargaining, rather than according to some other measure of the value of the settlement, Party's early-firm-commitment pattern deprives Opponent of some credit for any gains incorporated in the final outcome. It is not surprising, then, that the effect of this strategy on the relationship between Party and Opponent is likely to be negative.

Just as Opponent may resent the extreme early-firm-commitment strategy which is essentially a "final-offer-first" approach, he may also react adversely to an initial position which is extremely ambitious and bears no apparent relationship to a reasonable final settlement. Thus, attitudinal considerations probably place an upper and a lower limit on the commit-ment-concession patterns adopted for the primary purpose of distributive bargaining.

The considerations of intraorganizational bargaining generally lead to-ward a gradually increasing-commitment pattern. Fulfilling behavioral ex-pectations can be more easily executed by Party if he gradually modifies his explicit position. Indeed, the internal situation usually requires the negotiator to assume an initial position far more ambitious than what he expects to finally accept. Few negotiators operate within situations in which their principals are so realistic that it is possible for them to enter bargaining with a position that approximates their best estimate of the final settlement.[4]

The effect of Party's commitment strategy on Opponent's ability to in-fluence his principals is complex. On one hand, an early-firm-commitment pattern by Party entails making a "large" initial offer (relative to what Opponent expected as Party's initial position), which may result in rais-ing the expectations of Opponent's principals, making it more difficult for Opponent to revise them downward. On the other hand, the effect subse-quently of the persistence by Party in that position without concession or hint of concession could be helpful to Opponent in achieving internal consensus on more realistic objectives. Even this effect is not assured, be-cause Opponent's principals, as well as Opponent himself, may react emo-tionally against Party's violation of the norm that a concession by one side should be matched by a concession by the other. This reaction may take the form of a miscalculated commitment by Opponent or of an actual raising of the resistance point. Thus, Party's early-firm-commitment strat-egy could be responsible for frustrating Opponent's typical pattern of achieving consensus within his own organization.

**Degree of Openness in Communication.** A critical question for the ne-gotiator in integrative bargaining is the degree of openness he should as-sume in decision-making communications. How accurately and how com-pletely does Party report his underlying concerns in an effort to define problems; how open should he be about exploring alternatives; and how candid should he be about his own preference function?

From the point of view of increasing the effectiveness of integrative bargaining, there is no question that it would be preferable for Party to share all information. Problem solving succeeds with frankness.

---

[4] Peters distinguishes one class of negotiators who tend toward the early firm com-mitment—business agents in the craft unions often state their minimum terms at the outset. They tend to be more politically secure and more isolated from the rank and file than negotiators from industrial unions who usually follow the gradual commitment strategy. Edward Peters, *Strategy and Tactics in Labor Negotiations* (New London, Conn.: National Foremen's Institute, 1955), pp. 12–32.

However, the requirements of distributive bargaining suggest anything but complete openness in communication. Consider the amount of distortion, rationing, tactical timing, and ambiguity in meaning involved in the information exchanged in distributive bargaining. One need only recall some of the tactical operations of that activity: tactics to elicit cues, minimizing of cues, conveying deliberate impressions, selective withholding of information, communicating commitment, and interposing obstacles to communication.

On the other hand, openness of communication in the decision-making process does have favorable influence on attitudes and would be consistent with Party's efforts to improve his relationship with Opponent.

Open communication can create problems for intraorganizational bargaining. Often a negotiator needs to keep his principals in the dark about developments or to exaggerate the actual level of achievement—this cannot be done when negotiations are conducted on a completely open basis. Yet, problem solving succeeds when there is participation in the deliberations by persons closest to the problems, including diverse representation from the principal group. Theoretically it might be possible to be open with Opponent for the purposes of integrative bargaining and circumspect with principals for the purposes of intraorganizational bargaining, but, practically speaking, this is difficult to execute. Thus, he may be forced to forfeit some of the gains available through integrative bargaining.

**Degree of Trust.** The state of the union-management relationship involves many attitudinal dimensions, but a key element is the matter of trust. Many of the other favorable attitudes are important because they in turn affect the level of trust between the participants. How much effort, energy, and time should Party invest in raising the level of trust? How much risk should Party be willing to assume in attempting to create trust?

Clearly to the extent that Party's interests center on the relationship and the importance of improving it, he is willing to invest himself in the process of building trust and assume whatever risks are associated with this process.

In the distributive bargaining process trusting behavior or efforts at building trust can have associated costs. Distributive bargaining assumes a conflict of interest and is in nature a *self*-interest process. Moreover, it includes many tactical operations which tend to manipulate, deceive, and coerce. Party's efforts to build trust and be trusting need to take into account the nature of this activity.

While trust can have only a limited role, it still plays an absolutely essential part in distributive bargaining. It enables the parties to agree upon and enforce the rules of play of the game. Two parties will evolve a language of symbols and a book of rules regarding which conflict tactics can be used under which conditions. The net effect of trust in distributive bargaining can be stated simply: For Party, trust determines the degree of certainty that Opponent will observe the unwritten dictionary and ground rules wherever the latter might gain an advantage in violating them.

Trust plays a more central role in integrative bargaining. It does more than circumscribe conflict behavior of the participants; it enables them to increase their joint gain. The integrative process requires open communication, which in turn depends upon trust. Moreover, the more trust and other positive attitudes which exist in the relationship, the more sincerely motivated is each party to work on the problems of the other, irrespective of anticipated substantive or attitudinal payoffs.

Trust also plays a facilitating role in intraorganizational bargaining. Indeed, for Party to execute certain tactics (going through the motions, for example) without confusing Opponent and for Opponent to behave in a helpful way (maintaining a firm position, for example) so that Party can deal with his organization, considerable trust between the two negotiators is required.

The fact is that trust appears to be an unmixed asset in negotiations. There is little to commend a policy of fostering distrust, from either the perspective of attitudinal structuring or from that of the other processes.

**Degree of Internal Control.** How much control should the negotiator attempt to exercise over the principal group in establishing negotiation objectives, strategies, and tactics? Should his attempts to achieve internal consensus be pursued in an active or in a passive manner?

The amount of control influences how the negotiator will attempt to resolve intraorganizational conflict. With more general influence he may actively persuade the principals to adopt his views. With less control he is more likely to adopt a passive role, conforming to the behavioral expectations of the principals and relying upon Opponent or on a *fait accompli* to convince the principals of the limits of the situation.

Control is usually an advantage in distributive bargaining, but occasionally it is not. It means ability to command, and it means discipline. Organizational control is especially advantageous if the leadership desires gains beyond those insisted upon by the principals. The leaders can command certain behaviors and symbolic acts which increase the bargaining power of the organization. For example, the union membership might prefer not to strike but is willing to give real authority to leadership to call a strike if in the latter's opinion it is necessary on some occasion.

However, when the principals tend to be more ambitious than the negotiator, the latter may prefer to appear to have only limited influence with his organization, thereby increasing his bargaining power vis-à-vis his opponent.

Again, the implications which the negotiator's internal control have for integrative bargaining depend upon the tendencies of the principals. If the principals have positive attitudes, are favorably disposed toward problem solving, and have relevant information and preferences, then greater and more diverse participation and influence should increase the effectiveness of integrative bargaining. If these favorable conditions are not present, then reasonably centralized authority and discussions confined to chief negotiators and a few associates increase the chances of integrative bargaining.

Control—the ability to obtain intraorganizational discipline—is also important for engaging in purposive attitude change. Only if the negotiator can prevent provocative actions on the part of his own team or principals and only if he has the authority to make the timely gesture of trust or assistance, can he effectively pursue the attitudinal structuring process.

### Synthesis in the Context of Concrete Situations

Another way of synthesizing the four processes is to converge upon concrete situations and to observe interrelationships among the four processes in these settings. We have chosen several well-known union-management relationships for this purpose. By converging on specific negotiations and by using the tools of analysis simultaneously, we should be able to gauge the usefulness of the approach taken in this study.

While each of the processes contains its own inherent logics, its own character, and is of interest in its own right, an important purpose in developing these analytic frameworks has been to increase our understanding of the total process of labor negotiations. Consequently, the ultimate test of the theory has to be seen in its application to empirical entities.

An important advantage in choosing specific union-management relationships is that it is possible to deal with bargaining activities in a more aggregate way than has been feasible thus far. Up to this point we have focused on specific negotiations and examined the requirements and the general relationships among the subprocesses during the relatively short period of a single negotiation. Now we are in a position to expand our time horizon and analyze the character of negotiations over time.

There are several important reasons for analyzing the ongoing and evolving nature of specific union-management relationships. With a longer time perspective the true character of issues can be discerned more accurately. An item may be an issue in one negotiation, but over time the issue may be redefined. This point was made briefly in the discussion of attitudinal structuring but needs to be examined and elaborated at this point.

Moreover, the longer time span permits an analysis of the interrelationships between negotiations and the other activities of collective bargaining. In our work thus far, we have only incidentally touched on contract administration. It is time to place negotiations in the larger setting of collective bargaining, wherein grievance administration plays such an important role.

Several settings have been chosen within which to examine the negotiating process. They have been chosen for their diversity as well as their national interest. The first context, the relationship between GE and IUE, raises the important issue of Boulwarism. The next three situations involve the UAW and its bargaining relationships with International Harvester, Studebaker, and General Motors. Then we move to discuss bargaining in the steel industry, West Coast longshoring, and meat-packing.

**The International Union of Electrical Workers and the General Electric Company: Boulwarism.**[5] This relationship has received considerable attention. The company's approach to negotiations has been well publicized, and many other companies have emulated what has appeared to them to be a successful strategy. The union has bitterly attacked the company's style of bargaining, the issue coming into sharp prominence recently when a trial examiner of the National Labor Relations Board found GE guilty of an unfair labor practice.

The essence of Boulwarism involves "doing right by employees." To determine what constitutes a fair offer, the company conducts considerable research. This aspect of the plan can be seen from the following description of General Electric's approach during the 1960 negotiations:

> General Electric took six days to present its findings, calling on key location employee relations managers to explain problems and what was being done by their departments. General Electric later put its presentation in a booklet and distributed it to the union committee and then widely.[6]

The research phase usually continues through the early portion of the negotiations—during this period the company listens to the union's presentation and shapes its proposal accordingly. Once the offer is crystallized, it is presented in full form; in effect, the company uses an early-firm-commitment strategy. Communicating with employees is another key aspect of the program. Since the offer represents in management's judgment what

---

[5] Much of the data for this discussion has been taken from H. R. Northrup, *Boulwarism* (Ann Arbor, Mich.: Bureau of Industrial Relations, Graduate School of Business, The University of Michigan, 1964).

For a good description of Boulwarism in another context see the "Gardner Board and Carton" case in B. M. Selekman, S. K. Selekman, and S. H. Fuller, *Problems in Labor Relations*, 2d ed. (New York: McGraw-Hill Book Company, 1958), pp. 595–605.

[6] Northrup, *op. cit.*, p. 78.

is best for the employees (when all perspectives of the business are considered), the merits of the package must be communicated to the employees.

The differentiating feature of Boulwarism is the emphasis that it places during negotiations on the management-employee axis rather than on the management-union axis. The latter axis is not ignored; but it is inevitably deemphasized by the requirements of a final-offer-first strategy and an active communication program with employees.

In a certain sense Boulwarism can be viewed as a type of integrative bargaining between management and its employees. In a process similar to market research, the "job marketeers" at GE seek to discern the needs and preferences of the employees in order to design an optimum package. Further evidence of the integrative approach can be seen in the range of options that are usually presented during negotiations. The company does not seek to establish uniform benefit plans but rather prefers to let workers within different plants choose according to their preferences.

As we have noted elsewhere, integrative bargaining cannot take place without the presence of positive attitudes. Over the years a considerable amount of trust has been cultivated by GE management with its employee group. Attitudinal structuring tactics have been frequently used, as the following quote illustrates:

> General Electric puts a major effort into manager letters to the home "big brass," appearance at meetings, speeches, etc. This is an integral part of any effective communication program.[7]

The company does not completely ignore the management-union axis. Indeed, the company attempts in several ways to emphasize the importance of this channel of interaction. First, the company meets with union representatives throughout the year as it seeks to formulate its contract proposal. On several occasions the parties have also established preliminary or pre-negotiation conferences, during which problem areas have been discussed.

Second, once negotiations start, the company refrains from presenting its offer until it fully understands the union position. When the proposal is ready, it is previewed with the union negotiating committee before it is released.

Third, the company modifies its proposal as new information is presented. This has happened in almost every negotiation, although one must note that the modifications in the offers have not been as major as the bargaining adjustments typically made by other companies.

While the company does accord some consideration to the union, one must not assume that anything approaching integrative bargaining or co-

[7] *Ibid.*, p. 33.

operation takes place between GE and the IUE. On the contrary, deliberations along this axis are distributive. Evidence for the distributive character of the deliberations between the company and the union can be seen in the following: The company has taken an extremely firm stand on such issues as union security, cost-of-living adjustments, and extent of arbitration; and during the 1960 strike it kept its plants open and offered work to anyone who wanted to cross the picket lines.

In effect, the company develops its proposal by using problem-solving techniques along the management-employee axis and then, in bargaining with the union, attempts to preserve the integrity of this proposal by actively communicating with employees, to the end that they instruct their leadership to accept the company's offer. Since a considerable amount of work and research has gone into the design of this package, there is unlikely to be any substantial modification due to the union's presentation. Moreover, due to the problem-solving quality of the research, it is quite possible that management is wedded to its solution of employee needs.

The package, however, is usually very adequate; there is no desire to get off cheaply. The point is that many companies use the gradual-commitment strategy as a way of getting off as inexpensively as possible—they stop offering money when the union indicates acceptance. Contrastingly, GE, which wants to do well by its employees, lays on the table what it feels is the best offer.

In passing, one must note that certain environmental factors favor the distributive approach that the company has taken in bargaining. The IUE is far from being the dominant union at General Electric. Many plants are unorganized, and of those that are organized many are represented by other unions. Of the approximately 106,000 employees organized at General Electric, the IUE represents about 68,000.[8]

The impact of Boulwarism on Carey and the IUE can be seen in the attitudinal structuring and intraorganizational areas. Since Carey is not able to fulfill his role requirements as a union negotiator, he fights back belligerently and aggressively. Consider the following interchange that took place during 1960:

*Moore* (GE's chief negotiator) "Your items are inflexible?"

*Carey* "Yes, they are inflexible. We have an inflexible position on them. You can mess with the small items, but not with the principles. All of our items are important in the proposal. Mr. Moore, we're going to get all of them (demands) even if we have to walk over your face. Understand that? Even if we have to walk over your face, Mr. Moore." [9]

[8] *Ibid.*, p. 48.
[9] *Ibid.*, p. 82.

On another occasion Carey has said that he "owed General Electric a strike."

In the words of Northrup, "Carey talks incessantly, . . . often accompanied by loss of temper, foul and obscene language, and threats of what is to happen if IUE demands are not met forthwith. This sometimes humorous, often extremely unpleasant behavior is unique in this writer's experience or research." [10]

In certain respects the company experiences a type of self-fulfilling prophecy. In justifying its style of bargaining, the company cites the bombastic and unpredictable behavior of Carey. However, by giving primary attention to the management-employee axis, the company helps create the kind of behavior which it finds objectionable in Carey.

In passing, we should note that not all of Carey's unpleasant conduct is merely expressive. Some of it is instrumental for the type of distributive bargaining that he finds it necessary to conduct. Consider the following example of attitudinal behavior being used for a distributive result:

> On this occasion, July 21, Carey had set the stage by noting beforehand that he wanted to attend an afternoon union-management conference of General Motors which was being held in New York. Carey also had made it clear that he did not want the negotiations to continue without him. Suddenly, just about noon, and almost wholly out of context, he directed a screaming, twice-repeated command of obscenity at the chief company negotiator, Philip D. Moore. Moore said simply: "This meeting is over right now." A few days later, in negotiations, Carey boasted that now GE had joined Westinghouse and General Motors in adjourning meetings because of his foul, abusive and obscene language.[11]

Perhaps the greatest impact of Boulwarism is in the area of intraorganizational bargaining. At the outset it should be noted that some of the internal problems which Carey experiences stem from his own ineptness. But many of them result from the Boulwarism strategy.

Over the years Carey has been beset by back-to-work movements, rejection of strike votes, and internal factionalism—the recent dispute between Carey and Harnett (Secretary-Treasurer) is a prime example. Furthermore, Carey did not sign the 1952, 1954, 1960, or 1963 agreements. They were signed and endorsed by the IUE-GE Conference Board in opposition to Carey. This fact would suggest that the company's efforts at attitudinal structuring have extended to local union leaders, whom the company views as much as employees as officers of the IUE.

An important aspect of bargaining between IUE and GE is the role of

[10] *Ibid.*, p. 59.
[11] *Ibid.*, p. 84.

third parties. Despite the company's abhorrence of third-party influence,[12] the public and the NLRB have been very much involved in negotiations, at the urging of the IUE.

Carey, being frustrated in his dealings with GE, makes frequent use of public opinion.

> Long before a contract negotiation is due to begin, the attacks on General Electric from the IUE's Washington headquarters and from key local unions are stepped up. Carey himself inaugurates a speaking and writing campaign, which often converts numerous subjects into a vehicle for attacking the company, its policies, or its personnel.[13]

With regard to the role of the government, the IUE has quite frequently filed unfair labor practice charges before the NLRB. While in terms of the ideal of minimum government intervention and free collective bargaining the IUE action might be criticized (as it has been by several commentators), from the practical realities of distributive bargaining, it is only natural for Carey to involve a third party in negotiations in order to advance his objectives, which have been frustrated by the bargaining strategy of the company.

As of the writing of this study, GE has been found guilty of an unfair labor practice by a trial examiner of the NLRB. The issue will eventually be heard by the Supreme Court. In reaching his decision, the trial examiner placed great weight on the absence of significant concessions by GE during negotiations.

This important development can be analyzed in terms of the concepts used in this study. Clearly, the trial examiner felt that GE should be more flexible in its bargaining posture. But what does flexibility mean? Does it only entail a strategy of gradually increasing commitment, with the company clearly fixed on its resistance point at the start of negotiations? Or does it go further and imply that a company cannot have preconceptions about its point of ultimate resistance? In other words, a company should enter bargaining without a firm aspiration or at least with an aspiration that can be readily modified.

If the concept of bargaining in good faith only entails approaching the settlement in steps, then the NLRB is seeking to enforce a superficial type

---

[12] This is best illustrated by the rewriting of the arbitration clause during the 1963 negotiations to neutralize the effect of three labor cases. In 1960 the Supreme Court ruled in three important cases (which have been termed the "trilogy") that courts must order arbitration unless an express provision to the contrary appeared in the contract.

[13] *Ibid.*, p. 58.

of flexibility. It is certainly true that many companies which adopt a form of gradual commitment are well fixed on their final position before negotiations open. The fact that one company unveils its final offer at the outset while the other does it gradually does not seem to be a difference on which the charge of an unfair labor practice can be sustained.

If bargaining in good faith goes further and means that the company's inherent position must be flexible, it is questionable how this requirement could ever be enforced. The resistance point cannot be observed directly; it can only be inferred from circumstantial evidence. Consequently it would be difficult for this type of flexibility to be prescribed as a matter of public policy.

**The UAW and International Harvester: Shift from Containment-Aggression to Mutual Accommodation.**[14] During most of the postwar period, negotiations between IH and UAW were dominated by distributive bargaining and were marked by unfriendly and low-trust attitudes. This extreme adversary relationship had developed for several reasons: a long period of jurisdictional rivalry between the UAW and the Farm Equipment Workers (FE) helped foster competitiveness, the company's need to regain operating efficiency (tightening production standards, realigning classifications, etc.) created considerable resentment, and organizational weaknesses on both sides made it difficult for top officials to control developments within their organization as well as dealing with each other effectively.

The vigorous distributive bargaining that took place during these troubled years was at least partly an outgrowth of the poor relationship. Both parties saw each contract negotiation as a new opportunity to get even—to exact a price for some past injury—imagined or real. The union especially viewed contract negotiations as an opportunity to seize the initiative. During negotiations union officials recalled all the problems they had encountered—at the company's hands—during contract administration, and the power bargaining they pursued provided a way of achieving some symmetry in the situation.

However, the excessive use of strike action was less instrumental in terms of distributive bargaining than it was expressive of the animosity and embittered feelings of the union toward the company. This is not to

[14] Various aspects of the IH-UAW relationship have been described and analyzed in the following documents: R. B. McKersie, "Structural Factors and Negotiations in the International Harvester Company," in A. R. Weber (ed.), *The Structure of Collective Bargaining* (New York: The Free Press of Glencoe, 1961), pp. 279–306; R. B. McKersie and W. W. Shropshire, Jr., "Avoiding Written Grievances: A Successful Program," *Journal of Business,* vol. 35 (April, 1962), pp. 135–152; and "International Harvester Company: The 1955 Negotiations and Strike," in Selekman, Selekman, and Fuller, 2d ed., *op. cit.,* pp. 606–624.

say that the propensity to strike did not serve an important function in distributive bargaining. Even though it arose out of the poor relationship, it allowed the union to fully exploit its potential bargaining power which derived from structural factors. The union's power stemmed from the fact that most of the company's plants were located in the Midwest, making it easier for the union to develop cohesion and militancy for strike action. Moreover, the company was highly integrated, and a stoppage at one plant quickly affected overall operations. The union used its favorable power position to obtain settlements above the Detroit pattern.

Starting around 1955, top officials on both sides gradually engaged in more mixed bargaining. Policy statements were drawn up to resolve controversial areas, a third party (David Cole) was called in and provided help as a mediator in solving many of the persistent problems, and organizational arrangements were developed to stabilize the situation.

One might wonder why the union wanted to move away from distributive bargaining, since it enjoyed a superior contract. The union has often been asked this question and has a ready answer; "We had the best contract in the industry, but we had difficulty realizing these gains during contract administration." In other words, the union was able to gain better contract language but was not able to realize the benefits in practice. This suggests an important point about distributive bargaining; namely, when one side is forced to give up something, there will only be a grudging acceptance. Subsequent to formal negotiations the coerced party may find ways of offsetting its concession. This is exactly what happened in the IH situation.

From the company's point of view the motivation to move away from distributive bargaining and poor attitudes was manifold: it needed to regain control of the plant, and it needed to improve attitudes, since the troubled relations were having a serious effect on employee morale.

While considerable progress was made between 1955 and 1960 in moving toward mixed bargaining and in improving the relationship, the real breakthrough occurred with the inauguration of a grievance-prevention program that has been referred to as the "new look." In a remarkable way the parties stumbled upon a plan of action for improving relations. Both sides had grown fatigued from processing large numbers of written grievances; it was estimated that between 1954 and 1959 over 48,000 grievances had been appealed to the arbitration stage. In a completely informal and experimental way top officials agreed to suspend the writing of grievances at the Memphis plant. They pledged their energies to settling grievances on the spot and in an oral fashion. The results of the experiment were reinforcing, and therefore it was gradually extended to other plants. The success of the program has been noteworthy: for the first time in many years the parties have become current in their handling of grievances, the number going to arbitration has dropped to a trickle, and relations at the local level (between foremen, steward, and employee) have been improved dramatically.

The experience of the UAW and IH in dealing with their troubled grievance machinery and relationship suggests some important points about the sequence in which attitudinal structuring and integrative bargaining occur. The impetus for the new look came from the top. Among key officials a positive relationship had developed: they trusted each other and worked together in dealing with the troublesome problems. Thus, before an innovative solution to the grievance problem could emerge, a high degree of trust and accord needed to be present.

However, the connection between these two processes was reversed at lower levels in the organization. When top officials took the new program to the plants, it evoked considerable hesitancy and apprehension. Relationships at the plant level between the local union and management remained turbulent. As a result top officials had to induce their subordinates to engage in a new program, in part by invoking their authority and in part by pleading, "Let's give this a chance, fellows." As the problem-solving approach to grievances proved successful, attitudes changed at the plant level. In other words, lower-level people entered into the program on an experimental basis, and as it succeeded, their attitude changed.

The structuring of positive attitudes has been so successful that the parties negotiated in 1961 their first contract without a strike—not that the absence of a strike is always an indication of good attitudes. In the IH situation, however, it was, since every contract during the postwar period had been accompanied by a strike. Other more important attributes of an improved relationship were manifested during the 1961 negotiations. Behavior on both sides was characterized by integrative bargaining tactics: subcommittees were established and a degree of problem solving occurred, with some integrative or partially integrative solutions emerging.

Subsequently, the parties agreed to engage in discussions preliminary to the 1964 negotiations. They followed through with a liberal sharing of information which might well have been distorted and rationed in earlier negotiations. These preparations promise more integrative bargaining in the future.

The new look has been successful because it has embodied within it many of the important principles of attitudinal structuring. Hostile attitudes cannot be changed quickly or in a dramatic fashion. They have to be changed gradually and on a trial-and-error basis.[15] The genius of the

[15] In certain respects the tension reduction efforts of IH and UAW followed the prescription of C. E. Osgood, *Graduated Reciprocation in Tension-reduction: A Key to Initiative in Foreign Policy* (Urbana, Ill.: Institute of Communications Research, University of Illinois, 1960).

new-look program has been that it has singled out something that could be handled at the local level and in a step-by-step fashion. Both sides entered the program with little hope of any dramatic results. But as the union started to drop grievances, the company started to settle more grievances; as the company brought more staff people into the picture in order to handle grievances more expeditiously, the union began to act more responsibly in representing employees. Each time members of one party behaved in a friendly or more trusting way, members of the other party suffered some cognitive imbalance and tended to adopt more favorable views of the other. The most important point is that these tentative and testing overtures were reinforced.

The key point about the new look, and one that is perhaps generally applicable to attitudinal structuring, is that it is difficult to change hostile attitudes during contract negotiations alone. The tactical requirements as well as the stakes involved in distributive bargaining place real restraints on the amount of attitudinal structuring that can take place during a single negotiation. Trust can be created more readily in a situation in which the bargaining stakes are not so large.

The greater amount of attitudinal structuring which took place during contract administration occurred because of the frequent opportunities presented by grievance handling to initiate attempts at attitudinal structuring. Furthermore, contract administration involves many members of both organizations—which is not true of contract negotiations.

Nevertheless, we do not wish to play down the importance of attitudinal structuring during contract negotiations. Precisely because the stakes are high, the time period is short, the interactions are intense, and high officials from both sides are involved, contract negotiations provide a strategic opportunity for the restructuring of attitudes. Just this has started to occur in negotiations between UAW and IH. The tenor of deliberations is still not as accommodative as that during contract administration, but a decided shift has taken place in the character of contract negotiations.

For example, much less prenegotiation "softening-up" takes place. Union handbills are much more reserved in tone, and walkouts and heated sessions are noticeably absent from contract negotiations. It should not be inferred that negotiations have moved to a completely harmonious problem-solving process, but they are moving in that direction.

**The UAW and Studebaker: "Synthetic Problem Solving."** [16] The re-

---

[16] Most of the data for this analysis have been taken from R. M. MacDonald, *Collective Bargaining in the Automobile Industry* (New Haven, Conn.: Yale University Press, 1963). An earlier account can be found in F. H. Harbison and J. R. Coleman, *Goals and Strategy in Collective Bargaining* (New York: Harper & Row, Publishers, Incorporated, 1951).

lationship which existed between the UAW and Studebaker until 1964 was regarded by many people as a problem-solving and constructive one. A good statement about what people thought was happening at Studebaker during this period appears in a study of collective bargaining in the automobile industry by MacDonald.

> The notion that "we can settle anything by talking it over," that strikes (and coercion in general) are unnecessary, that problems should (and could) be resolved amicably through reasonable discussion, certainly expresses a noble sentiment.[17]

In reality, very little integrative bargaining occurred; rather the company got the good attitudes that were favorable in some sense and the union attained the good working conditions that it desired. The company's desire to avoid strikes and perpetuate harmonious relations provided the union with bargaining power, which it was quick to use in obtaining one of the best contracts and most liberal shop practices in the automobile industry.

A good illustration of the lack of problem solving can be seen in some excerpts taken from the 1950 negotiations when the company introduced the problem of excess manpower.

> *Mr. Vance (M)* Let's be frank about this thing. We can't tie up here to a five-year wage agreement (the industry pattern) unless we open the door to getting out some of the excess manpower in this plant. . . .

> *Mr. Hill (U)* If you've got a direct problem . . . why don't you tell us how many people are involved in this question of excess manpower in the plant and say to us that you're going to take them out? Then we can fight it out on that basis. . . .

> *Mr. Vance (M)* Can you suggest a better way to resolve this problem? . . .

> *Mr. Hartmann (U)* I think we went through this before when George Hupp was president. At that time, as I recall, this Committee told you that if you saw that there was too much manpower in these departments, then it was up to you and your supervision to study that, and it was up to you fellows to take it out. If you people find any spots where there's too much manpower, then that's your job . . . it isn't ours.

> *Mr. Vance (M)* This is a very serious matter . . . it's a problem we've had before us for three or four years, and we've talked about it repeatedly, as you know.

[17] MacDonald, *op. cit.*, p. 363.

*Mr. Hill (U)* And you're making a peculiar approach to the problem. You have said to us that you've got too many people in the plant. You're saying to us that you propose to take those people out of the plant by setting up a system . . . that is certainly opposed to the principles of our Union . . . the principle of all Unions.[18]

The above discussion clearly illustrates how the union viewed the manpower question as a purely distributive issue. While management showed some disposition to engage in problem solving, it, too, displayed a distributive orientation. In its frequent attempts to correct labor practices it placed primary reliance on the leverage of the increased rates and benefits in the new contracts.

On several occasions management succeeded in putting through some reductions, but it had to go to the employees to gain acceptance for the changes. No problem solving was involved; it was merely a matter of the company invoking the possibility of plant shutdown. Convinced that the company meant business, the employees went along.

By pushing through a tightening-up program, management instituted a type of reverse trade. The company had developed a deposit of goodwill with the employees, and on that basis it was asking for some changes in the working conditions in order that it might become more competitive.

While the workers may have trusted management and were inclined to think seriously about the company's problems, the union leadership displayed little positive regard. More was involved than merely a distributive orientation on the part of the union—in fact, a distributive orientation might have led the leadership to accept some tightening up in order to save the jobs in South Bend. Rather, what was involved was a lack of concern. Many union officials held Studebaker management in low regard. They viewed it as naive, compromising, and weak. Thus the behavior of union leadership must be explained as much in attitudinal terms as in a distributive orientation which sought to maximize short-run gains.

The interesting aspect about the Studebaker situation is that the parties executed many of the steps involved in integrative bargaining: they identified problems, they shared information (Studebaker went farther than most American companies in opening its books and showing the union and employees the "facts"), but little problem solving occurred. Why? The answer no doubt rests with the top officials on both sides. They lacked either sufficient trust or insight—they never moved to the stage of developing alternatives and talking about innovative solutions.

Importantly, the conciliatory attitudes of management did not facilitate problem solving. Concessions were made without insisting that these be reinforced, and, in general, attitudinal structuring did not possess a creative function.

[18] *Ibid.*, pp. 262–264.

The Studebaker experience makes one suspicious of many so-called "model relationships" that have been publicized within the last 10 or 15 years.[19] In the light of the Studebaker experience one wonders whether in many of these situations there has not been an exchange of good attitudes for loose working practices.

What can happen is the following: The positive attitudes that facilitated the problem-solving process become important in themselves, and the parties gradually devote excessive attention to attitudinal structuring. In effect, the attitudinal structuring no longer remains functional; it becomes an obsession.

Developments between the United Steelworkers and Inland Steel Container illustrate this point. At the time that Whyte wrote his story, negotiations had shifted from conflict to cooperation. The following excerpt documents the positive attitudes as well as the constructive solutions that emerged during the late 1940s:

> *Shafer (U)* Incidentally, the question of absenteeism was considered by the union; I can assure you that the union brings that up at their meeting. For example, last Sunday there was one of the things that was discussed and I might say a fine job was done for management by Lucius and his executive committee.
>
> *Gossett (M)* We are very happy to hear that.
>
> *Shafer (U)* Of course, I concurred with the chairman of the executive committee because I personally feel where absenteeism has a tendency to hamper production in any way whatsoever, when we are a party to an agreement we are partially responsible where our union people are at fault.[20]

The real breakthrough in the relationship occurred in 1949 on the issue of arbitrating rate changes. The union had insisted on arbitration of the rate determination, while management had opposed the use of a third party on rate grievances. The solution, which must be viewed as somewhat integrative, provided for arbitration on the appropriateness of the action in setting the new rate but not on the merits of the rate itself.

With the publication of Whyte's book in 1951 both sides found themselves basking in the attention of the nation. They were held up as a model relationship—as an example of how parties could deal with one another constructively. Unfortunately, the parties paid more attention to maintaining their image as a cooperative relationship than they did to the

---

[19] C. S. Golden and V. D. Parker (eds.): *Causes of Industrial Peace under Collective Bargaining* (New York: National Planning Association, Harper & Row, Publishers, Incorporated, 1955) and W. F. Whyte, *Pattern for Industrial Peace* (New York: Harper & Row, Publishers, Incorporated, 1951).

[20] Whyte, *op. cit.*, pp. 78–79.

matter of maintaining labor efficiency and the competitive position of the plant. By early 1960 the plant found itself uncompetitive, and around 1962 a new management team took over, a sizable number of people were laid off, and other drastic measures were instituted to improve labor efficiency. In effect, management had returned to a point of view which it had expressed during the 1949 negotiations. Consider this interesting exchange:

> **Shafer (U)** We have had many situations as Mr. Caples knows very well, on wildcats and what have you that happened, and as we grow older and we live with each other longer, we can exercise more control than we have exercised in the past . . . I feel that management and the union have been quite frank in our deliberations, and throughout all of the negotiations they have been fine. The union feels that there have been no cards dealt under the table, and we respect management's representation for that to the highest degree. . . .

> **Caples (M)** What we want is very obvious. We want, not promises, but a year or two of action.

The reason that many of these model relationships have stumbled and that the observers have erred in their analysis is that the process of integrative bargaining has not been differentiated from that of distributive bargaining. As soon as good attitudes begin to emerge, the observers assume that problem solving is taking place. Actually a form of distributive bargaining can still be occurring. As we have noted elsewhere, it is quite possible for distributive bargaining to take place in the presence of positive attitudes. Positive attitudes are required for integrative bargaining, but they are not a sufficient condition, only a facilitating condition. Ideally, one would like to revisit many of the relationships studied in *Causes of Industrial Peace* to see whether real integrative bargaining has occurred or whether the good relationship has been achieved at the expense of labor efficiency.

**The UAW and General Motors: Power Bargaining Modified by Reason.**[21] When one analyzes the relationship between UAW and GM, there is no suggestion of trading labor efficiency for good attitudes. The company's concern has always been directed at maintaining labor efficiency.

> To GM management, the test of a good labor relations practice, of a good solution to a labor problem is, in the last analysis, its soundness and workability, defined in terms of its contribution to the efficiency and profitability of the enterprise. There has been no con-

---

[21] Some of the material for this analysis has been taken from MacDonald, *op. cit.* An earlier account of this relationship appeared in Harbison and Coleman, *op. cit.* For a descriptive account of the major negotiations see Selekman, Selekman, and Fuller, 2d ed., *op. cit.*, pp. 441–465.

fusion of ends, no ambiguity of purpose. "Good labor relations are not an end in themselves," states the company's spokesman. "The end management seeks and is primarily responsible for is the successful business, to produce goods and service for customers at low cost and within increasingly better quality." [22]

An important point about GM management is that it has been sufficiently in control of its antagonistic emotions that it has been able to engage in businesslike mixed bargaining. However, it must be added that only a modest amount of spontaneous trust and virtually no friendliness have characterized the relationship.

On the union side the approach has been similarly sophisticated and hardheaded. Top UAW officials realize that their collective bargaining gains have not come from attitudinal structuring but from distributive bargaining. Good evidence about the distributive character of bargaining in the automobile industry can be discerned in the sequence of union breakthrough, management response, union breakthrough, etc. For example, in 1955 the UAW committed itself to obtain some form of GAW. Ford provided the answer with the SUB program, which was also adopted by General Motors and the other automobile companies. As the plan was initially framed, it paid benefits only to people unemployed in excess of one week. As a result, the auto companies scheduled short layoffs of less than one week as a way of minimizing SUB costs. Whereupon, in the next negotiations the union bargained a short work-week benefit to deal with the companies' response. With this "loophole" closed, the companies started to stabilize employment by working people overtime rather than by hiring temporary employees. As a result the union now faces the problem of having many unemployed members while others are working overtime. In the 1964 negotiations the UAW pledged itself to eliminate excess overtime.

The above reactions and counterreactions provide good evidence that distributive bargaining has been taking place. An important characteristic of distributive bargaining (one that was alluded to briefly in the analysis of the IH-UAW) is the following: if one side is forced into doing something that it would not otherwise do, once the settlement is achieved, it will look for ways in which it can recoup its losses. Contrastingly, if the settlement had been reached through integrative bargaining, a different orientation will be present and there will be less reason to continue the process of pressure. Each side will understand the workings of the plan much better, and there will be less tendency to subvert the meaning of the agreement.[23] Thus distributive bargaining in the absence of positive at-

[22] MacDonald, *op. cit.*, p. 351*n*.
[23] For some of these points we are indebted to Melvin Rothbaum, "Economic Dilemmas of Collective Bargaining," *Annals* (November, 1963), pp. 95–103.

titudes contains a cost, one that may be seen only subsequent to the negotiations.

One aspect of the automobile situation worthy of further comment is the critical importance of intraorganizational bargaining within the UAW. Since Reuther and the other top officials in the UAW have placed primary emphasis on making major breakthroughs in the economic and fringe area, it has been inevitable that local problems have been de-emphasized. A whole host of problems centering on production standards, relief time, seniority arrangements, etc. have been relegated to supplementary talks. The difficulty with this approach came into focus during the 1961 negotiations, when, after the major issues had been settled, a series of local strikes occurred over working conditions. In preparation for the 1964 negotiations Reuther gave top priority to working conditions and said that no agreement would be signed until the last local problem had been settled.[24]

It should be noted that Reuther was able to place primary emphasis on national items as long as he maintained considerable control and a secure leadership position. The cost of ignoring local problems only took its toll after a period of time. Eventually he found it necessary, in terms of his internal position, to tend to these issues in order to maintain the support and confidence invested in him.

The tensions within the UAW gave a particular twist to the talks which took place preliminary to the 1964 negotiations. Top officials within the UAW made no report to the rank and file about the deliberations that took place between the companies and the union. More was involved than merely keeping the deliberations secret (which can be quite functional for integrative bargaining). The top leadership realized that they were in danger of losing the support of many rank-and-file people. Consequently they did not want to give too much attention to the discussions that were taking place at the top.

In a union like the UAW, where the democracy theme is emphasized and practiced, an elected official has to be careful of the steps that he takes that are not fully authorized by the membership. Consequently, the UAW officials have told the companies that their preliminary discussions are strictly unofficial and do not constitute a form of bargaining. The fact remains, however, that both sides are learning about problems and getting a better picture of what will probably be possible during negotiations. The dilemma for the leadership is to make enough progress in these preliminary talks in order that the formal negotiations be as successful as possible (really exploiting the best of mixed bargaining) while at the same time keeping control of the rank and file, who feel that their leadership has

---

[24] It might be noted that the same promise was made as far back as 1957, although there was evidence in 1964 that the promise would be kept.

had a tendency to spend too much time in discussions with top company officials on glamour items.

In terms of the framework, the conflict comes between the dictates of integrative bargaining, requiring exploratory talks and a willingness to agree on solutions far in advance of the deadline, and the dictates of intra-organizational bargaining, requiring Reuther to bargain aggressively, to spend sufficient time on local problems in the central negotiations, and to press negotiations against the deadline in order to convince the membership that as much as possible has been achieved.

**The United Steelworkers and the Steel Industry: Power Bargaining with Poor Attitudes Changing to Integrative Bargaining and Good Attitudes.**[25] The steel industry provides an interesting contrast to the automobile industry. For many years negotiations in the steel industry were as predominantly distributive as those in the automobile industry, although they were characterized by considerably more hostile attitudes. The steel industry encountered more major strikes than the automobile industry did, and the tenor of bargaining was more antagonistic (the Fairless-MacDonald plant tours notwithstanding). The culmination of this pattern took place during the 1959 negotiations and the long accompanying strike. One outgrowth of that experience has been a greater respect for the power and determination of the other side, and as a consequence both sides have been motivated to deal with each other in a much more mature manner. The Human Relations Committee has been established, and two contracts have been negotiated without resort to deadline pressures or power plays.

The point of the steel experience is that hard and adamant distributive bargaining can set the stage for integrative bargaining. In the case of steel, the aggressive approach broke down during the 1959 negotiations. The long strike produced a catharsis as well as fatigue and demonstrated the inappropriateness of an approach that had been tried during the postwar period. The parties found it necessary to experiment with new methods, and one of these involved problem solving.

One might question whether real integrative bargaining has been taking place in steel, remembering the difficulties mentioned earlier with respect to Studebaker. The evidence suggests that real integrative bargaining *has* been occurring. For example, in the 1963 "experimental agreement" the parties established a pioneering subcontracting clause and also solved some long-standing difficulties in the seniority area. These clauses were written after considerable study and discussion on both sides. And more

---

[25] The most comprehensive study of bargaining in steel was undertaken by the Department of Labor after the 1959 steel strike. See E. R. Livernash, *Collective Bargaining in the Basic Steel Industry* (Washington, D.C.: U.S. Department of Labor, 1961). For a chronology of steel bargaining in case form see Selekman, Selekman, and Fuller, 2d ed., *op. cit.*, pp. 466–519.

importantly, since 1963 these clauses have not provoked grievance activity.[26] This is in line with the earlier point that for solutions reached by integrative bargaining there is less tendency for either side to press for additional gains during the period of contract administration.

One should also note the integrative quality of developments at Kaiser Steel. As an aftermath of the 1959 negotiations a tripartite committee was established to "recommend for the consideration of the parties establishment of a long range plan for the equitable sharing of the company's progress." The plan which has resulted is an imaginative solution to the often conflicting objectives of improving efficiency and safeguarding job security.[27] Not only is the Long Range Sharing Plan the product of integrative bargaining, but it will foster more integrative activity—the establishment of committees to solve operating problems and the sense of participation inherent in the incentive system should preserve the vitality of the integrative process at Kaiser.

The USW has handled internal relationships rather well while it has been engaged in integrative bargaining. Unlike the UAW, it has not experienced difficulty within the union about the question of preliminary talks with management—the members of USW appear to be more supportive of the new process being taken toward contract negotiations. No doubt, the difference stems from the different histories and structures of the two unions. The USW is much more centralized and has always had a tradition of top-down leadership. Therefore to the extent that these talks have taken place at the initiative of top officials, they are accepted.

More importantly, people from all levels of the union have been involved in the deliberations of the different subcommittees. These committees have visited individual plants and there has been a participation by local leadership. Moreover, the proceedings have not been kept completely secret. While minutes are not kept, the gist of what is taking place has been disseminated to the rank and file.

The major problem posed by the current approach in steel arises from an interesting side effect of integrative bargaining; namely, when people agree upon a solution as a result of problem solving, they are very vigorous in defending the solution. The ramification takes this form. The steel industry is heterogeneous—there are many subsidiary operations such as containers in which the conditions are quite different from those in basic steel. A sabbatical leave plan may make sense for the basic steel industry, where the work force is of a given age and where it is relatively easy to hire replacements during the extended vacations, but in a small pail plant, for example, the situation may be completely different.

[26] Speech by Ben Fischer before the Advanced Arbitration Seminar, sponsored by the Extension Division of the University of Chicago, June 5–6, 1964.

[27] For a good analysis of the plan see Harold Stieglitz, *The Kaiser-Steel Union Sharing Plan* (New York: National Industrial Conference Board, 1963).

One of the hallmarks of an integrative solution is that it takes into account all of the uniqueness of the specific situation. Many companies within the steel industry have long complained about the poor fit of particular compromise solutions arrived at in distributive bargaining which have been applied uniformly to all participating firms. The inadequacy of one solution for all is even greater when the solution emerges from what the parties have attempted to make a problem-solving process. As one official from a container plant put the matter, "We always faced difficulty in getting a deviation from the pattern, but since the Human Relations Committee has come into business, we cannot budge them from the standard plan."

What emerges as an integrative solution for one setting may become a distributive result for another group. In other words, container management has to bargain not only with the union but with its own company management as well.

Since problem solving is enhanced by stating the item in terms of specifics rather than principles, it is clear that, when there are diverse interests and constraints on each side, problem solving (more than distributive bargaining) is frustrated by multiemployer bargaining.

**International Longshoremen's and Warehousemen's Union and the West Coast Shipping Companies: A Dramatic Shift from Distributive to Integrative Bargaining.**[28] This example and the next (meat-packing) are presented to illustrate contrasting approaches to crisis situations. In both longshoring and meat-packing severe economic adjustments are taking place as the industries modernize. The differing styles of bargaining merit attention.

Kennedy describes the changeover in West Coast longshoring as follows:

> At the Portland caucus in 1957 the union started to change its policy towards mechanization from one of intermittent guerilla warfare directed against all changes which we anticipate which would reduce the need for men to one of co-operation in mechanization with the understanding that the workers' jobs would be protected and that they would receive a substantial share of the savings that would accrue from mechanization.[29]

The main problem has occurred on the intraorganizational front. Harry Bridges has experienced opposition from certain groups within the union who feel that he has "sold out" on the rights of workers. In the mechanization agreement the union gave its assent that the minimum crew size be reduced, that multiple handling could be eliminated, that the companies

[28] For an analysis of developments in West Coast longshoring see: Thomas Kennedy, *Automation Funds and Displaced Workers* (Boston: Division of Research, Graduate School of Business Administration, Harvard University, 1962), pp. 70–101.

[29] *Ibid.*, p. 76.

could introduce larger slings, etc. When a shipping company actually introduces the new methods, however, resistance usually occurs. From the viewpoint of Bridges the agreement is a *high-benefit* (a large mechanization fund with which to guarantee job security and to finance better pensions for the workers) as well as a *low-sacrifice* arrangement (the jobs would eventually be eliminated whether the union cooperated or not). But from the viewpoint of the affected worker the arrangement may appear highly distributive (he has to work harder for benefits that are not realizable, in large part, until he retires). Being a strong leader, Bridges has been able to deal with these difficulties, and one would predict that eventually most members of the union will come to view the mechanization fund as an integrative solution.[30]

**The United Packinghouse Workers and Armour: Mixed Bargaining.** The UPW has faced a crisis in the meat industry. Plants are being shut down in large urban centers, automation is shrinking the work force, and the opening of new plants in outlying areas is placing great pressure on the national wage structure. Unlike Harry Bridges and the approach of the ILWU, the UPW has decided not to cooperate with the changes. Rather it has fought a type of rearguard action, seeking to prevent plant shutdowns and any modifications in the existing wage structure.

The reason for the difference in approach must be seen in the area of intraorganizational bargaining. In both longshoring and meat-packing the union leadership faces constituencies with aspirations not in line with the realities of the situation. However, the leaders of the ILWU have dealt with the outlook of the membership directly and *actively*, while the leaders of the UPW have dealt with aspirations indirectly and *passively*. Why the difference? Several reasons can be given. First, in West Coast longshoring there is only one union, and it is extremely strong; while in meat-packing there are several unions, and the problem of union rivalry is always present. A second reason, and one just as important, is that in longshoring the total industry is organized, while in meat-packing there are many nonunionized plants. Consequently the leaders of UPW have to appear militant [31] and have to fulfill behavioral expectations in order to maintain their

---

[30] By contrast, the situation in East Coast longshoring has resisted solution. The difficulty appears to lie in the intraorganizational area; the leadership of the ILA has not been able to "sell" an innovative arrangement to the membership.

[31] Interestingly, the other major union in meat-packing, the Amalgamated Meatcutters and Butcher Workmen, has adopted a much more permissive attitude toward concessions. Faced with similar circumstances, the Amalgamated has approved rollbacks in wage and fringe benefits in order to prevent plant closings and preserve employment. To explain the respective responses, we would need to conduct a full analysis of the differences between the Amalgamated and the UPW—which would take us beyond the purposes of this section. Suffice it to say that the craft, conservative, and local autonomy character of the Amalgamated versus the industrial, aggressive, and national control character of the UPW can explain much of the contrast.

standing with the rank and file, while Harry Bridges has enjoyed a much stronger position and consequently has been able to reach integrative arrangements with the companies.

Not all bargaining by the UPW has been defensive; it has entered into automation funds with several meat-packing companies, the Armour Fund [32] being the best known. As a result of these automation funds a number of important arrangements have been developed to deal with the manpower problem inherent in technological change: retraining programs, advance notice, and manpower planning (eventually new plants will be opened as old plants are abandoned), etc. All of these solutions must be seen as integrative. Hence a mixed picture exists in meat-packing, the union behaving distributively on certain key matters such as wage rates and innovatively on arrangements for displaced personnel.

A final comment on the developments in the agricultural-implement, auto, steel, longshoring, and meat-packing industries: The integrative bargaining, which for the most part has increased, has not obviated the need for distributive bargaining between the parties. True, it has supplanted distributive bargaining in which the parties have been able to drop their earlier assumptions that most agenda items were issues. In most cases the main economic problems are still handled distributively, but the parties have been able to *add* integrative bargaining to the total process. They have increased their skill at mixed bargaining—devising ways of resolving some of the dilemmas, e.g., separating the processes by time, place, persons, agenda, ground rules, and so forth. We believe that if this book were written with greater perspective on these current developments in the field, the theoretical and illustrative treatment of integrative and mixed bargaining would assume a more dominant part in the elaboration of the total process.

[32] For a comprehensive account see Kennedy, *op. cit.*, pp. 129–160, and the various reports of the Armour Automation Fund Committee.

# CHAPTER XI

# SOCIAL NEGOTIATIONS IN INTERNATIONAL RELATIONS AND CIVIL RIGHTS

This chapter represents a brief exploration of how the theory might be applied in areas other than labor negotiations, specifically, in international relations and civil rights. The tasks of this chapter are first, to further define social negotiations, second, to analyze illustrative cases in international and civil rights in terms of the theoretical framework, and third, to identify those contextual factors in social negotiations which lead to different tactical content and emphasis.

**The Concept of Social Negotiations.** At the beginning of this study we presented the concept of social negotiations and suggested that labor negotiations was but one instance of this more general phenomenon. Since we would like to apply the theory to two other settings, we first need to be more specific about the defining properties of social negotiations.

It is most appropriate to build our conception of social negotiations on a cornerstone definition of bargaining. The following attempt to delimit the term "bargaining" is typical:

> There are at least two characteristics essential to bargaining situations: first, a conflict of interest of the parties cannot be satisfied completely and simultaneously; second, a possibility of mutual gain through cooperation—gain meaning more than each party could achieve by going it alone. . . . In order to differentiate this from all of politics, let us assume that bargaining applies to certain well-defined items or to a relatively fixed arena of common concern or behavior. . . . After mutual attempts to influence the choices of the parties in the most favorable manner, the successful outcome of the

bargaining process results in the movement of the parties to a commonly acceptable point of agreement. . . . The bargaining relationship arises out of scarcity of resources or satisfactions *and* interdependence.[1]

In effect, this definition fully embraces only one subprocess—distributive bargaining. Its function for the interacting parties is to influence the allocation of some scarce value between them. When the parties bring other needs to the situation and must work within certain other constraints, they require in turn that the interaction perform other functions for them.

Our definition of social negotiations involves a particular configuration of these other functions. In addition to (1) an awareness of the inherent conflict of interest in a decision-making situation, the parties must (2) wish to solve common problems or integrate their interest in other ways, (3) desire to maintain or change the basic attitudes of trust and friendliness between them, and (4) be responsible for achieving consensus or acceptance within their respective groups. When these four conditions are present, the complex set of activities which results is "social negotiations." When the first three conditions, but not the fourth, are present, the activities might be called "interpersonal negotiations." "Mixed bargaining," of course, results from the first two conditions.

The term social negotiations refers to the combination of, and interaction among, four subprocesses: distributive and integrative bargaining, attitudinal structuring, and intraorganizational bargaining. That definition, like all definitions, is somewhat arbitrary. Further justification for conceptualization of this combination of processes is provided by two other conditions which we believe are present. The first is that this combination is more than an additive one; it involves dynamic interaction among the analytic subparts. Our dilemma discussions are indicative of this characteristic. The second condition is that this combination is not unique to labor negotiations; it is encountered in other social settings.

We turn to this latter question by analyzing the nature of international relations and bargaining involving the civil rights movement. Are these two phenomena instances of social negotiations, in the sense that they embrace the several subprocesses?

---

[1] R. C. Snyder and J. A. Robinson, *National and International Decision-making* (New York: The Institute for International Order, 1961), p. 119. See also J. G. March and H. A. Simon, *Organizations* (New York: John Wiley & Sons, Inc., 1958); and N. W. Chamberlain, *A General Theory of Economic Process* (New York: Harper & Row, Publishers, Incorporated, 1955).

# PART 1 | SOCIAL NEGOTIATION CASES

### Analysis of an International Negotiation

**Introduction.** What types of international situations are most amenable to analysis as an instance of social negotiations? The Geneva disarmament negotiations and other scheduled discussions between two countries with distributive agenda items would come closest to the type of activities analyzed in labor negotiations. Equally suitable would be summit diplomacy —the occasional meetings of the heads of states or of foreign ministers. However, also appropriate would be crisis situations such as those in the post-World War II period that have developed over Berlin (1948), Korea (1950), Matsu-Quemoy (1954), Suez (1956), Congo (1960), Cuba (1963), and Vietnam (1963–1965). Of course, Berlin has been a crisis situation on several occasions since 1948. Such crises may not involve extended discussions between the countries, but our analysis of negotiating behavior is not confined to official verbal exchanges, rather it includes other public utterances and political, economic, and military moves of many types. The crisis situation makes analysis of this larger class of behavior more convenient.

In a crisis a large percentage of the behavioral output of the particular decision makers is related to a limited range of agenda items. In addition, much of the relevant behavior occurs during a comparatively short period of time. This not only facilitates observation but it increases the tensions among the subprocesses. For example, the tactical requirements of bargaining and attitudinal structuring with the opponent and the necessity of dealing with certain other incompatible expectations from within the country are more likely to be happening simultaneously in a rapidly developing situation.

**Background.** Our illustrative analysis centers on the crisis over Russian missiles in Cuba.[2] During the latter part of the summer of 1962, the United States, both its citizens and government, became apprehensive over a Soviet military buildup in Cuba. The events which transpired during the fall of 1962 are well known but probably require some recapitulation. The key events have been summarized in the following chronology:

> *August 25–29* The State Department reports that Russia has increased shipments of arms and military personnel to Cuba. The United States informs Russia that it is concerned and is watching. Russia replies that they are not doing anything foolish or suspicious; they are just shipping goods to Cuba.

[2] We are indebted to one of our students, William Jewell, for the following chronology and many of the insights about the Cuban crisis.

*August 30* President Kennedy bars invasion by the United States and tells the press that he "doubts" that the Soviet personnel are military.

*September 3* Russia announces that it has agreed to supply military personnel to train Cuban troops. The State Department says that this is nothing new. Several congressmen assail the administration for not taking a more aggressive position.

*September 5* President Kennedy pledges that the United States will act after any aggression from Cuba. Rusk assures Latin America that the United States is determined to stop the spread of communism.

*September 8* The administration requests authority to call up 150,000 reserves for one year but states that the buildup is for Berlin, not Cuba.

*September 9* The United States expresses concern about Allied ships carrying arms to Cuba. Great Britain responds that there are no arms on her ships.

*September 12* Russia warns that any attack on Cuban or Russian ships might bring on nuclear war. She also charges that the reserve buildup is an act of aggression.

*September 16* The United States attempts and fails to persuade the Allies and neutral countries to discontinue the use of their ships for shipment of arms to Cuba. Great Britain pleads that it has no control over long-term shipping contracts.

*September 17–21* A number of senators make speeches attacking the administration and warn President Kennedy against any secret deals. The Senate overwhelmingly passes a resolution sanctioning the use of force if necessary.

*September 22* Gromyko warns the United States that an attack on Cuba means war.

*September 29* The Senate moves to bar aid to countries transporting arms to Cuba. The administration begins threatening the Allies to conform to our position—persuasion has clearly failed.

*October 2* Several smaller countries including Greece and Turkey agree to stop sending arms.

*October 5* The United States sets tough penalities on ships transporting arms to Cuba, including loss of all United States cargoes and port privileges. Mexico calls Cuba an American problem and denies any obligation to help. Most countries are now cooperating on shipping with the major exception of Canada.

*October 11* Mexico changes its position and declares that the Cuban government is incompatible with the others in the Western Hemisphere. Senator Keating reports that missile bases are being built in Cuba. The administration denies knowledge of this.

*October 15–17* Several sources report that Russia has offered a more moderate course on Cuba in exchange for Berlin concessions.

*October 22* After a week of calm, President Kennedy announces a naval and air "quarantine" on shipment of offensive military equipment to Cuba. Responsibility is placed on Russia, and Gromyko is accused of giving the administration false assurances. The United States asserts that it will act alone if necessary. In addition it requests meetings of the United Nations Security Council and the Organization of American States. The announcement is backed up with the declaration that any missile launched from Cuba at any American nation will be regarded as an attack on the United States and will precipitate full retaliation against the Soviet Union.

*October 23* Stevenson requests a meeting of the UN Security Council in order to submit a United States resolution for immediate dismantling and removal of Russian missiles in Cuba under UN supervision. Congressional and Cabinet leaders fly to Washington, and civil defense preparations are under way.

*October 24* After an appeal by Rusk, the OAS unanimously approves use of force to carry out the quarantine. President Kennedy signs a proclamation putting United States quarantine into effect and authorizes force, if necessary, to enforce it. Russia challenges the right of United States to impose a quarantine and warns the United States of the risk of nuclear war. Moscow radio and press report that Russia would not attack unless provoked.

*October 25* U Thant asks the United States and Russia to suspend activities for two weeks. Russia agrees to the request, but the United States only agrees to talk with Thant. It refuses to enter discussions with Russia until the missile threat is dispelled. Russia returns our blockade proclamation without comment but pledges not to make any reckless decisions. Several Russian ships alter their course away from the blockade.

*October 27* Russia agrees to keep its ships away from the blockade, and the United States agrees to avoid confrontation. The United States points out that Russia has repeatedly stated since 1960 that they do not need foreign-based missiles, indeed, they can reach the United States from their own country.

*October 28* Russia proposes a trade of United States missiles in Turkey for Russian missiles in Cuba. President Kennedy immediately responds that Russia had made an earlier offer which did not involve a swap. United States officials report that the crisis is escalating by citing the firing on United States planes and other acts of Cuban belligerence.

*October 29* The United States and Russia agree on Russia's first offer: Russia pledges to stop work on the bases and dismantle the missiles under UN supervision; the United States promises to lift its blockade and not to invade Cuba. President Kennedy hails Khrushchev's "contribution to peace" and discloses that the alternative facing the United States was an air attack on the Cuban bases.

**Distributive Bargaining.** Preliminary to our analysis of the Cuban crisis we need to clarify our purpose. It is *not* to present a carefully documented, authoritative treatment of this important historical event. It is rather to present an illustrative analysis of the event which is merely suggestive of the use of the theoretical framework in international relations.

An analysis of the distributive bargaining that occurred over Cuban missiles can be divided into several phases: assessment, commitment, and convergence on an agreement.

*Assessing Opponent's resistance point.* During the period leading up to the announcement of the quarantine, each side was probing for the other's resistance point. The United States and Russia threatened and counterthreatened, each threat being a little stronger than the preceding one. During September the United States exhibited concern but also showed flexibility. The statement "we are watching" warned Russia not to do anything foolish. The statement that the administration doubted that the Soviet personnel were military suggested that a different view might be taken if they were military. As it later turned out, they were military and nothing was done, suggesting that the resistance point of the United States did not preclude that Russian move. The closest the United States came to stating its resistance point was in indicating that it would act after any aggression from Cuba and that it would use force if necessary in handling the Cuban situation.

Quite significantly, the United States implied that it was preparing to take a committed position more ambitious than that. Even before the United States action took place on October 22, it executed several confirming tactics, including the call-up of 150,000 reserve personnel and the Senate resolution on the use of force. In this case the execution of the confirming tactics did not wait upon the verbal statements of commitment but preceded and anticipated the position statement.

During the same period, Russia also remained flexible with respect to where it might make a firm tactical commitment: however, it did reveal a current resistance point, namely, that an attack by the United States on Cuba "meant war." Earlier Russia had said that an attack on Cuba "might" bring on "nuclear" war. Thus, as the crisis deepened, Russia increased its commitment about the certainty of a military response, but in neglecting to mention "nuclear," it became less specific about the nature of the war response.

Thus, it probably became apparent to the two negotiators that there was for the moment a positive range between their respective resistance points. But it was also apparent that the United States especially was likely to toughen its inherent resistance point. Both leaders knew that there was internal pressure on the government of the United States to take a stronger position and that the government would certainly gain more facts about the military buildup in Cuba. Since neither was willing to settle for his current resistance point nor to allow the other a clear field to revise his own minimum demands, the situation became "subject to negotiation."

*Making tactical commitment.* Russia advanced an offer to take a more moderate course on Cuba in exchange for Berlin concessions. Since the United States was moving toward a committed position and felt that it had accurately assessed the resistance point of Russia, it expressed no interest in the Russian offer.

On October 22 the United States clearly spelled out its committed position. The commitment was firm both in the finality of the position and the specificity of that position. In other words, it was clear that we *would* get the *Russian missiles out of Cuba.* The commitment did not overlap any previously made Russian commitments and thus did not require a move on Russia's part which she could not accept.

Significantly, the United States allowed two days to elapse between the announcement of its committed position and the executing of the first consequence, the blockade of ships going into Cuba. By giving the Russians a chance to think about possible moves, the United States was not forcing its opponent into any hasty, irrational decision.

Many additional confirming tactics were executed once the verbal commitment had been taken:

1. The United States announced its willingness to act alone, although it secured support from the OAS and moved to receive support from the world community through the United Nations.

2. Civil defense preparations were inaugurated.

3. Congressmen were brought back to Washington, and the entire nation put on a state of alert.

4. President Kennedy went before the American people on television and started to develop their support for the current position of the country and any future action which might be deemed necessary. President Kennedy was in effect informing Russia that his democratic government was developing commitment to its own citizens. Credibility for this was enhanced by many of the militant statements made throughout the earlier days of the crisis.

***Convergence.*** Having taken a fairly specific position and having begun the escalation of consequences, the United States found itself in the position of forcing convergence on its own terms. While Russia's first response warned of the risk of war, it was fairly moderate in tone and suggested that Russia had not yet decided on its next move and was keeping a fluid position. Although she did not immediately turn her ships around in the face of blockade, she made a subsequent statement, "we will not make any reckless decisions."

The United States maintained its firm position even in the face of the request from the United Nations for a cooling-off period. In refusing to accept U Thant's proposal, President Kennedy was apparently taking a page from Premier Khrushchev's bargaining book. In 1959, Khrushchev said that nations could not trade concessions for concessions with Russia because Russia had no concessions to make. President Kennedy sensed that he had the edge and had nothing to gain from a bargaining session with Russia, even under the auspices of the United Nations.

The first explicit move toward convergence came from Russia when its ships changed course and avoided the blockade. Then joint movement toward agreement occurred as Khrushchev agreed to avoid the blockade and Kennedy agreed to avoid confrontation.

With still no concrete action on the missiles, the United States then increased the pressure by citing Cuban belligerence and indicating that the crisis was escalating, even though the blockade was being observed.

Finally on October 29 Russia and the United States reached agreement, Russia pledging to stop work on the bases and to dismantle and to remove them under UN supervision and the United States promising to lift its blockade and not to invade Cuba.

Before this agreement on October 29 Khrushchev made a second offer, which was less favorable than the first offer. Why he made a second offer is not clear. It may be that Khrushchev was trying to force acceptance of his first offer by making a second and less agreeable offer, since the White House had not replied to his first offer. If this were the case, he succeeded. Another possibility is that Khrushchev felt that his first offer was weak and he feared being charged with appeasement. It is also possible that the first offer was a delaying tactic, which would have enabled Russia to complete its bases, thereby altering the bargaining situation.

The United States was able to move Russia back to its first offer by the buildup of pressure and the suggestion that attacks from Cuba on surveillance planes might be met in kind. In announcing the agreement, President Kennedy indicated that the alternative facing the United States was an air attack on the Cuban bases. This had an additional effect in suggesting to Khrushchev that he was wise in not having forced our hand;

in addition, it added credibility to any future threats that we might need to make in dealing with Russia.

While most of the bargaining maneuvers by the United States were commitment tactics, i.e., they communicated intentions, at least one tactic used was aimed at the other's perceptions of his own utilities. At a crucial point in the encounter, the United States pointed out to Russia that Russia did not need foreign-based missiles.

**Integrative Bargaining.** There was little, if any, opportunity for problem solving in this encounter. One area in which there might have been parallel interests between the United States and Russia was in constraining the Cubans from provocative behavior which might have heightened the hostilities between the major powers and increased the likelihood of war over issues that were not important to the Russians. If true, this was a coincidence of interests about how the situation might have been handled tactically. But this combination of interests may also have led to a continuation of Russia in Cuba, using its own personnel to man many of the defensive weapons allowed under the agreement.

Another related area of apparently parallel objectives was that the strategies employed and the outcome which resulted should minimize the gains of the Red Chinese—gains either as a challenger in the total Communist community or as a would-be participant in the affairs of Cuba.

Finally, there may have been some mixed bargaining around the substantive question of what weapons in Cuba are tolerable to the United States. President Kennedy's distinction between offensive and defensive missiles may have been part of an attempt to search for those features of an outcome which involved the lowest sacrifice for Russia and the highest gain for the United States.

This distinction possessed tactical advantages in the other processes, including distributive bargaining. It provided a point of prominence on the continuum from maximum war capability to no-war capability for Cuba. The distinction of defensive and offensive weapons also increased the legitimacy of our position to eliminate the class of weapons of most concern to us. The qualitative prominence of the point—even if it was not wholly operational—and the legitimacy attached to the distinction therefore had advantages for us in making a credible commitment to an intermediate objective. This intermediate point may have been as favorable as possible to us under the circumstances.

**Attitudinal Structuring.** Neither the United States nor Russia wanted to add to the hostilities between their countries. Although they both have felt compelled to pursue power strategies in the highly distributive game of world politics, they have frequently attempted to minimize the impact of these moves by cultivating a degree of trust and friendliness between their countries. Several aspects of the way in which the Cuban negotiations were handled had implications for attitudinal structuring.

The distinction between offensive and defensive weapons in Cuba and our tacit acceptance of the latter communicated some self-imposed limits to our objectives in those negotiations. Not to have done this would have been to create more fear and distrust on the part of Russia as well as Cuba.

Even though the United States commitment was meant to be firm, special effort was made to indicate that the United States was acting responsibly and was not taking a belligerent attitude. When the troops were called up, the United States indicated that the action was for the Berlin situation rather than for Cuba. Once the showdown stage arrived, the word "quarantine" rather than "blockade" was chosen to avoid sounding more provocative.

By citing Cuban belligerence, the United States hoped to dissociate its feelings toward Cuba from those toward Russia. At no time did the United States talk about Russian belligerence. On the other hand, the United States did hold Russia formally responsible for actions which the Cubans might take—in an effort to encourage as much internal discipline as possible on the Communist side.

The correspondence between President Kennedy and Premier Khrushchev which was made public frequently began by expressing appreciation for some act or by mentioning some object favorable to both parties. Moreover, when Premier Khrushchev moved to reduce tensions, President Kennedy followed—a reinforcement for Premier Khrushchev's cooperative move. Finally, when the settlement was reached, President Kennedy hailed Premier Khrushchev's "contribution to peace." Above all he did not try to make capital out of what at the time was generally regarded as a victory for Kennedy and a defeat for Khrushchev.

**Intraorganizational Bargaining.** Intraorganizational bargaining on the United States side can be analyzed at two levels: that taking place within the United States and that occurring within the Allied countries.

*Bargaining within the United States.* The task facing President Kennedy was twofold. During the reconnoitering period this meant keeping control of the militants or "hawks" (as they were referred to at the time) and preventing them from forcing the United States into an untenable position. And yet his task also involved mobilizing and keeping available enough public arousal so that he would have full support and commitment for any warlike move which might become necessary as the situation developed.

The administration experienced considerable pressure from many people: Senator Keating assailed the "do-nothing" policy, Senator Thurmond urged an invasion, Senator Goldwater recommended a blockade, and the American Legion urged the destruction of Castro.

President Kennedy sought to neutralize these pressures by indicating that the administration was acting as any American would expect it to act; it was fulfilling the behavioral expectations of the electorate. On occasion, President Kennedy sought to change the outlook by expressing doubt that Russian missiles were really present in Cuba.

In turn, several key constituents sought to prevent the use of a tactic commonly used in intraorganizational bargaining, namely, "keeping people in the dark," by warning the administration against making any secret deals with Russia.

Once the United States took a committed position, the problem of maintaining internal control shifted to dealing with the "doves." President Kennedy faced the task of raising the resistance point of most Americans to that of his own and also developing a will to fight on the part of the American people. He did this by going on television, calling in congressmen, and generally alerting the nation to the importance of the national objective which was involved.

The only problem he faced with the hawks was the necessity of rationalizing the earlier statements of the administration that people like Senator Keating were mistaken about the missile threat. The bad faith of Gromyko was used as the rationalizing device. In effect, the administration said: "We believed Gromyko's assurances that nothing belligerent was taking place within Cuba; once we learned that missiles were being installed, we quickly moved to take decisive action."

*Bargaining within the Allies.* During the reconnoitering period the United States tried with only moderate success to rally the Allies behind the United States position. Some of our closest allies, closest in terms of geography or common interest, such as Great Britain, Canada, and Mexico, refused to go along with us and said that Cuba was our own problem. The little support that we achieved came in response to pressure rather than to persuasion. Greece and Turkey agreed to go along after we had announced an embargo on ships supplying armaments to Cuba. While we did receive some verbal support (Mexico changed its position early in October and declared that the Cuban government was incompatible with those of the Western Hemisphere, and the OAS passed a mild resolution of support), at the level of specific action, such as controlling shipping movements, little concrete help was received.

The difficulty in getting support and consensus within the Allied group quickly changed after the United States announced its plan of action on October 22 and disclosed details of the missiles in Cuba. The OAS passed a resolution of full support, and the Allies backed the United States.

Once the United States had taken a committed position, it presented the Allies with a forced-choice situation. More importantly, they could support our plan of action because of the missiles in Cuba. During the reconnoitering phase any support for the United States might have appeared as giving in to the United States' obsession over Cuba. Thus, in terms of the political situation within the different countries it was easier for these governments to support us once they were presented with concrete evidence about missiles in Cuba, rather than merely on the basis of our assertion that a Russian-armed Cuba was an untenable part of the Western Hemisphere.

It was crucial for the United States to work with the Allies during the reconnoitering phase, even though strong support was not forthcoming. By discussing matters with the Allies, the United States was able to assess the prospects of support once the commitment stage arrived. In other words, the United States avoided the type of fiasco which occurred around Suez, in which Great Britain, not having consulted with its allies in advance, found itself acting alone.

### Analysis of a Civil Rights Negotiation

**Introduction.** Little is required by way of orientation to the civil rights movement, which achieved the proportions of a social revolution during the 1960s. The history of the Negro revolt, no doubt, goes back to the days of emancipation and earlier, but it was given particular impetus by the 1954 Supreme Court decision on school desegregation and by other critical events in Montgomery in 1955–1956. By 1963 the revolt had spread to the North, and during that year almost every large city witnessed sit-ins, demonstrations, boycotts, and other pressure tactics.

Many of the groups within the civil rights movement have a long history of service—the National Association for the Advancement of Colored People (NAACP) and the Urban League, to cite two. However, with the upsurge in activity many new groups have been formed, such as the Student Nonviolent Coordinating Committee (SNCC), Southern Christian Leadership Conference (SCLC), and Negro American Labor Council (NALC). Other activist groups which had been on the scene a little longer, such as the Congress of Racial Equality (CORE), also became very active.

The approaches of the various groups fall into three categories: persuasion, due process, and direct action. The Urban League best illustrates the persuasion and education approach. It advocates change through consensus and agreement. The NAACP best represents the due process approach, which effects change through the courts and legal redress. The newer groups use the direct-action approach. While they employ the term nonviolent, their approach often involves civil disobedience and embraces a variety of power tactics aimed at forcing change.

Our analysis will focus primarily on strategies involving direct action, since these methods also often involve negotiating activity. The direct-action groups have operated along a wide front: education, housing, public accommodations, and employment. This brief case illustrates an attempt to expand employment opportunities for Negroes.[3]

The encounter took place during the summer and fall of 1963. The company which was chosen as the target is a large national firm producing consumer, industrial, and military products. Several direct-action groups were involved: NALC, CORE, and SNCC.

During the early phase of the campaign the company refused to meet with the civil rights groups to discuss its employment practices. When the movement planned a demonstration directed against the company, management agreed to meet. Subsequently, four sessions were held between the company and representatives from the different direct-action groups. As a result of the deliberations, over 100 additional Negroes were hired, and many issues relating to their recruitment and introduction were discussed and resolved.

The details of the case will be developed as we analyze the episode in terms of the four subprocesses of social negotiations.

**Distributive Bargaining.** Preliminary to distributive bargaining the civil rights groups needed to ensure that they had adequate knowledge and understanding of the issue—they needed to know the nature and extent of the conflict of interest between themselves and the company. These groups knew that they wanted to change the *status quo*—in the direction of more and better employment opportunities in the company. But what was the *status quo*? And what would be the objective?

Beginning in the spring of 1963, several volunteers from the NALC, the lead group in the campaign, gathered data on the employment complexion of the given company. They did this by standing outside the employment gates and conducting a census of Negroes working at the company. They also secured information from the Urban League, which had been dealing with the company for several years on the question of how to introduce more Negroes.

When the NALC had convincing evidence that discrimination was being practiced by the company, they sent a letter requesting a chance to discuss the whole matter with the company. The company never answered the first letter or subsequent letters. This pointed up the critical problem in entering into negotiations—the civil rights groups had no inherent bargaining power.

The main task, then, facing the civil rights groups was to create a

[3] Portions of this case have appeared in the following study: R. B. McKersie, "The Civil Rights Movement and Employment," *Industrial Relations*, vol. 3 (May, 1964), pp. 1–21.

negotiating base with the target company. Commanding the attention of the recalcitrant employer took several months and involved direct-action tactics.

The first development toward this end took place at a rally held by the Coordinating Council of Civil Rights Organizations in Chicago (CCCO). At a workshop dealing with employment issues the chairman of NALC presented the facts on the target company. Participants were asked to volunteer to work on the project, and the chairman used the session for developing a sense of commitment on the part of the civil rights workers to do something about the situation in the company. At the meeting it was announced that a demonstration outside one of the company's show-rooms in downtown Chicago was being planned.

Subsequent to the meeting the leadership spent its time rallying support among interested labor groups and other direct-action groups for the demonstration. On the eve of the demonstration CCCO asked for a post-ponement, presumably in order to rally more support for the effort. The leadership agreed, and the demonstration was held in abeyance for several weeks.

At this point NALC released to the press a letter they had sent to the company:

> The policy of racial discrimination as practiced by your company is a well-known fact. You apparently violate the purpose, rules and regulations of the President's Committee on Equal Employment Opportunity, President Kennedy's Executive Order 10925, the Constitution of the United States, and in case of your plants, in the State of Illinois, The Illinois Fair Employment Practices Act.
>
> In regards to your plants in Chicago, we demand that you employ 1,000 Negroes by August 1st, 1964; at least 100 Negroes by October 1, 1963. A policy statement by you indicating compliance to these demands would be an important first step.

The company never responded directly to the leadership of the NALC but released a statement to the press.

> Our program for integration is reviewable by the Federal government and we are reviewed annually and have been found in compliance every year. We have Negroes on the payroll who have been with us for many years who share in the same benefits as other employees.
>
> To meet the objectives of the President's program we have accelerated the hiring of Negroes, such talent as Negro engineers, college-degree accountants, technicians, office and clerical employees and hourly workers.

It is clear that the NALC was trying to create a basis for bargaining by threatening to continue to publicly embarrass the company—damaging its image and good name in the community. For its part, the company sought to neutralize these attacks through its communication program. No direct contact had been established between the parties, and no basis for bringing the employer to the bargaining table had yet been created.

This basis came with the setting of a second date for the demonstration. On the eve of the demonstration the company finally communicated with the NALC and asked for a meeting date two weeks hence. The demonstration was suspended.

At the first meeting the company went to great lengths to explain why it had not communicated or met with the civil rights movement earlier. It maintained that company counsel suspected a union-organizing campaign in disguise of a civil rights drive. "When it became clear that the leadership was only interested in the area of civil rights, then the company was willing to meet." Obviously, the company felt it necessary to introduce some type of rationalization tactic as a way of abandoning its previous position of refusing to meet. It preferred not to be viewed as having conceded in the face of the demonstration threat.

At the first session distributive bargaining took place. The civil rights movement used the specter of the demonstration to drive home its point that the company must quickly hire many more Negroes. Specifically, the direct-action groups requested the following: the establishment of an employment office in the Negro section of Chicago, the insertion of advertisements in the Negro press, a public statement that discussions were taking place, and a statement that the company recognized its responsibility to hire without respect to color.

The company spokesman met the conflicts of interest by carefully handling the demands which would have been costly to the company. For example, he agreed to "consider" the idea of an employment office on the South Side, but he was thoroughly opposed to the idea, and as it turned out, nothing was ever done on this matter. (Such an employment office would have put the company in the embarrassing position of having to turn away thousands of Negroes, thereby creating considerable ill will.)

Similarly, the company delayed on the question of releasing a press statement. Again, the company wanted to avoid any disclosure that might create the impression that the company was giving in or initiating changes under pressure from the civil rights movement. The direct actionists preferred to give publicity to their successes in part for the benefit of Negroes and in part for the "lesson" value it might have for other reluctant employers.

The company did agree to inaugurate a program of advertising in the

Negro press—this had little cost and promised to produce a desirable stream of Negro candidates. This was the only instance of mixed bargaining in the first session. On the basic issue of expanding employment opportunities for Negroes, the parties were apart. The civil rights movement wanted a large number of Negroes hired very quickly. As they put the demand, "We have to report back to our people who are ready for direct action that something concrete is coming out of this meeting." The company spokesman met the demand by endorsing the objective, but saying, "You have to give me time to find the people and to prepare my organization for change."

**Integrative Bargaining.** During the second, third, and fourth sessions the character of the deliberations moved more and more toward mixed and integrative bargaining. During the first session the parties had agreed upon the objective of introducing more Negroes, but there was disagreement over the rate of progress. In addition, they had agreed on some implementing steps, such as advertising in the Negro press. During subsequent sessions the amount of collaboration increased. The parties started to talk about problems. Consider two examples:

*Recruiting Negroes.* During the second session the company reported that it was having problems attracting a sufficient number of qualified Negroes. The leaders of the civil rights movement responded that they would do what they could to inform the community—in particular, by placing churches and social service agencies in touch with the company. The suggestion was also made to the company that it should continue to use the resources of the Urban League, since this represented an excellent source of qualified manpower.

*Selecting Negroes.* During these sessions the subject of selection criteria and procedures was also discussed. The leadership inquired about the minimum qualifications for the available jobs so that they could be more effective in referring people from the Negro community. The discussion which followed produced sharp disagreement over the type of selection procedures which should be used. The civil rights representatives felt that the company was placing too much emphasis on experience and not giving enough attention to potential and ability to learn. As a result of these discussions the company at the next meeting spent some time discussing a new test procedure, which presumably discerned intelligence at a more basic level and gave the Negro without experience a chance to qualify for employment.

**Attitudinal Structuring.** The following comments pertain first to the attitudinal structuring conducted by the company official, the vice-president of industrial relations. The company representative wanted to create friendly and trusting attitudes. He was concerned about creating or preserving a positive image for the company with its current Negro employees, and with the Negro community in general. Moreover, he may have been personally sympathetic with the movement. In any event the company official engaged in balance and reinforcement tactics of the type identified in the discussion of attitudinal structuring.

His first bargaining tactic, which rationalized an earlier refusal to meet as a question about union involvement, also served to assure the civil rights representatives that he had not intended to reject them. Then as negotiations progressed, he attempted to convince the militants that he was on their side. "I agree completely with your objectives; you have to give me time, however, to prepare my organization for change." By talking frankly about the weaknesses and problems within the company, the vice-president actually gained respect from the militants.

He also exerted every effort to develop a personal acquaintance with as many civil rights leaders as possible. Between sessions he maintained contact with at least 30 different leaders. These leaders were asked to help in recruiting qualified applicants, and the company spokesman personally checked on each referral. When complaints were presented, he investigated and reported back either directly to the leader or during the joint meetings. In effect, the company executive allowed the representatives to serve as patronage posts. He told them about job opportunities and gave them first opportunity to refer their friends and associates from the Negro community.

The company official was also complimentary of civil rights leadership and emphasized its importance: "I've always gotten along fine with Negro leaders; I am counting on you people to help me solve my problem in recruiting more Negroes." He conducted the sessions in a way which enhanced the status of the civil rights representatives. The meetings were held in an elegant office belonging to the law firm serving as counsel to the company. Also, by holding the meetings away from the company and by appearing alone, the vice-president prevented his more reactionary colleagues in the company from aggravating the situation.

Compared with the company official, the civil rights groups were less interested in the attitudinal component of any relationship between themselves and management. This was especially true of the more militant members, who were interested in substantive gains "right now." The moderate members, however, were somewhat more concerned about the influence of their behavior on the level of trust and friendliness which existed between the civil rights movement and employers generally and this company in particular. They acted on their concerns in private and in supportive conversations with company officials, in civil rights strategy sessions with the direct-action groups by advising against the more provocative actions, and in negotiations by blunting the effect of certain militant and adamant statements from their own side.

**Intraorganizational Bargaining.** There was considerable occasion for internal differences to develop within each party to these negotiations. There must have been disagreement within management about whether and when to meet, about the posture the company should take in these sessions, about the general ground rules which should govern the discussions, about what agreements could be entered into, and so on. As the company spokesman said, he had to "prepare his organization for the changes." Unfortunately, we do not know all of the methods he used to cope with this internal conflict and how he eventually achieved sufficient consensus to proceed. We do know that he appeared in the negotiating sessions alone, and this allowed him to pursue his own tactics in these sessions without sanction and also enabled him to select and report back that characterization of the means and ends of the civil rights groups which tended to provide the most support for his own recommendations to his principals.

The most important differences in outlook within the civil rights movement existed between the militants (NALC, CORE, and SNCC) and the moderates (NAACP and the Urban League). The moderate representatives were men who had been working with the company over several years and would continue to work with them in implementing whatever agreement was reached. Although the moderates were not in control of the situation during the phase when the civil rights groups were building power and forcing the company to negotiate, a representative of their group did eventually assume the role of chief negotiator. Our analysis centers on how the moderates were able to maintain intracouncil influence and achieve a settlement with the company.

It should be recalled that when the militants had taken notice of the target company and were gathering information about its employment situation, several moderates provided the militants with accurate information concerning the number of Negroes employed by the company. These disclosures would not have been sanctioned by the top officials of the moderate group involved.

When the militants, who had not received an answer to any of their communications, were ready to take direct action against the company, the moderates attempted to get the demonstration by the militants postponed. They were successful, working through the pressure of the civil rights council to which both groups belonged.

Meanwhile the moderates, who had worked with officials of the company over the years, continued to meet with them and work toward changes in employment practices. The moderates still preferred their own approach—they regarded their own limited objectives as more realistic for the present, and they regarded persuasion, education, and assistance as more effective in the long run. Moreover, some moderates may have mildly resented the militants entering so boldly and unilaterally into an area in which they had been working.

When the militants rescheduled the demonstration (partly in response to pressure from constituents who were unhappy about the postponement), the moderates stayed in the background, although it was reliably reported that the moderates advised the company: "The direct-action people mean business; you had better deal with them." It was at this point that the company agreed to meet with militants and the demonstration was postponed.

When a bargaining team was chosen for the first meeting with the company, the moderates were not involved. However, a key moderate joined a strategy session held immediately preceding the first meeting with the company. Significantly, he emphasized the importance of taking a *hard* line with the company.

When the second meeting was held with the company, the moderate leader appeared and acted as spokesman. This shift had come about since the key militant had to be absent from the second meeting and had asked the moderate to plan it. The militant had been impressed by the sophistication and resources of the moderate and his organization.

The moderate felt free to appear, since deliberations had moved beyond the power-building stage (the demonstration possibility had receded from the foreground). The moderate guided discussions in a calm and deliberate way. He moved to squelch a militant who challenged several statements by the company spokesman; he vetoed the idea of releasing a press statement; and he dodged the issue of scheduling another meeting with the company after he felt that they had obtained adequate commitments from the company official.

Thus, in terms of the distinctions made in the chapter on intraorganizational bargaining tactics, the moderate who eventually spoke for the civil rights groups played a passive role at the outset, "going through the motions" when he was involved. Later when he was more secure in his position of influence, he was more active in his attempt to achieve internal acceptance of the goals and means he regarded as realistic under the circumstances. The main objective of the moderate was to keep control of the situation and to maintain his personal influence. At the beginning of the campaign this meant diverting the demonstration and generally refusing to support the direct action, but toward the end it meant actively leading the negotiations and bringing the deliberations to a conclusion.

## PART 2 | COMPARATIVE ANALYSIS

In this part we undertake a comparative analysis of collective bargaining, international relations, and civil rights. We shall give primary attention to the last two settings, assuming that the reader is already familiar with the setting of collective bargaining. We are interested in several questions. To what extent does each of the four subprocesses occur in these settings? What is the relative importance of given tactical operations in these different settings? Finally, how do structural factors in these several settings help explain these differences in importance of the processes and in the tactical mix within the processes?

Our exploration of these questions is organized in terms of the four subprocesses of social negotiations.

## Distributive Bargaining

As we have stressed before, this process is basic to negotiations. However, the relative dominance of distributive bargaining activity in negotiations and the form it takes depends upon many contextual factors.

**Basic Payoff Structure.** Some basis for negotiations must exist before the parties can be motivated to bargain. This dependency can come about in several ways. First, the parties may enjoy a mutual advantage or *positive sum* because of such factors as market rigidities. The area of common interest is defined for them by their respective alternatives or by resistance points. In game terminology the joint gain is *fixed,* that is, it is determined by marketlike forces rather than by the efforts of the parties. A fixed-sum configuration usually produces distributive bargaining as the parties seek to divide the joint gain.

Whether the parties utilize power tactics and active coercion depends upon whether their respective aspirations for sharing the joint gain are compatible. When the terms of trade or norms for sharing the joint gain are relatively well established, there is little that the parties can or try to do except to define the situation and decide whether to enter into it or not.

In many instances the parties share a dependency because the relationship between two parties is an exclusive one—neither party has another relationship which can perform the same function for the party, or alternate relationships are available only at a substantial cost. However, in other situations one party may enjoy another alternative, and his dependency upon the relationship can be rather small. Therefore the basis for bargaining must come in a different manner.

When the environment does not establish dependency, it is often possible through bargaining to create mutual gain. Such a prospect produces integrative bargaining. The parties start with a zero-sum situation, but through their efforts they create a positive sum. The amount of gain created depends upon the inherent nature of the issues and the effectiveness of their problem solving. Thus over time the game may be positive and *varying sum* in character.

Of course, both parties seldom enter voluntarily into real-world bargaining situations unless good prospects exist for the zero-sum game to be transformed into a positive-sum game. If no relationship and no joint gain exist, it may be difficult to create a basis for bargaining merely on the chance that something beneficial might result. In many situations an initiating party would like to bargain, but the responding party refuses, realizing that he only stands to lose.

In such situations the first party has to create an incentive for the second party to enter negotiations. If no relationship exists, which is usually the case, and the absence of a relationship means the absence of trust, it is unlikely that the prospect of increasing mutual gain (through integrative bargaining) can be used as a meaningful basis for negotiations.

The basis for negotiations may have to come from coercion. In effect, the initiating party creates the prospect of harm for his opponent, the size of this expected loss being greater than the expected cost of the first party's demands. The opponent finds himself in the difficult configuration of avoidance–avoidance conflict. He agrees to participate in the *negative-sum* game because his only alternative produces a larger expected negative value. In effect, the substantive issue is *zero sum,* but when the threat of harm is added, the game payoffs for the responding party are all zero to negative in sum.

*Labor negotiations.* This context usually represents the positive-sum game, either fixed or varying in character, depending upon the issues and the orientation of the parties. In labor-management negotiations, the parties are usually held together by a considerable area of joint dependency. Normally this dependency is balanced, and the union is as dependent upon management as vice versa.

However, there are certain situations in which the dependency in either direction can be rather thin. For example, the Teamsters are not dependent upon any small trucking company, and the area of mutual dependence is pretty much the dependence of the company upon the Teamsters. Contrastingly, in some industries in which the company is strong and the union is weak the area of dependency is very thin for the company. Some people feel that such is the case in the General Electric situation, in which the company has many alternatives (nonunion plants, etc.). Consequently, the union finds itself the dependent party.

The typical situation, however, is usually symmetrical both on positive gains (in the sense of both experiencing benefit from being in the relationship) and on the cost of a short-term breakdown (in the sense that both experience important sacrifices from a strike).

As we noted elsewhere, the incentive to negotiate may not come from market factors but from legislation. The requirements of the National Labor Relations Act (NLRA) may bring the parties together and induce them to negotiate an agreement.

The importance of this basis for bargaining can be inferred from the conduct of parties in situations not protected by the NLRA. For example, not-for-profit hospitals are exempted from the procedures of representation elections, designation of bargaining agents, and good-faith bargaining. Thus in 1959 and 1960 when a number of unions sought recognition for nonprofessional hospital workers, they were ignored in many instances. They possessed no means for creating a dependency on the part of the hospital management.

In New York City, the union created a basis for negotiations by striking against several hospitals and by disseminating to the public information about working conditions in hospitals. While most observers condemned these "strikes against the sick," the union's actions created such a severe crisis that the hospitals were forced to come to the bargaining table. The incentive to enter into negotiations did not come directly from the union but from the mayor and influential individuals who urged the hospitals to enter into discussions about employment conditions in order to end the crisis.

In Chicago at about the same time two hospitals were also struck. However, the campaigns were unsuccessful, since the striking workers allowed replacements and supplies to cross the picket line. Moreover, the mayor and influential citizens sharply criticized the union's action and thereby provided moral support for hospital management in its refusal to meet with the union.[4]

Thus a crucial factor in creating the basis for negotiations, as well as in affecting the outcome, is the role of third parties. We shall examine this structural factor shortly.

*International relations.* Although there are positive-sum possibilities, most manifest aspects of the payoff are zero sum with the presence of a negative-sum default alternative. An interesting point is that countries try to reduce areas of positive dependency and are particularly sensitive to asymmetrical structures. This is seen in the dispute between the United States and Panama over the arrangements for the Panama Canal. The United States has actively undertaken plans to build another canal in order to minimize its dependency upon the country of Panama for the Panama Canal. Shaping the area of dependency as the United States has done does not remove the basis for negotiations; it merely alters the resistance point for the United States and therefore the power equation.

The nuclear threat, however, creates mutual negative dependency insofar as both sides have a desire to avoid nuclear holocaust. In the Cuban crisis, as is typical in crisis encounters, the United States created the basis

---

[4] For an analysis of this campaign see: R. B. McKersie and Montague Brown, "Nonprofessional Hospital Workers and a Union Organizing Drive," *Quarterly Journal of Economics,* vol. 77 (August, 1963), pp. 372–404.

for negotiations between itself and Russia by convincing Russia that the cost of not entering negotiations (war) was greater than the cost of the concession involved.

*Civil rights.*[5] The substantive aspects of many civil rights encounters are also zero sum. A change in public accommodations results in gains in freedom and dignity valued by one group and the loss of an arrangement needed and valued (although pathologically, perhaps) by another group. Voting rights and political power gained by Negroes take place at the expense of the political power and control of another group. Employment concessions which involve unneeded hires or preferential treatment may cost the employer flexibility and the loss of prerogatives that he values.

Because such items in civil rights are likely to be zero sum and since the target parties are expected to grant concesssions, these groups are understandably reluctant to acknowledge the existence of a tacit bargaining situation, much less enter into explicit negotiations. Therefore, preliminary to establishing a bargaining relationship, the civil rights groups must first command the attention of the target party and also establish a basis for a *quid pro quo*. This usually involves threats of loss, inconvenience, or embarrassment.[6]

Although historically civil rights groups have had no negotiating base —no positive gains that they could offer nor any losses that they could threaten—this changed drastically during the 1960s. Most of the direct action that has taken place in the early 1960s must be seen as an attempt to create a situation in which the target eventually becomes dependent upon the civil rights movement, if only to have the demonstration or the boycott stopped.

An analysis of these direct-action techniques can be used to demonstrate both the variety of strategies for establishing a basis for negotiation and the range of contextual factors which influence the choice of strategy or weapon. A number of important weapons have been used: demonstrations, consumer boycotts, and sit-ins or lie-ins. In some respects these weapons possess similar characteristics, and in other respects they differ. They can be analyzed in terms of their leverage in creating immediate pressure on the target, their value in communicating degree of commitment, and their value in building internal strength within the protest group.

Of the three tactics the consumer boycott exerts the most leverage. Consumer acceptance is very important to most companies, and a boycott

[5] Much of the material contained in this section is based on the following study: McKersie, "The Civil Rights Movement and Employment," *op. cit.*

[6] J. Q. Wilson, "The Strategy of Protest: Problems of Negro Civic Action," *Journal of Conflict Resolution*, vol. 5 (1961), pp. 291–303.

can hurt sales substantially. Moreover, the boycott involves an important dimension of power which enhances its effectiveness. The target company needs the influence of the civil rights movement to restore the company's good name in the Negro community. As a result an incentive exists to negotiate with the movement. In the case of demonstrations and sit-ins much of the damage may have already been done, and the employer stands to benefit very little by agreeing to explicit negotiations, if he has already made the critical concession to end the demonstration or sit-in, or if the police have ended it. In other words there is no further *quid pro quo*. However, the sit-in can be effective if it succeeds in blocking production, as it did in several cases in the North.

In terms of commitment, however, a different ordering of the tactics is involved. The sit-in represents the most costly form of protest to the participants since it involves personal hardship, and consequently it exhibits the highest degree of commitment. On the other hand, because it is easy to participate in a consumer boycott (there is not much entailed in shifting purchases to another product), this tactic does not express as much feeling or communicate as much resolution. A demonstration falls somewhere in between, since some costs are involved, namely, the time and money to get to the site and the personal discomfort to many people at appearing in public. But it does not usually entail the danger of arrest and the physical suffering present in a sit-in.

The weapons can be differentiated along a third dimension, the cultivation of group spirit. As we noted in collective bargaining, the taking of direct action (a strike) may be primarily designed to develop group solidarity and to prepare the rank and file for future action rather than as essentially a pressure tactic against the employer. Similarly, some of the direct-action tactics in the civil rights area are more functional for the developing of the "will to act" than they are for winning immediate concessions. The demonstration represents a very effective device for building *esprit de corps*. By its very nature a type of religious experience is involved. Many people participate, and a strong group spirit can develop. On this count the boycott is least effective in developing group solidarity, since the participation is on an individual basis and little group action takes place. The sit-in develops great solidarity among the participants, but since so few are involved, the effect on the total civil rights movement may be small.

**The Number of Parties.** In most situations the number of participants or the number of prime organizations in the bargaining process is not fixed. To the extent that additional organizations enter the deliberations, some important implications are raised for the whole process of negotiations. The alteration of the game from a two-party to a three or more–

party configuration raises the possibility of coalition formation, which not only complicates the bargaining process for purposes of analysis but also opens up new avenues of influence. In a two-party confrontation, the only kind of instrumental power is that which works directly on the opponent, but in the three-party situation it may be possible to promise benefit or harm to the third party in order to enlist him in placing pressure on the opponent.

The third party can also take the initiative to change the sum of the game, by offering one or both parties some inducements in the way of bringing the negotiations to a conclusion. By offering positive inducements, he increases the sum of the game; negative inducements potentially subtract from the sum of the outcome.

**Labor negotiations.** The work-rules dispute in railroads, which reached a showdown during 1963–1964, provides a good illustration of an important change that can occur when three parties are involved in bargaining. The third party, of course, is the government and indirectly the public. As a result, each side (the brotherhoods and the carriers) directed its energies to winning support from mediation officials—Congress and the interested public. The forum for bargaining became the newspapers rather than the private meeting room.

The work-rules dispute was purely distributive as viewed by the unions and the companies. The unions felt that whatever changes took place in the work rules would be a direct loss to the membership in job security, income, etc. Similarly, the companies felt that whatever the unions blocked in the way of changes would be a direct impairment of their competitive position.

With the intervention of President Johnson in 1964 the nature of the game was affected quite fundamentally by the third party. The sum of the game changed—it increased. The President held out the possibilities to the companies that the Internal Revenue Service would reevaluate its tax policy on depreciation of tunnels and other "natural resources" owned by the railroads and that Congress would pass a bill giving the railroads greater flexibility in adjusting their rates in order to compete with other forms of transportation. Thus in terms of the direct transaction between unions and companies, the game remained fixed in sum, but in terms of possible side payments the game increased in value. The companies were induced to give up some of their key objectives (elimination of the 100-mile pay principle and freedom to operate interdivisional runs) in return for the promises by President Johnson.

**International relations.** The parallels in international relations to situations just described in collective bargaining are so numerous and familiar that we need not analyze them in detail. The Marshall Plan was a dramatic, massive, and relatively long-term effort by the United States to influence the negotiation outcome and process among European nations—we did this by contingent additions to the sums of their games. The United States and the United Nations have frequently used both techniques of military intervention and economic aid to influence the course of quarrels between small nations.

The United States and Russia are both conscious of world opinion, especially that of the neutral or uncommitted nations. To the extent that this third-party approval or disapproval is of value to the principal antagonists, the sum of the game is affected.

*Civil rights.* The public is almost always involved in encounters between the civil rights movement and the target group. How the public aligns itself is crucial to the outcome of a direct-action campaign. Thus, an important consideration in formulating strategy and tactics is to bring about a coalition between the movement, the public, and elected officials.

Some of the most effective campaigns have motivated public officials, perhaps against their will, to take action against employers. A demonstration at a construction site or a sit-in at a mayor's office, if properly publicized, can put an elected official under tremendous pressure to take action. Thus, the elected official may be induced to form a coalition with the civil rights movement. The role of the public is equally important; perhaps over the long run it is more important to the outcome of bargaining.

Being a minority force, the civil rights movement cannot achieve many of its objectives unless it wins the support of the larger community, which means the white public. The leadership of the movement knows that most white people endorse the objective of equal employment opportunity for Negroes. Thus, a key element in their strategy has been to play upon the conscience of the white community. The problem that they face, however, is that in dramatizing the lack of employment opportunities for Negroes, they cannot use means that violate the standards of the larger society. Thus, they are in a position of constantly testing the limits to which they can go in using extreme means to achieve noble ends.

What factors affect the response of the public? We can name several:

The first is the legitimacy of the objective—the more legitimate the objective, the more the public will tolerate questionable means. Civil disobedience has not been repressed as frequently in the North as in the South, since there is wider support for the idea of equal opportunity.

The same point can be made about the sit-down in the labor field.

> They were tolerated in 1937, and even received substantial public support, mainly because large segments of American industry refused to accept collective bargaining. Trade unions were the underdogs and they were widely represented as merely attempting to secure

in practice the rights that Congress had bestowed upon them as a matter of law.[7]

A second factor is the concreteness of the objective—when the objective is limited and stated concretely and is one that the target group can do something about, there is more tolerance for the tactics. This point explains the success of the Philadelphia ministers in securing employment opportunities through selective-buying campaigns and the lack of success of many of the New York City sit-ins. The latter gave the aura of general protest. By not stating their demands in concrete terms, they created an impression of anarchy.

A third matter is the duration of the disobedience—the more quickly the tactics can be accomplished, then the better the response by the public. One-shot demonstrations and short boycotts will be tolerated, while extended sit-ins will be disapproved. For example, when the sit-in demonstrators first appeared in Mayor Wagner's office, the public was not too opposed, but as the demonstrations continued, the public grew tired of the situation, and when Mayor Wagner had the demonstrators forcibly evicted, he was strongly supported by the public. In general one could say that the enthusiasm and interest of those who approve wanes, and the impatience and attention of those who disapprove mounts.

Fourth, the conduct of the participants is important. When the participants conduct themselves nobly and stand ready to accept punishment for their civil disobedience, there is less criticism of the movement. There is respect for participants when they express "the courage of their convictions," this courage being measured by the costs involved and the willingness of the participants to accept these costs. Thus there may be more public sympathy for "sit-iners" who stand (or sit) ready to be jailed than for the leaders of a consumer boycott who protect themselves through anonymity-creating devices.

A fifth factor is the representativeness of the organization conducting direct action. An organization like the NAACP speaks more authoritatively for the Negro community than narrowly based groups like CORE and SNCC do. As a result it may be less susceptible to public criticism when it initiates direct action.

A sixth factor is the prospect of greater turmoil—when the situation does not indicate still further disturbance, there will be a tendency to accept the tactics. The public often hopes that participation in the tactic will vent the displeasure of the minority and enable the society to return to normal. There may even be the hope that the means will be sufficiently successful to obviate the need for future action.

[7] Walter Galenson, *The CIO Challenge to the AFL* (Cambridge, Mass.: Harvard University Press, 1960), pp. 146–147.

On the other hand the specter of future trouble can be a powerful motivator for a third party to try to influence the underlying conditions. This was an important consideration in the thinking of the Supreme Court when it declared the NLRA legal,[8] and it has been extremely important in inducing governmental authorities to seek to expand employment opportunities for Negroes.

**Eliciting and Processing Clues.** Compared with labor negotiations, the need to elicit and process clues regarding the others' intentions and capabilities is probably more important in international relations and less important in civil rights. This condition derives from differences along two dimensions of the total negotiating situation.

First, there are questions about the uncertainty of the other party's negotiating objectives, the means he will use to achieve them, and the timing of such moves. In international negotiations is the greatest uncertainty. The chief decision makers in the United States and Russia must be prepared to meet all contingencies—tactical moves of several different varieties (economic and political as well as other strategies) pursuant to a variety of several agenda items, including Berlin, NATO, shipping rights, nuclear tests, Cuba, Vietnam, Japan, etc.

In a civil rights confrontation there are only a few points of pressure, and there is little uncertainty about the general objectives of each side. The difficulty in civil rights arises because of the diversity of decision makers, particularly within the civil rights movement. There are many decision makers on each side, and there is therefore less agreement about short-term objectives and strategies. There is also less likelihood of getting advance information about the other side, and if obtained, it is less likely to be reliable.

Second, there are questions about the extent to which negotiating moves can be identified and interpreted. The more highly institutionalized the setting, the easier it is to discern and process clues. In international relations especially, the parties have highly developed techniques for gathering and processing such data. Several departments and agencies in the Federal government have this as their primary task. Moreover, in international relations there is relatively greater use of probing and testing through feelers and tentative moves.[9]

**Concession Rules and Commitment Patterns.** Several of the descriptive

---

[8] "Experience has abundantly demonstrated that the recognition of the right of employees to self-organization and to have representatives of their own choosing for the purpose of collective bargaining is often an essential condition of industrial peace. Refusal to confer and negotiate has been one of the most prolific causes of strife." *National Labor Relations v. Jones and Laughlin Steel Corporation* 301 U.S. 1 (1937).

[9] See Daniel Schorr, "The Trojan Troika in Berlin," *Reporter* (Sept. 27, 1962), pp. 25–27.

statements about concession rules in labor negotiations, which we presented in the chapter on distributive tactics, appear to apply to the postwar disarmament negotiations, including the tendency for concessions to be reciprocated during the same or following rounds. Indeed if they are not reciprocated in the same round, the first nation usually reduces its concessions in the next.[10] One distinctive feature of the disarmament negotiation not encountered in collective bargaining is the large number of retractions of concessions made previously. These reversals of position may reflect the extent to which the parties are using this setting for broader purposes than arriving at a decision on the stated agenda items.

The typical commitment pattern in the civil rights arena is an interesting one. In a given encounter the civil rights groups will often execute what we referred to earlier as an early-firm-commitment strategy. Here the strategy cannot be explained in terms of knowledge about the opponent's resistance point but must be explained primarily in terms of knowledge about one's own resistance point. In direct-action groups with militant members the leadership is well aware of the minimum expectations of the constituents.

The choice of early firm commitment in civil rights is also consistent with another hypothesis offered in Chapter III: commitment will approach the early-firm-commitment form when mechanisms are available for communicating this commitment. The availability of high-commitment weapons like sit-ins and going to jail makes it possible for civil rights groups to take a firm position.

We should not overlook another important dimension, that is, the belief of many direct-action people that human rights are not negotiable. In other words, they do not start from a position of demanding more than they expect to receive. When there is a principle at stake and a moral fervor behind the campaign, one should expect to find the early-firm-commitment approach to distributive bargaining. When issues are non-principle in character and there is discretion about how much more or less of something one receives, such as money, then the bargaining is more likely to take the form of gradually increasing commitment.

### Integrative Bargaining

The main purpose of the discussion below is to explore the opportunities for this subprocess in different settings of social negotiations. Since we are already familiar with the problem agenda of collective bargaining, we turn directly to international relations and civil rights.

*International relations.* There is tremendous integrative potential among the nations of the world. Superordinate goals for at least a large

[10] Lloyd Jensen, "Soviet-American Bargaining Behavior in Post-war Disarmament Negotiations," *Journal of Arms Control*, vol. 1 (October, 1963), p. 622.

majority of these nations would include institutions for ensuring peaceful resolution of international disputes and progress in eliminating hunger, disease, poverty, and illiteracy. The UN is clear testimony in itself to these goals, and its agencies, conferences, committees, and programs are designed to facilitate problem solving and mixed bargaining toward these ends. UNESCO and its programs provide a well-known setting for integrative bargaining.

Shifting the focus to pairs of nations, integrative potential may arise because their interests have a consensual or symbiotic relationship for each other. An agricultural country and an industrialized country can readily increase their joint gain through mixed bargaining. Emigration-immigration offers integrative possibilities. For example, New Zealand, an underpopulated country, entered into an arrangement with the Netherlands, which is overpopulated, whereby they encouraged, subsidized, and supervised permanent migration to New Zealand. The decision processes which established the terms of this exchange must have been mixed bargaining. Both were interested in achieving migration but would have held different preferences for the characteristics of the migrants in terms of age, sex, skills, and family status as well as for the respective shares of the cost of transportation and other subsidies provided by the two governments.

In the examples above problem solving is likely to be the *main* process in the international interaction, distributive bargaining occurring as a complicating process. When the agenda contains mainly problems, the problem-solving process, not the distributive bargaining process, becomes the "cornerstone" for the theory. This emphasis is not inconsistent with the basic theory developed in this book, but it does require some reorientation to the theory.

It is significant that decision-making situations in international relations tend to have agendas which are either predominantly distributive or integrative. This appears to be a product of two tendencies. First, separate settings can be used to deal with issues and problems because they usually are not functionally interrelated. Second, they are separated out of an appreciation of the dilemmas created by dealing with a mixed agenda. Nevertheless, there are probably many matters which are mixed in nature and where progress can only be made by confronting the dilemmas.

Thus, we suspect that these areas of mixed agenda are not fully explored or exploited for additional reasons. The participants to international discussions may lack mixed bargaining skills (which are just now improving in labor negotiations). The limited trust which prevails between key nations like the United States and Russia is more constraining to mixed bargaining than to relatively pure problem solving. Finally, the complicated intraorganizational processes which the United States at least must contend with are major inhibitors in entering mixed bargaining.

Even though the mixed agenda is not typical, there are important examples. The series of meetings between the heads of the Allied countries before and after the end of World War II were classic examples of mixed bargaining. The postwar disarmament negotiations is another example of important and difficult mixed bargaining.

Still other important matters involving the basically antagonistic United States and Russia offer integrative possibilities. One which has been tentatively mentioned from time to time is the extremely costly exploration of space. The "space race" has been a competitive process, not only because of its military implications, but also because the parties chose to make it one. Space achievements could become a common venture, but only as a result of complex mixed bargaining.

Several matters of consensual interest are handled only tacitly thus far by the United States and Russia. There is a growing appreciation of the threat for both parties represented by Red China. A related matter is our joint interest in preventing the extension of nuclear weapons. These are part of the general desire held by the United States and Russia to preserve the *status quo,* growing out of the fact that both nations are prosperous and powerful. Although not discussed explicitly as agenda items, these matters are dealt with in tacit problem solving—even in the heat of such encounters as the Cuban crisis.

**Civil rights.** By and large integrative bargaining has been absent from the civil rights situation. However, the government's regulations and its increasing enforcement of equal opportunities for Negroes have created for companies many problems on which the moderate groups can provide assistance.

Here and there a few innovative solutions have emerged as racial moderates have met with cooperative businessmen or public officials. Particularly in the areas of recruitment, training, and selection of Negroes some imaginative arrangements have been developed to accommodate (in a varying-sum manner) the need of the direct-action groups for immediate change and the need of the employer to effect orderly transition and protect the rights of the majority. These problems entered into the illustrative civil rights case above. We shall elaborate on them here.

The first problem area is that of recruiting Negroes. Many companies do not have Negroes working for them, simply because Negroes have not applied for employment. In one negotiation the company frankly asked the civil rights group how it could get the word out to the Negro community. The leaders advised the company in these terms:

> Simply saying that you are an equal-opportunity employer will not do any good; Negroes have learned over time that industry does not really want them, and hence they are not going to put themselves

in the position of being embarrassed. You have to advertise in the Negro newspapers, you have to let us put the word out to the community, and you have to use other information posts in the ghetto such as churches, social service agencies, and fraternal organizations.

As a result of this advice, the company has been rather successful in generating a stream of Negro applicants.

After it has been made clear that a given company is interested in hiring Negro employees, the second problem becomes one of finding qualified applicants. At this point, an organization like the Urban League which has screening procedures can be helpful in referring qualified individuals to interested employers. But in many instances there are just not enough qualified Negroes to go around; the demand exceeds the supply. As a result, upgrading programs have been initiated to increase the supply of qualified Negroes. In Chicago, with the sponsorship of the Urban League, the Yellow Cab Company and the Shell Oil Company have run training programs for unemployed workers. These types of "prehire" programs have expanded rapidly around the country, and many of them have developed as a result of the search for solutions to the supply problem by civil rights leaders and employers.

A controversial issue is involved in the third problem, namely, selecting Negroes. The issue is one of preferential treatment for Negroes. All of the civil rights groups, including the Urban League, endorse some kind of preferential treatment for Negroes. As Whitney Young, of the Urban League, stated, ". . . white people have had special preference all along . . . it is time we instituted a special treatment for Negroes as compensation for generations of denial, at least for a while." [11]

Some interesting ideas have been advanced for fulfilling the spirit of preferential treatment but at the same time dealing with the inequities that may be involved. In one instance it was decided that preferential treatment could be achieved through extra effort and selective recruitment. In other words, whites would not be ignored, but extra attention would be given to developing a group of qualified applicants from the Negro community.

The "prehire" programs mentioned above represent another form of specialized attention to Negroes. The eligible group may be defined as the unemployed, but in most cities this means that the group will be heavily Negro.

Another solution which appears to be emerging, although it has not been put into practice, is the two-list system. This solution has relevance where there are whites on a waiting list. If Negroes are given exclusive

[11] *The New York Times* (Monday, Aug. 12, 1963), p. 10. © 1963 by The New York Times Company. Reprinted by permission.

preference, it means that they are advanced over the heads of whites who may have certain vested interests. One way of lessening this difficulty is to establish tandem lists from which applicants are taken in a stated proportion as openings develop.

## Attitudinal Structuring

Before considering several structural variables which affect the importance and character of attitudinal structuring, a few general remarks about international relations and civil rights are in order.

There is no question that officials are conscious of the attitudinal components of the relationships between their nation and other nations. For the United States and Russia many international programs are designed specifically to improve mutual understanding and goodwill between the peoples of these countries. These programs include cultural and scientific exchange ventures as well as certain trade arrangements. However, the question is whether these international moves which effect substantive outcomes are also made with some thought about their influence on attitudes between the countries.

Certain treatments of the problem of tension management and attitude change in international relations are especially suggestive that attitudinal structuring is often a goal of officials engaged in international decision making.[12] The relationship between attitudinal and bargaining processes is pointed up by some of the balance tactics that have been suggested for changing United States–Russian relations: (1) renunciation by one party of an avowed objective having significance for the other party, (2) reduction in the absolute level of military forces and capabilities, (3) removal of provocative features of weapons or weapons systems, and (4) avoidance of certain subjects of discourse during negotiations.[13]

In the early 1960s attitudinal structuring was a part of social negotiations in the civil rights area but was not the dominant process by any means. In those geographic regions and with respect to those issues where there remained an assumption of basic conflict of interests, the civil rights groups were more concerned about building power and creating a negotiating base. In those instances in which the parties have actually entered into discussions or working arrangements, both sides have given more attention to the level of trust and friendliness. However, entering this phase

[12] See C. E. Osgood, *Graduated Reciprocation in Tension-reduction: A Key to Initiative in Foreign Policy* (Urbana, Ill.: Institute of Communications Research. University of Illinois, December, 1960); and J. D. Singer, "Threat-perception and the Armament-tension Dilemma," *Journal of Conflict Resolution,* vol. 2 (1958), pp. 90–105.

[13] R. C. Snyder and J. A. Robinson, *National and International Decision-making* (New York: The Institute for International Order, 1961), p. 136.

does not signal the end of the need to create power and use it in bargaining over further objectives; therefore, in this phase there is an increase in the tension between the bargaining and the attitudinal structuring processes.

What we explore below are a few of the basic dimensions of the settings for social negotiations which affect the importance of attitudinal structuring within the overall process.

**Nature of the Agenda.** If the agenda contains a relatively larger proportion of problems to issues, relatively greater attention will be paid to the attitudinal structuring subprocess. The parties will tend to resolve tactical dilemmas between distributive bargaining and attitudinal structuring in favor of the latter process. Similarly, they are more likely to follow the dictates of attitudinal structuring when they clash with intraorganizational bargaining.

Beyond the question of whether the agenda contains items which are inherently fixed sum or variable sum is the question about the emotional overtones involved in many issues. More may be at stake than economic resources allocation—human dignity, political freedom, rule of law, social class mobility, etc. Because of the critical nature of the stakes, the objectives of one party may go beyond usual self-interest; they may involve weakening or destroying the other. Thus, an important dimension of the agenda is the implication of the items for attitudinal structuring.

As we have stressed throughout this book, many collective bargaining issues have strong emotional overtones; they involve questions of personal dignity, personal security, managerial prerogatives and status, and democratic procedures. The labor movement is in large part a struggle for power and influence—a social revolution. Virtually the same general point applies to international relations and civil rights. Thus, the character of bargaining in all three settings is directly affected by the latent as well as explicit meanings in the agenda items.

**Uncertainty of Performance under Agreement.** In some bargains the transaction may be on the spot, immediate, or at least self-enforcing. This is the condition of many commercial transactions. In other cases it may involve understandings about rights and obligations and other conditions of future performance. Even if put into writing, the expectation may not be enforceable in any meaningful or complete way. What results then is uncertainty about fulfillment of the agreement terms.

Our assumption is that in those social negotiations in which performance under the agreement is relatively difficult to enforce and where it depends upon more or less voluntary compliance, the relatively greater attention will be paid to attitudinal structuring activities. Further, the tactical dilemmas between attitudinal structuring and other subprocesses will more frequently be resolved in favor of the attitudinal process.

In signing a labor contract, the union does not agree to deliver a depersonalized good or service. Rather, it agrees to a defined pattern of rights and obligations within which the employer can "expect" employee performance. The actual patterns and the performance delivered will be strongly conditioned by the attitudes of all concerned and the relationship which exists between the parties.

Similarly, in international relations some agreements contain great uncertainty about performance under any agreement. Nothing could illustrate that point better than the implementation of the four-power agreement on Berlin made at the end of the war. Moreover, in the Cuban situation we have had to continue overflights in order to be sure that the missiles were dismantled and removed from that island. An agreement without the presence of trust represents only a piece of paper. It is for this reason that the disarmament negotiations have proved to be so difficult. Since the feeling exists within the United States that "the Russians cannot be trusted," it has been the objective of the United States to negotiate a disarmament plan that would be fully enforceable through inspection, etc.

Sometimes the object of the transaction in civil rights agreements is specific and material: Negroes can take seats in the front of the bus; they can swim with police protection on certain beaches previously closed to them; a firm agrees to the immediate employment of five additional Negroes, etc. While in some cases these practices become self-enforcing, in many instances they raise issues of compliance, especially when more subtle objectives are involved, such as equal employment opportunity in white-collar jobs.

In passing, we should note that the presence of mechanisms for raising questions about compliance and intent under the agreement can eliminate much of the uncertainty about performance and thereby have an impact on the role of attitudinal structuring. In the labor area considerable emphasis has been placed on the right of the parties to submit grievances and in many cases to have these disputes about performance decided by a third party.[14]

Civil rights groups have expressed great concern that employers would not honor agreements, that they would grant concessions only to neutralize direct action, and that once the crisis passed, they would renege on their promises. Examples of this uncertainty about performance occurred frequently during the early days of the current civil rights revolution. For example, it was the practice of the Philadelphia ministers not to end a

---

[14] For a study of the bargaining process inherent in grievance administration see J. W. Kuhn, *Bargaining and Grievance Settlement* (New York: Columbia University Press, 1961).

boycott until the requisite number of Negroes had been hired. A company's statement that it intended to hire a specified number of Negroes was not honored. In New York City when the referral committee of the construction industry made its first report about progress in introducing minority members, a civil rights spokesman commented: "self-serving rationalizations and half-truths."

In the international field, the UN and the World Court can serve to some extent the same function by handling complaints and misunderstandings between countries, although there is no way for the injured party to compel the other party to participate in the adjudication process. In the civil rights area, few formal mechanisms exist. Various human relations commissions attempt to mediate disputes, but they have little authority; they only operate at the pleasure of the parties. Where compliance mechanisms are largely absent or ineffective, attitudinal structuring performs a crucial function.

The acceptance of due process mechanisms by the parties reveals the extent of accommodation and the amount of attitudinal structuring that has already taken place. In other words, a measure of trust must be present before the parties will consent to live under a constitutional arrangement with established procedures for handling complaints about performance.

**Pattern of Interaction.** An important variable affecting the opportunities for attitudinal structuring is the interaction setting, especially whether the parties are face to face or removed, and whether the bargaining is continuous or one-shot.

Attitudinal structuring can take place much more readily when the negotiators meet in person than when they communicate through dispatches or intermediaries and also when the encounter is frequently repeated rather than when it represents an isolated transaction.

Labor negotiations, which are face to face and where there is a succession of contracts, present the most opportune setting for attitudinal structuring.

In international relations the chief negotiators seldom come face to face. While some of the encounters, such as the Cuban negotiations, are one-shot in character, diplomatic contact is maintained on a continuous basis, thereby providing some opportunity for attitudinal structuring.

The civil rights context has the most limited potential for attitudinal structuring. Very often the protagonists never come together—the encounter is an exercise in raw power without any face-to-face deliberations. However, once actual negotiations begin, there may be considerable attitudinal structuring, as the earlier case study illustrated. Moreover, a type of continuous interaction takes place between the civil rights movement and the general business community, the key leaders from both sides often developing a working relationship.

The pattern of interaction, its frequency and intensity, has another bearing on attitudinal structuring, particularly in its interrelationship with the other subprocesses. Continued interaction may produce positive attitudes, but it may also produce negative attitudes. It is unlikely that attitudes will remain neutral in the face of frequent encounters.

The tendency for extended interaction to move toward extreme states has been documented by various experimental studies. The important finding is that bargaining often follows a stochastic process, Party's actions being more a reaction to Opponent's than a predisposition to act in a certain way. As a result of the response-counterresponse dynamics, the tenor of bargaining evolves to either the stable state of cooperation or to defection.[15]

More importantly, frequent interaction also produces a pairing of distributive bargaining with hostile attitudes, and integrative bargaining with friendly attitudes. The point is that in a setting of frequent and intense interaction it is difficult for the configuration of distributive bargaining with positive attitudes to emerge. Either the self-oriented character of the distributive process produces hostile attitudes which are held stable by a type of reinforcement process between the parties, or the positive attitudes lead to a new approach to the substantive matters, i.e., integrative bargaining begins to emerge, and this also achieves stability through a type of reinforcement process.[16]

One would expect to find the hybrid arrangement, distributive bargaining with positive attitudes, only in situations in which the interaction could be carefully controlled, either because the parties communicated by dispatch, or because they negotiated agreements infrequently, or occupied highly specified roles which required emphasis on the self-interest objectives of the organization.

## Intraorganizational Bargaining

Again, we turn directly to international relations and civil rights.

*International relations.* The extent to which the international decision maker must attend to the problem of achieving internal consensus while he also acts appropriately in the international context is certainly an

---

[15] See Marc Pilisuk and Anatol Rapoport, *A Non-zero-sum Game Model of Some Disarmament Problems* (Ann Arbor, Mich.: Mental Health Research Institute, University of Michigan, 1963).

[16] R. E. Walton, "Theory of Conflict in Lateral Organizational Relationships," paper presented to the International Conference on Operations Research and the Social Sciences, Cambridge, England, September 14, 1964.

empirical question. Snyder and Robinson cite the divergent views on this matter when they report that

> To talk to some policy-makers is to come away with the impression that public opinion is a highly volatile force, omnipresent, unpredictable, a combination of shifting searchlights within which the policy-maker must function and which constitutes a basic limitation on what he can do. On the other hand, there are both poll data and frequent observations which suggest that the policy-maker is largely free to do what he wishes, and will do what he wishes, regardless of what those outside the government think or want.[17]

These two descriptions are applicable to the extreme cases, and the majority of international decision-making situations probably fall somewhere along a spectrum of public-opinion influence. Thus, we assert the generality of our assumptions made initially regarding the labor negotiator that "he occupies a position which has influence" but that "the activities and influence of the chief negotiator are constrained and shaped by internal organizational forces," and finally that "even with respect to the potential influence he does possess, he must choose and time his tactics wisely."

We can cite two ways in which the principals can affect the way the international negotiator conducts himself in integrative and distributive bargaining.

The negotiator, more than his principal, is cognizant of the need for the other to avoid losing face. In the Cuban crisis President Kennedy was more aware of this than the United States public was. Thus, he was less likely to insist upon an outcome which would be a victory for him and a defeat for the other. Contrastingly, the militants within the United States pressed for an all-out effort against Cuba. If Russia had not conceded, it would have been difficult for President Kennedy to have opposed the escalation of sanctions.

The negotiator, more than his principal, is aware of the possibility of an integrative solution in which neither side loses or in which one does not necessarily lose what the other gains. The American public and presumably other publics tend to keep almost daily score of the wins and losses in the diplomatic encounters between the United States and Russia, and the effect of this public preoccupation is to limit the negotiators' activity in mixed bargaining.

*Civil rights.* The leader of a direct-action organization experiences many of the pressures and problems felt by a labor leader representing militant constituents. The Negro activist often finds himself in a role-

[17] Snyder and Robinson, *op. cit.*, p. 228.

conflict situation. As negotiations unfold, he becomes more cognizant of the problems of the employer, and he sometimes realizes that his extreme position is no longer tenable. Meanwhile, the constituents remain adamant and demand full measure for their position.

One technique for coping with this conflict involves "going through the motions," that is, acting aggressively and giving the constituents some release for their intense feelings. Such an approach works only when the employer understands that the outburst is for the benefit of constituents.

> The furthering of race pride and racial solidarity is a means of diminishing internal strivings in the Negro community and of lining up the community into a working unity. Whites sometimes understand this, and there is, therefore, also a certain amount of "tolerated impudence," which a trusted and influential Negro can get away with even in the presence of whites.[18]

A second technique also similar to labor negotiations is to keep the constituents "in the dark" about developments in the bargaining room. In one situation in which the Negro leader was under pressure to obtain immediate concessions from the company, he spoke as a militant when confronted with the constituents but as a moderate when confronted by the employer. When challenged by his constituents, he scheduled additional meetings with the employer, but inside the meeting he acted in a moderate fashion. In many respects this approach resembles the first technique of going through the motions; the basic difference is in keeping the constituents in the dark about the approach being used on the employer.

A third technique is to avoid responsibility for a decision which may entail compromise by throwing the matter back to the constituency, in effect allowing them to experience the "essence of the situation." During discussions about the situation in the construction field in New York, James Farmer of CORE emerged from the bargaining room and predicted a settlement in the near future, but he added, "there will be no behind-the-door settlement, we will take it to the members for approval or rejection."

Intraorganizational bargaining operates at another level within the civil rights movement, namely, between groups within the movement. While it is the militant who experiences the brunt of intraorganizational pressures within a particular direct-action organization, it is the moderate who is sensitive to pressures within the movement.

The racial moderate faces a dilemma in maintaining his position in the larger Negro community. In many instances, the militants have seized

[18] Gunnar Myrdal, *An American Dilemma* (New York: Harper & Row, Publishers, Incorporated, 1944), p. 771.

the initiative and have forced the moderates into the background. The moderate becomes particularly troubled when the protest gets to the talking stage, especially when the militants have been successful in getting the attention of an employer with whom the moderates have been working for some time.

Confronted with this challenge, the moderate can ignore the activities of the direct-action group. The threat of direct action may even work to his advantage, since the company, convinced that it must do something, may rather make changes with the moderate on a calm, rational basis.

However, there comes a point at which the moderate must vie for control of the direct-action campaign. His personal position as well as the reputation of the institution he represents are at stake. How this was done in one situation was described earlier.

**Size of Negotiating Group.** The size of the organization is a crucial variable in affecting the complexity of the internal process and the extent to which intraorganizational bargaining is involved. Parties may be more than individuals; they may be complex social entities—groups, organizations, nations, coalitions, etc. The groups may be composed of more or less heterogeneous populations, in which subgroups hold differing biases and concerns about the issues of negotiations. The membership may have considerable influence over the objectives and strategies pursued in negotiations and varying degrees of opportunity for surveillance of the proceedings.

Generally speaking, larger organizations are more compartmentalized and are more likely to be characterized by divergence in outlook between the negotiators and the constituent groups. The larger the organization, then the more apt there is to be vertical and horizontal separation and the more prominent intraorganizational bargaining will be.

The size of the bargaining group in labor negotiations falls somewhere between international relations and civil rights. If the bargaining group is relatively large, e.g., multiunion councils or employer associations, then there are bound to be many internal differences, and the whole matter of achieving consensus within the organization becomes an important activity for the negotiator. On the other hand, if the effective decision-making unit includes only a few individuals, e.g., a small union or an authoritatively organized management group, there is likely to be little intraorganizational bargaining.

In the international relations field the size of the group is extremely large, often being the extent of the nation. It is for this reason that intraorganizational bargaining is such an important aspect of negotiations in this context.

The direct-action groups in the civil rights area are usually rather small, and the extent of intraorganizational bargaining is consequently limited.

However, even within small cohesive groups, some people are not present at the deliberations, and the conduct of the negotiator may have to be shaped accordingly. At the level of the overall civil rights movement many differences exist in style between the moderates and the militants. Some interesting illustrations of divergence both within an individual direct-action organization and within the movement were presented earlier.

# BIBLIOGRAPHY

## Books

Adorno, T. W., et al.: *The Authoritarian Personality* (New York: Harper & Row, Publishers, Incorporated, 1950).

Bakke, E. W.: *Mutual Survival: The Goal of Unions and Managements* (New Haven, Conn.: Labor and Management Center, Yale University, 1946).

Bambrick, J. J., and M. P. Dorbandt: *Preparing for Collective Bargaining,* Studies in Personnel Policy no. 172 (New York: National Industrial Conference Board, 1959).

Barbash, Jack: *Labor's Grass Roots: A Study of the Local Union* (New York: Harper & Row, Publishers, Incorporated, 1961).

Blake, R. R., and J. S. Mouton: *Group Dynamics: Key to Decision-making* (Houston: Gulf Publishing Company, 1961).

Boulding, K. E.: *Conflict and Defense: A General Theory* (New York: Harper & Row, Publishers, Incorporated, 1962).

Cartter, A. M.: *Theory of Wages and Employment* (Homewood, Ill.: Richard D. Irwin, Inc., 1959).

Cartwright, Dorwin, and Alvin Zander (eds.): *Group Dynamics,* 2d ed. (New York: Harper & Row, Publishers, Incorporated, 1960).

Chamberlain, N. W.: *Collective Bargaining* (New York: McGraw-Hill Book Company, 1951).

Chamberlain, N. W.: *A General Theory of Economic Process* (New York: Harper & Row, Publishers, Incorporated, 1955).

Coser, Lewis: *The Functions of Social Conflict* (New York: The Free Press of Glencoe, 1956).

Derber, Milton, et al.: *The Local Union-Management Relationship* (Urbana, Ill.: Institute of Labor and Industrial Relations, University of Illinois, 1960).

Douglas, Ann: *Industrial Peacemaking* (New York: Columbia University Press, 1962).

Dunlop, J. T.: *Wage Determination under Trade Unions* (New York: A. M. Kelley, 1950).

Dunlop, J. T. (ed.): *The Theory of Wage Determination* (London: International Economic Association, Macmillan & Co., Ltd., 1957).

Dunlop, J. T.: *Industrial Relations Systems* (New York: Holt, Rinehart and Winston, Inc., 1958).

Dunlop, J. T., and J. J. Healy: *Collective Bargaining: Principles and Cases,* rev. ed. (Homewood, Ill.: Richard D. Irwin, Inc., 1953).

Follett, Mary Parker: *Dynamic Administration: The Collected Papers of Mary Parker Follett,* H. C. Metcalf and L. Urwick (eds.) (New York: Harper & Row, Publishers, Incorporated, 1942).

Galenson, Walter: *The CIO Challenge to the AFL* (Cambridge, Mass.: Harvard University Press, 1960).

Ginzberg, Eli: *The Labor Leader* (New York: The Macmillan Company, 1948).

Golden, C. S., and V. D. Parker (eds.): *Causes of Industrial Peace under Collective Bargaining* (New York: National Planning Association, Harper & Row, Publishers, Incorporated, 1955).

Gross, Neal, W. S. Mason, and Alexander McEachern: *Explorations in Role Analysis: Studies of the School Superintendency Role* (New York: John Wiley & Sons, Inc., 1957).

Harbison, F. H., and J. R. Coleman: *Goals and Strategy in Collective Bargaining* (New York: Harper & Row, Publishers, Incorporated, 1951).

Hare, A. P.: *Handbook of Small Group Research* (New York: The Free Press of Glencoe, 1962).

Heider, Fritz: *The Psychology of Interpersonal Relations* (New York: John Wiley & Sons, Inc., 1958).

Hickman, C. A., and M. H. Kuhn: *Individuals, Groups, and Economic Behavior* (New York: Holt, Rinehart and Winston, Inc., 1956).

Hicks, J. R.: *The Theory of Wages* (Gloucester, Mass.: Peter Smith Publisher, 1948).

Hilgard, E. R.: *Introduction to Psychology,* 3d ed. (New York: Harcourt, Brace & World, Inc., 1962).

Homans, G. C.: *The Human Group* (New York: Harcourt, Brace & World, Inc., 1950).

Homans, G. C.: *Social Behavior: Its Elementary Forms* (New York: Harcourt, Brace & World, Inc., 1961).

Kahn, R. L., D. M. Wolfe, R. P. Quinn, J. D. Snoek, and R. A. Rosenthal: *Organizational Stress: Studies in Role Conflict and Ambiguity* (New York: John Wiley & Sons, Inc., 1964).

Kennedy, Thomas: *Automation Funds and Displaced Workers* (Boston: Division of Research, Graduate School of Business Administration, Harvard University, 1962).

Kornhauser, Arthur, et al. (eds.): *Industrial Conflict* (New York: McGraw-Hill Book Company, 1954).

Kuhn, Alfred: *Labor Institutions and Economics* (New York: Holt, Rinehart and Winston, Inc., 1958).

Kuhn, J. W.: *Bargaining and Grievance Settlement* (New York: Columbia University Press, 1961).

Lester, R. A.: *As Unions Mature: An Analysis of the Evolution of American Unionism* (Princeton, N.J.: Princeton University Press, 1958).

Lindzey, G. (ed.): *Handbook of Social Psychology* (Reading, Mass.: Addison-Wesley Publishing Company, Inc., 1945).

Livernash, E. R.: *Collective Bargaining in the Basic Steel Industry* (Washington, D.C.: U.S. Department of Labor, 1961).

Luce, R. D., and Howard Raiffa: *Games and Decisions: Introduction and Critical Survey* (New York: John Wiley & Sons, Inc., 1957).

MacDonald, R. M.: *Collective Bargaining in the Automobile Industry* (New Haven, Conn.: Yale University Press, 1963).

Maier, N. R. F.: *Problem-solving Discussions and Conferences* (New York: McGraw-Hill Book Company, 1963).

March, J. G., and H. A. Simon: *Organizations* (New York: John Wiley & Sons, Inc., 1958).

Moser, G. V.: *Problem Solving Conferences*, Studies in Personnel Policy no. 176 (New York: National Industrial Conference Board, 1960).

Myrdal, Gunnar: *An American Dilemma* (New York: Harper & Row, Publishers, Incorporated, 1944).

National Industrial Conference Board: *Preparing for Collective Bargaining: II*, Personnel Policy Study no. 182 (New York, 1961).

Newcomb, T. M.: *The Acquaintance Process* (New York: Holt, Rinehart and Winston, 1961).

Northrup, H. R.: *Boulwarism* (Ann Arbor, Mich.: Bureau of Industrial Relations, University of Michigan, 1964).

Osgood, C. E.: *Graduated Reciprocation in Tension-reduction: A Key to Initiative in Foreign Policy* (Urbana, Ill.: Institute of Communications Research, University of Illinois, 1960).

Parnes, H. S.: *Union Strike Votes: Current Practice and Proposed Controls* (Princeton, N.J.: Industrial Relations Section, Department of Economics and Sociology, Princeton University, 1956).

Parsons, Talcott, and R. F. Bales: *Family, Socialization and Interaction Process* (New York: The Free Press of Glencoe, 1955).

Pen, Jan: *The Wage Rate under Collective Bargaining*, translated by T. S. Preston (Cambridge, Mass.: Harvard University Press, 1959).

Peters, Edward: *Strategy and Tactics in Labor Negotiations* (New London, Conn.: National Foremen's Institute, 1955).

Pigou, A. C.: *The Economics of Welfare*, 4th ed. (New York: The Macmillan Company, 1950).

Pilisuk, Marc, and Anatol Rapoport: *A Non-zero-sum Game Model of Some Disarmament Problems* (Ann Arbor, Mich.: Mental Health Research Institute, University of Michigan, 1963).

Rapoport, Anatol: *Fights, Games, and Debates* (Ann Arbor, Mich.: The University of Michigan Press, 1960).

Rees, Albert: *The Economics of Trade Unions* (Chicago: The University of Chicago Press, 1962).

Rosenberg, M. J., et al.: *Attitude Organization and Change* (New Haven, Conn.: Yale University Press, 1960).

Ross, A. M.: *Trade Union Wage Policy* (Berkeley, Calif.: University of California Press, 1948).

Sayles, L. R.: *The Behavior of Industrial Work Groups* (New York: John Wiley & Sons, Inc., 1958).

Sayles, L. R., and George Strauss: *The Local Union: Its Place in the Industrial Plant* (New York: Harper & Row, Publishers, Incorporated, 1953).

Schelling, T. C.: *The Strategy of Conflict* (Cambridge, Mass.: Harvard University Press, 1960).

Selekman, B. M.: *Labor Relations and Human Relations* (New York: McGraw-Hill Book Company, 1947).

Selekman, B. M., S. K. Selekman, and S. H. Fuller: *Problems in Labor Relations,* 1st and 2d eds. (New York: McGraw-Hill Book Company, 1950 and 1958); 3d ed. (1964) by B. M. Selekman, S. H. Fuller, T. Kennedy, and J. M. Baitsell.

Sherif, Muzafer (ed.): *Intergroup Relations and Leadership* (New York: John Wiley & Sons, Inc., 1962).

Sherif, Muzafer, et al: *Intergroup Conflict and Cooperation: The Robbers Cave Experiment* (Norman, Okla.: University Book Exchange, 1961).

Shultz, G. P.: *Pressures on Wage Decisions* (Cambridge, Mass.: The Technology Press of the Massachusetts Institute of Technology, 1951).

Siegel, Sidney, and L. E. Fouraker: *Bargaining and Group Decision Making* (New York: McGraw-Hill Book Company, 1960).

Simon, Herbert: *Administrative Behavior* (New York: The Macmillan Company, 1959).

Skinner, B. F.: *Science and Human Behavior* (New York: The Macmillan Company, 1953).

Slichter, S. H., J. J. Healy, and E. R. Livernash: *The Impact of Collective Bargaining on Management* (Washington, D. C.: The Brookings Institution, 1960).

Snyder, R. C., and J. A. Robinson: *National and International Decision-making* (New York: The Institute for International Order, 1961).

Sorokin, P. A., and W. A. Lunden: *Power and Morality: Who Should Guard the Guardians?* (Boston: P. Sargent, 1959).

Stevens, C. M.: *Strategy and Collective Bargaining Negotiation* (New York: McGraw-Hill Book Company, 1963).

Stieglitz, Harold: *The Kaiser-Steel Union Sharing Plan* (New York: National Industrial Conference Board, 1963).

Stock, Dorothy, and H. A. Thelen: *Emotional Dynamics and Group Culture,* Research Training Series no. 2 (Washington, D.C.: National Training Laboratories, 1958).

Taylor, G. W., and F. C. Pierson (eds.): *New Concepts in Wage Determination* (New York: McGraw-Hill Book Company, 1957).

Thibaut, J. W., and H. H. Kelly: *The Social Psychology of Groups* (New York: John Wiley & Sons, Inc., 1959).

Ulman, Lloyd: *The Government of the Steel Workers' Union* (New York: John Wiley & Sons, Inc., 1962).

Von Neumann, J., and O. Morgenstern: *Theory of Games and Economic Behavior,* 2d ed. (Princeton, N.J.: Princeton University Press, 1947).

Waller, W. W., and R. Hill: *The Family: A Dynamic Interpretation* (New York: Holt, Rinehart and Winston, Inc., 1951).

Walton, R. E.: *The Impact of the Professional Engineering Union* (Boston: Division of Research, Graduate School of Business Administration, Harvard University, 1961).

Weber, A. R.: *Union Decision-making in Collective Bargaining* (Urbana, Ill.: Institute of Labor and Industrial Relations, University of Illinois, 1951).

Weber, A. R. (ed.): *The Structure of Collective Bargaining: Problems and Perspectives* (New York: The Free Press of Glencoe, 1961).

Whyte, W. F.: *Pattern for Industrial Peace* (New York: Harper & Row, Publishers, Incorporated, 1951).

Whyte, W. F.: *Men at Work* (Homewood, Ill.: The Dorsey Press, Inc., and Richard D. Irwin, Inc., 1961).

Zeuthen, F.: *Problems of Monopoly and Economic Welfare* (London, England: Routledge and Kegan Paul, Ltd., 1930).

## Journal Articles

Abelson, R. P.: "Modes of Resolution of Belief Dilemmas," *Journal of Conflict Resolution,* vol. 3 (December, 1959), pp. 343–352.

Adams, J. S.: "The Reduction of Cognitive Dissonance by Seeking Consonant Information," *Journal of Abnormal and Social Psychology,* vol. 62 (January, 1961), pp. 74–78.

Allen, L. E.: "Games Bargaining: A Proposed Application of the Theory of Games to Collective Bargaining," *The Yale Law Journal,* vol. 65 (April, 1956), pp. 679–693.

Atkinson, J. W.: "Motivational Determinants of Risk-taking Behavior," *Psychological Review,* vol. 64 (November, 1957), pp. 359–372.

Bauer, R. A.: "Problems of Perception and Relations between the United States and the Soviet Union," *Journal of Conflict Resolution,* vol. 5 (September, 1961), pp. 223–229.

Beier, E. G.: "The Effect of Induced Anxiety on Flexibility of Intellectual Functioning," *Psychological Monographs,* vol. 65, no. 9 (1951), pp. 3–26.

Blake, R. R., and J. S. Mouton: "Comprehension of Own and Outgroup Positions under Intergroup Competition," *Journal of Conflict Resolution,* vol. 5 (September, 1961), pp. 304–310.

Blum, A. A.: "Collective Bargaining: Ritual or Reality?" *Harvard Business Review,* vol. 39 (November-December, 1961), pp. 63–69.

Cohen, A. R.: "The Effects of Individual Self-esteem and Situational Structure on Threat-oriented Reactions to Power," *Dissertation Abstracts,* vol. 14 (1954), pp. 727–728.

Dearborn, D. C., and H. A. Simon: "Selective Perception: A Note on the Departmental Identification of Executives," *Sociometry,* vol. 21 (June, 1958), pp. 140–144.

Deutsch, Morton: "An Experimental Study of the Effects of Cooperation and Competition upon Group Process," *Human Relations,* vol. 2, no. 3 (1949), pp. 199–231.

Deutsch, Morton: "Trust and Suspicion," *Journal of Conflict Resolution,* vol. 2 (December, 1958), pp. 265–279.

Deutsch, Morton: "Trust, Trustworthiness, and F-Scale," *Journal of Abnormal and Social Psychology,* vol. 61, no. 1 (1960), pp. 138–140.

Deutsch, Morton: "The Effect of Motivational Orientation upon Trust and Suspicion," *Human Relations,* vol. 13 (May, 1960), pp. 123–140.

Edwards, Ward: "Behavioral Decision Theory," *Annual Review of Psychology,* vol. 12 (1961), pp. 473–498.

Festinger, Leon: "A Theory of Social Comparison Process," *Human Relations,* vol. 7, no. 2 (1954), pp. 117–140.

Festinger, Leon: "Cognitive Dissonance," *Scientific American,* vol. 207 (October, 1962), pp. 93–106.

Galtung, Johan: "Pacifism from a Sociological Point of View," *Journal of Conflict Resolution,* vol. 3 (March, 1959), pp. 67–84.

Garfield, Sidney, and W. F. Whyte: "The Collective Bargaining Process: A Human Relations Analysis," *Human Organization,* vol. 9, part I (Summer, 1950), pp. 5–10; part II (Fall, 1950), pp. 10–16; part III (Winter, 1950), pp. 25–29; vol. 10, part IV (Spring, 1951), pp. 28–32.

Gerard, H. B.: "Some Effects of Status, Role Clarity, and Group Goal Clarity upon the Individual's Relations to Group Process," *Journal of Personality,* vol. 25 (1957), pp. 475–488.

Getzels, J. W., and E. G. Guba: "Role, Role Conflict and Effectiveness: An Empirical Study," *American Sociological Review,* vol. 19 (April, 1954), pp. 164–175.

Gibb, J. R.: "Defensive Communication," *Journal of Communication,* vol. 11 (September, 1961), pp. 141–148.

Gross, Edward: "Symbiosis and Consensus as Integrative Factors in Small Groups," *American Sociological Review,* vol. 21 (April, 1956), pp. 174–179.

Haire, Mason: "Role Perceptions in Labor-Management Relations: An Experimental Approach," *Industrial and Labor Relations Review,* vol. 8 (January, 1955), pp. 204–216.

Harsanyi, J. C.: "Approaches to the Bargaining Problem before and after the Theory of Games: A Critical Discussion of Zeuthen's, Hicks', and Nash's Theories," *Econometrica,* vol. 24 (April, 1956), pp. 144–157.

Harsanyi, J. C.: "Bargaining in Ignorance of the Opponent's Utility Function," *Journal of Conflict Resolution,* vol. 6 (March, 1962), pp. 28–38.

Haythorn, William: "The Influence of Individual Members on the Characteristics of Small Groups," *Journal of Abnormal and Social Psychology,* vol. 48, no. 2 (1953), pp. 276–284.

Haythorn, William, et al.: "The Behavior of Authoritarian and Equalitarian Personality Groups," *Human Relations,* vol. 9 (February, 1956), pp. 57–74.

Heise, G. A., and G. A. Miller: "Problem Solving by Small Groups Using Various Communications Nets," *Journal of Abnormal and Social Psychology,* vol. 46 (July, 1951), pp. 327–335.

Hildum, D. C., and R. W. Brown: "Verbal Reinforcement and Interviewer Bias," *Journal of Abnormal and Social Psychology,* vol. 53 (January, 1956), pp. 108–111.

James, Ralph, and Estelle James: "Hoffa's Acquisition of Industrial Power," and "Hoffa's Leverage Techniques in Bargaining," *Industrial Relations,* vol. 2 (May, 1963), pp. 67–95 and vol. 3 (October, 1963), pp. 73–93.

Janis, I. L., and Daniel Katz: "The Reduction of Intergroup Hostility: Research

Problems and Hypotheses," *Journal of Conflict Resolution,* vol. 3 (March, 1959), pp. 85–100.

Jensen, Lloyd: "Soviet-American Bargaining Behavior in Post-war Disarmament Negotiations," *Journal of Arms Control,* vol. 1 (October, 1963), pp. 616–635.

Jordan, N.: "Behavioral Forces That Are a Function of Attitudes and of Cognitive Organization," *Human Relations,* vol. 6 (August, 1953), pp. 273–287.

Joseph, M. L., and R. H. Willis: "An Experimental Analog to Two-party Bargaining," *Behavioral Science,* vol. 8, no. 2 (1963), pp. 117–127.

Katz, Daniel: "Consistent Reactive Participation of Group Members and Reduction of Intergroup Conflict," *Journal of Conflict Resolution,* vol. 3 (March, 1959), pp. 28–40.

Katz, Daniel, Irving Sarnoff, and Charles McClintock: "Ego-defense and Attitude Change," *Human Relations,* vol. 9 (February, 1956), pp. 27–45.

Kelman, Herbert: "Compliance, Identification and Internalization: Three Processes of Attitude Change," *Journal of Conflict Resolution,* vol. 2 (March, 1958), pp. 51–60.

Kerr, Clark: "Industrial Conflict and Its Mediation," *The American Journal of Sociology,* vol. 60 (November, 1954), pp. 230–245.

Kogan, N., and R. Tagiuri: "International Preference and Cognitive Organization," *Journal of Abnormal and Social Psychology,* vol. 56 (January, 1958), pp. 113–116.

Kuhn, H. W.: "Game Theory and Models of Negotiations," *Journal of Conflict Resolution,* vol. 6 (March, 1962), pp. 1–4.

Lasswell, H. D.: "Compromise," *Encyclopedia of the Social Sciences,* vol. 4 (New York: The Macmillan Company, 1937), pp. 147–149.

Leavitt, H. J., and R. A. Mueller: "Some Effects of Feedback on Communication," *Human Relations,* vol. 4, no. 4 (1951), pp. 401–410.

Levinson, D. L.: "Authoritarian Personality and Foreign Policy," *Journal of Conflict Resolution,* vol. 1 (March, 1957), pp. 37–47.

Levinson, H. M.: "Pattern Bargaining by the United Automobile Workers," *Labor Law Review,* vol. 9 (September, 1958), pp. 669–673.

Levinson, H. M.: "Pattern Bargaining: A Case Study of the Automobile Workers," *Quarterly Journal of Economics,* vol. 74 (May, 1960), pp. 296–317.

Mander, George, and W. K. Kaplan: "Subjective Evaluation and Reinforcement Effect of a Verbal Stimulus," *Science,* vol. 124 (1956), pp. 582–583.

McKersie, R. B.: "The Civil Rights Movement and Employment," *Industrial Relations,* vol. 3 (May, 1964), pp. 1–21.

McKersie, R. B., and Montague Brown: "Non-professional Hospital Workers and a Union Organizing Drive," *Quarterly Journal of Economics,* vol. 77 (August, 1963), pp. 372–404.

McKersie, R. B., and W. W. Shropshire, Jr.: "Avoiding Written Grievances: A Successful Program," *The Journal of Business,* vol. 35 (April, 1962), pp. 135–152.

McMurry, R. N.: "War and Peace in Labor Relations," *Harvard Business Review,* vol. 30 (November-December, 1955), pp. 48–60.

Mellinger, G. D.: "Interpersonal Trust as a Factor in Communication," *Journal of Abnormal and Social Psychology,* vol. 52, no. 3 (1956), pp. 304–309.

Meyer, Arthur S.: "Function of the Mediator in Collective Bargaining," *Industrial and Labor Relations Review,* vol. 13 (January, 1960), pp. 159–165.

Milburn, T. W.: "The Concept of Deterrence: Some Logical and Psychological Considerations," *Journal of Social Issues,* vol. 17 (July, 1961), pp. 3–12.

Naess, Arne: "A Systematization of Gandhian Ethics of Conflict Resolution," *Journal of Conflict Resolution,* vol. 2 (June, 1958), pp. 140–155.

Nash, John: "Two-person Cooperative Games," *Econometrica,* vol. 21 (January, 1953), pp. 128–140.

Newcomb, T. M.: "An Approach to the Study of Communicative Acts," *Psychological Review,* vol. 60 (September, 1953), pp. 393–404.

Newcomb, T. M.: "The Prediction of Interpersonal Attraction," *The American Psychologist,* vol. 11 (November, 1956), pp. 575–586.

Pen, Jan: "A General Theory of Bargaining," *American Economic Review,* vol. 62 (March, 1952), pp. 24–42.

Pilisuk, Marc: "Cognitive Balance and Self-relevant Attitudes," *Journal of Abnormal and Social Psychology,* vol. 65 (August, 1962), pp. 95–103.

Pruitt, D. G.: "An Analysis of Responsiveness between Nations," *Journal of Conflict Resolution,* vol. 6 (March, 1962), pp. 5–18.

Raiffa, Howard: "Arbitration Schemes for Generalized Two-person Games," *Contributions to the Theory of Games, II,* Annals of Mathematics Study no. 28 (Princeton, N.J.: Princeton University Press, 1953), pp. 361–387.

Rapoport, Anatol: "Lewis F. Richardson's Mathematical Theory of War," *Journal of Conflict Resolution,* vol. 1 (September, 1957), pp. 249–299.

Rapoport, Anatol, and Carol Orwant: "Experimental Games: A Review," *Behavioral Science,* vol. 7 (January, 1962), pp. 1–37.

Reder, M. W.: "The Theory of Union Wage Policy," *The Review of Economics and Statistics,* vol. 34 (February, 1952), pp. 34–45.

Rees, Albert: "Industrial Conflict and Business Fluctuations," *The Journal of Political Economy,* vol. 60 (October, 1952), pp. 371–382.

Riecken, H. W., and G. C. Homans: "Psychological Aspects of Social Structure," in G. Lindzey (ed.), *Handbook of Social Psychology* (Reading, Mass.: Addison-Wesley Publishing Company, Inc., 1954), pp. 786–832.

Rokeach, Milton: "Political and Religious Dogmatism: An Alternative to the Authoritarian Personality," *Psychological Monographs,* vol. 70, no. 18, whole no. 425 (1956), pp. 1–43.

Rosen, H. M., and R. A. H. Rosen: "The Union Business Agent Looks at Collective Bargaining," *Personnel,* vol. 33 (May, 1957), pp. 539–545.

Rothbaum, Melvin: "Economic Dilemmas of Collective Bargaining," *Annals* (November, 1963), pp. 95–103.

Schein, E. H.: "The Effect of Reward on Adult Imitative Behavior," *Journal of Abnormal and Social Psychology,* vol. 49 (July, 1954), pp. 389–395.

Schelling, T. C.: "An Essay on Bargaining," *American Economic Review,* vol. 46 (June, 1956), pp. 281–306.

Schorr, Daniel: "The Trojan Troika in Berlin," *Reporter* (Sept. 27, 1962), pp. 25–27.

Scott, W. A.: "Rationality and Non-rationality of International Attitudes," *Journal of Conflict Resolution,* vol. 2 (March, 1958), pp. 8–16.

Seltzer, George: "Pattern Bargaining and the United Steelworkers," *Journal of Political Economy,* vol. 59 (August, 1951), pp. 319–331.

Shackle, G. L.: "The Nature of the Bargaining Process," in J. T. Dunlop (ed.), *The Theory of Wage Determination* (London: International Economic Association, Macmillan & Co., Ltd., 1957), pp. 292–314.

Simon, H. A.: "A Behavioral Model of Rational Choice," *The Quarterly Journal of Economics,* vol. 69 (February, 1955), pp. 99–118.

Singer, J. D.: "Threat-perception and the Armament-tension Dilemma," *Journal of Conflict Resolution,* vol. 2 (1958), pp. 90–105.

Sorokin, P. A.: "Some Activities of the Harvard Research Center in Creative Altruism," *Journal of Human Relations,* vol. 2 (Spring, 1954), pp. 12–17.

Speroff, B. J.: "Group Psychotherapy in Labor Relations: A Case Study," *Personnel Journal,* vol. 39 (1960), pp. 14–17.

Starbuck, W. H.: "Level of Aspiration Theory and Economic Behavior," *Behavioral Science,* vol. 8 (April, 1963), pp. 128–136.

Steiner, I. D., and E. D. Rogers: "Alternative Response to Dissonance," *Journal of Abnormal and Social Psychology,* vol. 66 (February, 1963), pp. 128–136.

Stone, J. J.: "An Experiment in Bargaining Games," *Econometrica,* vol. 26 (April, 1958), pp. 286–296.

Stouffer, S. A., and J. Toby: "Role Conflict and Personality," *Journal of Sociology,* vol. 56 (March, 1951), pp. 395–406.

Thibaut, J. W., and John Coules: "The Role of Communication in the Reduction of Interpersonal Hostility," *Journal of Abnormal and Social Psychology,* vol. 47 (October, 1952), pp. 770–777.

Toby, Jackson: "Some Variables in Role Conflict Analysis," *Social Forces,* vol. 30 (March, 1952), pp. 323–327.

Verplank, W. S.: "The Control of the Content of Conversation: Reinforcement of Statements of Opinion," *Journal of Abnormal and Social Psychology,* vol. 51 (November, 1955), pp. 668–676.

Weschler, Irving R.: "The Personal Factor in Labor Mediation," *Personnel Psychology,* vol. 3 (Summer, 1950), pp. 113–132.

Wilson, J. Q.: "The Strategy of Protest: Problems of Negro Civic Action," *Journal of Conflict Resolution,* vol. 5 (1961), pp. 291–303.

Wolfe, D. M., and J. D. Snoek: "A Study of Tensions and Adjustments under Role Conflict," *Journal of Social Issues,* vol. 18 (July, 1962), pp. 102–121.

Zaninovich, M. G.: "Pattern Analysis of Variables within the International System: The Sino-Soviet Example," *Journal of Conflict Resolution,* vol. 6 (September, 1962), pp. 253–269.

## Pamphlets, Unpublished Material, and Other Sources

AFL-CIO Collective Bargaining Report, "Strikes," vol. 3 (November, 1958).

Bok, Derek, and Max D. Kossoris: *Methods of Adjusting to Automation and Technological Change* (Washington, D.C.: U.S. Department of Labor, no date).

Brandt, Floyd, John Glover, B. M. Selekman: "Gray Manufacturing Company (C)," (Copyright by the President and Fellows of Harvard College, 1959).

*Business Management:* "The Story of a Pioneer in Crisis-free Bargaining" (March, 1964), p. 43 and ff.

Fischer, Ben: Speech before the Advanced Arbitration Seminar (Extension Division, The University of Chicago, June 5–6, 1964).

Goldstein, Bernard: *Unions for Technical Professionals: A Case Study,* Ph.D. thesis (Chicago, Ill., University of Chicago, Department of Sociology, August, 1957).

Jacobs, A. T.: "Some Significant Factors Influencing the Range of Indeterminateness in Collective Bargaining Negotiations," Ph.D. thesis (Ann Arbor, Mich., University of Michigan, 1951).

Raskin, A. H.: "Non-stop Talks Instead of Non-stop Strikes," *The New York Times Magazine* (July 7, 1963).

Steiner, G. A.: "The Creative Organization," Selected Paper no. 10 (The Graduate School of Business, University of Chicago, Chicago, Ill., no date).

United Automobile Workers: *Worker's Problems Are Democracy's Problems* (Detroit, Mich.: Solidarity House, 1961).

U.S. Department of Labor: *Recent Collective Bargaining and Technological Change,* BLS Report no. 266 (Washington, D.C., 1964).

*The Wall Street Journal:* "Union Workers Rising Rejection of Pacts Imperils Labor Leaders and Management" (June 3, 1963).

Walton, R. E.: "Theory of Conflict in Lateral Organizational Relationships" (paper presented to the International Conference on Operations Research and the Social Sciences, Cambridge, England, September 14, 1964).

# AUTHOR INDEX

Note: All names appear in footnotes on the pages indicated—in some cases the names also appear in the text.

# SUBJECT INDEX

*435*